Camouflage

Camouflage

Modern International Military Patterns

Eric H Larson

Pen & Sword
MILITARY

First published in Great Britain in 2021 by
Pen & Sword Military
An imprint of
Pen & Sword Books Ltd
Yorkshire – Philadelphia

ISBN 978 1 52673 857 8

A CIP catalogue record for this book is available from the British Library.

Typeset by Mac Style
Printed and bound in India by Replika Press Pvt. Ltd.

FSC www.fsc.org MIX Paper from responsible sources FSC® C016779

Pen & Sword Books Limited incorporates the imprints of Atlas, Archaeology, Aviation, Discovery, Family History, Fiction, History, Maritime, Military, Military Classics, Politics, Select, Transport, True Crime, Air World, Frontline Publishing, Leo Cooper, Remember When, Seaforth Publishing, The Praetorian Press, Wharncliffe Local History, Wharncliffe Transport, Wharncliffe True Crime and White Owl.

For a complete list of Pen & Sword titles please contact

PEN & SWORD BOOKS LIMITED
47 Church Street, Barnsley, South Yorkshire, S70 2AS, England
E-mail: enquiries@pen-and-sword.co.uk
Website: www.pen-and-sword.co.uk

Or

PEN AND SWORD BOOKS
1950 Lawrence Rd, Havertown, PA 19083, USA
E-mail: Uspen-and-sword@casematepublishers.com
Website: www.penandswordbooks.com

Contents

Acknowledgements

This book is a culmination of thirty-five years of research and continuous exposure to military personnel and culture. Although it is a product of my own creation, I would be remiss if I took all the credit for the research and information provided in this volume. Much of the historical information can be credited to the generation or two of professionals and hobbyists that came before mine, as well as to historians that had the foresight to keep good records on a subject that is quite often overlooked.

Those of us who developed an interest in military camouflage more than twenty years ago owe a huge debt of gratitude to Dr Jean-Francois Borsarello, one of the pioneering researchers on this subject and the publisher of some of the first reference materials in English on camouflage uniforms. Likewise, I believe we are equally indebted to the multitude of military photographers and combat photojournalists out there who are largely responsible for recording many of the images that analysts such as myself have relied upon as primary source material for our research. Of these individuals, I would single out Yves Debay as the single most influential and critical recorder of military conflicts in the latter part of the twentieth century, whose dedication to combat photojournalism ultimately cost him his life in 2013.

My personal gratitude extends to a lot of other individuals. Some of these folks have generously assisted me personally by sharing their own research or helping to collect data and locate source material, while others can still be thanked for their indirect contributions to the fields of camouflage studies and the history of military conflict in the post-war world. While I have made every effort to include as many people that I feel have made a significant contribution to this book in the list that follows, there are a select group of people that must remain anonymous and whose names will not be mentioned here. These folks know who they are, and I hope they also know how valuable I consider their contributions to my work, and to the greater field of knowledge that is camouflage studies.

Herewith follows a list of people that have helped, directly or indirectly, make this book possible. My thanks go out to each and every one of you.

Beni Antares (Indonesia)
Andreas Arphan (Malaysia)
Filippo Buccaro (Italy)
Mark Campbell (Canada)
Henrik Clausen (Denmark)
Kenneth Conboy (USA-Indonesia)
Dion Desembriarto (Indonesia)
Dennis Desmond (USA)
Peter Erickson (USA)
Marco Garofalo (Italy)
Gilles Gorgues (France)
Jim Hooper (USA)
Dominic Hyde (United Kingdom)
Alex Iide (Brazil)
Richard D. Johnson (USA)
Carlos Caballero Jurado (Spain)
Leo Karlin (USA)
Samuel Katz (Israel)
Marko Kocoljevac (Serbia)
Michal Koníĉek (Czech Republic)
John Laffin (United Kingdom)
Thomas Lundberg (USA)
Salvatore Mascoli (Italy-USA)
D. Matz (Brazil-USA)
Santiago Medina (Spain)
Juan Morales (Spain)
Eric Micheletti (France)
Piet Nortje (South Africa)
Werner Palinckx (Belgium)
Jorge Panuncio (Uruguay)

Daniel Peterson (USA)
Ben Playford (Australia)
Riaan Rossouw (South Africa)
Maksim Savochkin (Uzbekistan)
Amin Allah Shakeri (Iran)
Shelby Stanton (USA)
Peter Stiff (United Kingdom)
Gani Sunglao (Philippines)
Juan Pablo Tessiere (Argentina)
Philip Thum (Austria)
Andress Vargas (Mexico)
Al Venter (South Africa)
Steven Wende (South Africa-USA)
Martin Windrow (United Kingdom)

Introduction

What is Camouflage?

A typical definition of the term camouflage might render 'a way of hiding soldiers and military equipment, using paint, leaves, or nets, so that they look like part of their surroundings.' In terms that apply specifically to military personnel, we typically think of camouflage as articles of clothing printed in designs that, under the correct conditions, will render the wearer invisible to a casual observer.

Historically, this would have been a perfectly acceptable way to think of military camouflage, given the fact that its purpose from inception was to disguise or conceal the wearer. It may seem perplexing to the reader, then, to discover that we must really arrive at a much broader definition of the word, if we are to delve more deeply into the variety of designs and color combinations that comprise military camouflage in the second half of the twentieth century and to the present day.

Up to the late 1970s, it would be accurate to say that camouflage designs were almost exclusively of a pragmatic nature. That is, the developers intended for the wearer to be disguised or hidden when wearing or employing it. However, at some point in the 1980s, national laboratories, private companies, and individual camoufleurs began playing around with the color schemes of typical camouflage patterns, so that the wearer ended up standing out rather than becoming more obscure. The earliest of these non-functional patterns were the so-called 'urban' camouflage designs (usually employing shades of grey and blue in combination with black). While it might be argued that these initially had a functional purpose in mind, in practice the brighter blues and lighter greys tended to distinguish rather than disguise the wearer, becoming more a mark of pride instead of a functioning operational garment. In the latter part of the twentieth century, blue and grey camouflage became a mark of distinction for many law enforcement agencies throughout the world.

Straying even further from the practical aspects of camouflage design, by the late 1990s we see numerous distinctive patterns emerging whose sole purpose is to immediately identify the wearer either as coming from a particular unit or entity, or at least stand out and be easily identified – whether in a crowd of people, or in extreme situations such as search and rescue missions or firefighting. Purists will insist that true camouflage must be functional and, as a linguist, I am prone to agree with them, up to a point. Yet, we cannot deny the fact that colorful (or even garish) designs that utilize traditional shapes, drawings, and geometrical patterns have some relationship with the more functional, traditional camouflage designed for the typical infantry soldier. There is a relationship, and if you were to query the average collector of camouflage uniforms from any part of the world, I am sure they would admit they have included at least some examples of non-functional camouflage patterns in their collections.

As the world emerged from the Second World War, the concept of military camouflage was still in its infancy. It is possible to count on one's hands the number of countries that actually employed unique camouflage designs during the war, and from there we would need to subtract quite a handful that continued to use it once hostilities had ended. Camouflage, at least in the eyes of most Europeans, was equated with the war and not with peacetime service, and in many cases was associated with wartime combat units that had a sinister reputation, such as the Waffen SS. Olive drab remained the color of most Army service uniforms, with camouflage being retained most often only for elite units such as paratroopers, commandos, reconnaissance personnel, and snipers. Many camouflage designs that emerged in the post-war years were in fact based on those developed during the war, and it was really not until the world began to experience a new type of warfare – on a smaller scale, waged by ragtag forces (freedom fighters, or terrorist insurgents, depending on one's perspective) – that the need arose for better disguising the ground personnel operating in places across Africa, Asia and Latin America.

In Europe, camouflage designs arose from three main traditions – Britain, Germany and Italy. Although Italian camouflage had been around for the longest period of time, it probably had the narrowest influence on camouflage designs in the twentieth century. Britain, whose 'brushstroke' design was essentially a quick-fix solution to the need for disguising commandos and paratroopers, would go on to influence the series of French 'lizard' patterns, the Southeast Asian 'tiger stripe' designs, the UK's own Disruptive Pattern Material (which would spread across the globe), as well as a host of other brushstroke-derivative patterns that would populate at least five continents. At the same time, Germany's wartime patterns, although stigmatized by their association with the Nazi Schutzstaffel, would nevertheless influence not only future patterns in Germany, but those in neighboring Central, Eastern and Northern European nations as well.

Meanwhile, in the Americas, the use of camouflage was relegated to the back burner, particularly by the United States. Although American military developers would continue to experiment with designs, it would be nearly twenty years after the end of the Second World War before the usefulness of infantry camouflage was embraced, and then it would still be largely relegated to troops with specific duties, such as intelligence gathering and reconnaissance. Likewise, Canada would retain the use of olive-green combat fatigues for the majority of its armed forces until long after the rest of the world had adopted some sort of camouflage design for its ground personnel.

The remainder of the world's armed forces were largely influenced by a select few camouflage traditions, then – those of Britain, wartime Germany, pre-war Italy, Russia and the United States. Pattern concepts then branched out to influence the traditions of other nations, beginning initially with what remained of European colonial possessions in Asia, Africa and the Americas, and later to the armed forces of nations that fell under the heavy political influence of superpowers like the Soviet Union and the United States. Although there are camouflage designs that may not fit easily into the 'camouflage family tree', for the most part the concept holds true until the development of so-called 'digital camouflage designs'.

The idea of multi-scale camouflage is to combine patterns or shapes utilizing two or more scales in order to create a camouflage design that is effective at disrupting the wearer's shape over a range of distances. Although the concept took root in the mid-twentieth century and had been touched on by the Germans, Russians, and independent designers such as Timothy O'Neill, it did not really take off until the first truly pixilated camouflage design was developed for the Canadian Armed Forces and issued in 2002. From that initial CADPAT design evolved an entire range of functional pixilated and fractal camouflage designs, often developed with the aid of computer technology, as well as a host of knock-offs which are essentially just recolored versions of CADPAT or other popular designs. Although 'digital' patterns have replaced more conventional designs in many armed forces around the world, it can be argued that the vast majority of them function no more effectively than old-fashioned hand-drawn designs, or even solid colored uniforms and have become fashion statements in their own right.

What does this book cover?

My intention has been to create a single-volume reference work that covers the majority of camouflage designs issued by the world's military and paramilitary forces since the end of the Second World War. Additionally, when evidence has documented substantial use of patterns or designs by unconventional forces (insurgents, freedom fighters, terrorists, or whatever you wish to call them), I have attempted to document these as well, or at least mention their usage. The reader should be able to find the majority of camouflage designs with which they are familiar within these pages, as well as a host of additional designs or usages which may be new to them. What you will not find here, at least not with any degree of focus or attempt at encyclopedic coverage, are experimental or test camouflage patterns. Although the subject of experimental camouflage is both fascinating and far-reaching, its scope is far too great to attempt in this volume. Indeed, I would hypothesize that it would be nearly impossible to address the subject of experimental camouflage designs (except, perhaps, by individual nations that have kept prolific and accurate records) simply due to a lack of resources and accessible documentation. In a few cases where an experimental design was issued to a large number of military personnel deployed in combat, there may be some mention in this volume, but even in situations where a well-known design saw very limited use by special operations personnel I am leaving the subject for another time, and probably another author.

Chapter 1

Africa

ALGERIA

Algeria is today officially known as the People's Democratic Republic of Algeria (الجمهورية الجزائرية الديمقراطية الشعبية), though historically it has been a part of many subject territories, including the Carthaginian, Roman, Byzantine, Spanish and Ottoman empires. The French seized control of Algiers in 1830 and lead a military campaign that ended in complete control by 1848. Once under French control, Algeria was considered an integral part of France, with tens of thousands of Europeans emigrating there.

The Algerian War was launched by the Front de Libération Nationale (FLN) in 1954 with the aim of liberating Algeria from French control. French forces were pitted against the Armée de Libération Nationale (ALN), the armed wing of the FLN. The war was primarily a guerilla campaign, but it evolved into a civil war as well, with loyalist Algerians supporting the nation remaining French and the insurrectionists favoring independence. Combat even spilled over into France, in the form of the so-called 'Cafe Wars', bombings and assassinations that centered around cafes, perpetrated both by the FLN and the rival Mouvement National Algérien (MNA). France ultimately capitulated after nine years of war and Algeria achieved its independence in 1963.

During the period of French administration, the only use of camouflage by native Algerian military personnel was by specialized units such as the commandos, although captured stocks of French uniforms were also worn by the ALN during the war. Algeria has continued to utilize French-inspired camouflage into the present era; however, a greater number of non-French inspired designs have been adopted as well, particularly during the latter part of the twentieth century and into the present era.

French Camouflage

Algeria was considered France's tenth Military District and was populated by a number of native Algerian units such as Tirailleur infantry, Spahi mechanized cavalry regiments, and an assortment of commando units. The French-designed tenue du leopard or 'lizard' camouflage design was worn by some of these specialist units, such as the Commandos de Chasse, who, in addition to issue military garments, adopted special, locally-produced caps and berets. For the length of the Algerian War, and for a period of time following independence, an assortment of native French 'lizard' designs could be found in use with Algerian units. These included the full array of designs up to and including the standardized 'F1' found on the Mle 1948 Tenue Toutes Armes (TTA) and the Mle 1947/56 Troupes Aéro Portée (TAP) uniforms.

For full details of French lizard camouflage produced during this era, see the section on France.

Algerian Camouflage

Several camouflage patterns arose during the 1960s, although photographic documentation of their use with Algerian forces is limited. Of these, the most notable are a copy of the Spanish rocoso (rocks) pattern – possibly made from imported fabric – as well as a curious blotch or spot pattern of undetermined origins.

During the late 1980s or early 1990s a number of additional camouflage patterns came into use with Algerian forces, including additional designs inspired by French, British, Belgian and American patterns. The earliest of these is a 'lizard' pattern with very dark coloration incorporating purple and very dark olive stripes on an medium olive green background. At this point, uniform styles followed closely the original French TAP design.

Spanish-manufactured camouflage fabric in rocoso (rocks) pattern was exported to Algeria for production into combat clothing, circa 1960s

Algerian Marines wearing a DPM variant pattern in use since at least 2007. (*Private collection*)

This purple-dominant 'lizard' variant pattern camouflage is of 1980s vintage.

Algerian Army officers wearing a green-dominant, woodland derivative camouflage design. (*Private collection*)

Algerian Special Forces soldier circa 2013 wearing 'brushstroke' pattern uniform; the design appears to be influenced by Belgian patterns. (*Private collection*)

Algerian paratroops wearing a grey dominant lizard pattern. The lizard was reintroduced circa 2010–12. (*Private collection*)

Introduced circa 2012, this mottled or spotted camouflage design has an arid colorway. (*Private collection*)

Members of the elite Garde Republicaine wear a splinter-inspired camouflage design with a woodland color palette. This pattern was adopted relatively recently. (*Private collection*)

ANGOLA

The Republic of Angola (República de Angola) has a long history of association with Portugal through its status as a colonial possession. A post-war wave of African nationalism took root here in the 1950s, leading to civil war in 1961 involving the Portuguese Armed Forces as well as the MPLA (Popular Movement for the Liberation of Angola), the FNLA (National Front for the Liberation of Angola), and UNITA (National Union for the Total Independence of Angola). Although complete independence was granted in 1975 (following a change in government from military dictatorship to liberal democracy within Portugal), internal fighting in Angola continued into the 1990s as the three factions, each supported by foreign governments, vied for control.

During the 1970s, FNLA and UNITA forged a shaky alliance against the MPLA, in response to which the Soviet Union and Cuba channeled increasing military assistance to the Forças Armadas Populares de Libertação de Angola or FAPLA (the armed wing of the MPLA), aid that would continue well into the 1990s. The United States initially countered by supporting Daniel Chipenda's FNLA, with South Africa offering its support to both the FNLA and Jonas Savimbi's UNITA. This overt military support, however, was short-lived, with US aid ending in December 1975 and the South African Defense Force leaving the country in February 1976. Meanwhile, as many as 11,000 Cuban advisors remained in Angola, along with a number of Soviet military personnel, and a large assortment of war materiel. The MPLA subsequently became the de facto government of the nation, with UNITA and the FNLA continuing an insurgency campaign against the FAPLA. Although they would still receive covert support from several nations, including the United States, South Africa, and Zaire, the FNLA eventually capitulated, leaving UNITA to continue waging its war against FAPLA. Many FNLA personnel would later be transformed into 32 Battalion of the SADF, a Portuguese-speaking special operations unit with a fierce reputation and more cross-border combat experience than any other unit of the SADF. As for UNITA, when its leader, Jonas Savimbi, was killed during combat operations in February 2002, the group negotiated a ceasefire shortly thereafter and by August of that year had given up the armed struggle, declaring its intent to focus on political means of change. Approximately 4.28 million people were displaced over the course of the twenty-seven-year Angolan Civil War, with as many as 500,000 people killed.

Camouflage from the Angolan Civil War

Originally issued to units serving in Africa, the m63 'vertical lizard' camouflage pattern was worn by Portuguese and Colonial personnel throughout the Angolan War for Independence. Remaining stocks ended up in the hands of FAPLA, UNITA and the FNLA, when they were liberated from supply houses after Portuguese military personnel abandoned the country. Limited stocks would remain in usage with FAPLA into the late twentieth century.

Several types of Portuguese lizard camouflage were worn by both Portuguese military forces and by insurgent forces of FAPLA, the FNLA and UNITA.

MPLA/FAPLA insurgents wearing Portuguese Army issued lizard camouflage during the war. (*Private collection*)

Cuban military personnel initially brought great numbers of 'grey lizard' pattern camouflage uniforms with them when deployed to Angola. The pattern was so popular with Angolan forces that it remained in service long after the Cubans left, with subsequent contracts being fulfilled by manufacturers in South Korea. The pattern fell into disuse in the 1990s. (*Private collection*)

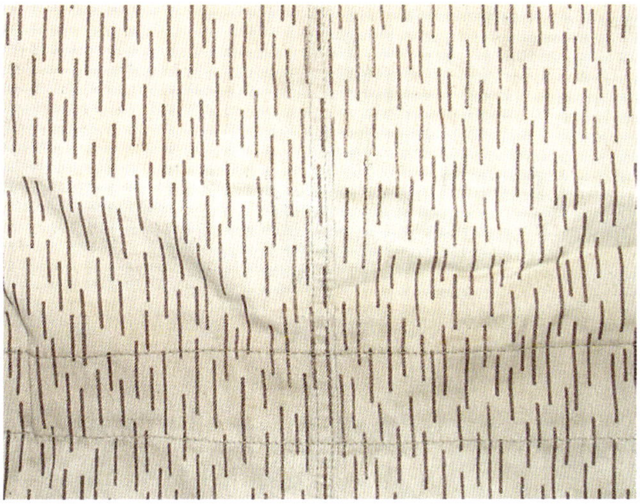

FAPLA personnel also wore export uniforms in East German strichtarnmuster (rain pattern) camouflage. These uniforms were mostly seen in the early part of the war.

UNITA personnel for a brief period wore ex-Rhodesian pattern camouflage uniforms. Use was extremely limited, as UNITA personnel were typically outfitted in various shades of olive green.

Limited use of French lizard pattern camouflage was seen by UNITA commanders when making public appearances, but does not appear to have been worn on combat operations with any degree of frequency.

Angolan Camouflage

The Angolan Armed Forces (FAA, or Forças Armadas Angolanas) have procured nearly all of their military uniforms from foreign sources in Asia. This practice continues into the present era.

Angolan soldier wearing a lime-green based woodland pattern uniform circa 2002. (*Private collection*)

Two Angolan Commandos wear the current Multicam pattern, adopted as the standard camouflage pattern beginning in 2014. (*Private collection*)

Several variations of US woodland pattern camouflage have been worn by Angolan military personnel since the 1990s. It has probably seen the most use of any camouflage design within the FAA. (*Private collection*)

Of Chinese origin, this unique pattern of swirling amoeba shapes saw service with the FAA in the 1990s.

Also supplied by EO in less substantial numbers were French-inspired camouflage uniforms in DPM pattern camouflage.

When the South African-based company Executive Outcomes (EO) became involved in training and equipping the FAA in the 1990s, they introduced a number of camouflage uniforms that would be dispersed among several Angolan units. The Chinese-made copy of French lizard camouflage was particularly popular with the EO trainers.

Formerly known as Dahomey, the République du Bénin has had a long association with France, both before and after being granted complete independence in 1960.

Between 1960 and 1972, several coups d'etat and regime changes dominated the political scene in Dahomey. In October 1972, Lieutenant Colonel Mathieu Kérékou overthrew a presidential council created by previous political rivals and declared himself president of a Marxist state under control of the Military Council of the Revolution (CNR). On 30 November 1975, the country was renamed the People's Republic of Benin. Riots broke out in 1989 over the Kérékou regime's failure to pay its army. Shortly thereafter, the nation renounced Marxism, ratified a new constitution, and renamed the country the Republic of Benin in March of 1990. Kérékou lost the presidential election in 1991, but regained it by popular vote in 1996, and again in 2001.

Copies of the French leópard (or 'lizard') pattern camouflage have been in use by the Armed Forces since the 1980s, and quite probably earlier. The majority of its military personnel continue to wear this pattern.

Armored personnel NCO wearing typical lizard pattern uniform of Benin Armed Forces. (*Private collection*)

A unique camouflage design incorporating animal heads and footprints is worn by personnel of the paramilitary park rangers of the Special Brigade, charged primarily with anti-poaching operations.

At least some Benin personnel have worn a copy of the US m81 woodland pattern.

The Customs Service of Benin (Douanes Béninoises) also has its own camouflage pattern, loosely based on the US-designed six-color 'chocolate chip' desert pattern. (*Private collection*)

BIAFRA

During the early 1960s, ethnic violence had claimed thousands of lives as several coups d'etat vied for control of Nigeria, and military leaders from one tribe vented their anger on civilians from rival tribes. During the July 1966 coup, as many as 30,000 Igbos had been killed in northern Nigeria. Unable to reconcile their regional differences and share power, the south-eastern and ethnically Igbo region seceded and declared itself the Republic of Biafra on 26 May 1967. Large oil reserves that had recently been discovered in the east, however, necessitated in the minds of the Federal government that the region be restored to Nigerian control, and a military invasion (termed a 'police action') was launched to that end.

At the beginning of the civil war, military resources in Biafra were minimal and only around 3,000 personnel served with the Biafran Army. Many arms and munitions were fabricated locally from scrounged resources, as no support would be openly forthcoming from any other nations. A number of Europeans and Southern Africans ultimately served with the Biafran Army, and by the war's end as many as 30,000 troops would have swelled its ranks. Frequently termed 'mercenaries', a number of the more prominent figures were in fact émigrés with considerable military experience who believed in the Biafran cause and were granted Biafran citizenship. Nevertheless, a fair number of foreigners were simply warriors for hire. Supported financially and militarily by the United Kingdom, USSR, Saudi Arabia, Syria, and the USA, the Nigerian Federal Army eventually defeated the Biafran forces, who surrendered on January 13, 1970.

The standard combat uniform of Biafran forces was olive green, but a number of troops did acquire the Nigerian-issue 'vertical lizard' pattern camouflage uniform during the war. (*Private collection*)

Seen here on senior commander General Odumegwu Ojukwu, a locally produced duck hunter or 'spot' camouflage pattern was also commonly found among some Biafran personnel. (*Private collection*)

BOTSWANA

The Republic of Botswana (Lefatshe la Botswana) was previously the British protectorate of Bechuanaland. Between 1885 and 1964, the land was administered by Britain, but when proposals were made for democratic self-government they were granted, with general elections and ratification of a constitution leading to full independence in September 1966. Botswana is one of very few nations in Africa to have never suffered a coup d'etat, dictatorship, civil war, or armed conflict with any of its neighbors. It has maintained strong ties with the United Kingdom and the Botswana Defense Force (BDF) follows the British model.

Members of Special Support Group (SSG) currently wear a mottled grey camouflage pattern seen here. (*Private collection*)

British DPM has been the standard camouflage pattern of the BDF since the mid-1980s and continues to be worn today. (*Private collection*)

BURKINA FASO

Formerly a colonial territory of France, this region became the self-governing Republic of Upper Volta in December 1958. The first president of Upper Volta was Maurice Yaméogo who, shortly after coming to power, banned all political parties other than his own Voltaic Democratic Union. His government lasted until 1966, when he was deposed in a military coup d'etat which suspended the constitution, dissolved the National Assembly, and placed Lieutenant Colonel Sangoulé Lamizana at the head of a government of senior army officers. A new constitution was ratified in 1970, but Lamizana remained in power as president until November 1980, when he was overthrown in a bloodless coup headed by Colonel Saye Zerbo. Two years later, Zerbo was himself overthrown by Major Dr Jean-Baptiste Ouédraogo, who only managed to retain power until August 1983, when yet another coup installed former Prime Minister Captain Thomas Sankara as president. The nation changed its name to Burkina Faso (Land of Honest People) under Sankara.

In use since the 1980s, variations of the French leópard or 'lizard' camouflage pattern continue to be worn into the present period. Seen here is a very early French-style M1964 pattern uniform. (*Private collection*)

A more recent variation of the French lizard pattern features bolder colors and varied shapes from the historical French designs. (*Ministère de la Défense Nationale*)

The Gendarmerie Nationale have worn a leaf pattern camouflage design with a blue-purple colorway, and having the 'Gendarmerie Burkina' logo embedded within the pattern. (*Gendarmerie Burkina Faso*)

A variation of the horizontal stripe pattern worn in desert/arid conditions is also in use with Burkinabe personnel, since around 2015. (*Private collection*)

In use by regular army personnel since 2012, this horizontal stripe pattern consists of green and rust-colored shapes on an orange earth-colored background. (*Private collection*)

Seen here worn by the commander of the Garde Présidentielle, a kind of 'duck hunter' pattern with brown and green spots on a yellow-tan background is worn by members of this unit. (*Ministère de la Défense Nationale*)

The Mobile Brigade of the Customs Service (Douanes de Burkina Faso) wear a 'grey lizard' pattern camouflage design, very similar to that produced in Cuba and later in Angola and Yugoslavia. (*Private collection*)

The Garde de Sécurité Pénitentiaire have worn a light blue-grey digital camouflage design since at least 2016. (*Private collection*)

In October 1987, Sankara and twelve other political officials were assassinated in another coup d'état organized by his former colleague, Blaise Compaoré, who has remained in power as president ever since.

Although this nation maintains loose connections to France, its use of camouflage is quite varied and shows influence from a number of sources, as well as designs unique to the country itself.

BURUNDI

Although once part of German East Africa, Burundi became part of the Belgian mandate following the First World War and has maintained ties to that country since obtaining independence in 1962. Like its neighbor Rwanda, the République du Burundi is home to two primary ethnic groups, the Tutsi and the

Belgian 'jigsaw' pattern camouflage was worn both by certain local units during the colonial era, and for a period of time thereafter.

A variation of the army jigsaw with a blue colorway was worn by the National Gendarmerie for a period of time but has since been replaced. (*Private collection*)

A jigsaw variant pattern, unique to Burundi, was in service with this country since at least the early part of the twenty-first century. Note the colors are much darker than those of the Belgian versions.

Units serving with the OAU, as well as commando personnel adopted a copy of the US m81 woodland pattern until recent years.

The Police de Sécurité Intérieure (a unit of the National Police) also adopted a variation of the 'leaf' design with a blue colorway, in service until approximately 2017. (*Private collection*)

The Armed Forces adopted a new 'pixelated' camouflage design incorporating black, brown and foliage green shapes on a khaki background since approximately 2016. (*Private collection*)

The Police de Sécurité Intérieure began wearing a digital pattern with a grey colorway in 2017, although many units continue to wear the old blue pattern. (*Private collection*)

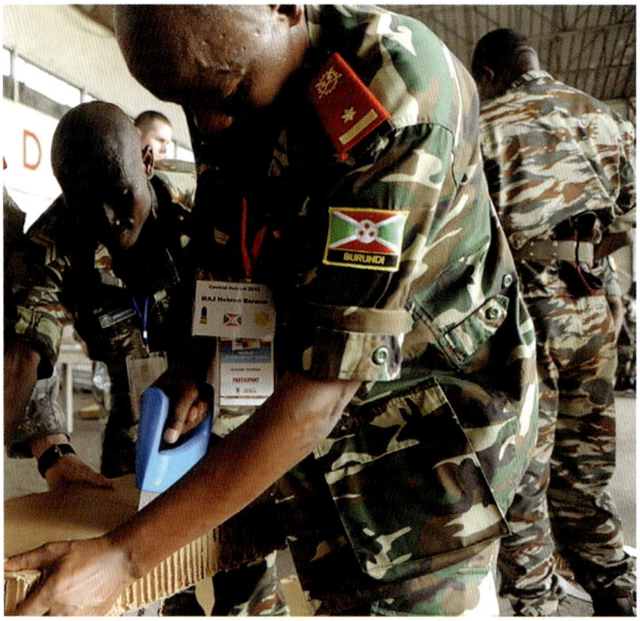

Seen here worn by an Army officer in 2013, this 'leaf' type camouflage design saw extensive service with the Burundi Armed Forces until quite recently. (*Private collection*)

Hutu, which has given rise to periodic episodes of inter-tribal violence and government-sponsored oppression. Following the assassination of the first Hutu head of state, Melchior Ndadaye, in October 1993, a civil war erupted in which more than 300,000 people were killed over a period of three years. Only after a military coup d'etat seized power in 1996 was peace restored, although it took an additional four years of negotiations before a transitional government was created.

Although retaining strong ties to Belgian military traditions, Burundi has slowly broken out on its own with regards to the use of military camouflage designs. Since 2016 the armed forces and gendarmerie have both embraced the so-called 'pixel age' of camouflage which has taken hold in so many parts of the world.

CAMEROON

The present day République du Cameroun has an interesting colonial history involving Germany, France and the United Kingdom. Following a period of colonial war, independence was granted by France in 1956, and in 1961 the British Cameroons joined the new territory to form the Federal Republic of Cameroon. However, an ongoing conflict with the Union of the Peoples of Cameroon (UPC) party continued into the 1970s. During the late 1980s and early 1990s, Cameroon suffered a severe economic crisis, in part due to years of corruption and mismanagement within the government. With the reintroduction of multi-party politics in December 1990, the former British Cameroons pressure groups called for greater autonomy, with some advocating complete secession as the Republic of Ambazonia. In February 2008, Cameroon experienced its worst violence in fifteen years when a transportation union strike in Douala escalated into violent protests in thirty-one municipal areas.

Use of the French leópard or 'lizard' pattern uniform within the Cameroon armed forces has been documented since at least the 1980s, and probably much earlier. Several variations are documented, although it appears most of these were phased out by the 1990s. (*Private collection*)

Variations of 'woodland' type camouflage are worn by certain units within the armed forces, particularly the Naval Infantry and the Anti-Terrorist Unit of the Army. (*Private collection*)

This member of the Marine Nationale wears a copy of the US tricolor desert pattern in typical M1964 uniform design. (*Private collection*)

Cameroon has also made significant use of a Chinese-made copy of the 'lizard' pattern, having less well-defined stripes but more consistent coloration. These members of the Rapid Intervention Battalion (Battalion d'intervention rapide) wear a uniform modeled after the French Army's design for airborne personnel. (*Private collection*)

A different woodland pattern is currently worn by the Bataillon d'Intervention Rapide (BIR), having dark brown, dark green and black shapes on a pale green background. (*Private collection*)

The islands comprising the Republic of Cape Verde (República de Cabo Verde) were reputedly uninhabited prior to being colonized by Portugal in the fifteenth century. During that period, the islands became an important part of the slave trade, and were a target for infrequent raids from pirates and other European nations. After the decline of the slave trade, Cape Verde became an important commercial center and re-supply stopover. During the 1950s, growing nationalism and a desire for independence spawned the creation of the Partido Africano da Independência da Guiné e Cabo Verdeor or PAIGC (African Party for the Independence of Guinea and Cape Verde), which waged a guerilla campaign against the Portuguese in the mainland colony of Portuguese Guinea. Yet the insurgency did not disrupt life on Cape Verde. The nation eased into its independent status, which was officially granted in July of 1975.

Like many Francophone countries in Africa, a Chinese-made copy of the French 'lizard' pattern has been in use with the FARP for many years. Although replaced by other designs in some parts of the armed forces, this pattern continues to be worn by some units, including the Fuzilieros Navais (Marine Corps). (*Private collection*)

The Partido Africano da Independência de Cabo Verde (PAICV), or African Party for the Independence of Cape Verde, was created in 1980 as a response to a coup in Guinea-Bissau, and ruled the nation as a one-party state until 1990. Growing political pressure, however, brought about multi-party elections in September 1990, which the nation has retained ever since.

The armed forces were originally known as the Forças Armadas Revolucionarias do Povo (FARP) or People's Revolutionary Armed Forces, but in the early 1990s this changed to Forças Armadas Cabo Verdeanas (FACV). The Force consists of only about 1,200 personnel, divided into the Army and Coast Guard. The FACV was restructured around 2016, with the Army being replaced by a National Guard consisting of three branches: Military Police, Naval Infantry, and an Infantry Battalion. Camouflage has primarily been copied from Portuguese-speaking countries until very recently.

Brazilian Army vertical lizard pattern camouflage has been documented in service with units of the FARP, particularly those having a public function, such as military police and presidential honor guards.

These two Fuzileiros Navais (Naval Infantry) personnel wear the Brazilian Navy vertical lizard pattern. (*Private collection*)

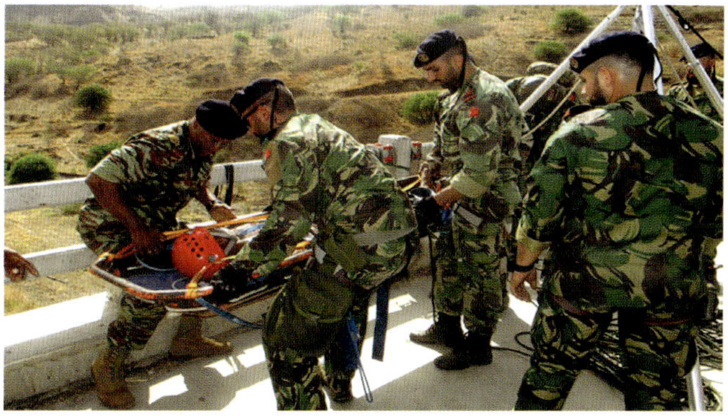

These Coast Guard personnel are wearing Portuguese DPM pattern, which appears to have replaced the earlier lizard designs. (*Private collection*)

These French-style uniforms in CE Woodland pattern have been fielded by the Guarda National since at least 2016 (*SAPO*).

CENTRAL AFRICAN REPUBLIC

The present day République Centrafricaine was incorporated into the area known as French Congo during the latter part of the nineteenth century. On 1 December 1958 the region of Ubangi-Shari became an autonomous territory within the French Community and took the name Central African Republic; it was granted full independence on 30 August 1960.

The country has seen a number of regime changes since independence, the first merely two years after it was originally achieved. A one-party state was established in 1962 by David Dacko, who was subsequently overthrown in 1965 by a military coup led by Colonel Jean-Bédel Bokassa. Bokassa declared himself President for Life in 1972, and later Emperor Bokassa I of the newly renamed Central African Empire, on 4 December 1976. Accusations of cannibalism and feeding his political opponents to animals kept in a personal zoo prompted France to intervene militarily in 1979, re-establishing Dacko as president. Two years later, he was again overthrown by General André Kolingba, who suspended the constitution and ruled until 1990. Under intense international and local pressure, Kolingba resisted the holding of free elections until 1993. Under newly elected president Ange-Félix Patassé, a new constitution was approved in December 1994. Nevertheless, protests, ethnic tension and vandalism marked the next few years until January 1997, when the Bangui Peace Accords were signed, providing for the deployment of an inter-African military mission. It would later be replaced by a UN peacekeeping force, the Mission des Nations Unies en RCA (MINURCA).

Ethnic and political violence again erupted in May 2001, sparked by a failed coup attempt in Bangui, and leading to two years of violence in the capital that resulted in the destruction of many homes and thousands killed. A new president was again elected in 2005. On 12 June 2008, the Central African Republic became the fourth country to be placed on the agenda of the UN Peacebuilding Commission, which was set up to help countries emerging from conflict avoid sliding back into war or chaos.

As with many former French colonies, the CAR employed copies of the leópard or lizard pattern for a period of time, which has seen limited use even into the present day.

Several variations of 'woodland' camouflage have been worn by the Forces Armées Centrafricaines (FACA), obtained through a variety of sources. (*Private collection*)

In the current era, copies of both French Daguet desert and CE Woodland pattern can be found among FACA. (*Private collection*)

These FACA soldiers are wearing a DPM pattern of undetermined origins. (*Private collection*)

This 'leaf' variant pattern saw at least limited use with the Republican Guard, and possibly by units of FACA as well.

Within the ranks of the Republican Guard a copy of the US-developed tricolor desert pattern has been documented.

Although France had claimed much of North Africa as its territory and established the Territoire Militaire des Pays et Protectorats du Tchad in 1900, the region was administered rather loosely and considered primarily a source of raw cotton. Chad was granted independence on 11 August 1960, following the French process of releasing most of its former colonial possessions that had begun in the early 1950s. The country has unfortunately been plagued with civil war, and has struggled against external aggression since shortly after gaining its independence. The first of these internal wars was instigated by a coalition of Muslim groups who overthrew the government and executed François Tombalbaye, the first president of Chad, in 1965. A state of sporadic civil warfare would subsequently exist from 1978 until 1987, with Libya involving itself in military matters on four separate occasions. The Libyans would ultimately be defeated and expelled in what is often called the Toyota War (16 December 1986 to 11 September 1987), when Chadian forces pulled together under the leadership of Hissène Habré. Habré governed the nation as a dictator until 1990, when he was overthrown by General Idriss Déby. A short period

From the late 1970s until perhaps the late 1980s, some Chadian government forces wore the Egyptian-made 'rocks' pattern camouflage, undoubtedly imported from that country.

The Belgian-influenced 'jigsaw' type camouflage seen here was adopted by Chad in the 1980s. Of undetermined origin, the pattern and fabric may have originated in Europe. Some of these uniforms would later end up in the hands of Libyans.

French leópard or 'lizard' pattern was also a frequently encountered camouflage design during the late 1970s and early 1980s period. (*Private collection*)

of stability and peace lasted until 2003, when a new civil war broke out, pitting the Chadian government against various dissident groups such as the United Front for Democratic Change, United Forces for Development and Democracy, Gathering of Forces for Change, and the National Accord of Chad. The country continues to struggle with war into the present period.

The Armed Forces of Chad are today called the Forces Nationale Tchad (FNT).

Seen here worn by a member of the BTAP (Airborne Forces), another variation of the French 'lizard' pattern made in Asia has seen extensive use with Chadian forces, even into the present era. (*Private collection*)

A copy of the US-designed six-color 'chocolate chip' camouflage has been worn since the very late 1980s. (*Private collection*)

Unique four-color woodland and desert patterns were produced for Chad, both based around the US m81 woodland design. (*Private collection*)

Seen here are two slightly different copies of the US-designed tricolor desert pattern in use with FNT officers. (*Private collection*)

A copy of both temperate and desert MARPAT has seen some sporadic use by FNT. (*Private collection*)

The same camouflage pattern developed for Kuwait's National Guard has been worn by FNT.

Copies of the pixilated designs made specifically for use by the Jordanian Armed Forces are also in use with Chad. These patterns were reputedly illegally copied by Chinese factories and made available on the commercial market to other countries.

A yellow-based woodland pattern was seen on Chadian participants during exercise Flintlock 2015. (*US Department of Defense*)

FNT have also adopted a copy of Norwegian desert pattern camouflage, as seen here. (*Private collection*)

Some members of the FNT special operations, as well as anti-poaching units of the Gendarmerie, have been observed wearing a copy of UCP. (*Private collection*)

The three-color desert pattern seen here also first appeared during exercise Flintlock. (*US Department of Defense*)

As with many other countries in the modern era, an Asian-made copy of Multicam is in use with some units of the FNT. (*Private collection*)

The island nation known as the Union of the Comoros (Union des Comores) achieved independence from France in 1975, but the next thirty years were a period of political turmoil, with the islands experiencing more than twenty coups or attempted coups. These began with an armed coup d'etat led by the infamous mercenary Robert Denard in August 1975, which removed the legitimate president from office and replaced him with United National Front of the Comoros (UNF) member Prince Said Mohammed Jaffar. A few months later he was ousted in favor of the Minister of Defense Ali Soilih. In May 1978, Denard returned with another band of mercenaries to lead a second coup and reinstate Abdallah as ruler. An authoritarian with a belief in the strict adherence to Islamic law, Abdallah renamed the country the Federal Islamic Republic of Comoros, and in 1989 ordered the Presidential Guard (under Denard) to disarm the armed forces. Shortly thereafter he was assassinated by a member of the military.

Following Abdallah's death, Said Mohamed Djohar (Ali Solih's brother) became president, serving until September 1995, when Denard returned again to attempt another coup. He was forced to surrender after the intervention of French military personnel.

In the early 2000s, the armed forces re-adopted a variation of the French tenue du leópard, no doubt obtained from Asian sources. (*US Army*)

The Comorian Army and the Defense Force wore a Chinese-made copy of French 'lizard' pattern in the 1990s.

Around the mid-2000s, a DPM pattern similar to that worn by Tanzania was adopted but did not last very long. (*Private collection*)

A faithful copy of the US woodland camouflage design was adopted by the AND circa 2010 and continues to be worn by many personnel. (*US Army*)

A copy of French CE woodland is also in use with some personnel of the AND. (*Private collection*)

Circa 2015, personnel of the AND adopted a leaf-type pattern unique to the country. (*Ministère de la Défense Nationale*)

The islands of Anjouan and Mohéli declared their independence from the Comoros in 1997 which sparked confrontations between federal troops and rebels. The insurrection was quelled, but in 1999 Army Chief of Staff Colonel Azali Assoumani seized power from an interim president, although he was unable to re-establish control over the entire country. The official name was changed to the Union of the Comoros, and Azali stepped down in 2002 to run in the democratic election of the president of the Comoros, which he won. He was succeeded in 2006 by Ahmed Abdallah Mohamed Sambi, a Sunni Muslim cleric.

The Comorian armed forces are called the Armée Nationale de Développement, consisting of a small Army, National Police force, and small Defense Force.

DEMOCRATIC REPUBLIC OF CONGO (CONGO-KINSHASA)

The present day Democratic Republic of Congo (République Démocratique du Congo) or DRC has experienced a number of name changes over the course of its history, which may prove quite confusing to those not intimately familiar with African history. To differentiate it from the former French Congo (now Republic of Congo), the nation has at various times been called Belgian Congo, Congo-Leopoldville (vice Congo-Brazzaville), Republic of the Congo, Congo-Kinshasa, or simply Congo. Between 1971 and 1997, the nation was known as Zaire (see later entry), and between 1960 and 1963 a breakaway state existed within its borders known as Katanga (also a separate entry).

The former Belgian colony was declared République du Congo in June 1960, but was immediately faced with a crisis as the southern province of Katanga declared its intent to secede. At nearly the same time, a mutiny of the Force Publique led to looting and terrorization of the European population, with thousands fleeing the country. Following a Belgian military intervention to secure the safety of the remaining European population, most Belgians left the country (including officers and senior Army NCOs), leaving a newly renamed Armée Nationale Congolaise (ANC) with little trained leadership.

Initially supported by local Belgian businesses and several thousand Belgian military personnel, the State of Katanga was declared on 11 July 1960, to the violent opposition of the Congolese government. Congolese PM Patrice Lumumba was shortly thereafter kidnapped and executed under mysterious circumstances, leaving

Joseph Kasavubu as president, but with real power in the hands of Joseph Mobutu, who controlled the Armée Nationale Congolaise (ANC). The resulting war involved a sizeable number of European Katangese and mercenaries on the side of Katanga, and eventually led to a military intervention by the United Nations on the behalf of the Congolese government. Under intense international and military pressure and with little outside support, Katanga eventually capitulated after its capital fell on 15 January 1963.

In November 1965, Mobutu seized power from president Kasavubu and declared a one-party state. A series of mutinies in 1966 and 1967 involving former Katangese gendarmes and European mercenaries were both quelled, and in 1971 the name of the country would be changed to Zaire. Mobutu ruled the nation with an iron fist until 1997 when he was deposed during the First Congo War by a coalition of militias and friendly foreign governments (Uganda, Angola and Rwanda) calling themselves the Alliance des Forces Démocratiques pour la Libération du Congo-Zaïre (AFDL). Under the leadership of Laurent-Désiré Kabila, the ANC was defeated and the country renamed Democratic Republic of Congo, with Kabila as president.

Following his victory, Kabila thanked all foreign military personnel for their help and requested they

Camouflage Patterns of Congo-Kinshasa (Congo-Leopoldville): 1960-1970

Both the Force Publique (FP) and the later Armée Nationale Congolaise (ANC) wore olive green as a standard combat uniform, but some units (in particular the Para-Commando Battalion) were issued Belgian camouflage uniforms, including both types of brushstroke and the early Belgian jigsaw pattern. There is some evidence to suggest locally-made or imported uniforms were also worn, made of the same fabrics. (*Private collection*)

Camouflage Patterns of Congo-Kinshasa (Congo-Leopoldville): 1960-1970

A substantial amount of Portuguese camouflage was worn by the ANC in the early 1960s. (*Private collection*)

Other early units of the ANC during the 1960s have been documented wearing various French lizard designs, some of which appear to be ex-French surplus, but many of which were probably either locally produced from imported fabrics, or imported from European companies.

return to their countries of origin. Not wishing to relinquish what power they had taken, however, Rwandan troops organized the Rassemblement Congolais pour la Democratie (RCD) to wage an insurgency campaign. Ugandan soldiers did the same, forming the Movement for the Liberation of Congo (MLC). Thus between August 1998 and July 2003, the Second Congo War raged between the transitional government of the new DRC and the two aforementioned rebel militias. The largest war in modern African history, it directly involved eight African nations, as well as approximately twenty-five different armed groups. By 2008 the war and its aftermath had claimed the lives of 5.4 million people, mostly from disease and starvation. The government of the DRC was assisted by Angola, Chad, Namibia and Zimbabwe, while the insurgents were aided by the governments of Rwanda, Uganda, and Burundi. Kabila was assassinated in 2001, but was succeeded by his son, Joseph Kabila, who shortly thereafter managed to arrange a ceasefire agreement, and a United Nations mission to restore peace (MONUC). However, the war was reignited in January 2002, with both Uganda and Rwanda sending troops back into the country. The conflict officially ended in 2003, although the death toll would continue to mount due to cases of malnutrition and disease.

Camouflage Patterns of the DRC: 1997–present

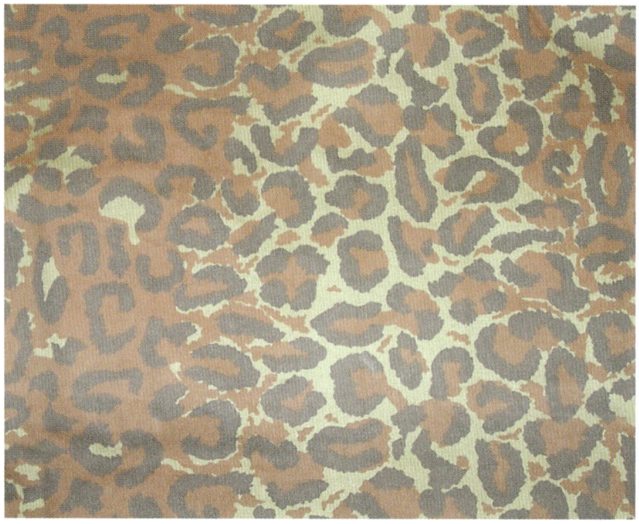

Units of the FARDC have worn a variety of camouflage patterns, including many worn during Mobutu's regime, when the country was still called Zaire. Even in recent years, scattered examples of the 'leopard spot' and Zairean jigsaw pattern can be found both among government units and within the ranks of rebel militias.

Chinese-produced 'woodland' type camouflage has been worn by the FARDC since the early part of the twenty-first century. (*Private collection*)

In use with both the government forces and some insurgent units, commercial tiger stripe patterns have been popular for years.

Similar to the Norwegian m/98 pattern, the four-color design seen here is the standard combat uniform of the FARDC. (*Private collection*)

Elements of the Garde Presidentielle wear this unique 'grasslands' camouflage pattern. (*Private collection*)

REPUBLIC OF CONGO

République du Congo is often called Congo-Brazzaville in order to differentiate it from its neighbor, the Democratic Republic of Congo. Once administered as part of French Equatorial Africa, the nation achieved independence in August 1960.

A coup d'etat in August 1968 established Marien Ngouabi as president of the newly proclaimed People's Republic of Congo. During this period, strong relations were established with the USSR, China, North Korea, and North Vietnam. Ngouabi was assassinated on 16 March 1977 and replaced by Joachim Yhombi-Opango, who in turn was ousted two years later, with Denis Sassou Nguesso assuming the position of president. Under Sassou, the country became even further aligned

During the 1960s, some units wore a copy of the French leópard or 'lizard' pattern camouflage, although it appears to have fallen into disuse by the late 1970s.

The East German M58 Flachtarnenmuster camouflage was in use with some Congolese forces during the 1980s.

A copy of US m81 woodland is currently the standard camouflage pattern of this nation. (*Private collection*)

The Republic of Congo Eco-guards, operating primarily in the vast Odzala-Kokoua National Park, wear DPM pattern camouflage uniforms. (*Private collection*)

with the Communist Bloc and signed a twenty-year friendship pact with the Soviet Union. This dictatorship would continue well into the present era.

In June 1997, a four-month armed conflict sparked by political rivalries destroyed much of the capital (Brazzaville) and cost tens of thousands of civilian lives. A military intervention by Angola in October of that year reinstalled Sassou as president. He would be re-elected in 2002, but discontent over the one-party system and questionable electoral processes instigated a rebellion in the Pool region which ended by peace treaty signed in April 2003. Sassou remains president of the Republic of Congo amid continued accusations of fraud and irregularities.

CÔTE D'IVOIRE

Once considered a part of French West Africa, the present day République de Côte d'Ivoire (Ivory Coast) became fully independent from France in 1960. The nation was ruled under a one-party system by its first president, Félix Houphouët-Boigny, until his death in 1993. He was succeeded by Henri Konan Bédié, who retained control until forced into exile in 1999.

In September 2002, military personnel from the north, loyal to General Guéï, mutinied and launched attacks on several cities including the capital of Abidjan. Although government forces maintained control over the south and the capital, insurgents wrested control of most of the north and based themselves in the city of Bouake. France intervened, sending 2,500 personnel to maintain a peace line and requested the assistance of the United Nations, but fighting raged until late in 2004. In addition to the National Army (FANCI), the government was supported by nationalist militias calling themselves Young Patriots, and mercenaries recruited from Liberia and Europe. The Forces Nouvelles (FN) or New Forces, was the name taken by the insurgent northerners. Although a peace agreement was reached in 2004, it proved short-lived as the FN refused to disarm or give up control of the north. An ongoing peacekeeping mission to the nation, the United Nations Operation in Côte d'Ivoire (UNOCI), has been in place since April 2004, although a new peace accord was signed in March 2007, with a transitional government including rebel leader Guillaume Soro as prime minister. Violence erupted again following the November 2010 elections, which were contested by supporters of Gbagbo.

French lizard pattern saw widespread use in this country until the 1990s, and was phased back into service circa 2010–11.

This unique 'veins' design incorporating dark green or black lines on a grey green background was in service primarily in the 1980s.

A copy of the French CE woodland pattern has been in service with this nation since 1990s.

Seen here worn by several FANCI officers, several types of woodland camouflage have also seen service with this nation. (*Private collection*)

One interesting woodland-type design from the 2007 period incorporated the letters FANCI into the pattern. (*Private collection*)

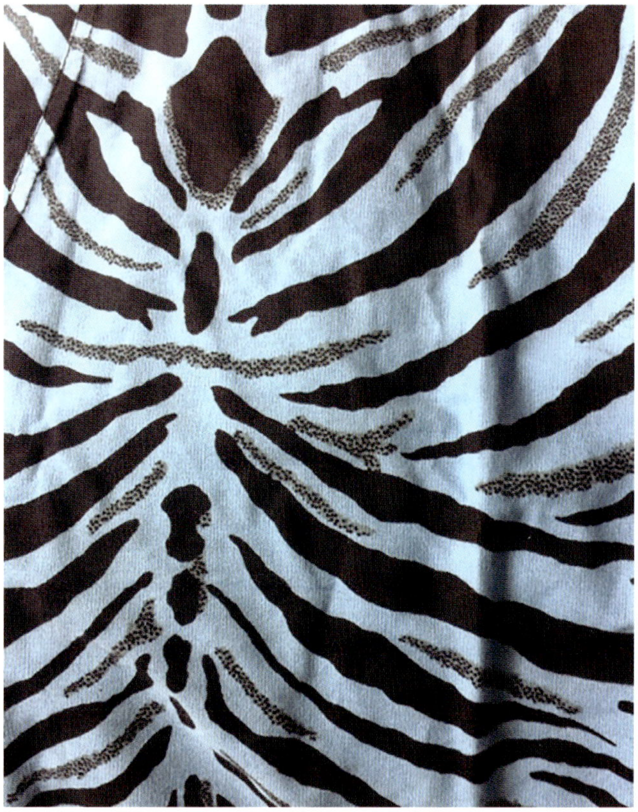

The Brigade Anti-Emeute (Anti-riot Brigade) of the Gendarmerie has worn a 'zebra stripe'-like design seen here consisting of midnight blue or black stripes on a white or pale grey background. A variation of the pattern with a pale blue background was still being worn in 2017. (*Private collection*)

The Police Maritime wear a unique 'blue lizard' camouflage design, of which at least two variations have been documented. One version has the 'Police Maritime' logo stamped over the camouflage design itself.

The Gendarmerie Nationale have worn a blue-green woodland derivative pattern, incorporating the national coat-of-arms into the design. (*DGPN*)

Circa 2010–11, members of the FRCI (particularly members of the Garde Republicaine) adopted a copy of the Universal Camouflage Pattern (*UCP*).

Some members of the FRCI and the Gendarmerie have been documented wearing commercial tiger stripe patterns such as the one seen here circa 2010.

In mid-2012, a new pattern for Ivory Coast appeared in public for the first time, inspired by splinter camouflage designs such as that worn in Sweden. The first of these patterns features black and light-brown splinter shapes on a grass green background, with the national coat-of-arms incorporated into the design in black ink. A second version of this colorway has been documented featuring a reduction of the overall shape size by at least 50 per cent. The green variant is now the standard issue pattern of the Army. (*Ministère de la Défense Nationale*)

A variation of the above, with light brown and black shapes on a white background, is in service with the Garde Presidentielle. A variant exists with the size reduced by 50 per cent as well.

An additional variation of the splinter pattern, also in use with the Gendarmerie Nationale is shown here, having a primarily dark blue-black colorway with pale blue contrasting background. As with most other splinter variants, this one has been produced in both large and reduced size versions. (*DGPN*)

For operational deployment, the Brigade Anti-Emeute (Anti-riot Brigade) of the Gendarmerie wear a fourth variation of the splinter pattern with a grey colorway. The splinter shapes in this version are solid black with additional shapes in a composite of black dots, both on a pale blue or light grey background. (*Private collection*)

The Police Maritime have their own variation of the splinter design incorporating blue and medium brown shapes on a pale grey background, with the coat of arms embedded into the design as in other versions. (*Private collection*)

An interesting variation of the French 'Daguet' desert pattern is in service with the FRCI, the distinguishing feature being the incorporation of the Ivorian coat-of-arms into the design. (*Private collection*)

An Asian-made copy of Multicam is now in use with the FRCI Special Forces. (*Private collection*)

Some members of the Police Nationale (under the Ministry of the Interior) wear camouflage-like dark striped print pattern uniform. The design actually incorporates the title 'Police Nationale RCI' into the pattern, the title being printed in light grey or pale blue on a midnight blue background. It is worth noting that some versions appear to have larger lettering than others. (*Private collection*)

The Customs Service of Ivory Coast (Douanes de Côte d'Ivoire) issue a unique camouflage-like uniform having a yellow-green colorway. This uniform is worn by regular personnel of the Customs Service. Two versions of the pattern have been documented, one having a brighter concentration of yellow. (*Private collection*)

Members of the Customs Service Special Brigade wear a variety of camouflage designs, including a copy of the USMC MARPAT, a copy of the Colombian Army pixelado pattern, commercial 'desert tiger stripe' pattern, and some unique designs with yellow colorways. (*Private collection*)

Up until April of 2011, the armed forces were called the Forces Armées Nationales de Côte d'Ivoire or FANCI. Under this umbrella are included the Army (broken into five military regions), a brown-water Navy (essentially a Coast Guard) called the Police Maritime, a largely ineffective Air Force, and the National Gendarmerie. With approximately 14,000 active duty personnel, the FANCI were defeated during the Second Ivorian Civil War (November 2010 to April 2011) and have since been replaced by the Forces Nouvelles de Côte d'Ivoire (New Forces of the Ivory Coast), under which the armed forces themselves are now called Force Republiques de Côte d'Ivoire or FRCI.

DJIBOUTI

The present day Republic of Djibouti was formerly known as French Somaliland. The nation gained its independence from France in 1977. Djibouti was involved in a civil war between 1991 and 1994, when the Front for the Restoration of Unity and Democracy (FRUD) – an ethnic Afar rebel group – mounted a

During the 1970s and 1980s, this nation wore French leópard or 'lizard' pattern camouflage uniforms.

Seen here in a photo from 2011, the Armed forces transitioned to a copy of US 'chocolate chip' desert at some point in the 1990s. (*Private collection*)

The Armed Forces also wear a copy of US tricolor desert as seen here. (*Private collection*)

Djiboutian personnel serving in Central Africa wore a copy of the French CE woodland pattern. (*Private collection*)

Various copies of US m81 woodland pattern have been worn in the modern era. (*Private collection*)

A copy of the Italian desert vegetato pattern has been worn by Djiboutian forces since 2015.

The Garde-côtes (Coast Guard) wear a grey-dominant version of the six-color 'chocolate chip' desert pattern, similar to that worn by UAE and Saudi Arabia. (*Private collection*)

Naval Forces have worn a woodland-derivative pattern with a blue colorway. (*US Navy*)

Some Djiboutian military personnel have adopted the Yemeni Republican Guards arid camouflage pattern, both the earlier organic and the later pixelated design. The uniforms seem to be overruns, as they have Velcro patches in the same position as the Yemeni version. (*US DOD*)

military operation against the government in response to a lack of Afar representation in government. The nation also clashed briefly with Eritrea over a border conflict in 1996, and again in 2008.

The Djibouti Armed Forces (Ciidanka Jabuuti) consist of several branches of service, including the National Army, Navy, Air Force, and the Gendarmerie (Gendarmerie Nationale Djiboutienne) In 2013, the Garde-côtes (Coast Guard) was formed, primarily to protect territorial waters from piracy.

EGYPT

Egypt became a British protectorate following the First World War, but the revolution of 1919 led to its being declared an independent state, one of the first nations in Africa to achieve this status in the twentieth century. The present Republic came into being in 1953 and was followed shortly thereafter by a brief union with Syria known as the United Arab Republic (1958–61).

The modern Egyptian armed forces have been involved in numerous crises and wars since independence, including the 1948 Arab–Israeli War, Egyptian Revolution of 1952, Suez Crisis, North Yemen Civil War, Six-Day War, Nigerian Civil War, War of Attrition, Yom Kippur War, Egyptian bread riots, 1986 Egyptian conscripts riot, Libyan–Egyptian War, Gulf War, War on Terror, Egyptian Crisis, Second Libyan Civil War, War on ISIL and the Sinai insurgency.

Egypt's first post-war involvement was the 1948 Arab-Israeli War, which ended in Egyptian occupation of the Gaza Strip. This was followed by the Suez Crisis in 1956, resulting in Israeli occupation of the Suez Canal. In the early 1960s, the nation became involved in the North Yemen Civil War (1962–70) on the side of the Yemeni republicans. Egypt became further embroiled in the Six-Day War (1967) with Israel, during which the Gaza strip was lost.

The October War (Yom Kippur War) of 1973 lasted only nineteen days, but allowed Egypt to regain some of the Suez territory previously occupied by Israel. A peace treaty signed with Israel in 1979 resulted in complete Israeli withdrawal from the Sinai as well as the Multinational Force and Observers (MFO) which has maintained a continuous presence there since.

A series of regime changes occurred between 2011 and 2014, beginning with the resignation of President Hosni Mubarak and the adoption of a new constitutional referendum in 2012. New president Mohammed Morsi

One of the earliest camouflage patterns produced in Egypt is frequently called the 'rocks' pattern (often to discern it from the 'sand' pattern), which is believed to have emerged in 1956. The design can be seen to derive from the German Wehrmacht 'Planetree' pattern (hence is sometimes called 'Egyptian Plane Tree'), although certainly the Egyptian version is much more crude. Variability within production runs is considerable, even more so when factoring in that the pattern remained in production well into the 1990s period. The 'rocks' pattern was historically printed on one side of a reversible fabric, with a two-color desert 'sand' pattern (see below) on the other side. This practice continued into the later years of its production, but contemporary uniforms are no longer designed to be worn reversibly; they are either sewn together with a single side permanently out, or made from single-sided fabric. This pattern is generally associated only with Airborne and Commando units. Egyptian manufacturers have exported this pattern to Sudan, Somalia, Niger, Libya, and Yemen, among others.

Introduced in the 1960s or 1970s, the two-color 'sand' camouflage design was also worn primarily by Egyptian airborne and commando units, and continues to be issued today in a slightly darker print. (*Private collection*)

was instantly unpopular due to his association with the Muslim Brotherhood. Violence ensued in December 2012, resulting in another temporary coup d'etat and interim government. A new constitution was finally approved in 2014 and former military general Abdel Fattah el-Sisi was overwhelmingly elected president, under protest from the Muslim Brotherhood and secular activist groups.

The Egyptian Armed Forces today consist of four branches: the Army, Navy, Air Force and Air Defense Forces. In addition, the Ministry of the Interior has its own paramilitary forces, including special police and SWAT-type units.

Another very early pattern, also dating to around 1956, is the 'oakleaf' camouflage. This design is unquestionably copied from the German Wehrmacht Waffen SS Beringt-Eichenlaubmuster (ringed oakleaf), although again the printing is much more crude than the original.

A variation of the desert pattern was produced during the First Gulf War and is missing the green elements. The fabric may have been mis-printed, but evidence indicates the uniforms were worn anyway during that operation.

A vertical stripe or 'lizard' pattern first emerged in use among Egyptian forces in the mid-1980s, and was restricted to use by units of the Presidential Guard. The design is unquestionably influenced by earlier patterns worn in Syria, Lebanon and Palestine in the 1970s and 1980s. (*Private collection*)

A darker copy of the US woodland camouflage design was adopted by Egyptian Forces in the 1990s and issued to personnel serving abroad, such as with KFOR, when attending foreign military courses, and by special operations personnel such as the individuals seen here. (*Private collection*)

Egypt introduced a new desert camouflage pattern beginning in the 1980s consisting of amoebic shapes in dark brown, olive green and dusty rose on a khaki background. This densely concentrated design was later replaced by a similar pattern with sparse concentration of shapes but essentially the same color palette (although there has been considerable variability among fabric lots). As seen in this photo, the two designs were often worn interchangeably. (*Private collection*)

Copies of US tricolor desert and Air Force Digital Tiger Stripe pattern have also been adopted by Egyptian Forces, the latter worn strictly by members of Egypt's own Air Force. (*Egypt Ministry of Defense*)

A locally produced copy of the US 'chocolate chip' (six color) desert pattern with a more orange/rust coloration was adopted by Egypt in the late 1990s. (*US DOD*)

By 2015, the Navy had changed to a blue-dominant camouflage pattern with smaller, more 'leaf' inspired shapes. (*Egypt Ministry of Defense*)

A woodland-type camouflage with blue colorway was adopted by the Egyptian Navy at some point during the late 1990s. (*Egypt Ministry of Defense*)

Other variations of the US woodland pattern began to appear among Egyptian military forces in the early 2000s. As seen in the photo there is considerable variability in shades. By this period, Egypt was sourcing its uniforms in Eastern Asia. (*Egypt Ministry of Defense*)

A two-color black/grey pattern first seen in use among Iraqi forces has also been adopted by the Egyptian Central Security Forces (قوات الأمن المركزي) and sourced through China.

EQUATORIAL GUINEA

Formerly known as Spanish Guinea, the country is known today as the República de Guinea Ecuatoria (Republic of Equatorial Guinea). Independence from Spain was achieved in 1968. The Fuerzas Armadas de Guinea Ecuatorial are the armed forces of Equatorial Guinea, consisting of the Army, Navy and Air Wing, with approximately 1,300 active duty personnel. A Gendarmerie and National Police force are tasked with internal security and law enforcement respectively. A Presidential Guard of approximately 350 personnel is comprised primarily of Moroccans.

Woodland camouflage is worn by members of all branches of service. In addition, a unique blue lizard pattern is worn by members of the Navy. (*Private collection*)

The Army of this nation has worn a variation of the French 'lizard' pattern also, as well as m81 woodland and a blue DPM pattern by the police. (*Private collection*)

ERITREA

This nation was once a part of the Italian colonial possessions of North Africa, which also included Somaliland and Ethiopia. The country came under British mandate following the Second World War but was federated with Ethiopia in 1952, becoming essentially a province under its protection. Subsequently the Eritrean War of Independence was sparked, lasting thirty years (from 1961 to 1991) and ultimately ending with success for the Eritrean People's Liberation Front (EPLF) and full independence from Ethiopia.

The Eritrean Defense Forces is one of the largest military entities in Africa, consisting of around 320,000 active duty personnel within the Army, Navy and Air Force.

Copies of both US woodland and six-color desert (with suitable color variations depending on source) have been worn by this country since obtaining its independence from Ethiopia. (*Private collection*)

As seen here, this country also wears a copy of the US tricolor desert pattern. (*Private collection*)

For most of its history, the territory comprising modern Ethiopia was ruled as a monarchy. Briefly federated with its neighbor Eritrea from 1952 to 1961, the connection was dissolved by emperor Haile Selassie, leading the country down a path of war which lasted for more than thirty years. Selassie was deposed in 1974 by a military junta known as the 'Derg' which established a one-party communist state (the People's Democratic Republic of Ethiopia) supported by the Soviet Union and Eastern European communist countries.

A brief war with Somalia (the Ogaden War, 1977–78) ended in Ethiopia's loss of the Ogaden region, which was only regained by the assistance of the USSR, North Korea and Cuba. A period of internal strife, the

In this photo from 1994, DPM pattern camouflage is worn by Ethiopian troops deployed on a UN mission to Rwanda. This may have been the only time such camouflage was worn by this nation. (*Private collection*)

This 'waves' pattern, produced in South Korea for export, was worn under the 'Derg' regime but disappeared from service after democratic elections in 1993. (*Private collection*)

A two-color desert pattern is also worn by some special units of the national police. (*Private collection*)

Variations of US m81 'woodland' camouflage have been worn by this nation since the 1990s. (*Private collection*)

This woodland pattern with a blue colorway is worn by special units of the national police. (*Private collection*)

Ethiopian Red Terror, was then followed by a series of famines that affected as many as 8 million Ethiopians. In response, an opposition movement, the Ethiopian People's Revolutionary Democratic Front (EPRDF), waged a guerilla war which ultimately collapsed the military junta and set up a transitional government in 1991. Eritreans voted for and achieved independence in 1993, and the first free and democratic election took place in May 1995. The country is today known as the Federal Democratic Republic of Ethiopia.

In May 1998, Ethiopia again went to war with Eritrea over a border dispute that continued until 2000. Ethiopia continues to occupy the territory gained during the conflict, despite a UN determination that the land actually belongs to Eritrea.

The armed forces of Ethiopia are today called the Ethiopian National Defense Force (ENDF), and consist of the Army and Air Force. The Ethiopian Navy existed from 1955 until 1991, but was dissolved after the independence of Eritrea as the country is now landlocked. It is estimated there are as many as 182,000 active duty personnel in the ENDF.

Field Rangers that protect the natural resources of Ethiopia's parks and national reserves wear a camouflage design based on the US tricolor desert but with a slightly more grey color palette. (*Private collection*)

GABON

This nation was considered French territory from the late nineteenth century and became one of the four territories of French Equatorial Africa, all of which were granted independence in 1960.

Although its first president, Léon M'ba, was elected in 1961, the country was run as a dictatorship thereafter, with suppression of the press, political opposition, and freedom of expression. When a military coup sought to remove M'ba in 1964 and restore parliamentary democracy, the French government intervened militarily, imprisoned the opposition, and restored its favored politician to power. Omar Bongo Ondimba replaced M'ba as president when he died in 1967, and declared Gabon a one-party state as an effort to subvert the regional and tribal rivalries that traditionally divided African national politics. Partisan politics would gradually make their way back into Gabon, but despite political opposition and some violent protests, Bongo was re-elected as president in 1975, 1979, 1986, 1993, 1998, and 2005, but died in 2009 of cardiac arrest. His

A copy of the French CE woodland pattern replaced lizard in the 1990s and is seen here worn by a member of the Naval Commando unit. (*Private collection*)

Seen here worn by members of the Parachute Battalion, French 'lizard' pattern can be dated to the 1980s, although it was probably used earlier. The design is still worn by some units. (*Private collection*)

Seen at the far right in this photo, a tricolor variation of CE woodland incorporating dark brown and olive green shapes on a sandy background is worn by the Garde Republicaine. Also note the 'leaf' pattern at the far left, which has been observed in use by some Gabon military personnel. (*Private collection*)

Both blue- and a grey-dominant versions of the CE woodland are in use with National Police units. (*Private collection*)

Unique to the National Military Health Service is this red-dominant variation of CE woodland. (*US DOD*)

A copy of the US m81 woodland pattern has seen some use with Gabon military personnel in recent years. (*Private collection*)

A unique jungle pattern camouflage uniform is worn by members of the Agence Nationale Des Parcs Nationaux. (*Parcs Gabon*)

A variation of the French 'Daguet' tricolor desert pattern has been observed in use since 2015. (*Private collection*)

son Ali Bongo Ondimba was declared winner of the presidential election in October of the same year.

The armed forces of Gabon consist of the Army, Navy, Air Force, Presidential Guard, National Gendarmerie, and the National Police. There are approximately 5,000 active duty personnel.

GAMBIA

Gambia was ruled as a British Crown Colony until granted self-governance in 1962. In February of 1965, Gambia achieved full independence as a constitutional monarchy within the Commonwealth of Nations. Five years later it became a republic.

After seeking military assistance from neighboring Senegal in 1981 following a failed coup attempt, Gambia joined briefly with its neighbor to form the Senegambia Confederation, which combined the armed forces and currencies of the two nations and lasted until 1989. In 1994, the Armed Forces Provisional Ruling Council (AFPRC) deposed the legitimately elected government and banned opposition political activity, but announced shortly thereafter a plan to return to democratic civilian government. Finally in December 2001, a new president took the oath of office.

The Gambian armed forces consist of the Army, National Guard, a small Navy and the National Police, with approximately 2,300 active duty personnel. During the Liberian civil war, members of the Gambian Armed Forces participated in the ECOMOG effort to stabilize the nation in 1990.

Seen here in a photo from 2008, DPM pattern camouflage has been in use with this country since the 1990s. (*Private collection*)

A copy of US m81 woodland camouflage has been worn by this nation since the 1990s, but is now primarily used only by the National Republican Guard. (*Private collection*)

An Asian-made copy of Multicam was adopted by the National Republican Guard but apparently was only worn for a short period of time.

This Navy officer wears a variation of the pixilated design with a blue colorway. (*Private collection*)

This pixilated camouflage pattern was adopted by the armed forces in 2012. (*Private collection*)

A pixilated design with a bright green base color has been adopted by the National Republican Guard seen intermixed with woodland and DPM. (*Private collection*)

This dark blue-dominant pattern is worn by a variety of units, including some members of the Republican Guard, Military Police and others. (*Private collection*)

The limited use of a blue-dominant tiger stripe pattern has been documented with the Ghana Police Service, circa 1990s. (*Private collection*)

This nation was formed under European auspices by merging the region known earlier as Gold Coast with British Togoland, achieving full independence in 1957. In February 1966, the democratic government of Dr Kwame Nkruma was overthrown in a coup led by the armed forces under Colonel Emmanuel K. Kotoka. Ghana was subsequently governed by an alternating succession of military and civilian governments until 1981, when the constitution was suspended and all political parties were banned under the Provisional National Defense Council of Jerry John Rawlings. Restoration of multi-party politics did not occur until 1992.

The use of woodland camouflage by the GAF began in the late 1990s and has continued to the present day, with some variation in colors and hue. (*Private collection*)

Seen here worn by the Director of the Ghana Immigration Service is a 'leopard spot' pattern issued to officers of this government agency. (*Ghana Immigration*)

The Ghana Armed Forces (GAF) consists of the Army, Air Force and Navy, as well as a Border Guard Unit and a battalion-sized Presidential Guard Regiment. Law enforcement is administered by the Ghana Police Service, consisting of numerous regional and divisional commands. Historically the use of camouflage was limited, with the standard working uniform being simple olive drab.

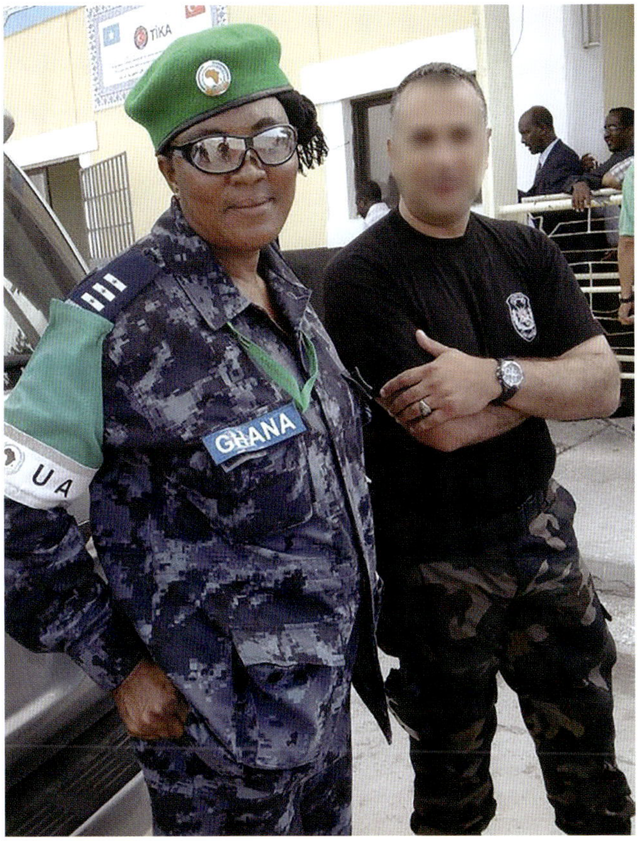

First seen in 2012, the Ghana Police Service have adopted a copy of the Jordanian Police digital camouflage pattern. (*Ghana Police Service*)

This bright red and black woodland-type camouflage design is worn by members of the Ghana Fire Service. (*Private collection*)

Below (l & r): The Ghana Prison Service have issued both brown dominant 'desert lizard' pattern and a woodland variant utilizing the same color palette. (*Private collection*)

REPUBLIC OF GUINEA

This country was formerly known as French Guinea, part of the greater region known as French West Africa. It is sometimes referred to as Guinea-Conakry to distinguish it from its neighbor Guinea-Bissau. For most of its history, Guinea has been governed by a one-party system under the Democratic Party of Guinea, noted for strong socialist policy, intolerance of dissent and censorship of free speech.

In 1970, Portuguese forces from neighboring Portuguese Guinea staged a raid in support of exiled opposition forces. Although successful in achieving some of its goals, the Portuguese were unable to depose leader Sékou Touré, who in retaliation arrested and executed many that were deemed a part of the plot. Shortly after Tourés' death in 1984, the government was overthrown in a bloodless coup, and Lansana Conté assumed the

Seen here worn by Lansana Conté during the successful 1984 *coup d'etat*, a variation of the French leópard or 'lizard' pattern with a grey colorway was worn by this nation during this period. (*Private collection*)

A Chinese-designed 'woodland' type pattern has been worn to some limited extent by the Army. (*Private collection*)

role of president and retained control of the country until his own death in 2008. Moussa Dadis Camara then seized control in another military coup, leading to violent protests and numerous atrocities committed by the military. A free election was finally held in 2009 with former opposition leader Alpha Condé emerging as winner. Since this time, the nation has been marred by political violence as well as the deadly outbreak of Ebola, responsible for thousands of deaths.

Guinea's armed forces are divided into five branches: the Army, Navy, Air Force, National Gendarmerie and the Republican Guard. Law enforcement and internal security is largely overseen by the Sûreté National. (National Police).

A copy of the US m81 woodland pattern has been in use by this nation since 2000, and possibly earlier. (*Private collection*)

This Commander of the Army Special Forces wears a lizard pattern camouflaged uniform. (*Ministère de la Défense Nationale*)

US tricolor desert pattern camouflage uniforms were worn by Guinean personnel serving in Mali, circa 2010. (*Private collection*)

The pattern here is worn by members of the Garde Presidentielle, and possibly other units. (*Private collection*)

Since around 2010 the Army has worn copies of the French CE woodland pattern. (*Ministère de la Défense Nationale*)

This member of the Forces Speciales wears a variation of the Italian Army's vegetato pattern. (*Private collection*)

As seen in this photo, a copy of the US Marine Corps temperate MARPAT design is in use with some units of the Sûreté National and also by members of the armed forces. (*Private collection*)

This nation was formerly known as Portuguese Guinea (Guiné Portuguesa). Beginning in 1956, the Partido Africano da Independência da Guiné e Cabo Verde or PAIGC (African Party for the Independence of Guinea and Cape Verde) was established, and by 1961 was waging a guerilla war against the Portuguese. Although the insurgency never managed to secure control of more than a fraction of the interior of the country, independence was granted following the change in government that occurred in Portugal in 1974.

The nation was controlled by a revolutionary council until 1984. The first multi-party elections were held in 1994, but an army uprising in 1998 led to the president's ousting and sparked a civil war pitting government forces against guerilla elements from June 1998 to May 1999. Elections were held again in 2000 and Kumba Ialá was elected president; he was removed from office and arrested in 2003, leaving the country again in military hands until new elections were held in 2005. João Bernardo Vieira succeeded to office, under protest from his opponent who claimed election tampering had occurred. In 2009, Vieira was assassinated by members of the military, and his previous opponent Malam Bacai Sanhá won the new presidential election in June of that year. However, the nation was again faced with military unrest in April of 2010 when Prime Minister Carlos Gomes Junior was placed under house arrest and his PAIGC supporters protested in the capital. Later that year the European Union sent a mission to reform the armed forces, which ended in August.

Under Portuguese colonial administration, African troops wore the same camouflage uniforms as regular Portuguese military personnel. African Commando troops in Portuguese Guinea were some of the most effective jungle fighters in all of Portuguese Africa.

The tradition of wearing Portuguese-style 'vertical lizard' camouflage has continued into the present era, with several Asian-made variations having been documented in use by the armed forces of Guinea-Bissau. (*Private collection*)

The armed forces adopted a copy of the DPM camouflage worn by Portugal in the 1990s.

Seen here worn by Army Chief of Staff in 2009, significant use has been made of the Asian-produced 'lizard' camouflage seen throughout Africa. (*Private collection*)

These high ranking officers in 2015 wear a copy of US m81 woodland pattern, which has been in use with this nation for at least ten years. (*Private collection*)

KATANGA

Katanga is a province in the Democratic Republic of Congo that proclaimed its independence on 11 July 1960, sparking a war with the Congolese government. Although technically an 'unrecognized state', the government of Katanga had a legitimate leader in president Moise Tshombe, and was initially supported by Belgian business interests and as many as 6,000 Belgian military personnel. Katanga was one of the richest and most developed areas of the Congo, with profits from copper, tin, gold and uranium mining contributing significantly to the nation's coffers. This was one of the primary reasons for Congolese resistance to the secession. Katanga was also accused, in January 1961, of orchestrating the torture and execution of deposed Congolese president Patrice Lumumba, which provided an excuse for military intervention of the Armée Nationale Congolaise (ANC). In February of that year, the United Nations passed a resolution that authorized 'all appropriate measures' to prevent civil war. This resolution would, in fact, be utilized as justification for a military intervention on the part of UN forces, effectively putting Katangan forces at war on two separate fronts.

Katangese Gendarme wearing a surplus Belgian Force Publique issue 'brushstroke' camouflage uniform, a common sight during the conflict. As a former Belgian colony, Katangan forces made considerable use of camouflage uniforms provided by Belgian military advisors who initially remained in country to train the Gendarmerie. (*Torsten Dahlén collection*)

Although less common, the Belgian jigsaw pattern has also been documented in use by Katangese forces.

La Force Terrestriale Katangaise, trained and commanded by officers on loan from the Belgian Army, formed the bulk of the fighting force. Formed with the assistance of a handful of European emigres and Belgian advisors, the Katangan Gendarmerie was converted into an effective military force, augmented by several hundred mercenaries recruited in Europe and southern Africa. Without the intervention of the United Nations, Katanga might well have been able to resist the poorly trained and largely undisciplined ANC, who had recently lost most of their European officers and NCOs following a mutiny that impelled most Europeans to flee the country. Under intense international pressure, continuous military incursions from a numerically and technologically superior UN coalition, and with little outside support, Katanga eventually capitulated after its capital Élizabethville fell on 15 January 1963.

Also widely used by Katangan forces were original or locally-made uniforms of French lizard pattern. These were primarily worn by soldiers of European origin.

Kenya came under British administration in the latter part of the nineteenth century, when significant portions of land were cleared for the production of coffee and tea. Under British law, many native Africans gradually became landless and were forced into labor merely to

Above: During the 1970s the Army's twentieth Parachute Battalion wore a copy of the British Army Denison smock; a similar pattern has also been worn by Armored Car personnel.

Above/Below: British DPM has been the Army's standard combat dress since the 1980s, although a wide variety of colorways have been employed over time. (*Private collection*)

The Kenya Police Service has worn a vertical 'lizard' pattern based on the Portuguese M64 since the early 2000s. (*Private collection*)

subsist. By the 1950s, widespread dissatisfaction with these laws and a general resistance to colonialism brought about a popular uprising known as the Mau-Mau Rebellion (1952–56). The counter-insurgency war, which pitted British and African troops against the tribal guerillas, cost more than 10,000 African lives. Despite defeating the Mau-Mau, Britain eventually conceded to popular elections resulting in a new

A DPM variant pattern with a unique color palette was introduced in the early 2000s for the Air Force. (*US DOD*)

government under the Kenya African National Union (KANU) of Jomo Kenyatta. In December 1963 Kenya achieved independence, and declared the new Republic of Kenya one year later, with Kenyatta as president. After

The Kenyan Navy also introduced its own DPM variant at roughly the same time as the Air Force. (*Private collection*)

Kenya's Wildlife Service Guards wear a DPM pattern very similar to the desert designs found in Kuwait and Iraq in the late 1980s. (*Private collection*)

his death in 1978, Kenyatta was succeeded by Daniel arap Moi, who remained in office for twenty-four years. Mwai Kĭbakĭ was elected president in 2002, and remains in office today. The country was embroiled in a period of civil unrest between December 2007 and February 2008, following the re-election of Kĭbakĭ . Both violent and non-violent demonstrations took place, resulting in as many as 1,500 deaths and approximately 600,000 displaced people.

The Kenya Defense Forces consist of the Army, Navy and Air Force. The armed forces have regularly deployed as peacekeepers with the United Nations, although in the aftermath of the 2007 elections allegations of human rights violations were lodged against it. Law enforcement is largely overseen by the Kenya Police Service, with protection of wildlife and natural resources falling under the jurisdiction of the Kenya Wildlife Service.

LESOTHO

The Kingdom of Lesotho (Muso oa Lesotho) is a landlocked nation that is completely surrounded by South Africa. Formerly known as Basutoland, the region was a British protectorate that achieved independence in 1966.

In the 1970s, members of the Basotho National Party (BNP) who had lost power in Parliament formed the Lesotho Liberation Army (LLA), which was trained in Libya. A largely ineffective guerilla campaign was waged against the government into the early 1980s. In 1986, a military coup d'etat deposed the president and handed power to King Moshoeshoe II, hitherto only a ceremonial monarch. His son was installed as King Letsie III one year later when he went into exile. The nation returned to a democratically elected government in 1993, but was again overthrown in another coup led by Letsie in August the following year and Moshoeshoe reinstated as head of state.

As seen on this officer in 2010, other versions of DPM are also worn, including at least one produced in Southern Africa. (*Private collection*)

Lesotho has always worn some variation of DPM. In this photo from 2014, troops appear to be wearing ex-British Army surplus uniforms. (*Private collection*)

A unique brown-dominant DPM variant is worn by the Special Operations Battalion of the Lesotho Mounted Police. (*Private collection*)

In 1998, tensions rose over a rift in the ruling Basotho Congress Party (BCP), sparking protests and ultimately leading to the involvement of troops from both the Botswana Defense Force and the South African National Defense Force (SANDF). Order was finally restored, but not before a number of Basotho and South Africans had died.

Formed in 1978, the Lesotho Defense Force consists of the ground forces and the Air Wing.

LIBERIA

Modern Liberia began to take shape in 1822, when the American Colonization Society began working to repatriate former slaves to Africa. Known as Americo-Liberians, many chose to emigrate and on 26 July 1847, these settlers declared the independence of the Republic of Liberia. The Americans did not integrate easily into African society, preferring instead to establish many of their own American style institutions. The nation retained its independence during the European 'Scramble for Africa' and enjoyed large-scale support from the United States and American businesses throughout much of the twentieth century.

In 1980 a group of NCOs, under the leadership of Master Sergeant Samuel Kanyon Doe, staged a military coup d'etat and wrested power from the legitimately elected leaders, claiming marginalization of tribal societies at the hands of the Americo-Liberian descendants. In 1985 new elections were held, but the results were nullified by Samuel Doe's National Democratic Party of Liberia, which in turn claimed his own victory as president. The First Liberian Civil War erupted in 1989, pitting two, non-cooperating movements – the National Patriotic Front of Liberia (under Charles Taylor) and the Independent National Patriotic Front of Liberia (under Prince Johnson) – against the government forces of Doe's regime. In August 1990 an intervention force sponsored by the Economic Community of West African States Monitoring Group (ECOMOG) entered the country to impose a ceasefire. Doe was captured, tortured and executed the next month, and an interim government established in November succeeded in ending hostilities for only a few days. The United Liberation Movement of Liberia for Democracy (ULIMO) was formed in June 1991 by supporters of former President Doe and former members of the Armed Forces of Liberia (AFL). Although another peace agreement was brokered in September 1993, renewed hostilities erupted in May 1994. The experience was essentially repeated in August 1995, with a new agreement signed but having effect only until April of the following year. In August 1996, the warring factions finally agreed to and upheld a peace agreement that included demobilization and disarmament. In 1996, Charles Taylor was elected president of Liberia.

Taylor's regime was no more liberal or democratic than government under Doe, and in 1999 a Second Liberian Civil War broke out. Supported by Sierra Leone and Guinea, two rebel groups, Liberians United

A mixture of US ERDL pattern camouflage was worn by the Liberian Army during the 1980s. (*Private collection*)

The Liberian Army also wore variations of 'tiger stripe' pattern camouflage during the 1980s, and later combatants such as those in these photographs continued to do so as well. (*Private collection*)

The US Army has donated a significant number of woodland pattern camouflage BDUs to the Liberian armed forces over the years, such as that seen here. (*US DOD*)

The Bureau of Immigration and Naturalization (BIN) wears the US tricolor desert pattern, probably also donated by the US government. (*Private collection*)

Since 2014, some personnel of the BIN began wearing a pixelated camouflage design that seems to be loosely based on the desert MARPAT camouflage of the USMC. (*Private collection*)

for Reconciliation and Democracy (LURD) and Movement for Democracy in Liberia (MDL), fought the newly constituted Armed Forces of Liberia under Charles Taylor. After four years of fighting, culminating in a military intervention by the USA and ECOMOG, as well as non-violent demonstrations by the Women of Liberia Mass Action for Peace, Taylor accepted asylum in Nigeria and a transitional government established in 2003. A United Nations Mission in Liberia (UNIMIL) has since been in place.

With the aid and assistance of the United States, the Armed Forces of Liberia were restructured in 2005, and presently stands at a strength of 2000 personnel.

LIBYA

Once considered a territory of Italy, in the aftermath of the Second World War Libya came under the administration of both the United Kingdom and France. A United Nations resolution in 1949 recommended granting independence, and on 24 December 1951 the United Kingdom of Libya came into being under the rule of King Idris.

Fueled by Nasserism and Arab Nationalism, a small group of military officers led by 27-year-old Muammar al-Gaddafi staged a coup d'état against King Idris in 1969, launching the Libyan Revolution. The officers abolished the monarchy and proclaimed the new Libyan Arab Republic. Gaddafi was declared Revolutionary Leader and retained the position of national leader into the present era. Publicly supportive of Arab nationalist and sovereignty movements, Libya served as supporter and host to a number of training camps for international terrorist organizations. Libyan forces have intervened militarily in Chad on several occasions, but were defeated and expelled during the Toyota War (16 December 1986 to 11 September 1987).

Gaddafi played a prominent role in creating the African Union (AU), established in 2002, and in February 2009 was selected to be chairman for a year. Among the objectives of the AU are to achieve peace and security in Africa, and to promote democratic institutions, good governance and human rights. To this end, the AU has provided both intervention and peacekeeping forces to various nations in Africa.

Responding in large part to the Arab Spring movement, in 2011 anti-government protests and clashes with security forces swiftly turned into a full-scale Civil War. Between February and October of 2011, forces loyal to Gaddafi battled against the National Liberation Army, insurgent

As seen in this photo, Libyan troops wore a copy of the Egyptian 'sand' or two-color desert camouflage pattern in the late 1970s. (*Private collection*)

Variations of m81 woodland pattern, such as seen here on Gadaffi's personal female guard, have been in circulation since the mid-1990s. (*Private collection*)

As far back as the late 1970s a copy of the German sumpftarnmuster or 'marsh' pattern camouflage was worn by some Libyan units. Interestingly enough, this pattern was still circulating among the Libyan armed forces during the recent Civil War. (*Private collection*)

A copy of the US tricolor desert pattern has also been in use with Libyan forces since the 1990s, but continued to be seen up until the time of the Civil War.

Seen here on two insurgents during the uprising in 2011, a four color desert DPM pattern and 'barbed wire' variation of chocolate chip camouflage can both be dated to the earlier, Gadaffi period. (*Private collection*)

Many variations of the US-designed six-color camouflage pattern were worn by Libyan forces under Gaddafi. The examples seen here illustrate the varied color palettes. (*Private collection*)

forces composed largely of civilians fortified by defectors from the regular Libyan Army. The brutal and draconian methods employed by loyalist forces did nothing to enlist international support for the Libyan government, and within weeks a coalition of mostly NATO countries actively engaged in a military intervention with the aim of toppling the Gaddafi regime. Following the capture and execution of Colonel Gaddafi on 20 October 2011, the war was largely over.

Under Muammar Gaddafi, the armed forces of Libya consisted of the Army, Air Force, Navy and the People's Militia, with an estimated 119,000 active duty personnel in early 2011. Today's military forces are known as the Libyan National Army. They comprise ground forces, an air force and navy, and are estimated at approximately 35,000 personnel as of May 2012.

The two photographs here illustrate the use of a variant six-color desert pattern known as 'barbed wire' for the use of a shape that resembles the barbs on steel fencing. Like many of the designs shown from the Civil War, these patterns were probably interspersed throughout the armed forces, and later were obtained by various insurgent factions. (*Private collection*)

Seen here again worn by an insurgent during the Civil War, this pattern saw use primarily by the Libyan Police before 2011. (*Private collection*)

Although quantities of this South Korean designed pattern were in use with Libyan forces under Gaddafi, the pattern has since been discarded.

Copies of the US-designed Universal Camouflage Pattern (UCP) first appeared among anti-Gadaffi forces in 2011, and the pattern later came into official use with the Libyan National Army (LNA) in 2012. (*Private collection*)

This digital desert pattern came into use with the LNA in 2012 as the standard uniform of the reconstituted army. It is essentially the same pattern worn by the UAE.

A copy of the US Marine Corps desert MARPAT design was also adopted by the new Libyan National Army circa 2012.

Seen here worn by Military Policemen in 2013, a pattern loosely based on the USMC temperate MARPAT design is also fielded by the LNA. (*Private collection*)

Seen here is a photo of a LNA soldier wearing a copy of the Jordanian Army's KA2 desert digipat camouflage in 2013. Use of this design seems to have been relatively short-lived, or was perhaps limited to a specific unit. (*Private collection*)

These commandos of the Ministry of the Interior Police wear a black and brown-dominant 'woodland' type camouflage pattern that probably originated in Turkey. (*Private collection*)

Designed specifically for use by personnel of the African Union, six different color-palette versions of the pattern were produced by factories in China. A few of these have been seen in use among Gadaffi-era personal guards and military personnel.

This island nation came under French control in 1896. Following approximately ten years of armed insurrection, the French government granted autonomous republic status in 1958, followed by full independence for the new Malagasy Republic (aka the First Republic) in 1960. The nation remained relatively stable until 1972 when a state of national emergency was declared after rioters were fired upon by the Force Républicaine de Sécurité and control of the country was turned over to the Army. What followed was a period of instability and transition lasting nearly three years and four separate heads of state. This era involved, successively, an attempted coup d'etat, the assassination of the second military leader, Colonel Richard Ratsimandrava, and the declaration of martial law. In December 1975 the National Military Directorate appointed Vice Admiral Didier Ratsiraka as head of state, ushering in a new socialist-Marxist Second Republic (the Democratic Republic of Madagascar) lasting until 1992. During this period, the country aligned itself with Eastern Bloc countries.

In 1991, presidential guards opened fire on unarmed protestors, leading to the election of Albert Zafy as president of the Third Republic in 1992, and adoption of a new constitution establishing the country as a multi-party democracy.

Formerly known as the Malagasy Defense Force (Tafika Malagasy), the Madagascar People's Armed Forces consist

This photo from 2017 of several high-ranking Army personnel illustrates the intermingling of yet another lizard pattern variation with at least two different copies of French CE woodland pattern. (*PRM*)

Several variations of the traditional French 'lizard' camouflage design have been worn by this nation over the years. Seen here, these Para-Commando personnel wear a version having strong similarities to the French originals. (*Private collection*)

These personnel, also airborne qualified (but not Para-Commandos) wear a unique brown-dominant lizard pattern that was worn in the 1990s. (*Private collection*)

The soldier at the forefront of this photo wears a Chinese-made woodland-type camouflage pattern that has been exported around the world. (*Private collection*)

of the Army (Intervention Force), Aeronaval Force (navy and air wing), and the Development Force. Internal security falls under the jurisdiction of the Ministry of the Interior, which administers the National Civil Police, Gendarmerie Nationale, a Presidential Security Regiment, and the Secret Police (DGIDE).

The oldest known camouflage patterns worn by the Tafika Malagasy (Malagasy Defense Force) were variations of the French tenue de leópard or lizard pattern, which has been in use at least since the 1980s, if not earlier. Several variations have been documented, some with more green, yellow or brown domination of the design. The lizard camouflage has in large part been phased out by more contemporary designs, but is still occasionally encountered.

MALAWI

The region comprising present-day Malawi came under British control in the nineteenth century and was known as Nyasaland until 1964. Between 1953 and 1963 it was part of the Federation of Rhodesia and Nyasaland. The Republic of Malawi became a fully-independent nation in 1964. Under president Hastings Banda, the country was ruled as an autocratic one-party state until Banda was replaced in 1994 by the current president Arthur Peter Mutharika. A democratic, multi-party government is now in control.

The Malawi Defense Force consists primarily of the Army, which includes two Rifle Regiments (Malawi

Originally introduced as USA military aid, woodland pattern camouflage is now standard issue to Malawi personnel and also obtained from various sources. (*US Army*)

DPM camouflage was officially introduced in the 1980s and is still in circulation, obtained from a variety of sources. (*Private collection*)

This variation of DPM is worn by Malawi Police Service. (*Private collection*)

Rifles) and one Paratroop Battalion, as well as a Support Battalion, Air Wing and a Small Naval Detachment (which patrols Lake Malawi). The Malawi Police Service is tasked with law enforcement and internal security duties, falling under the Ministry of Internal Affairs and Public Security.

Numerous other camouflage patterns have been documented in use by this country, although in small numbers. These include copies of Rhodesian brushstroke camouflage (possibly sourced in Zimbabwe), Zambian camouflage, and some unique designs that may have been very short-lived.

MALI

This region came under French control in the nineteenth century, when it was considered a part of French Sudan. In 1959 this territory joined with Senegal and formed the Mali Federation, which lasted only two months before splitting up. The Republic of Mali was formally established on 20 June 1960. Modibo Keita, the first elected president of Mali, promptly established a one-party state with a socialist orientation. His regime was overthrown in a bloodless coup d'etat in 1968, and Moussa Traoré was then installed as president. This period was marked by political turmoil, drought, famine and repression of political dissent which lasted for years. Continued protests culminated in the March Revolution of 1991. Despite the brutal suppression, arrest and torture of dissidents, increasing support from workers and members of the military for the pro-democracy movement led to the arrest of Traoré, the drafting of a new constitution, and the formation of a pro-democracy transitional government.

Variations of French leópard or 'lizard' camouflage have been worn by this nation since at least the 1990s.

Here an officer of the Medical branch wears a commonly-seen 'lizard' variant produced in Asia. (*Private collection*)

A continued period of internal conflict has existed in Mali since 2012, initially stemming from a desire by Toureg people of the north to establish their own independent homeland (referred to as Azawad by the insurgent population). The National Movement for the Liberation of Azawad (Fr. MNLA), heavily populated

Various types of m81 woodland camouflage can be found intermixed within the armed forces. (*Private collection*)

This picture from 2004 shows army personnel being instructed by a US Army Special Forces NCO. The tricolor desert pattern uniforms were provided as part of military aid. (*US Army*)

Seen here in a photo from 2014, this three-color arid DPM variant pattern is the same as worn by Lebanese security forces of the General Security Directorate. (*Private collection*)

A copy of the French CE woodland pattern was adopted by this country in the early part of the 2000s and continues to see considerable use. (*Private collection*)

Personnel from the Armée de l'air du Mali (Mali Air Force) have adopted a blue/purple dominant DPM variant pattern camouflage. (*US Army*)

Copies of the US-designed six-color 'chocolate chip' desert pattern have been worn by the Garde Nationale.

As seen here a variation of the six-color pattern with pale blue background is worn by the Gendarmerie Nationale. (*Private collection*)

This unique woodland variant with blue/black/red colorway is worn by the Police Nationale. (*Bamada.net*)

La Douane (Customs Service) wears a pixilated camouflage design with blue/black colorway, as seen here. (*Private collection*)

Here a Para-Commando wears a unique brown woodland-type camouflage design, seen only within this unit. (*Private collection*)

Members of the Federal Forest and Wildlife Service wear this copy of the USMC Standard 'wine leaf' camouflage design. (*Private collection*)

This photo from 2017 shows high-ranking officers of the Army wearing a copy of Italian vegetato pattern camouflage, as well as later issue tricolor desert uniforms in service with the Army. (*Private collection*)

by Toureg veterans that fought in the 2011 Libyan Civil War, took control of the north and declared an independent state in the early stages of the war. Shortly thereafter, however, Islamist movements such as Ansar Dine and Al-Qaeda in the Islamic Maghreb (AQIM), which had supported the MNLA initially, betrayed it and took control of the north themselves. Malian government forces, with French military assistance, were able to regain control of much of the north in early 2013, turning over peacekeeping operations to the UN in April of that year (MINUSMA). Hostilities were renewed in September 2013, reigniting conflict between the government and the MNLA.

The armed forces of Mali consist primarily of the Army and Air Force, as well as the National Guard (formerly the Republican Guard). The Sûreté Nationale (National Police) and the Gendarmerie share responsibility for internal security and law enforcement.

Beyond its use of French-inspired camouflage patterns, Mali has no political or cultural standards insofar as the use of camouflage goes. They have utilized many different designs, including some unique to this nation and others borrowed from foreign military and paramilitary organizations.

MAURITANIA

Once part of a territory known as French West Africa, Mauritania achieved its independence in 1960. The country has a long history of ethnic discord and social discrimination, particularly between the Arab Mauritanians and black sub-Saharan elements of the population, with Arabs traditionally dominating politics and blacks often relegated to low social status. The diverging worldviews of Arab-dominated Mauritania contributed significantly to poor relations with neighboring Senegal and in April 1989 the Mauritania-Senegal Border War erupted. Lasting just over two years, the conflict resulted in thousands being forcibly expelled from both countries and hundreds of deaths. Forces de Libération Africaines de Mauritanie (FLAM), a paramilitary group supporting sovereignty in Mauritania for the Wolof ethnic group, still operates out of Senegal. Mauritania has experienced a number of regime changes by coup d'etat, the latest orchestrated by General Mohamed Ould Abdel Aziz in August of 2008.

The armed forces of this nation include the Army, Navy, Air Force, Gendarmerie and the Presidential Guard. In addition, there is a National Guard and national Police force that fall under the Ministry of the Interior.

A variation of the standard 'lizard' design with arid colorway first appeared in use with this nation in the late 1980s and can still be observed. (*Private collection*)

Copies of French 'lizard' camouflage have been in use with this country for many years and continue to see service. (*Private collection*)

This general wears a lizard camouflage variant pattern found across Africa and sourced in Asia. (*Private collection*)

A copy of the Italian pattern is in use with some units of the armed forces, including the Garde Présidentielle. (*Private collection*)

This soldier serving with the UN is wearing a copy of the French CE woodland pattern, commonly found among Mauritanian forces. (*Private collection*)

Also worn by the Garde Présidentielle. is a desert DPM variant, seen here. (*Private collection*)

The soldiers in this photo from 2014 show use of m81 woodland pattern as well as a copy of the Italian Army's arid vegetato design. (*Private collection*)

A loose copy of the USMC temperate MARPAT camouflage design is worn by National Gendarmerie personnel on foreign missions. (*Private collection*)

MAURITIUS

The British crown colony of Mauritius historically included a number of islands in the Indian Ocean, including the present Republic of Mauritius. Having adopted its own constitution in 1968, the island nation retained Queen Elizabeth II as head of state until 1992, when it was proclaimed an independent republic within the Commonwealth. Mauritius has been fortunate in that it has not participated in, or been drawn into, any external conflicts in its twenty-five years of existence, nor have there been any significant periods of civil unrest.

The country has no standing Army, its security and law enforcement falling under the jurisdiction of the National Police Force, National Coast Guard and the paramilitary Special Mobile Force (SMF).

Only the SMF and Coast Guard have been observed wearing camouflage, a copy of the British DPM pattern. (*Private collection*)

MOROCCO

The area comprising Morocco was under the administration of France in the earlier parts of the twentieth century, except for the area stretching into the Sahara, which was part of what was known as Spanish Morocco. By the 1950s, a growing sense of nationalism and dissatisfaction with the colonial system led to violent outbreaks and, ultimately, the granting of full independence by 1956. The nation has been ruled as a constitutional monarchy and has largely avoided involvement in external military operations, but has had a long history of documented human rights violations under the rule of King Hassan II (1961–1999).

Morocco claims ownership over the region known as Western Sahara, an area that had continued under

Moroccan forces have worn French 'lizard' or leópard pattern since the 1980s and possibly earlier. Several variations have been documented, from early versions with highly detailed stripes to more modern copies with a darker color palette and less definition to the stripes. (*Private collection*)

The camouflage pattern seen here has seen some use with the La Garde Royale, and is part of a stylized uniform particular to this organization. (*Private collection*)

Spanish administration through the 1960s. In 1973, native Sahrawi people formed the Polisario Front (Frente Polisario), aimed at establishing an independent state. Spain agreed to turn over administrative control of Western Sahara to Morocco (and neighboring Mauritania) in 1975 following the 'Green March' demonstration, but tensions with the native Sahrawi escalated into war in October of that year, a conflict that lasted for more than fifteen years. Known as the Western Sahara War, militias of the Sahrawi Arab Democratic Republic (supported by Algeria) continued a low intensity war against both Moroccan and Mauritanian forces (although a treaty was signed with that nation in 1979) until a peace agreement was reached in 1991. Although roughly 75 per cent of the territory in Western Sahara is under control of Morocco, passive/civilian resistance continues to push for a sovereign state.

Defense of the country falls to the Royal Moroccan Armed Forces, which consists of the Army, Navy, Air Force, Royal Moroccan Gendermarie, and the Moroccan Royal Guard. During peacetime, the latter two branches fall under the administration of the Ministry of the Interior. A paramilitary force, the Auxiliary Forces, can be called upon to support the armed forces in times of national emergency, to maintain public security, or during wartime.

Morocco has long maintained its military links to France, which can be seen in its continued use of the tenue de leópard or lizard patterned camouflage uniforms. These have been worn as far back as the 1970s, and possibly earlier.

A variation of the lizard pattern in desert coloration was introduced in the 1990s and has been worn by Moroccan forces deployed abroad or on peacekeeping missions. (*Private collection*)

A woodland-derivative pattern with blue colorway is worn by the Groupe Aéro Maritime/Groupe d'Intervention Maritime, which is part of the Gendarmerie Royale. (*Private collection*)

From the 1950s onwards, Mozambique was considered an overseas province of Portugal. Despite the Portuguese policy of assimilation and a greater degree of administrative autonomy, however, the push for universal African independence reached the nation in the early 1960s. This manifested primarily in the Frente de Libertação de Moçambique or FRELIMO (Liberation front of Mozambique), a Marxist-Leninist political party which organized an armed guerilla movement to wrest control away from the Portuguese. From 1964 until 1974, European and African units of the Portuguese Armed Forces effectively held the guerilla army at bay, despite FRELIMO's support from both the USSR and Communist China. The Colonial War (which Portugal was fighting concurrently in Angola and Portuguese Guinea as well) eventually took its toll on Portugal, and in April 1974 when a military junta wrested control of the government from the nation's Estado Novo regime, liberation for the province was not far away. On 25 June 1975, Mozambique became independent.

The original Portuguese M64 lizard camouflage design was in use with Portuguese and African colonial units in the 1960s, and later adopted by both Frelimo and RENAMO. Versions of this design continue to be worn by this country into the present day.

These engineers in 2011 wear a close copy of the original Portuguese design. (*US Navy*)

These Naval Infantry troops in 2013 wear a slightly darker version of the lizard design, similar to that worn by the Portuguese Navy Fuzilieros. (*US Marine Corps*)

The new government, under the leadership of Samora Machel, would proceed to lend its assistance to a number of other revolutionary insurgency movements, notably the Zimbabwe African National Union (ZANU) operating in Rhodesia, and the African National Congress (ANC) in South Africa. In turn, the governments of Rhodesia and South Africa sponsored and supported an anti-Communist paramilitary movement called Resistência Nacional Moçambicana (Mozambique National Resistance) or RENAMO. Founded in 1975, RENAMO guerillas would wage a continuous civil war against the government of Mozambique from 1977 until 1992, when peace talks and movements towards a multi-party political system based on capitalism sponsored by the country's new president Joaquim Chissano brought an end to hostilities. With more than 1.7 million people displaced during the ten year civil war, it took nearly three years for the majority of these people to be repatriated. Since 2013, the RENAMO insurgency has again gained momentum.

The armed forces are known as Forças Armadas de Defesa de Moçambique or FADM, and consist of the Army, Naval Command, Air & Air Defense Forces, and localized militia. In addition the Ministry of the Interior controls the Polícia da República da Moçambique (PRM), which consists of the Public Order and Security Police, Criminal Investigative Police, and Special Forces Police (including Rapid Reaction Force, Protection Forces, and Border Guards).

These Navy personnel wear a grey-dominant camouflage design adopted after the turn of the millennium and unique to this branch of service. (*Private collection*)

Seen here again, Naval Infantry troops in 2009 illustrate several versions of lizard worn at the same time and within the same unit. (*Private collection*)

In 2014, both Police and Provincial Police adopted a copy of the old East German strichtarn pattern as a standard operational uniform. (*Private collection*)

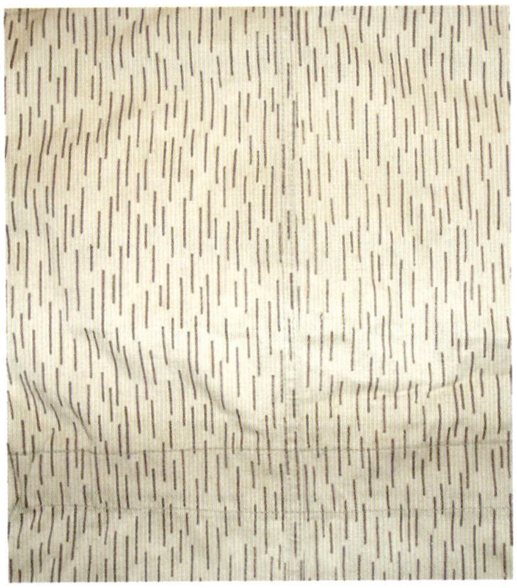

The 'rice fleck' or strichtarn camouflage design was worn by both FRELIMO and RENAMO forces at various times.

This South-African produced DPM pattern was supplied in limited numbers to Renamo by SADF special forces.

The Soviet solnechnye zaychiki (sunshine rays) pattern was supplied to FRELIMO by the USSR during the civil war.

NAMIBIA

The present Republic of Namibia emerged out of the twenty-three-year insurgency waged by African nationalists against the South African government, which had been the administrator of South West Africa since the end of the First World War. Known locally as the Namibian War of Independence, in South Africa it has most often been referred to as the Border War. The People's Liberation Army of Namibia (PLAN), the military arm of the South West Africa People's Organization (SWAPO), received financial and military support from the USSR and Cuba, as well as neighboring Zambia and Angola, but it was largely as a result of international political pressure that South Africa agreed to a peace accord in 1988, followed by free elections and a declaration of independence in 1990.

Namibia is considered a parliamentary democracy and has promoted a policy of national reconciliation since its independence. In 1998, the Namibia Defense

These officers wear a 'lizard' type camouflage introduced in 1991. Although there have been some changes to the design over the years, it has remained in service well into the present period. (*Private collection*)

When it first became an independent nation, neither the police nor the defense force had their own camouflage design with which to equip its personnel. Instead, British DPM pattern was issued over this period of time.

This DPM variation with an orange color palette was adopted by the Namibian Police Special Field Force in the late 1990s. (*Private collection*)

These officers of the NAMPOL Special Reserve Force (SRF) wear a tan DPM pattern highly suited for operations in the Kalahari. (*Private collection*)

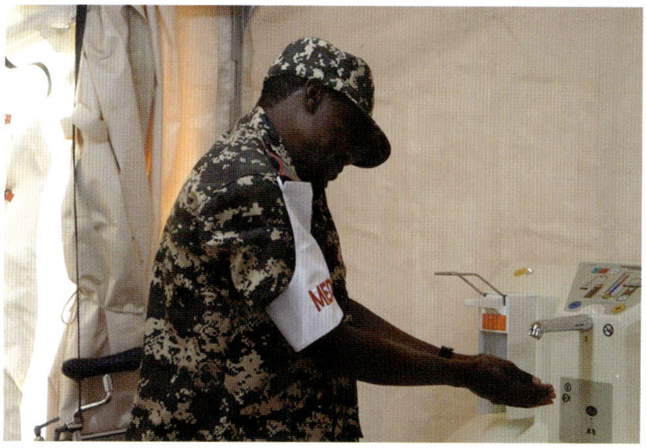

The standard 'lizard' pattern was pixilated and reissued in 2017 and has begun to replace the earlier Defense Force patterns. (*Private collection*)

Adopted by the Namibian Air Force circa 2015–16, the variation of the standard DF lizard pattern incorporates blue stripes instead of brown. (*Private collection*)

In 2014, the recently formed Namibian Marine Corps adopted a pixilated camouflage pattern of its own. (*Private collection*)

Force (NDF) sent troops to the Democratic Republic of the Congo as part of a Southern African Development Community (SADC) contingent. In 1999, the national government successfully quashed a secessionist movement aimed at sovereign nationhood for the northeastern Caprivi Strip. The Caprivi conflict was initiated by the Caprivi Liberation Army (CLA), an insurgent group led by Mishake Muyongo.

The Namibian Defense Force (NDF) consists of the Army, Navy and Air Force, which were formed in 1990 by combining elements of the South West Africa Territorial Force (SWATF) and the PLAN. Law enforcement is the duty of the Namibian Police Force (NAMPOL) as well as the Police Special Reserve Force (SRF).

NIGER

Niger came under control of France at the beginning of the twentieth century and became an autonomous state within the French Community in 1958. The country was granted full independence in 1960. During its first years as a nation, Niger was governed by a single-party regime, but corruption and mismanagement brought about a military coup d'etat in 1974 that continued to govern the nation until 1990. A transitional government was established in 1991, but political rivalry prevented a permanent democratic administration from making any progress, and in 1995 the government was again overthrown by the military under the leadership of Colonel Ibrahim Baré Maïnassara. Colonel Baré reputedly engineered his own victory in a 'democratic' election, and assumed the presidency until 1999, but was killed in a coup led by Major Daouda Malam Wanké. A new constitution was drafted in 1999, and for the first time Niger held truly democratic elections resulting in the election of Mamadou Tandja. However, in February 2010 another coup d'etat wrested power from Tandja after he was accused of extending his political term through constitutional manipulation.

The only major military operation conducted by troops from Niger in the modern era has been a counter-insurgency campaign against ethnic Tuareg that began in 1985 and led to the organization of two primary rebel organizations in 1990, the Front for the Liberation of Aïr and Azaouak (FLAA) and the Front for the Liberation of Tamoust (FLT). Peace accords were finally signed in 1995, ending most of the fighting, but a second Tuareg rebellion instigated by the Mouvement des Nigeriens pour la Justice (MNJ) began in 2008. In 1991 the Niger sent a small 400-man military contingent to join American-led allied forces during the Persian Gulf War. The Armed Forces have

The French leópard or 'lizard' camouflage design has been in use with FAN since the 1960s or 1970s, although today it has largely been replace except in ceremonial units.

US m81 woodland pattern has been in service with FAN since the 1990s, some supplied as military aid through the US military but also via independent supply contracts.

FAN personnel deploying with the United Nations continue to wear a version of the 'lizard' pattern that has been reproduced in Asia.

Initially worn by a small contingent of personnel sent to support Operation Desert Storm in 1991, variations of the six-color 'chocolate chip' desert pattern continue to be worn by FAN troops into the present day. (*US DOD*)

This colonel of the FAN wears a modern copy of French CE woodland pattern during Exercise Flintlock in 2017. Variations of the pattern have been worn throughout the modern period. (*US Africa Command*)

These military policemen wear a copy of the US tricolor desert pattern, which has been in service since the late 1990s.

also participated in a number of peacekeeping missions, including those with ECOMOG (Liberia and Guinée-Bissau), the African Union (Burundi – MIOB, Comoros – MIOC), and the United Nations (Saudi Arabia – Iraq War, Rwanda – MINURCA, Democratic Republic of Congo – MONUC).

The Forces Armées Nigeriennes (FAN) are the armed forces of Niger, consisting of the Army, Air Force, National Gendarmerie and a Republican Guard. The latter was known as the Garde Republicaine from 1963–97, Forces Nationales d'Intervention et de Securité from 1997–2011, and currently as the Garde Nationale du Niger. The Police Nationale, along with the Gendarmerie, are tasked with law enforcement.

NIGERIA

During the earlier part of the twentieth century the Colony and Protectorate of Nigeria was administered by Britain as separate northern and southern provinces. Both educational and economic opportunities spread more rapidly in the south, which has affected the nation's political life into the present era. Full independence was granted in 1960, at which time the two provinces were joined into a single nation. Almost immediately, the northern and southern regions of Nigeria began expressing their divergent cultural and religious identities in the form of three predominating political parties: the Nigerian People's Congress (NPC) in the Islamic north, the National Council of Nigeria and the Cameroons (NCNC) in the largely Christian south, and the Yoruba-dominated Action Group (AG). In 1961, Southern Cameroon broke away to join the Republic of Cameroon, while Northern Cameroon remained with Nigeria, which declared itself a Federal Republic two years later.

In 1966, the nation was shaken by several back-to-back military coups d'etat, sparked initially by alleged corruption in the electoral and political processes. The resulting oppression and violence against certain ethnic groups, in particular the Igbo, led to the secession of Eastern Nigeria and the declaration of a new nation, the Republic of Biafra, under the leadership of Lieutenant Colonel Emeka Ojukwu. When the Federal Army launched attacks against Biafra, it sparked a civil war that lasted from 6 July 1967 to 15 January 1970. Made famous by the Biafran government's reliance on foreign mercenaries from Europe, Southern Africa, and Israel, the fledgling republic was unable to sustain a continued onslaught by the much larger Nigerian military, backed as it was by the support of such states as the UK, Egypt, the USSR, Syria, Saudi Arabia, Niger, and Chad. It is estimated that more than one million people died during the Nigerian Civil War.

The nation continued under military control throughout most of the 1970s, 1980s, and 1990s, with several additional regime changes facilitated by coups d'etat. In 1999 the first president in thirty-three years to be freely elected took office.

The Nigerian Armed Forces consist of the Army, Navy and Air Force. The principle law enforcement agency is the Nigeria Police (formerly the Nigeria Police Force).

A 'vertical lizard' camouflage pattern was in use with the Federal Army as far back as the 1960s. At what point it fell into disuse is unknown. (*Private collection*)

The earliest use of desert camouflage by Nigerian personnel was desert DPM pattern, worn by troops deploying to Dharfur, Sudan in 2011. (*Private collection*)

Variations of US m81 woodland have been in use with Nigerian forces since the late 1980s and include a wide range of color differences. (*Private collection*)

There are two patterns worn by the Nigerian Police Service since around 2012 onwards – one with a blue colorway, and the other with a grey colorway. (*Private collection*)

A copy of the old Chinese Navy blue/green camouflage design was adopted by the Nigerian Navy SBS Commandos in the 2010s. (*Private collection*)

Also in use since at least 2014, copies of the US tricolor desert have been worn by Nigerian troops both at home and on deployments abroad. (*Private collection*)

The Nigerian Army adopted a new camouflage design to replace its earlier woodland derivative in 2012. (*US Army*)

A desert version of the 'blotch' pattern was adopted in 2014 and, like its predecessor, is worn both at home and on missions abroad. (*US Army*)

Some members of the Nigerian Air Force wear this blue-grey camouflage design based around shapes found in Chinese PLA camouflage from the 1980s. (*US Air Force*)

The Nigerian Customs Service also has its own camouflage design, with a grey colorway. (*Private collection*)

Independently of the SBS Commandos, the by Nigerian Navy wear a copy of the current Chinese PLA Navy pattern, which is a pixilated design.

RHODESIA

Once part of a larger, British controlled territory, this nation became Rhodesia in 1964 and issued its Universal Declaration of Independence (UDI) one year later, effectively severing ties with the UK. Lacking support from Europe, North America, and most of its African neighbors, Rhodesia struggled to maintain its independence, made worse with the emergence of two African nationalist movements, the Zimbabwe African National Union (ZANU), and the Zimbabwe African People's Union (ZAPU). Between 1972 and 1979 a state of civil war existed between Rhodesian Security Forces and the military wings of ZANU and ZAPU, the Zimbabwe African National Liberation Army (ZANLA), and the Zimbabwe People's Revolutionary Army (ZIPRA). Although the Rhodesian security forces were militarily far superior, and insurgent casualties exponentially greater, the Rhodesian government was unable to hold out indefinitely against worldwide pressure and lack of support. In 1979 an interim government for a new nation, Zimbabwe-Rhodesia, was agreed to by the Smith government, but so-called 'free' elections in 1980 saw ZANU's Robert Mugabe win the office of prime minister, a position he held continuously (by electoral 'victories') until his death in 2019. In 1980 the name of the nation was officially changed to Zimbabwe.

The Rhodesian security forces consisted of the Army and Air Force, supplemented by the British South African Police (BSAP) and the Ministry of Internal Affairs (INTAF) Guard Force, a localized militia.

Members of C Squadron, Rhodesian Special Air Service serving in Malaya wore British-produced 'brushstroke' camouflage smocks; the pattern would later be reproduced locally and continue in service until the formal adoption of a Rhodesian design.

In the 1960s, members of the SAS also wore ex-British Army issue 1942 pattern windproof camouflage.

The Rhodesian 'brushstroke' camouflage pattern was introduced in 1965 and became the default and standard camouflage of all services in 1970, including the BSAP and Guard Force. (*Private collection*)

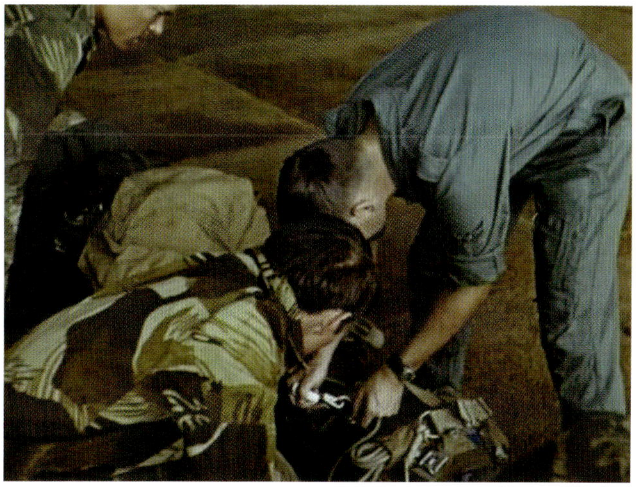

Introduced between 1965 and 1969, an experimental 'winter season' camouflage with a golden color palette was tested but never officially adopted. (*Private collection*)

Some units of the BSAP initially wore South African Police pattern camouflage, although eventually this would be replaced by the standard Rhodesian design.

Camouflage Worn by Insurgent Groups

ZIPRA and ZANLA received considerable military support from other African nations as well as Eastern European and Chinese sources. Although uniforms and equipment were never standardized, some trends in camouflage have been documented and are illustrated here.

Known as 'rice fleck' in Southern Africa, 'rain' pattern camouflage uniforms were supplied by Poland and East Germany to ZIPRA forces.

The Soviet issue 'sun bunnies' or berezhka pattern was supplied to ZIPRA by Russia.

Some use of Egyptian camouflage such as this 'rocks' design has been documented in use by ZIPRA.

Limited use of grey 'lizard' pattern camouflage, supplied by Cuban and/or Angola, was also seen amongst ZIPRA forces.

Both ZIPRA and ZANLA obtained some quantities of old Portuguese lizard pattern camouflage uniforms, probably via Angola or Mozambique.

A significant number of photos from this period show ZANLA troops wearing what appear to be Ethiopian uniforms in South Korean 'waves' pattern camouflage.

This region came under Belgian administration following the First World War but was plagued with tribal rivalry between Hutu and Tutsi, leading to a violent period known as the Rwandan Revolution lasting from 1959 into the 1960s. After abolishing the traditional monarchy, Belgium granted independence but split its territory into two nations, Rwanda and neighboring Burundi. Continued periods of violence afflicted the country despite changes in government.

The Rwandan Civil War began in 1990, sparked by an invasion of the north by the Front Patriotique Rwandaise or Rwandan Patriotic Front (RPF). When president Habyarimana's plane was shot down in 1994 by unknown perpetrators, the Hutu population blamed the Tutsi and this rapidly escalated into one of the worst periods of genocide in recent African history. In response, the RPF renewed its military offensive and eventually took control of the nation.

The Forces Armées Rwandaises (Rwandand Armed Forces) or FAR was the national army's name from 1960 to 1994, consisting of a national Army and a much smaller national Gendarmerie. Several units with 'elite' status, including the Presidential Guard, Para-Commando Battalion, and a Reconnaissance Battalion were in existence at this time. Following the RPF victory the armed forces were reformed and renamed to Forces Rwandaises de Défense or Rwanda Defense Forces.

Belgian 'jigsaw' pattern camouflage was in use with elite units of the FAR in the period immediately following independence into the 1990s. Initial stocks were leftover from the Belgian government, while later uniforms were procured from various sources in Asia.

This three-color DPM derivative pattern, produced in Asia, saw use in the FAR from the late 1980s to 1990s, at least with the Para-Commandos and possibly with other units as well.

An Asian-produced copy of the traditional French 'lizard' pattern saw limited use with FAR, and continued in use with the FRD. (*Private collection*)

Available cheaply on the international surplus market in the early 1990s, ex-East German strichtarn camouflage uniforms were quickly adopted by the RPF as a combat uniform, but discarded following their victory. (*Private collection*)

Seen here in a photo from 2011, these Rwandan Army personnel wear variations of woodland, which was adopted in the early 2000s for all FRD personnel. (*Private collection*)

These OAU personnel in 2006 wear newly issued uniforms in a darker variation of the US six-color 'chocolate chip' desert pattern that has been seen on other Rwandan deployments as well. (*Private collection*)

This Rwandan general is wearing a copy of the USMC temperate MARPAT camouflage seen sporadically among FRD personnel since 2017. (*Private collection*)

A new pixilated camouflage pattern was adopted by the FRD in 2015 having a similar color palette to some variations of woodland previously issued in this country. (*Private collection*)

SÃO TOMÉ AND PRÍNCIPE

This small island nation in the Gulf of Guinea was a former colonial territory of Portugal. Following the overthrow of the Caetano dictatorship in 1974, the Movement for the Liberation of São Tomé and Príncipe (MLSTP) took control after the country was granted independence along with the rest of Portugal's former African colonies. Since 1990, the country has embraced a multiparty, democratic system of government, and was one of the first African nations to do so.

This undated photo illustrates the continued use of Portuguese lizard pattern camouflage by this nation. (*Private collection*)

The armed forces of this nation are called Forças Armadas de São Tomé e Príncipe (FASTP), and consist

At least some usage has been made of French lizard pattern, as seen here. (*Private collection*)

A photograph from 2012 illustrates the wearing of Portuguese DPM pattern. (*Private collection*)

of the Army, Naval element (Coast Guard) – which includes a small Marine Corps – a National Guard, and a Presidential Guard.

Maintaining close military ties to Portugal, the armed forces have largely retained the use of traditional Portuguese camouflage patterns. Since colonial times, variations of Portuguese 'vertical lizard' have seen use with both land and naval forces. In more recent times, copies of the Portuguese DPM pattern have also been used.

SENEGAL

Once part of French territorial possessions in Africa, Senegal became an independent nation in August 1960, following the dissolution of the Mali Federation. In 1982, the nation joined with Gambia to form the Senegambia Confederation, which dissolved amicably in 1989. Senegal's main internal conflict involves the southern Casamance region, which has been the heart of a separatist movement called the Mouvement des forces démocratiques de Casamance (MFDC). An ongoing, low-level state of conflict has existed in this region since 1982, with periodic ceasefires but no permanent resolution.

Senegal has been involved in a number of military actions since the early 1980s. In 1981, Senegalese forces assisted in putting down an attempted coup d'etat in Gambia. In 1990, a battalion of Senegalese troops were sent to take part in the Persian Gulf War. As part of a ECOMOG peacekeeping force, 1,500 personnel were sent to Liberia in 1992, and a battalion-sized unit was sent to Rwanda in 1994; peacekeepers were also sent to the Central African Republic in 1997. One year later, Senegalese military personnel intervened in the Guinea-Bissau Civil War at the request of President Vieira. In

Senegalese forces have used French leópard or 'lizard' pattern camouflage since 1963, although it has gradually been replaced with other, more contemporary designs.

The use of m81 woodland camouflage by some Senegalese units began in the period 2000–01 (possibly earlier) and may have been sparked by aid from US military training teams (MTTs). (*Private collection*)

Some units of the Gendarmerie Nationale wear a DPM variant with blue/purple colorway. (*Private collection*)

Also worn by some units of the Gendarmerie is this vertical lizard design with unique colorway. The pattern first appeared in 2014 and may be strictly ceremonial. (*Private collection*)

By the early 2000s, the majority of Senegalese ground forces had adopted a copy of French CE Woodland. (*US DOD*)

Certain units of the National Police wear a woodland-type camouflage pattern with blue colorway. (*Private collection*)

2017, Senegal again deployed troops to Gambia to support the newly elected president Barrow.

The Forces Armées du Sénégal consists of the Army, Navy, Air Force and the Gendarmerie Nationale. The latter shares law enforcement and internal security duties with the National Police. The armed forces initially followed a French model as regards styles of camouflage and uniform cut, although there has been far less consistency in the twenty-first century.

SEYCHELLES

This small nation consists of about 115 islands situated 1,500 miles off the east coast of Africa in the Indian Ocean. During most of the colonial period it fell under British control and was granted independence as part of the Commonwealth in 1976. The nation made international news in 1981 after security forces put down an attempted coup d'état led by Thomas Michael 'Mad Mike' Hoare, who had gained fame twenty years previously as commander of 4 Commando in Katanga and later of 5 Commando (the Wild Geese) in the Congo. Several additional coup attempts were made in the 1980s.

These members of the Tazar Special Forces unit wear Multicam pattern uniforms, which have been in use with the unit since 2013. (*US Navy*)

These members of the Seychelles Coast Guard wear a copy of British DPM, which has been in service since the turn of the century, and possibly earlier. (*Private collection*)

The Seychelles People's Defense Force consists of an Infantry Unit, Coast Guard, Air Force and a Presidential Protection Unit. Training and materiel have largely been provided by India, but in terms of camouflage British DPM has been the standard for most units that wear it.

SIERRA LEONE

A former British colonial possession, Sierra Leone became a repository for resettling Britain's 'black poor' following the abolition of slavery. As a result, the population includes a vast number of non-indigenous immigrants from Asia, the West Indies and North America, the origins of its Krio culture. Decolonization was a gradual process beginning in the early part of the twentieth century, but by 1961 full independence had been achieved. Sierra Leone saw a series of successful and attempted coups d'etat beginning in 1967 and continuing into the 1970s. A multi-party system of government and a new constitution were approved in October 1990, but lack of faith led to the formation of the Revolutionary United Front (RUF), a paramilitary army that gained a reputation for committing atrocities and using child soldiers. Civil war wracked the country

Asian produced 'lizard' camouflage uniforms were supplied by EO and worn by SLA during the civil war.

Seen here in a photo from 2012, a mixture of DPM and woodland pattern camouflage with a variety of color palettes have been in use with both SLA and RSLAF since the 1990s. (*US DOD*)

for eleven years, during which time the legitimate government of Sierra Leone was replaced in a coup d'etat by a group of young soldiers calling itself the National Provisional Ruling Council (NPRC) in 1992. Instability ensued as the NPRC lost control of territory to the RUF, leading to the enlistment of several hundred private military contractors from Executive Outcomes in 1994 to assist in training and boost its military capabilities; control was quickly restored to the NPRC. Several additional coups d'etat followed, but it was not until 1998 that a democratically elected government

Various types of tiger stripe pattern camouflage were in use with SLA up until the end of the civil war.

A 'leaf' type camouflage design was worn by some elements of the SLA during the civil war.

was reinstated with the assistance of ECOMOG forces. From 1999, the United Nations involved itself in peacekeeping efforts, sending as many as 13,000 troops by February 2000. Initial attempts to disarm the RUF failed and as many as 500 peacekeepers were taken hostage, resulting in a UN-sponsored rescue operation known as Operation Khukri. Stability was not restored to the country until the British Armed Forces intervened in Operation Paliser; the war was finally declared over

Since the restructuring and formation of the RSLAF, the standard combat uniform has been British DPM as seen here. (*Private collection*)

A RSLAF contingent deployed to Somalia as part of UNOSOM wears surplus US Army issue tricolor desert uniforms. (*Private collection*)

in January 2002. To this day, elements of the British Army remain in country to assisting with training of the armed forces.

Historically known as the Sierra Leone Army (SLA), the armed forces of this nation are today called the Republic of Sierra Leone Armed Forces (RSLAF), and consist of ground, air and naval elements, following a British model. The Sierra Leone Police (SLP) is responsible for law enforcement and includes a heavily armed unit known as the Operations Support Division.

Members of the Operational Support Division of the Sierra Leone Police have been documented wearing several types of 'woodland' camouflage with blue colorways.

SOMALIA

The country was known as British Somaliland prior to the Second World War, but came under Italian control briefly in 1940 until recaptured by the British in 1941. Nevertheless, after the war, the League of Nations returned control of Somaliland to Italy, which was not relinquished until 1960 when the nation became the Somali Republic.

Following a brief period of democratic government, a coup d'etat seized power in 1969, suspended the constitution, and declared a new Somali Democratic Republic with strong socialist leanings. Between July 1977 and March 1978, Somali forces waged war against neighboring Ethiopia in an attempt to seize its Ogaden region, but were repelled by a massive intervention involving several thousand Soviet and Cuban personnel. Somalia thereafter shifted its alliance to the United States, receiving training and military aid (which officially ended in 1988).

Evidence indicates that the Somali government obtained quantities of Egyptian 'rocks' pattern camouflage during the 1980s.

The Pakistani-produced 'arid brushstroke' pattern seen, on these two Somali soldiers in 1983, was also worn by some elements of the Somali National Army. (*Private collection*)

Woodland pattern camouflage has been in use with Somali government personnel since the 1980s and continues to be worn. (*Private collection*)

Growing dissatisfaction with the socialist regime and increasing encouragement from Ethiopia resulted in the formation of several anti-government resistance movements, including the Somali Salvation Democratic Front (SSDF), United Somali Congress (USC), Somali National Movement (SNM) and the Somali Patriotic Movement (SPM). Fuel shortages, massive inflation, power outages and curfews contributed to the emerging anti-government sentiment, and in 1991 a coalition of opposition groups backed by Ethiopia and Libya removed the administration of Mohamed Siad Barre. The country rapidly descended into civil war, and has remained in some state of conflict ever since. In 1992, the United Nations authorized a limited peacekeeping presence (UNOSOM I) which was largely ineffective, thus

This Somali soldier in 1985, possibly a military policeman, wears a one-piece coverall in a different kind of 'brushstroke' pattern camouflage, often associated with Iraq. (*Private collection*)

Another pattern worn during the 1980s was the Egyptian sparse desert, or 'scrambled eggs' pattern shown here.

This photo from 2006 shows several camouflage patterns being worn by Somali military personnel, including a copy of US six-color desert pattern, and an interesting two-color desert design. (*Private collection*)

leading the United States to organize a military coalition (UNITAF) to stabilize the nation. When the United States withdrew in 1993, the second UN peacekeeping mission (UNOSOM II) replaced it, remaining in the country until 1996, but never succeeding in the restoration of government rule. Although a Transitional Federal Government was established in 2004, Somalia remains in a state of civil war between warring militias.

The Somali Armed Forces (SAF) were once the largest and most capable military force on the continent, and consisted of the Army, Air Force, Navy, Police Force and the National Security Service. These forces were effectively disbanded once the civil war began. Since 2008, efforts by the European Union to train a new military force have produced a new Somali National Armed Force (SNAF), which is still in the process of training and formation. At present the SNAF is largely land-based and includes six Infantry Brigades, a Commando Brigade, and a special operations battalion. In addition, the regional governments of Somaliland and Puntland maintain their own security and police forces.

Military cadets in 2014 were supplied with camouflage uniforms by their Turkish trainers. (*Private collection*)

In a photo from 2004, a Somali soldier wears a leaf pattern camouflage similar to that produced in Syria. The soldier is part of the Transitional Government forces. (*Private collection*)

These Danaab commandos, part of the National Intelligence and Security Agency, wear a Chinese-produced copy of the US Marines Corps MARPAT camouflage design in 2016. (*Private collection*)

Members of the Gaashaan or 'Shield Force', also attached to the NISA, wear a copy of A-TACS® arid pattern during a training exercise in 2015. (*Private collection*)

Somaliland Defense Force

The 'leaf' pattern camouflage design seen here is worn by the Somaliland Defense Force. (*Private collection*)

Also worn by the Somaliland DF is this arid pattern from Yemen.

Puntland State Armed Forces

These members of the Punland State Armed Forces wear 'desert tiger stripe' pattern uniforms in 2014. (*Private collection*)

The British government lost control of South Africa prior to the beginning of the Second World War, although the country remained a part of the Commonwealth until declaring itself a republic in 1961. The historic policy of apartheid (institutionalized segregation) became an increasingly distinctive part of society in the late 1940s, but faced opposition both internally and externally. Growing internal discontent in the 1960s, fueled by increasing feelings of African nationalism, spawned the growth of a number of anti-apartheid movements, most notably the African National Congress (ANC), Azanian People's Organization, and the Pan Africanist Congress. The government's policy of brutal suppression contributed to these movements embracing more violent, direct action solutions to their political problems, resulting in nearly thirty years of insurgency pitting government forces against the military wings of the African nationalist movements. South Africa further endured numerous boycotts and embargoes from nations throughout the world, impelling it to become relatively self-sufficient with regards to the development of technology and military equipment.

Most famous of the insurgency groups, Umkhonto We Sizwe (Spear of the Nation), representing the ANC, was responsible for numerous acts of sabotage and many civilian and military deaths during its military campaign. The Azanian National Liberation Army (AZANLA) also engaged in acts of sabotage and violence, and in the 1980s also found itself in armed opposition to the ANC. Numerous foreign military governments, as well as nationalist insurgency movements from neighboring countries, gave financial and military support to both the ANC and AZANLA.

The South African Defense Forces (SADF) and South African Police (SAP) were also involved in military operations outside the country during the apartheid era, including the Rhodesian Bush War. The ongoing Border War (1966–90) in Southwest Africa drew many South African military personnel into its theater of operations, and many SADF units also saw service in Angola, Mozambique, and Zaire. These military involvements largely came to a halt after universal elections in 1994 in which the ANC won an overwhelming majority. The old SADF was then combined with the Umkhonto we Sizwe and Azanian People's Liberation Army, as well as the former Bantustan defense forces to create the new South African National Defense Force (SANDF). Since then the South African military has largely become a peacekeeping force, serving in Lesotho, the Democratic Republic of Congo, and Burundi.

From 1957 until 1994, the South African Defense Force consisted of the Army, Navy, Air Force and South African Medical Service. Law enforcement and internal security were overseen by the South African Police as well as the South African Railways Police (SARP), although the latter was disbanded in 1986 and its remaining elements were incorporated into the SAP. Following the 1994 elections, the South African National Defense Force was reorganized, with some units being disbanded and new ones created. The SANDF today consists of the Army, Navy, Air Force and the Military Health Service. The SAP was also reorganized and is now the South African Police Service (SAPS).

We can separate Southern African camouflage patterns into three separate groups based on who wore them. In addition to designs developed for and utilized by the SADF/SANDF, a separate category can exist for the SAP/SARP, and for paramilitary and insurgent groups. Despite its relative isolation from the rest of the world, South Africa did produce some of the most interesting and effective camouflage patterns of any country prior to 1994.

SADF and SANDF Camouflage

Prior to the 1970s, the use of camouflage by the SADF was virtually non-existent. The oral history of Hunter Group, a self-supplied, all-volunteer, counter-insurgency unit trained in guerrilla warfare, patrolling, tracking, bushcraft, and intelligence gathering, states that commercially designed camouflage uniforms were obtained privately by individuals. Additionally, the documented history of 5 SAI indicates Col. Hannes Botha designed a camouflage pattern specifically for this unit; this is the same pattern associated with Hunter Group. Although never produced officially by the SADF it was purchased privately.

These are the three camouflage patterns associated with Hunter Group. The first pattern was also worn by 5 SAI for a period of time.

Originally developed for the Reconnaissance Commandos between 1970 and 1976, this camouflage pattern was later supplied to 32 Battalion's Reconnaissance wing. It has often been referred to as 'Recce wet season' camouflage.

32 Battalion was a specialized counter-insurgency unit formed mostly of Portuguese-speaking Angolans that had fled that country following FAPLA's provisional victory. Two variations of the same camouflage design were produced specifically for this unit, known colloquially as summer or 'wet season', and winter or 'dry season'.

Light machine gunner of 32 Bn wearing the 'wet season' or summer camouflage pattern. (*Private collection*)

32 Battalion wet season camouflage pattern.

32 Battalion dry season camouflage pattern.

Owing to the clandestine nature of its work, the Reconnaissance Commandos utilized a vast array of camouflage designs for work inside and outside the nation, often posing as enemy combatants by wearing the same camouflage uniforms. This led to the secret production of at least a dozen 'copy' patterns that remained in inventory for use by units on clandestine operations.

Some members of 32 Battalion Recce Wing were also provided with a DPM pattern having a bright green element that appears to have some connection with the Reconnaissance units of the 1980s, who provided many uniforms in this pattern to RENAMO in Mozambique.

Developed and trialed between 1991 and 1993, the SANDF officially adopted Soldier 2000 pattern camouflage in 1994, replacing virtually all the previous camouflage designs issued to individual units or organizations. As illustrated in these photos, all services of the SANDF wear the identical camouflage pattern. (*US DOD*)

Rhodesian pattern camouflage was worn by some Recce personnel operating alongside the Rhodesian SAS.

Recce copy of the Cuban 'grey lizard' design.

Recce copy of the Cuban 'elm leaf' design.

Recce copy of the East German strichtarn or 'rice fleck' camouflage, found throughout Southern Africa.

Recce copy of an Egyptian 'vertical lizard' camouflage pattern.

Recce copy of the French leópard or 'lizard' camouflage pattern.

Recce copy of the so-called 'Lebanese' pattern.

Recce copy of the so-called 'Libyan' camouflage pattern that was actually produced in Yugoslavia and supplied to SWAPO/Plan.

Recce copy of the Portuguese M64 lizard camouflage pattern.

Recce copy of the Tanzanian DPM pattern produced in Canada for export.

Recce copy of the Zimbabwe 'dry season' camouflage pattern.

Known as P90 or 'cabbage patch' design, this camouflage design was printed on waterproofed nylon cloth and was made into various items of kit, including a variety of field equipment.

South African Police/SARP

The SAP began producing its own camouflage in 1969. The pattern changed slightly after 1972 and has continued in production ever since.

The 1st pattern of the South African Police has a few unique features, such as the 'pinwheel' shape and a 'smear' effect, where it looks like the screens were shifted during the inking process.

The 2nd camouflage pattern of the SAP was changed a bit but essentially uses the same color palette. Although worn by a variety of Police units prior to 1994, after the agency became the South African Police Service, the use of camouflage was largely restricted to the Special Task Force (STF).

Between 1975 and 1986, the Special Task Force of the South African Railway Police (SARP) were issued a horizontal stripe pattern of black, reddish-brown and dark olive green on a nutria background.

Paramilitary/Insurgent Groups

The Afrikaner Weerstandsbeweging (AWB) or Afrikaaner Resistance Movement, a right wing extremist group that advocated for the continued practice of apartheid, among other things, often wore two camouflage designs based loosely on DPM drawings. (*Private collection*)

The Mkonto We Sizwe (MK) of the ANC and the AZANLA had no official camouflage design, but instead wore various uniforms provided to them from foreign governments or insurgent movements operating in neighboring countries. (*Private collection*)

SOUTH AFRICA – TRIBAL HOMELANDS

The South African government set aside parcels of territory within its borders during the apartheid period to establish tribal homelands (Bantustans) for the major black African ethnic groups that made up its population. Established in 1951 and given semi-autonomous status in 1959, the tribal homelands consisted of the following: Bophuthatswana, Ciskei, Gazankulu, Ka Ngwane, Kwa Ndebele, Kwa Zulu, Lebowa, Qwa Qwa, Transkei, and Venda. Ultimately, four of these (Bophuthatswana, Ciskei, Transkei and Venda) were officially declared independent, self-governing states with their own defense forces (although unrecognized outside of South Africa), while the remaining three received only partial autonomy. As part of an effort to set their defense and police forces aside from those of South Africa, many of the homelands adopted their own unique camouflage designs.

Bophuthatswana

The Bophuthatswana Defense Force (BDF) was formed in 1976. During the later years of its existence, this homeland dealt with a number of attempted coups d'etat. In 1994, an incident involving the BDF firing upon civilians led to an intervention by Afrikanner extremists from the AWB and resulted in several deaths.

A variation of the SAP 2nd pattern camouflage was produced between 1978 and 1983 and worn by the Bophuthatswana Police.

The SAP style camouflage was replaced in 1983 by a kind of 'grasslands' design, worn by the Police until 1994.

Ciskei

The Ciskei Defense Force was established in 1981. A camouflage uniform was adopted in 1990, the pattern having been based partially on the design originally worn by the South African Railways Police (SARP).

The Ciskei DF camouflage design differs from the SARP design in having a much more olive green color and the fact that the orientation of the green and brown shapes is flipped.

Gazankulu

Although never a fully-independent homeland, the basis of a Gazankulu Defense Force was formulated from 113 Battalion, raised in Eastern Transvaal from members of the Tsongas Tribe in 1980. A Police force was formed in 1982. Elements of 113 Battalion did adopt camouflage based on the Portuguese m63 vertical 'lizard' design. Three separate pattern variations have been documented, including surplus stocks of the original Portuguese pattern.

A DPM camouflage pattern was adopted after 1990, replacing the earlier plain olive green uniforms worn by the Defense Force.

Some members of 113 Battalion were issued with original, Portuguese M64 pattern 'lizard' camouflage.

A locally-produced variation of the 'red lizard' pattern was later fabricated for issue to the Battalion. Two different prints of this pattern have been documented, one with red stripes over green, and the other with green stripes over red.

The last variation of the 'red lizard' camouflage pattern was produced in very small numbers, and may never have made it to the Battalion at all. (*Author's collection*)

Ka Ngwane

A fledgling infantry battalion was issued with 'giraffe spot' pattern camouflage fatigues, although the homeland never saw a fully-formed Defense Force.

Kwandebele

115 Battalion was raised in 1984 in Central Transvaal with the intent of forming a regular Defense Force for Kwa Ndebele. A distinctive camouflage pattern was created, having dark brown and orange-tan blotches on a nutria brown background, despite the fact that the battalion remained a part of the SADF.

Kwa Zulu

This homeland for the Zulu never had its own defense force.

The Kwa Zulu Police force was issued with a camouflage design based on that of the South African Police, but with a grey colorway.

Transkei

The Transkei Defense Force was founded in 1975 with the assistance of the SADF. In 1978 the homeland broke off diplomatic ties with South Africa over a border dispute. The TDF later obtained assistance from a number of ex-Rhodesian Security Forces personnel and even appointed former Lt. Colonel Ron Reid-Daly as its General Officer Commanding. Relations with South Africa were eventually restored. In 1987, a coup d'etat replaced the legitimate elected leader with a military figurehead. Thereafter the region became a safe haven for African National Congress paramilitary members.

The Transkei Police also had a camouflage design created for it by elements of the South African Police in 1983, but evidence suggests it was never fully adopted and probably only entered the trial stage.

Loosely based on a camouflage design produced in Zimbabwe, the TDF adopted this pattern with green printed over brown. (*Private collection*)

The Republic of South Sudan became an independent state in July 2011, following protracted periods of civil war with the government of Sudan that began in the 1950s and ended only in 2005. Accusations of a plotted coup d'etat from President Kiir against his deputy Riek Machar resulted in the latter leaving the government to lead the Sudan People's Liberation Movement – In Opposition (SPLA-IO). A state of civil war has existed in this country ever since.

The South Sudan People's Defense Forces are the current armed forces of the government of South Sudan, consisting of the Army and Air Force. The military was formed out of the Sudan People's Liberation Army (SPLA), the guerilla movement that waged its lengthy civil war against the government of Sudan.

A wide number of camouflage designs have been worn by the SPLA and SSPDF, including stocks of uniforms from the Sudanese Army as well as patterns sourced from independent distributors.

Originally worn by elements of the SPLA, this 'woodland' type camouflage pattern continued to be worn by the new SSPDF for several years, as illustrated by this photo from 2012. (*Private collection*)

These soldiers of the Presidential Republican Guard wear a tiger stripe camouflage pattern, based on designs produced in South Vietnam in the 1960s. (*Private collection*)

Seen here in a photograph from 2013, these members of the South Sudan Police Service wear a blue 'leaf' type camouflage pattern. (*Private collection*)

A similar pattern but with larger shapes, more 'woodland-like,' is worn by the SSPS here in 2016. (*Private collection*)

This contingent of Presidential Republican Guard personnel wear a copy of the US 'Universal Camouflage Pattern' or UCP in 2014. (*Private collection*)

The South Sudan Wildlife Police wear a variation of desert DPM having bright, yellowish tones. (*Private collection*)

The Auxiliary Forces of the SSPS wear this unique DPM-based camouflage with pink and orange tones. (*Private collection*)

SOUTH WEST AFRICA

South West Africa (Suidwes-Afrika) was the former name of the present nation of Namibia. Historically part of the German Empire, the territory was captured by South Africa during the First World War and retained as a fifth province. Growing successes of African nationalist movements led to the formation of the South West African People's Organization (SWAPO) in 1960, and its paramilitary wing, the People's Liberation Army of Namibia (PLAN). Between 1966 and 1989 a state of armed conflict existed within the borders of South West Africa – the Border War or Namibian War of Independence, pitting the combined South African military and police forces against those of PLAN and its allies in Angola, Cuba and Zambia. Responding to international pressures, South Africa came to the negotiating table in 1988 and reached a peace accord which led to free elections in the following year and the establishment of the independent country of Namibia in 1990.

The South West African Territorial Force (SWATF) was the armed forces during this time, modeled after that of South Africa. Unlike many of the units in the SADF, SWATF did not have a tradition of wearing camouflage at all. The South West African Police (SWAPOL) are the only organization to have regularly used camouflage.

Both 1st and 2nd pattern SAP camouflage designs were worn by SWAPOL Koevoet on operations, often intermixed with other types of attire.

The distinctive pattern of the SWAPOL was introduced in 1980 and worn by constables of the regular units and Koevoet until just before the disbandment of the latter in 1989.

Camouflage of PLAN

Owing to its support from a variety of Eastern Bloc nations and sympathetic African movements, a terrific variety of military camouflage uniforms were utilized by PLAN at various times. Those represented here have been documented in significant enough numbers as to be representational.

This undated photograph illustrates Swapo leader Sam Nujoma wearing what appears to be East German strichtarn pattern camouflage fatigues, while behind him another Plan insurgent wears Portuguese M64 lizard camouflage. (*Private collection*)

During the 1988–89 period, PLAN personnel were observed wearing what appear to be privately procured DPM camouflage uniforms made in Kenya. It is uncertain whether the uniforms were actually Kenyan military issue, but there is strong evidence supporting the theory that uniforms were supplied by Kenyan military forces serving at that time in SW Africa under UNTAG.

Produced in Bulgaria specifically for export, this pattern of branch-like shapes in ochre and russet on a grey background was worn by Plan troops exclusively.

Seen here again worn by former FAPLA leader Sam Nujoma, this vertical stripe pattern is probably of Egyptian origins and saw limited usage by insurgents during the war. (*Private collection*)

The Cuban-made 'grey lizard' camouflage pattern was often seen among PLAN insurgents throughout the conflict.

Another pattern of Eastern European origins, although called 'Libyan' by many South African sources, this is another Plan design that saw significant usage.

The land comprising the Republic of Sudan fell under British administration at the end of the nineteenth century, with self-governance being granted in 1953 and full independence in 1956. With independence from Britain came concerns from the largely Christian tribal areas in the south that the new country would be completely dominated by the Muslim north, concerns that would prove well-founded. A period of civil war followed (lasting from 1956 to 1972), ending only in a ceasefire. Following ten years relatively free of armed conflict, the Second Sudanese Civil War erupted in 1983, with the Sudan People's Liberation Army (SPLA) mounting a full scale guerilla war against the Sudanese armed forces of the north. The war lasted twenty-two years and is believed to have claimed the lives of 2 million Sudanese, as well as spawning innumerable human rights violations including torture and slavery. From 1989 onwards, Sudan was effectively a one-party state under military control, with open ties to Islamic fundamentalist groups.

In February 2003, the north was beset with a second military conflict in the Darfur region, mounted by the Sudan Liberation Army (SLA) and the Justice and Equality Movement (JEM). The conflict is largely based around accusations of oppression by the government against non-Arab Sudanese. Since 2011, various factions

In this photo from 1983, Sudanese soldiers wear Egyptian-made uniforms of reversible camouflage fabric. (*US DOD*)

A copy of the French 'lizard' pattern has been in use with Sudanese forces since the 1980s.

Seen here in a photo from 2008, this 'leaf' pattern camouflage has been documented in use with Sudanese Army since the early 2000s. (*Private collection*)

These Sudanese Army officers wear a light-hued woodland type camouflage pattern, in use since the 1990s. (*Private collection*)

A copy of the US 'chocolate chip' desert pattern has been in use with Sudan for some time. (*Private collection*)

The US 'tricolor desert' pattern has also seen extensive use in the Sudanese Army. (*Private collection*)

This Sudanese Air Force general, photographed in 2017, wears a unique 'splinter' type camouflage pattern that was adopted several years earlier. (*Private collection*)

This Sudanese Police Force officer in 2007 wears two different camouflage designs, each having a blue colorway. Several variations have been worn by this service for at least twenty years. (*Private collection*)

This pattern that was originally developed for Jordan was also worn by Sudanese airborne personnel in 2008.

These officers of the Central Reserve Police wear a two-color desert camouflage design, in use since 2009. (*Private collection*)

Another pixilated pattern adopted by the 9th Airborne Division is seen here. (*Private collection*)

This desert 'digital' camouflage pattern appears to be worn primarily by the Sudanese Army Special Forces.

These members of the 9th Airborne Division wear a camouflage design loosely based on the US Marine Corps MARPAT, first observed in 2012. (*Private collection*)

Members of the newly formed Rapid Support Forces in 2013 adopted their own green-tinted digital pattern, seen here worn by Sudanese President Bashir. (*Private collection*)

These Sudanese Military Policemen illustrate the widely practised habit of mixing camouflage patterns within the same unit. Shown here is a copy of British desert DPM, a Sudanese 'woodland' type pattern, and a copy of the US 'Universal Camouflage Pattern'. (*Private collection*)

This digital pattern was first seen on Sudanese members of the Saudi-led coalition forces operating in Yemen in 2015. (*Private collection*)

such as the SLA and JEM have joined forces under the banner of the Sudanese Revolutionary Front (SLF). The war in Darfur has continued into the present era.

A peace agreement between the Sudanese government and the SPLA was signed in 2003, leading to a 2011 UN resolution and a unanimous vote for the secession of South Sudan, which became in independent state in July.

The Sudanese Armed Forces today consist of the Land Forces, Navy, Air Force, paramilitary Popular Defense Forces, and the Republican Guard. The Sudan Police Force is responsible for law enforcement and falls under the administration of the Ministry of the Interior.

The pattern seen here is worn by Sudanese special forces. (*Private collection*)

Camouflage of the SPLA

A wide number of camouflage designs were worn by the Sudanese People's Liberation Army during the civil war, of which the following are only representational.

(*Private collection*)

Early DPM camouflage was imported, possibly from the UK, and manufactured into uniforms of a localized style.

This vibrant blue/purple DPM pattern is associated with the Royal Squadron, a unit assigned to protect the King and the Royal Household.

The Kingdom of Swaziland (Umbuso weSwatini) is a landlocked nation in Southern Africa, also called kaNgwane in the local dialect. Following South Africa's independence from Britain, Swaziland continued to be under administrational control of Britain until the 1960s, when the nation was encouraged to pursue self-governance. Following the ratification of its own constitution and the creation of a Legislative Council, elections were held in 1967 and official independence granted in 1968. The nation is presently an absolute monarchy, under King Mswati III.

A standardized DPM with brighter colors has been worn by the USDF since the early 2000s, and possibly earlier. (*US Africa Command*)

Formed in 1979, the armed forces of this nation are known as the Umbutfo Swaziland Defense Force, and comprise approximately 3,000 active duty personnel. The USDF has never been involved in a foreign conflict. An elite security unit called the Royal Squadron provides ceremonial and protective details for the monarchy. The Royal Swaziland Police Service is responsible for internal security, border security and customs control.

TANZANIA

The area comprising the modern United Republic of Tanzania consists of the island of Zanzibar and land historically known as Tanganyika. The island was once claimed by the Sultan of Oman, while the continental portion was once incorporated into what was considered German East Africa. In 1954, the Tanganyika African National Union (TANU) was founded with the purpose of gaining independence for the mainland territory. Britain granted this in 1961 and Joseph Nyerere was appointed Prime Minister, and later elected President. Shortly thereafter, Nyerere committed the new state to socialism and a Pan-Africanist doctrine. The Sultan of Zanzibar was overthrown in 1964 by African revolutionaries, and the island merged with its mainland neighbor to form Tanzania on April 26.

The nation's armed forces are known as the Tanzania Peoples' Defense Force (TPDF), and consist of the Land Forces Command, Naval Command, and Air Force Command. The military engaged in a brief war with Uganda between October 1978 and April 1979 over a territorial claim made by Ugandan President Idi Amin, ending in defeat for Uganda. The Army has been involved in several UN missions in recent years, including those to the Democratic Republic of Congo, and the Sudan. Law enforcement is overseen by the Tanzanian Police Force (TPF).

A contract with the Canadian company 'Peerless' in the 1980s provided the TPDF with a quantity of Canadian-style uniforms in the 'Reversed DPM' pattern that was created for the Airborne Regiment's parachutist smocks. The same style uniform was still being worn in the early part of the 2000s.

This DPM variant pattern was produced in Zambia for the TPDF, probably in the late 1980s or early 1990s.

A number of DPM variations are worn by TPDF forces in the current period. These Navy personnel in 2010 wear a version with more subdued tones. (*US DOD*)

General officers in 2015 are wearing a version with much brighter tones, and a uniform style similar to the US BDU. (*US DOD*)

TOGO

Once a protectorate of Germany, following the First World War this region came under a joint mandate of Britain and France known as Togoland. British Togoland would become Ghana in 1957, while French Togoland became an autonomous republic of the French Union in 1959, and an independent republic in 1960. The country

A copy of the French tenue de leópard or 'lizard' pattern was historically used by FAT ground forces, particularly by the Régiment Para Commando (RPC) and the Régiment Commando de la Garde Présidentielle (RCGP).

Elements of the Police wear a blue DPM pattern, such as these officers photographed in 2007. (*Private collection*)

These members of the para-Commando Regiment wear a pattern influenced by the USMC temperate MARPAT design in 2009. (*Private collection*)

Various woodland patterns have been worn by this nation since the turn of the millennium, and were probably adopted earlier. (*Private collection*)

Elements of the Police currently wear a blue pixilated pattern, which is also worn by the Presidential Guard. (*Private collection*)

This DPM variant pattern, initially worn by the Lebanese General Security Directorate, is also in service with the Presidential Guard Commando Regiment.

is now known as the Togolese Republic (République Togolaise). The first president, Sylvanus Olympia, served only three years in office before he was assassinated during a coup d'etat in January 1963. An interim government resumed civilian control until 1967, when another coup d'etat put former Army NCO Eyadéma Gnassingbé in the presidency – a position he retained until his death in 2005. His son, Faure Gnassingbé, assumed the presidency and has maintained control of the country since that time. Anti-government protests in 2017 led to heavy-handed measures by security forces, which have been condemned by the UN.

The Forces Armées Togolaises (FAT), are the armed forces of Togo, and include the Army, Navy, Air Force and Gendarmerie Nationale. A shared responsibility for internal security falls to the Gendarmerie and the national Police.

TUNISIA

The Tunisian Republic (الجمهورية التونسية) was a former colonial possession of France, granted independence in 1956. The country has remained remarkably free from external threats and internal conflict, and has been credited as one of the most modern countries in the Arab world; however, there have been numerous accusations of human and political rights abuses. Governmental corruption, inflation and high rates of unemployment sparked a campaign of civil resistance from December 2010 to January 2011, often referred to as the Tunisian Revolution. This resulted in the overthrow of the old, repressive government, new elections, and, ultimately, sparked the Arab Spring throughout other parts of the Arab world.

A number of 'lizard' patterns have been by Tunisian forces since the 1960s, including this one modeled after the early French shelter design.

This photo of a Tunisian officer serving with the UN, illustrates another variant with bright orange stripes. (*Private collection*)

Yet another variant has darker brown and green stripes, with an overlap that is almost black.

The Tunisian Armed Forces consist of the Land Forces, Air Force, and the Navy. These are augmented by the Garde Nationale (National Guard), and the Directorate of National Security (Sûreté Nationale), which includes special units such as the Brigade Anti-Terrorisme (BAT), Brigade Nationale d'Intervention Rapide, and the Brigade Nationale de Détection et de Neutralisation d'Explosifs (BNDNE). The nation's military have participated in peacekeeping efforts with the United Nations since the 1960s, including missions to the Congo, Cambodia, Namibia, Somalia, Rwanda, Burundi, and the Western Sahara.

The nation gradually began to adopt woodland pattern camouflage in the 1980s, first with elite units such as the commandos of the Garde Nationale and the Presidential Guard, and later with conventional forces. This undated photo illustrates a crossover period where members of the Special Forces wear both lizard and woodland pattern together. (*US Army*)

Another woodland variant is seen here worn by a Naval Infantryman being trained by US personnel. (*US DOD*)

These members of the Groupement Territorial Saharien (GTS) wear a unique two-color desert pattern.

The elite Groupe d'Intervention Presidentielle (GIP) wear a hybrid woodland-leaf pattern with urban colorway of grey and black. (*Private collection*)

Multicam is also worn by a number of elite units in Tunisia, including the Unite Speciale and the BNIR of the Garde Nationale. (*Private collection*)

A DPM pattern virtually identical to the British Army's S95 camouflage has been in use with the anti-terror unit of the Garde Nationale.

These members of the Brigade Nationale d'Intervention Rapid (BNIR), a specialized unit of the Garde Nationale, wear a pixilated urban pattern based on UCP. (*Private collection*)

A new camouflage pattern was adopted in June 2017 by armed forces. The design has many similarities to the Russian SURPAT. (*Private collection*)

Uganda achieved independence from Britain in 1962, but remained a member of the British Commonwealth. Traditional kingdoms were abolished in 1967, after which the nation was declared a republic. In 1971, President Milton Obote was deposed by Army General Idi Amin in a coup d'etat; Amin then declared himself as president. Suspending the constitution and setting up military tribunals in place of civil law, Amin created a military government that used violence, torture, intimidation, and outright murder to persecute political rivals, intellectuals, professionals, and foreign nationals, often for no reasons whatsoever. Between 80,000 and 300,000 people were killed during his eight-year reign, and as many as 80,000 foreign nationals were expelled from the country. In 1978, Amin attempted to annex the Kagera province of Tanzania, leading to war between the two countries. Although supported by Libya and some members of the PLO, Ugandan forces were defeated by a coalition of Tanzanian Defense Forces and the Uganda National Liberation Front (UNLF), a militia of exiled Ugandans. Amin fled into exile in 1979 as new democratic elections were organized by the UNLF.

This photo from 1974 illustrates General Idi Amin wearing a version of French 'lizard' camouflage that was in use with some units of the Ugandan Army at that time. (*Private collection*)

The reconstituted government did not last long, as the National Resistance Army (NRA) soon began a guerilla war (often called the 'bush war' or Luwero War) against the government, which lasted from 1981 until

A copy of Portuguese M64 'vertical lizard' camouflage was worn by some Ugandan forces during the bush war. The majority of photos that emerged from this period suggest it may have been primarily used by the NRA rather than the Ugandan government.

A copy of British DPM was used by Uganda during the 1980s.

This interesting, three-color 'blotch' pattern also dates to the 1980s, and was in service with Uganda land forces. (*Private collection*)

1986. Late in the conflict, President Milton Obote was again deposed (by Tito Okello), but the war continued and the old government eventually crumbled. Yoweri Museveni, former leader of the NRA, was installed as president and has remained in this position into the present era. The army was then reorganized into the Uganda People's Defense Force, which has been engaged since 1987 in a guerilla campaign waged by the Lord's Resistance Army based in Northern Uganda. The latter have been accused of multiple

Various types of 'woodland' camouflage have been worn by the UPDF (and by the NRA) since the 1990s. This photo from 2007 shows an African Union contingent of Ugandans wearing a darker version. (*Private collection*)

Another version seen here from 2012 has a color palette more faithful to the US original. (*Private collection*)

First seen circa 2012, this 'leopard spot' pattern is in service with the elite Presidential Guard unit – the Special Forces Group (SFG) – now the Special Forces Command. (*US DOD*)

Adopted in the early 2000s, this woodland variant with a pale blue background color is worn by Ugandan Air Force personnel. (*US Air Force*)

Two different pixilated camouflage designs were adopted by the UPDF in 2014: green-dominant version for most regions, and brown-dominant version for drier regions of Uganda like Karamoja. (*US DOD*)

The Field Force Police of the Uganda National Police wear a blue/purple variation of DPM pattern seen here. (*Private collection*)

Additionally a different pixilated pattern was adopted for the Ugandan People's Defense Air Force. (*US Air Force*)

These Field Force riot police units of UNP wear a 'wavy' camouflage design with a blue colorway. (*Private collection*)

This officer of the Special Forces Command wears a DPM pattern camouflage that was adopted in 2014. (*Private collection*)

human rights violations, including child slavery and genocide. Ugandan forces have frequently and illegally crossed the border into neighboring Congo to pursue LRA insurgents who have sought refuge there. Uganda has also deployed military personnel in a peacekeeping capacity to places including the Democratic Republic of Congo, Somalia, the Central African Republic and South Sudan.

Seen here in 2014, the Police Presidential Guard (PPG) of the UNP wear a blue pixilated pattern similar to that previously issued to the US Navy. (*Private collection*)

The Ugandan Wildlife Authority (UWA) wears a Multicam clone pattern seen here. (*Private collection*)

The armed forces are currently known as the Uganda People's Defense Force (UPDF), formed in the aftermath of the Lowero War, mostly from elements of the NRA. The UPDF consists of the Land Forces, Air Force, and the Special Forces Command. Ugandan forces have a long history of using camouflage, but interestingly enough the designs have come from all manner of different sources.

ZAIRE

Zaire was the name of the Democratic Republic of Congo from 1971 until 1991. Following a period of intense internal conflict, a coup d'etat in 1965 put Joseph-Désiré Mobutu in power. In 1971 he changed the name of the country to the Republic of Zaire, from the Kongo word nzere or nzadi, meaning 'the river that swallows all rivers'. Under Mobutu, Zaire was governed with an iron fist, with a single party political system and zero tolerance for communist or socialist ideals. Between 1977 and 1978, exiled rebel forces living in Angola launched a military offensive into the Shaba (formerly Katanga) region of Zaire, hoping to revive the popular

Worn here by Colonel Daniel Lusadusu as an officer of the Paratroopers, this leopard spot pattern is frequently associated with the Zaire Kamanyola division, but was worn by other units as well, including commandos, paratroops and Mobutu's personal guard. (*Private collection*)

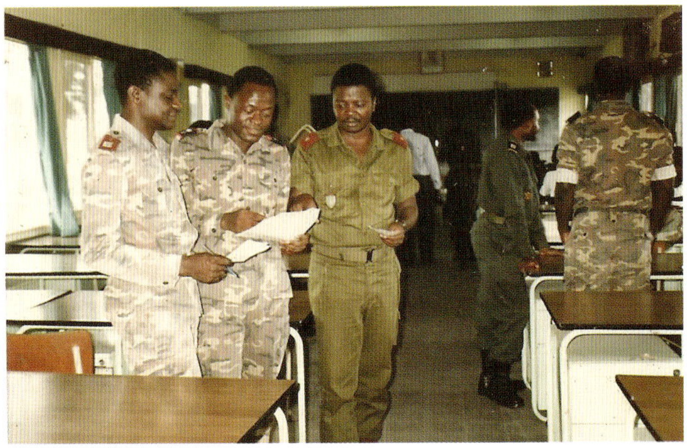

Worn by some officers of the DSP as well as others, this leaf pattern uniform was not encountered as frequently but did see service with FAZ. (*Private collection*)

These officers of the Division Spéciale Présidentielle (DSP) wear the Belgian-influenced Zairean 'jigsaw' camouflage pattern, worn extensively by FAZ well into the 1990s. (*Private collection*)

movement for an independent Katanga. Unable to quell the rebellion by itself, Zaire sought the aid of Belgian and French paratroopers, who eventually routed the insurgents and returned the region to relative stability.

By the 1990s, Mobutu's pattern of environmental exploitation, political repression, corruption, and human rights violations spurred increasing demands for political reform. In November 1996, an insurrection led by Laurent-Désiré Kabila sprang out of eastern Zaire, leading to the First Congo War. The Alliance of Democratic Forces for the Liberation of Congo (AFDL) combined local Zairian militias with Tutsis that had crossed the border from Rwanda during its recent ethnic cleansing, with additional aid coming from Angola, Rwanda, Burundi and Uganda. By May 1997 the war was essentially over, after which Mobutu went into exile in Morocco and Kabila was named president. At this point the country was renamed the Democratic Republic of Congo.

The Armed Forces of Zaire were known as the Forces Armées Zaïrois (FAZ) and consisted of the Army, Navy, Air Force, and several paramilitary organizations. In addition to a Special Presidential Division, the Army's ground forces consisted of the Kamanyola Division, 31st and 32nd Parachute Brigades, the 41st Commando Brigade (Kisangani), three Infantry Brigades, and an Armored Brigade. Zaire would produce some interesting and distinctive camouflage patterns during its tenure, but would also incorporate patterns from the old Belgian and French colonial periods.

This photograph of President Mobutu shows the use of French lizard as far back as 1977 within the FAZ. (*Private collection*)

The use of woodland pattern uniforms by the ADFL during the war has been well-documented. (*Private collection*)

The Republic of Zambia emerged out of the British-controlled region known in colonial times as the Federation of Rhodesia and Nyasaland (est. 1953). At this time, rumblings of African nationalism were already being heard from many parts of Africa, and in Northern Rhodesia civil unrest led to crisis in the early 1960s. The push for independence largely came from the United National Independence Party (UNIP) under Kenneth Kaunda. The federation dissolved in December 1963, and Kaunda won the race for prime minister of a separate Northern Rhodesia in January 1964. One of his first tasks was quelling the Lumpa Uprising in the north. In October 1964, the nation changed its name to the Republic of Zambia.

The Zambian government has a long history of supporting African nationalist movements, including UNITA (Angola), the Zimbabwe African People's Union (ZAPU), the African National Congress (ANC), and the South West Africa People's Organization (SWAPO). It also established close relations with both the Soviet Union and communist China. Zambia's endorsement of the Patriotic Front (PF) guerillas waging a guerilla war against the government of Rhodesia to the south led to a militarization of its border with that country. Incursions by Rhodesian security forces into Zambian territory were common and continued until that country became Zimbabwe. Kenneth Kaunda remained president until 1991, when civil discontent escalated into riots and an attempted coup d'etat. When multiparty elections were finally held, Kaunda was ousted.

Dating to the 1980s, the pattern seen here is a kind of DPM hybrid.

The Zambian Defense Force (ZDF) consists of the Army, Air Force and the Zambian National Service. The latter is an internal defense type organization. Law enforcement is overseen by the Zambian Police Service. In recent years, Zambian forces have taken part in peacekeeping operations to other African nations.

A vertical 'brushstroke' camouflage design was worn by the ZDF during the 1970s and is seen here.

These women soldiers wear a pattern adopted by the ZDF in 1990s, having some brushstroke elements. (*US DOD*)

The Zambian Air Force makes use of a woodland pattern as seen here on these security forces personnel. (*US Air Force*)

This vertical 'grasslands type' camouflage pattern is worn by the Zambia Wildlife Authority. (*Private collection*)

Elements of the Zambian Police Service (ZPS) wear a zigzag pattern design, which could possibly be classified as camouflage. Although uniformly grey from a distance, a close-up view shows there is obviously a pattern. (*Private collection*)

This blue-green camouflage design is worn by the Zambia National Service branch of the armed forces. (*Private collection*)

ZIMBABWE

The Republic of Zimbabwe emerged out of the Rhodesian Bush War which pitted the Rhodesian Security Forces against the Zimbabwe African National Liberation Army (ZANLA) operating primarily out of neighboring Mozambique, and the Zimbabwe People's Revolutionary Army (ZIPRA) operating out of training camps in Zambia. The majority of the war lasted from 1972 until 1978, when the Rhodesian government was brought to the negotiating table by international pressure. Following 'free' elections held in 1979, ZANU leader Robert Mugabe was elected president and remained in power until tendering his resignation in November 2017. The Mugabe administration has a long history of voter intimidation and electoral fraud, but all political opposition has either been ignored or suppressed by government forces. The nation has meanwhile fallen into a steady decline, plagued by a gradual decrease in food production, the rampant spread of HIV/AIDS and cholera, a general degeneration of living standards, and one of the highest infant mortality rates in Africa.

The Zimbabwe National Army was created by integrating elements of the old Rhodesian Army with elements of ZANLA and ZIPRA in 1980. Many units of the old Rhodesian Army were retained, including several of the old Brigades and the Special Air Service. The Rhodesian Light Infantry became the Commando Regiment, and a new Parachute Regiment was formed along the lines of the British regiment. The old Grey's Scouts became the Zimbabwe Mounted Infantry regiment. The Army has primarily been involved in border conflicts, particularly against Renamo operating out of Mozambique.

Although there are rumors still floating around that the Zimbabwe government burned original stocks of Rhodesian camouflage, they were worn by the ZNA until around 1983–84, particularly by units operating in Mozambique to protect the pipeline.

A copy of the old Rhodesian brushstroke camouflage pattern was reintroduced in the 1990s, and has been the standard camouflage pattern of the ZNA since that time. These paratroopers in 2015 even wear camouflaged load-bearing vests. (*US DOD*)

Two types of vertical 'brushstroke' pattern were introduced in 1984, known colloquially as 'monkey hand' camouflage. A version with green background color was reputedly produced for use in the wet season, while a sand or khaki-based version was produced for the dry season. This pattern was worn into the 1990s. (*Private collection*)

Chapter 2

Americas

ANTIGUA AND BARBUDA

This small island nation in the Caribbean emerged as an independent state within the British Commonwealth in 1981. The Antigua and Barbuda Defense Force is one of the smallest in the world, with less than 300 personnel, and consists primarily of the Antigua and Barbuda Regiment, a separate Coast Guard unit, and a small cadet corps.

This member of the ABDF wears a US woodland pattern BDU style uniform in 2013. (*USARNG*)

ARGENTINA

Argentina was governed by a military dictatorship from 1966 until 1982. During this period the country received clandestine military and technical support from the United States, as part of its Operation Condor, largely a project of US Intelligence services. The so-called 'Dirty War' was a campaign of state terrorism aimed at suppressing left-wing political dissidents. Thousands of individuals disappeared during this era.

In April 1982, Argentine forces occupied the British Falkland Islands, declaring its intent to incorporate the islands into Argentine territory. The British government responded with military force, leading to the two-month-long Guerra de Malvinas (Falklands War), which ended with the defeat of Argentine forces and the restoration of British sovereignty. The war was followed by a return to democratic rule in 1983.

These paratroopers wear a copy of the US M1942 pattern camouflage pattern as helmet covers. Historic photographs also suggest a similar pattern was issued to small amphibious commando units and the NCO school of the Marines during the 1970s. (*Private collection*)

The Armed Forces of the Argentine Republic (Fuerzas Armadas de la República Argentina) fall under the control of two primary departments: the Ministry of Defense and the Ministry of the Interior. Under the Ministry of Defense are the Army (Ejército Argentino), Air Force (Fuerza Aérea Argentina) and the Navy (Armada Argentina). In

Another version of 'duck hunter' pattern camouflage can be seen here, worn by two members of the Infanteria de Marina. This pattern also dates to the 1970s. (*Private collection*)

This unique camouflage design was introduced in 1975, and worn primarily as helmet covers, although some individuals also used it for scarves (*Juan Pablo Tessiere collection*)

Shown here in a photo from the Malvinas War, this camouflage pattern primarily appeared on camouflage helmet covers and possibly individual scarf material. (*Private collection*)

A woodland-type camouflage pattern, having completely different shapes than the US m81 design, is worn here by members of Army 601 or 602 Commando Company in the 1980. (*Private collection*)

Another kind of woodland design is seen here, issued to Naval Infantry in the 1980s.

A Chinese-produced 'woodland' style camouflage was imported for use by commando, airborne and elite infantry units in 1990s, although the fabric was not rugged and it tended to fade and deteriorate very quickly. (*Private collection*)

This 'jigsaw' style camouflage, made by the Belgian firm Salik, was utilized by 601 & 602 Commando Companies during the Malvinas War, and also by some Marine commandos. (*Private collection*)

Seen here in a photo from 2012, the mimetizado selva or jungle camouflage is a DPM-based design issued primarily to mountain troops, some cavalry and peacekeepers in 1990s but also worn later. (*Private collection*)

addition to national defense, these forces are fully committed to peacekeeping roles with the United Nations. The Ministry of the Interior administers several Federal paramilitary services, including the Gendarmeria Nacional Argentina (GNA), Prefectura Naval Argentina (PNA), Policia Federal Argentina (PFA), and the Policia Seguridad Aeroportuaria. The Gendarmeria Nacional functions as the primary security force of the nation, providing both internal security and border protection functions. Although subordinate to the Ministry of the Interior, the GNA is distinguished from other Federal agencies in being truly paramilitary in organization and function (in this regard, functioning almost as a fourth branch of the military). The GNA has also served in peacekeeping/observation roles outside the borders of Argentina, and provides embassy security personnel.

Additionally, each of the twenty-three provinces maintains its own provincial police agency (Policia de la Provincia), all of which have some tactical or special operations unit that employs specialized uniforms and equipment.

Various copies of the US m81 woodland have been in circulation with Argentine forces since the mid-1990s and have continued to be worn into the present day. This camouflage pattern eventually became the standard uniform of the armed forces and some federal agencies. (*Private collection*)

A DPM variant is seen here worn by mechanized infantry personnel. Known colloquially as Camuflaje Patagonico (also called 'Pampa' pattern), the design is primarily worn by personnel serving in the Patagonia and Cordillerana regions. (*Private collection*)

A copy of the US six-color 'chocolate chip' pattern camouflage is issued to some units, including Air Force Tactical Support Squadron, Army 601 and 602 Commando Companies, and the National Police GOE (Grupo de Operaciones Especiales). (*Private collection*)

Units serving outside Argentina, particularly those on missions with the United Nations, often wear a copy of the US tricolor desert pattern. This photo from 2013, shows several personnel attached to UNFICYP in Cyprus. The pattern is also worn locally by the Coast Guard Grupo Albatro. (*Private collection*)

The Naval Infantry adopted a pattern modeled on the USMC temperate MARPAT design in the 2000s; this design is also worn by 601 and 602 Commando companies and the Special Operations Group of the air force. (*Private collection*)

The Naval Infantry also wear a desert version of the MARPAT design, seen here on this member of the Comandos Anfibios. (*Private collection*)

The Army adopted a version of Multicam in 2014, which is worn primarily by units serving in the Patagonia region, although it has also been seen with special operations personnel. (*Private collection*)

These members of the Grupo Especial de Operaciones Federales or GEOF of the Federal Police wear a tiger stripe camouflage pattern that has been in service for a number of years. (*Private collection*)

Police and Federal Forces Camouflage

These members of GE-1, the Infantry Special Group of the National Police, wear a copy of the Universal Camouflage Pattern (UCP). (*Private collection*)

The unique selva digital pattern is worn by the Grupo Alacran of the National Gendarmerie. (*Private collection*)

A blue camouflage design was worn by the Brigada Halcon (Fuerzas Especiales Halcon) of the Buenos Aires Provincial Police in the 1980s. (*Private collection*)

A bright blue DPM variant design is worn by several provincial units, including the Cordoba Provincial Police, Salta Provincial Police, and the Brigada de Operaciones de Rescate y Antitumulto (BORA) of the Rio Negro Provincial Police seen here. (*Private collection*)

This unique blue 'waves' design is worn by the Cuerpo Guardia de Infantería of the Buenos Aires Provincial Police.

Another unique camouflage design worn by the Brigada Especial Operativa Halcón of the Buenos Aires Provincial Police.

A DPM variant pattern with a grey colorway is worn by the Grupo de Apoyo Departamental (Departmental Support Group) or GAD unit of the Buenos Aires Provincial Police.

The Unidad de Prevención Bancaria (Bank Crimes Unit) or UPB of the Buenos Aires Provincial Police wear this unique orange camouflage design.

These members of the Tropas de Operaciones Especiales (TOE) or Special Operations Troops of the Sante Fe Provincial Police wear a grey urban type woodland camouflage.

BAHAMAS

The Bahamas are a nation of more than 700 islands in the Caribbean and has been an independent member of the British Commonwealth since 1973. The Royal Bahamas Defense Force (RBDF) is primarily a naval force supplemented by a small Air wing, Special Operations Unit and a Commando Wing.

This soldier of the RBDF wears the copy of the USMC temperate MARPAT camouflage design adopted in 2012. (*US Air National Guard*)

Members of the Special Operations Unit and the Commando Wing previously wore a copy of US m81 woodland camouflage.

BARBADOS

Barbados is another island nation in the Caribbean and member of the British Commonwealth. The Barbados Defense Force (BDF) is the combined armed forces of this nation, and consists of the Barbados Regiment (an infantry unit), Barbados Coast Guard, Force Headquarters and a cadet corps.

These members of the Barbados Regiment wear a copy of British DPM during a training exercise. (*US Army National Guard*)

Some members of the Coast Guard wear m81 woodland camouflage, as seen here. (*US Marine Corps*)

BELIZE

This small nation on the northeast coast of Central America was formerly a British protectorate known as British Honduras. Belize was granted full independence in 1981, although units of the British Armed Forces (British Forces Belize) would continue to remain in country for many years to come. The British presence is officially to provide protection against possible incursion by neighboring Guatemala, with whom the country shares a border and a long-standing territorial dispute. The Belize Defense Force (BDF) was founded in 1978, following the disbanding of two territorial units the year before – the Belize Volunteer Guard and the Police Special Force. The BDF is concerned with ground and air defense, the Belize Coast Guard with maritime matters, and the Belize Police Department with internal security and law enforcement.

More commonly encountered in the BDF is British DPM, as seen here in a joint training exercise with a number of Caribbean nations. (*US Army*)

Photographed in 2010, this general of the BDF wears a copy of m81 woodland camouflage, in service for many years. (*US Army*)

These members of the Belize Special Assignment Group (BSAG) wear Multicam pattern while on exercise in 2011. (*US Army*)

A copy of the Russian armed forces green pixilated camouflage was adopted by the BDF in 2011, although it has not been universally adopted as many personnel continue to wear the old DPM design. (*US DOD*)

BOLIVIA

The Revolutionary Nationalist Movement (MNR), a broad-based political party, secured control of Bolivia in 1952, introducing land reform, universal suffrage, and nationalizing key industries. This government was overthrown in 1964 by a military junta, which heralded in a long period of rule by military dictatorship. Through its friendship with the United States, Bolivia received considerable training, aid and war materiel. In 1967, a team of Bolivian Army Rangers captured and executed revolutionary leader Che Guevara, under the leadership

Members of the Special Boat Unit (SBU) previously wore a blue woodland pattern seen here. (*Private collection*)

Special Ranger Companies, trained and outfitted by US advisors, wore duck hunter spot pattern uniforms during the 1960s and 70s. (*Private collection*)

Since approximately 2011, the Special Boat Unit (SBU), the Anti-Drug Unit, and the newly formed Navy SEAL Team of the Coast Guard have worn a digipat design with a blue colorway. (*US Marine Corps*)

These members of the 12th Special Forces Regiment pose in their woodland pattern camouflage uniforms, universally adopted by the armed forces in the 1990s. (*Private collection*)

Based on the US ERDL camouflage pattern drawings, two distinctive 'leaf' patterns were adopted by some units of the armed forces in the 1980s. (*Private collection*)

Several elite units of the National Police wear a copy of the UCP (Universal Camouflage Pattern), including the UTARC (Tactical Crisis Resolution Unit) and the Grupo de Investigaciones de Casos Especiales. (*GICE*)

The Bolivian Naval Infantry have been outfitted in six-color desert pattern camouflage, as seen here. The design has also been worn by some units of the Bolivian Police, such as the Unidad Táctica de Resolución de Crisis – UTARC. (*Private collection*)

A darker version of the UCP is worn by the La Unidad Táctica de Operaciones Policiales (UTOP) or Police Tactical Operations Unit. (*Private collection*)

Some units of the Army and Police have worn copies of the USMC temperate and desert MARPAT patterns since 2013. (*Private collection*)

These officers of the Bolivian Air Force (FAB) wear a recently adopted blue digital pattern similar to the US Navy's NWU-1 design. (*Private collection*)

of a CIA officer. Between 1979 and 1981, several coups d'etat and counter coups foisted weak leaders and weaker governments on the population. A transition to democracy began with the election of Hernán Siles Zuazo in 1982.

The Bolivian Armed Forces (Fuerzas Armadas de Bolivia) consist of the Army, Navy and Air Force. Law enforcement is the responsibility of the Bolivian National Police Force (Cuerpo de Policía Nacional), which includes a number of specialist paramilitary units.

BRAZIL

The government of Brazil in the post-war years vacillated between democratically elected and military junta governments. By 1964, a military regime was firmly in place and would retain power for more than twenty years. The Brazilian military government was noted for its repressive treatment of political opponents, which included guerillas, artists, journalists, and anyone whose opinion differed from that of the regime. The country began a slow return to democracy in the 1980s.

The Brazilian Armed Forces (Forças Armadas Brasileiras) consist of the Army, Navy and Air Force and is the largest in South America. Since 1994 all three branches of service have been heavily active with United Nations peacekeeping missions. The Polícia Militar (PM) or Military Police are a national gendarmerie of independent agencies responsible for maintaining order within the individual states. Conventional law enforcement such as criminal investigations is handled by the Civil Police.

Seen here worn by a group of Brazilian Army paratroops, this 'amoeba' pattern was introduced in 1967 for use by the Brazilian Army. (*Private collection*)

Heavily influenced by the US-designed M-1942 'spot' pattern and introduced in the 1960s, the camuflagem bolinhas pattern was worn primarily by airborne and commando units, as well as some police special operations units throughout the 1960s and 1970s. (*Private collection*)

Based on some of the Portuguese M64 lizard patterns worn in Africa, this design was introduced in 1980s for use primarily by Mountain troops.

Another variation of lizard pattern from the 1980s is seen here, for use by Caatinga troops operating in extremely arid parts of the country.

A more standardized version of the lizard pattern was produced in 1980s for use by the conventional units of the Army, although minor color variations are documented as the pattern has been in production for so many years. (*US Army National Guard*)

Although variations exist, a standardized pattern was issued in the 1980s for use by Navy and Marines also, having a very green color palette. (*Private collection*)

The Air Force had also standardized a camouflage design by the 1980s, worn primarily by personnel engaged in ground defense and special operations. (*Private collection*)

Police Patterns

A lizard variation using a dark green color palette is worn by the São Paolo State Police Shock Battalion COE. (Special Operations Company). (*Private collection*)

A woodland-type camouflage design with grey-black colorway is worn by a number of Shock Battalions (Batalhão de Choque) within some of the State Police agencies. (*Private collection*)

This grey dominant variation of the lizard pattern is worn by Bahia and São Paolo State Police Shock Battalion COE. (*Special Operations Company*)

Another urban type camouflage design seen here is worn by Goias State Police GATE unit, Rio Grande do Sul State special police, and Rio de Janeiro police. (*Private collection*)

This grey-dominant digital camouflage design is used by the Força Nacional de Segurança Pública. (FNSP – National Public Security Force). (*Private collection*)

A locally-produced copy of the US six-color 'chocolate chip' camouflage pattern has been worn by the Batalhão de Operações Policiais Especiais (BOPE) or Police Special Operations Battalion of the Rio de Janeiro State Police, as well as by some Caatinga personnel.

These members of the BOPE wear a copy of the USMC temperate MARPAT design, which is now standard issue, in addition to the solid black fatigues commonly worn by this unit. (*Private collection*)

These members of the TIGRE unit of the Parana State Civil Police wear a dark tiger stripe pattern camouflage. (*Private collection*)

This leaf camouflage design is worn by the Goias State Wildlife Police. (*Private collection*)

Members of the Espirito Santo PM Ambiental (Environmental Police) unit wear a copy of the US m81 woodland camouflage pattern. (*Private collection*)

This vertical lizard camouflage design was adopted by the Mato Gross de Sul PM Ambiental unit. (*Private collection*)

Members of the Rio de Janeiro PM Ambiental unit wear this variation of woodland camouflage. (*Private collection*)

A member of the Comando de Operações Táticas (Tactical Operations Command) or COT of the Polícia Federal wears Multicam pattern. (*Private collection*)

A bright green digital camouflage pattern is worn by the Amazon State Police Ambiental unit. (*Private collection*)

Canada was a founding member of the United Nations and contributed a significant number of military personnel to the Korean War. The country took part in the Persian Gulf War in 1991, and ten years later sent personnel to Afghanistan in 2001 as part of the International Security Assistance Force (ISAF). Canada has a poor record of dealing fairly with its indigenous population, which has contributed to a number of violent confrontations between Canadian Forces and First Nations communities.

The Canadian Armed Forces (or Canadian Forces – CF) consist of the Army, Navy and Air Force, and retain many of the traditional regimental designations inherited from the British Army. Additional elements falling under the umbrella of CF include the Canadian Special Operations Command, Information Management Group, and the Canadian Forces Health Services Group. Canadian Forces have contributed substantially to peacekeeping missions with the United Nations, including Cyprus, Croatia, Bosnia, and Kosovo.

Canadian paratroopers wore vintage Denison smocks for several years after the Second World War, but they were phased out after wartime stocks were depleted and

Canadian DPM was produced in the 1970s and 1980s for the Canadian Airborne Regiment and issued only as a smock worn for training and formation purposes. This photo from 1987 illustrates the 2nd pattern, which was enlarged by about 30 per cent over the shapes in the 1st pattern. (*Henrik Clausen*)

Members of the 1st Canadian Parachute Battalion wore British-made Denison camouflage smocks during the Second World War and throughout the 1950s.

The No. 4 Garrison Dress was introduced in 1989 and worn until 1995. The distinctive Canadian Garrison Dress Land Forces (LF) jacket was never intended to be used as combat dress, but nevertheless was printed in a woodland-type camouflage pattern. (*Henrik Clausen collection*)

The Canadian Temperate Weight digital camouflage pattern, or CADPAT (TW), was introduced in 1996 as the standard combat design for all personnel operating on the ground. This design set the standard for other 'digital' patterns that came after, many of which are simply recolorations of the original. (*NATO*)

A desert version of this pattern was introduced in 2002, known as CADPAT (AR), for use in arid environments such as Afghanistan. (*US Navy*)

CADPAT (WA) was likewise introduced for snow/arctic conditions (*Dept National Defense*)

A Master Warrant Officer of the Canadian Special Operations Regiment commemorates Menton Day at Joint Base Lewis-McChord in 2017, wearing the Multicam pattern chosen by this unit as a working and operational pattern. (*US Army*)

never replaced. Indeed, aside from solid white outer clothing worn by military personnel operating in arctic or snow-covered regions, the Canadian Armed Forces did not utilize any camouflage uniforms at all until the mid-1970s. In 1975, the Canadian Airborne Regiment was issued its first camouflage garment in nearly twenty-five years, a DPM pattern camouflage airborne smock. Although the Regiment experimented with other items, such as special windproof trousers, the DPM smock remained the only item of issue camouflaged clothing worn by the Regiment until its disbandment in 1995. The standard combat uniform remained olive green for the next quarter century, with a tan version for desert deployments seeing very brief trials in the mid-1990s. Then, in 2001, after several months of research and experimentation, the Canadian Armed Forces adopted their very own camouflage pattern, a computer-designed scheme incorporating a pixelated pattern known as CADPAT (TW). This pattern was shortly thereafter complemented by its desert counterpart, CADPAT (AR), and a snow/arctic version, CADPAT (WA).

Chile experienced severe political polarization in the 1960s and 1970s that culminated in a 1973 coup d'etat that placed General Augusto Pinochet in power. The nation remained firmly under military control until 1990, during which time all political activity considered left wing was brutally repressed and several thousands were imprisoned or simply disappeared. The military junta received covert military assistance from the United States, particularly through the Central Intelligence Agency, although publicly it maintained a strongly critical attitude.

The Armed Forces of Chile (Fuerzas Armadas de Chile) consist of the Army, Navy and Air Force. Between 1974 and 2011, the Carabineros de Chile (national police) were also considered a branch of the armed forces. In addition to internal security, the Carabineros are responsible for maritime and border security.

Chile's use of camouflage can be traced to the 1970s and is strongly influenced by early US designs such as the M1942 'spot' and M1948 ERDL 'leaf' patterns. Nevertheless, early Chilean camouflage patterns have a distinctive flavor of their own and would be regarded only as derivative, rather than copies. In the modern era, the Armed Forces have embraced US designs a bit more literally.

This spotted pattern, nicknamed rana (frog), was issued to Army and Marine units operating in the Central Military zone from the 1970s to the late 1980s. Several color variations are documented, including those shown here.

Another version of the rana pattern, having completely different series of shapes to the design, was also worn in the Central Military zone during this time period.

Having similar shapes to the first *rana* pattern, but a different colorway, and often referred to as *pantera rosa* (pink panther), this variant of the spot design was issued to Army and Marine units operating in the North Military zone where the terrain is arid and desert-like (*Private collection*)

Yet another pattern worn in the North Military zone and having similar coloration to the pantera rosa is seen here. Shapes are similar to the second rana pattern, but not exactly the same.

Having similar shapes to the first rana pattern, but a different colorway, and often referred to as pantera rosa (pink panther), this variant of the spot design was issued to Army and Marine units operating in the North Military zone where the terrain is arid and desert-like. (*Private collection*)

These Chilean Marines wear the same 'turtle shell' camouflage design developed in South Korea, introduced in the 1970s for use by Chilean Army and Marine units operating in the South Military zone. A reversible poncho was printed in a unique variant on the opposing side. Also note the South Korean 'waves' pattern helmet covers being worn in this photo. (*Private collection*)

This blue or purple 'leaf' pattern was adopted by the Chilean AF personnel in the 1980s and worn into the early 2000s. (*Private collection*)

A copy of US m81 woodland camouflage was universally adopted for most units of the Chilean Armed Forces serving in the Central and South Military zones in the 1990s. (*Private collection*)

These snow camouflage patterns have been worn by Army and Marine units operating in the Andean Military zone. (*Private collection*)

The US tricolor desert pattern was also universally adopted in the 1990s by units serving in the North Military zone.

Some elements of the Chilean AF and Special Operations Brigade wear a copy of the UCP pattern, as seen in this photo from 2012. (*Private collection*)

This Chilean Commando team, photographed in 2014, is wearing a copy of the USMC desert MARPAT camouflage, first issued in 2007 to Army and Marine units operating in the North Military zone. (*Private collection*)

This copy of USMC temperate MARPAT camouflage began replacing the previously issued woodland pattern worn by units operating in the Central and South Military zones in 2009. (*US Army National Guard*)

A copy of Multicam was universally adopted by most special operations units of the Army, Navy and Air Force beginning in 2007. (*US Marine Corps*)

The period of the 1940s and 1950s was marked by extreme violence between the Liberal and Conservative parties in Colombia, known as La Violencia. By the late 1950s, an agreement between the parties to share power was brokered, but in spite of this, several paramilitary guerilla groups emerged during the 1960s. The most notable of these were the Fuerzas Armadas Revolucionarias de Colombia (FARC), Ejército de Liberación Nacional (ELN) and Movimiento 19 de Abri*l* (M-19) – all of whom claimed to follow Marxist doctrines. A low-intensity conflict has existed in the country to this day, involving the armed forces, right wing paramilitary groups, and leftist revolutionary guerilla organizations. When powerful drug cartels emerged during the 1980s and 1990s, most were supported by their own paramilitary organizations, which added to the conflict. The United States has been a staunch ally and supporter of the Colombian government since the 1950s, and has always encouraged its military operations against communism. Under the administration of President Alvaro Uribe, right wing paramilitaries were disbanded and increased security measures taken to combat terrorism. A peace agreement with FARC was finally signed in 2016, ending more than fifty years of conflict.

The Colombian Armed Forces consist of the National Army, Navy (including the Naval Infantry) and Air Force, historically supplied and heavily influenced by the United States. In addition to its long counter-insurgency campaign at home, the armed forces have contributed observers to the Multinational Force and Observers mission in the Sinai since 1978, and have participated in United Nations peacekeeping efforts abroad. The National Police (Policía Nacional de Colombia) are also administered by the Ministry of Defense, although not technically part of the armed forces. The use of camouflage by its armed forces has also been heavily influenced by designs from the United States.

Unquestionably based on the US M1942 spot camouflage pattern, the Tigrillo design was adopted by the armed forces in the 1970s and continued to be worn well into the 1990s. The top photograph clearly illustrates the two major color variations, the green background and tan/khaki background. (*Private collection*)

A copy of the US m81 woodland design was introduced in the 1990s and became the standard pattern of the armed forces for a number of years to come. (*US Marine Corps*)

These Comandos Urbanos, photographed in 2013, wear another woodland variation having a darker grey colorway. (*Private collection*)

The pixelado (pixelated) camouflage pattern was introduced in 2006 and developed specifically for the Colombian armed forces. Although some branches of service since replaced the design, this continues to be worn by the Army. (*US Army National Guard*)

A variation of the woodland pattern worn by the Unidades de Alta Montaña del Ejército (Special Mountain Warfare units) was suited for use in high altitudes with heavy snow conditions.

The matching desert version is seen here, which his worn primarily by personnel operating outside of Colombia, such as with the MFO or United Nations missions. (*Private collection*)

A grey-dominant camouflage design, having pixilated shapes with a 'mesh-like' overlay design, was adopted by the Colombian Air Force in 2015. (*Private collection*)

The Infanteria de Marina (Colombian Marines) also adopted its own version of the 'mesh' type camouflage pattern in 2015. (*Private collection*)

The Instituto Nacional Penitenciario y Carcelario (INPEC) or National Penitentiary and Prison Institute has issued a brown/black woodland camouflage design in the past. (*Private collection*)

INPEC later adopted the blue pixilated camouflage pattern seen here. (*Private collection*)

COSTA RICA

Following the annulment of presidential election results in February 1948, a brief civil war erupted in March and ended with the government being overthrown by the army, commanded by José Figueres Ferrer. Costa Rica endured rule by military junta for the next year-and-a-half, during which time the armed forces were abolished, and a new constitution was drafted by a democratically elected assembly. Control of the government was relinquished to the new government in November 1949.

In place of regular armed forces, Figueres established the Fuerza Publica (Public Force) which consisted of the Guardia Civil (Civil Guard), the Rural Assistance Guard, and the Frontier Guards (border patrol units). The Guardia Civil was a gendarmerie-type force combining

The Guardia Civil made limited use of US m81 woodland camouflage pattern while it was still in existence. (*Private collection*)

The Organismo de Investigación Judicial (OIJ) intervention unit, known as Servicio Especial de Respuesta Táctica, wear the two 'urban woodland' type camouflage patterns seen here.

This grey-black digital camouflage design is worn by some members of the Fuerza Publica. (*Private collection*)

The Unidad Especial de Apoyo teams of the Public Force have deployed in a copy of the USMC temperate MARPAT camouflage. (*Private collection*)

Currently the SERT Teams of the OIJ seem to prefer wearing Multicam uniforms, when not outfitted in their traditional black assault suits.

The PF Unidad Especial Intervención and the OIJ SERT teams have both worn the US-designed UCP camouflage pattern on some occasions. (*Private collection*)

the functions of army, air force, navy, national police and coast guard, with a strength of no more than 2,000, and extremely limited military capacity. The primary duty of the Civil Guard was internal security, but they were involved in the long standing border dispute with Nicaragua which came to a head in 1955. During the Nicaraguan Civil War, the CG patrolled the border in order to prevent guerillas from using Costa Rican territory.

The Fuerza Publica was completely reorganized in 1996, and the old units including the Guardia Civil were eliminated. The present Force functions primarily as a national police agency with ground security, law enforcement, counter-narcotics, and border patrol as its primary duties. Costa Rica also maintains a small special operations unit, the Unidad Especial de Intervencion (UEI) or Special Intervention Unit.

CUBA

The Republic of Cuba (República de Cuba) came into existence following the Cuban Revolution (1953–59), in which armed revolutionaries under Fidel Castro successfully overthrew the government of Fulgencio Batista. Displeased with the socialist leanings of the new government, the United States trained and supported a military force of Cuban exiles to lead an assault on the fledgling Cuban Army in April 1961. This operation was a complete failure and did nothing to destabilize Castro's control over the island nation. By 1963 the new government was moving towards a Communist system based on that of the USSR, with whom the nation would have strong ties for many decades.

During the 1970s, thousands of Cuban military personnel were dispatched to Africa to assist in propping up Soviet-sponsored insurrections. Cuban 'advisors'

Although not part of the FAR, Cuban exile troops of the Brigade 2506 were provided with 'duck hunter' pattern uniforms (supplied by the CIA) during the Bay of Pigs operation in 1963. (*Private collection*)

Probably introduced in the late 1960s, this camouflage pattern was worn by the Tropas Especiales (Special Troops) of the Cuban Ministry of the Interior as well as by some Cuban advisors deployed to Africa.

A variation of the French 'lizard' pattern with a grey colorway and brown or orange stripes was worn by Cuban advisors serving in Africa in the 1970s and 1980s. In more recent years it has also been worn by Border Guards serving in Guantanamo Bay. (*Private collection*)

This three-color 'amoeba' camouflage design has been worn by the Tropas Especiales of the FAR from the 1990s onwards. (*Private collection*)

Another pattern associated with the Tropas Especiales of the FAR is this vertical 'brushstroke' design.

were particularly prevalent in Angola and Ethiopia, and remained in Angola until after the end of the South African Border War in 1990.

The Fuerzas Armadas Revolucionarias (FAR) are Cuba's armed forces, comprising the Army, Navy, Air and Air Defense Forces. Additional paramilitary units can be found within the Ministerio del Interior de la República de Cuba (MININT), Civil Defense and National Reserves. Most units of the FAR and MININT do not wear camouflage uniforms. Exceptions to this rule have been those units deployed overseas as advisors, and the special operations and airborne forces of the army.

The Dominican Republic was a dictatorship controlled by Rafael Trujillo prior to the Second World War and remained under his iron fist until his assassination in 1961. The Trujillo regime received considerable assistance from the United States, but this was withdrawn shortly before the assassination. A democratically elected government was established in 1963, but overtaken in April 1965 by a military junta, sparking a brief civil war involving loyalists and constitutionalists. Fearful of a communist takeover, the United States, along with several small contingents from the Organization of American States, intervened. Supervised elections in 1966 put Joaquín Balaguer in the presidency, although this period has been criticized for human rights

The US m81 woodland camouflage was adopted in the late 1980s or early 1990s and remained in service until approximately 2008. (*Private collection*)

The earliest camouflage pattern in documented use with this nation is a copy of the US ERDL or 'leaf' pattern that was introduced circa 1971.

A small contingent of Dominican personnel deployed to Iraq in 2003-04. These men were outfitted in a combination of US six-color 'chocolate chip' and tricolor desert pattern camouflage uniforms.

The Dominican National Police SWAT Team (Unidad SWAT) wear tiger stripe pattern camouflage uniforms, some having a more green colorway and other more black. (*Private collection*)

The Naval Infantry Battalion adopted the American UCP pattern in 2008, replacing the earlier solid tan uniforms worn by this unit. (*US Marine Corps*)

A copy of the USMC temperate MARPAT camouflage design was adopted by the Dominican Army in 2008 and is now worn by most units. (*US Army*)

The Dominican Air Force (FAD) is now wearing a copy of the US ABU 'grey tiger stripe' pattern. (*Private collection*)

abuses and repression of civil liberties. The Dominican Republic remains a staunch ally of the United States but has a strained relationship with its neighbor Haiti due to mass migrations of Haitian citizens across its border.

The Fuerzas Armadas de la República Dominicana consists of the Army, Navy and Air Force and are heavily modeled after those of the United States. Uniforms and equipment have largely copied those of the USA, and in many cases are exactly the same. This has been particularly true for camouflage combat uniforms. A small contingent of Dominican personnel was deployed to Iraq between 2003 and 2004.

ECUADOR

A military junta under General Guillermo Rodríguez took control of Ecuador in 1972 and retained power until 1976, when he was replaced in another coup d'etat orchestrated by Admiral Alfredo Poveda. The military government responded to increased calls for a return to democracy in April 1979.

Beginning in the 1990s, the country began to issue a copy of the US m81 woodland pattern which was adopted as a general service pattern for the armed forces. Color or hue variations of this design have also been documented. (*Private collection*)

A unique tiger stripe pattern was adopted by this nation in the 1970s and worn primarily by elite units of the Army and Navy. There are a number of documented variants, some with very strong, defined colors, and some with a more muted appearance. (*Private collection*)

Units of the Ecuadorian Air Force such as the Infantry wore a woodland variant pattern with blue colorway in 1990s.

Another woodland variant worn by the Guias Penitenciarios (prison guards) is seen here, with a brown/black colorway.

These members of the Grupo de Operaciones Especiales (GOE) and the Grupo de Intervención y Rescate (GIR) of the National Police wear a woodland camouflage pattern with a grey colorway as seen here. (*Private collection*)

This blue digital pattern is worn by the Instituto Nacional Penitenciario y Carcelario (INPEC) or National Penitentiary and Prison Institute. (*Private collection*)

These commandos wear a copy of USMC temperate MARPAT pattern with a slightly modified colorway, universally adopted by the Armed Forces in 2007. (*Private collection*)

Since approximately 2008, both the GOE and GIR of the National Police began wearing a digital camouflage design with the same grey colorway. (*Private collection*)

A long-standing border dispute with neighboring Peru has resulted in periods of armed conflict between the two nations. A brief skirmish lasting a week in 1981 was followed in 1995 by the Cenapa War, lasting just over a month. The dispute was finally resolved in October 1998 by means of a pact.

The armed forces of Ecuador consist of the Army, Navy and Air Force. The nation has provided military observers to the United Nations missions around the world since 1948. Subordinate to the Ministry of Interior, the Policía Nacional del Ecuador are responsible for law enforcement, counter-insurgency and internal security duties.

In an attempt to quell a rising revolutionary movement, a military junta seized power in 1979, but was dissolved shortly thereafter due to popular pressure. With the aid of the United States, a second junta under Napoleon Duarte was then installed in 1980; however, the government was unable to stifle an insurrectionist movement in time, and so the nation degenerated into war. The Salvadoran Civil War raged from 1980 to 1992, fought between the military government of El Salvador (supported by the United States) and a coalition of

Following its departure from Southeast Asia, the United States donated considerable quantities of surplus equipment and uniforms to El Salvador, including M1964 ERDL pattern camouflage uniforms. (*Private collection*)

As supplies of US-made uniforms dried up, locally-produced copies of the ERDL pattern were manufactured and made into uniforms worn by regular and elite status units throughout the Civil War.

Another variant of the above was produced, printed in very dark colors on a stiff, canvas-like fabric. These saw extensive use during the war. (*Private collection*)

leftist groups known as the Farabundo Martí National Liberation Front (FMLN). Under US direction, the Salvadorian government invoked a 'scorched earth' policy combining airstrikes and counter-insurgency techniques learned from their American advisors. The government was also known to deploy 'death squads' that kidnapped, tortured and executed suspected FMLN members and their supporters. Following the revolutionary principles of Che Guevara, Mao Zedong and the Viet Minh, the FMLN were proponents of economic sabotage, intimidation of the rural population, and using civilians as human shields. After twelve years of war, in which the

Local manufacturers also produced their own version of 'tiger stripe' printed on heavy fabric using poor-quality dyes that faded rapidly. Like most camouflage of this period, the tiger patterns were worn primarily by units with elite status.

Camouflage uniforms were also imported from South Korea and issued to units with special status, such as this 'waves' pattern worn by airborne and elite infantry personnel.

This spot or 'duck hunter' camouflage design is associated with the Atlacatl Battalions, and may have been around during the Civil War, although this photo is from 1993. (*Private collection*)

FMLN made some territorial gains, a truce was finally reached in January of 1992.

Under the peace accords of 1992 the size of the Salvadoran army was reduced, and the National Police, Treasury Police, National Guard and Civilian

Seen here with an Iraqi Army officer, two Salvadoran officers serving in Iraq wear US tricolor desert pattern. (*Private collection*)

This photo from the late 1980s illustrates the wide range of uniform styles worn at the same time by members of a single unit during this period. This is also when local copies of the US m81 woodland pattern were originally fielded by this country. (*Private collection*)

The Army's Comando de Fuerzas Especiales or CFE, the Special Forces Command, has worn US 'chocolate chip' desert pattern during the dry season since the 1990s. (*J. Montes collection*)

A blue version of m81 woodland pattern was adopted by Salvadoran Air Force personnel in 1990s. (*Private collection*)

A pixilated camouflage design with blue/black colorway was adopted by the National Police Grupo de Reaccion Political or GRP. (*Private collection*)

Shown here in 2012, these Marines of the Salvadoran Navy (Infanteria de Marina) wear a copy of the USMC temperate MARPAT design (also worn by Army Special Operations teams). (*Private collection*)

The Army also adopted its own digital pattern circa 2016, similar to that of the Navy but with lighter shades of brown. (US Army)

These Salvadoran airmen in 2016 wear a new blue digital pattern adopted by the Air Force. (US Air Force)

Defense militia were all dissolved. The armed forces of El Salvador consist of the Army, Navy and Air Force, which includes a number of special operations units. A small contingent of Salvadoran military personnel deployed as part of the Multinational Force – Iraq between 2003 and 2009. Since 1992, the re-formed Policía Nacional Civil is responsible for internal security and law enforcement.

GUATEMALA

Guatemala has a long history of dictatorial rule dating from the pre-war period. A brief period of democracy was brought to an end in 1954, when a US-backed coup installed yet another military leader. Mounting dissatisfaction with right-wing governments, human rights abuses, and racial and socio-economic discrimination spawned the formation of several insurgency movements. By 1960, the country was

Seen here in a photo from 1983, this unique 'duck hunter spot' camouflage pattern was employed by some Guatemalan units. (*Private collection*)

This South-Korean-made 'waves' camouflage design saw extensive use during the Civil War period, particularly by elite infantry and special forces units. (*Private collection*)

Loosely based on US M1948 ERDL, the pattern in this photo was produced locally for use by the army, where it was nicknamed hoja de platano (banana leaves). (*Private collection*)

Woodland pattern camouflage was introduced in the mid-1980s for general issue and worn well into the 2000s. (*Private collection*)

The US tricolor desert pattern has been worn by the Fuerzas Especiales de Policia (FEP) of the National Police.

A new digital camouflage pattern was introduced in 2007 for use by the Army, loosely based on the USMC temperate MARPAT design. (*Private collection*)

embroiled in a civil war that lasted for thirty-six years and resulted in as many as 200,000 civilian deaths, many of these attributed to government-coordinated assassinations and executions. In 1996, a peace accord was reached, involving United Nations military observers to monitor implementation of the peace process.

The Armed Forces of Guatemala have received substantial assistance from the United States since the 1940s. The Army, Navy, Air Force and Presidential Honor Guard comprise the Fuerzas Armadas de Guatemala. During the Civil War period, a number of secret police organizations existed, most of which have since been disbanded.

This blue digital pattern is now worn by the Policia Nacional Civil (PNC). (*Private collection*)

The Guatemalan Navy has also adopted its own camouflage design, seen here, although the blue appears much brighter than the version worn by the PNC. (*US Navy*)

GUYANA

The Cooperative Republic of Guyana (formerly British Guiana) achieved its independence from Britain in 1966, and is a member of the British Commonwealth. The country has never been to war and does not participate in international peacekeeping efforts. The Guyana Defense Force (GDF) includes land, air and naval elements (GDF Coast Guard).

A tiger stripe camouflage pattern, seen here in 2012, was introduced in the late 1980s or early 1990s and has been a standard uniform of the GDF since that time. (*US DOD*)

HAITI

Over the course of its history, Haiti has endured thirty-two coups d'etat that have claimed tens of thousands of lives, and greatly hampered the nation's economic growth. The period from 1957 to 1986 was dominated by the hereditary dictatorship of the Duvalier family. Although hugely popular with the black population, Dr François 'Papa Doc' Duvalier (1957–71) and members of his Milice de Volontaires de la Sécurité Nationale (MVSN) (Tonton Macoutes) established a legacy of arrest, torture and brutal executions of all their political opponents. His son, Jean-Claude 'Bébé Doc' Duvalier, continued the tradition but was forced into exile in 1986. The 1990s were then marked by another coup d'etat and the establishment of a military government, which in 1994 was removed both through political and military intervention led by the United States. A ten-year period of relative stability ensued, but a rebellion in 2004 again tumbled the nation into unrest. In order to restore stability, the United Nations Stabilization

This rare photo shows members of the elite Corps des Leopards wearing their distinctive 'duck hunter spot' pattern uniforms. (*Private collection*)

At least one specialist unit of the Haitian Police has been documented wearing US tricolor desert since 2004.

US m81 woodland camouflage was worn to a limited extent by the Haitian Army in the last couple of decades of its existence.

The specialist Groupement d'Intervention of the Haitian National Police also wore a grey-dominant woodland camouflage pattern during the early part of the 2000s.

A grey-dominant 'tiger stripe' pattern uniform has been worn by National Police trainees as well as SWAT teams. (*Private collection*)

The newly reformed Haitian Army have adopted a USMC temperate MARPAT-like camouflage pattern, although with a much greener color palette. (*Private collection*)

These members of the Corps d'Intervention et de Maintien de l'Ordre (CIMO) of the National Police wear a copy of the USMC desert MARPAT camouflage design. (*Private collection*)

The A-TACs series of camouflage patterns is worn by some units of the National Police. (*Private collection*)

Mission in Haiti (MINUSTAH) has remained in the country to this day.

The historical Forces Armées d'Haïti or FAd'H consisted of the Army, Navy, Air Force, Coast Guard, and a small Gendarmerie. After years of military interference in politics, including dozens of military coups, Haiti disbanded its military in 1995. The security of the nation was handled solely by the Haitian National Police (Police Nationale d'Haïti) and the Haitian Coast Guard until 2013, when the nation began to rebuild its military. The Armed Forces were officially remobilized in 2017.

HONDURAS

A coup d'etat ousted President Ramón Villeda Morales in 1963, putting the country under the control of a military junta for the next sixteen years. The interference of the United States in Honduran politics that began in the early part of the twentieth century continued, reaching a height in the 1980s, when the country was utilized as a staging ground for the US military presence in El Salvador as well as for the Contra movement battling the leftist Nicaraguan government. The US also assisted the Honduran military in conducting its own campaign against Marxist-Leninist militias such as the *Movimiento Popular de Liberación (Chichoneros)*. In 2009, a military coup d'etat removed President Manuel Zelaya

These officers, photographed during an exercise in 1983, wear a locally produced copy of the US M1942 spot pattern that came into existence in the late 1970s. (*US DOD*)

Paratroopers of the 2nd Infantry Battalion in 2007 wear the m81 woodland pattern that was adopted in the 1980s and worn by all members of the armed forces for the next twenty-five or more years. (*Private collection*)

Two woodland variations have been worn by the National Police Cobra squadron since the late 1990s until recently – one having a primarily blue colorway, and the other a grey colorway. (*Private collection*)

A new digital camouflage pattern was adopted by the Armed Forces in 2008, seen here worn by paratroopers of the 2nd Infantry Battalion. (*US Army*)

A blue dominant digital pattern was adopted by special units of the National Police in 2009, including the Cobra and Tigres units. (*Private collection*)

and replaced him with another civilian politician, a move that was internationally denounced.

The Honduran Armed Forces consist of the Army, Navy and Air Force. It has historically received substantial military aid from the United States and many of its uniform traditions are based on those of the US military. The National Police are responsible for local law enforcement, internal security, counter-terrorism and special investigations.

JAMAICA

Jamaica achieved independence from Britain in 1962 but remains a member of the Commonwealth. The Jamaica Defense Force (JDF) is the armed forces of this nation, descended from the old British Army's West India Regiment of the colonial period. The JDF follows a British model and consists of an Infantry Regiment (the Jamaica Regiment), Engineer Regiment, Support Services Battalion, Air Wing, Coast Guard, and Combat Support Battalion. The JDF receives training from the United States and Canadian governments. Law enforcement duties, including counter-narcotics operations, are tasked to the Jamaican Constabulary Force.

Copies of the US m81 woodland pattern were adopted in 1986 and were worn by the JDF until very recently. This photo illustrates several variations being worn at the same time. (*Private collection*)

A digital pattern was adopted by the JDF in 2015 for reasons of security, as woodland camouflage was deemed too easy to procure on the civilian market. (*US Air Force*)

A blue variation of the digital pattern was also adopted for the JDF Coast Guard in 2015. (*US DOD*)

MEXICO

Mexico was governed under a single party system until 2000, a situation that bred authoritarianism and oppressive policies, particularly against indigenous minorities and those with leftist political views. The country has also experienced increasingly high incidents of violence and murder stemming from the activities of drug cartels that wield an uncanny degree of power and influence in parts of the country. Although the Mexican government has embraced a zero-tolerance policy with regards to organized crime, corruption, human trafficking and drug-related violence continue to be among the nation's greatest concerns.

The Fuerzas Armadas de México or FAM (Mexican Armed Forces) is comprised of two branches, the Mexican Army (which includes the Air Force) and the Mexican Navy (including Naval Infantry and Naval Aviation).

Copies of the US M1942 spot were introduced for use by some units as early as the 1950s. This photo of infantry personnel in the 1970s illustrates the minimal use of insignia. (*Private collection*)

Specialist units of the armed forces, including the Army's Grupo Aeromóvil de Fuerzas Especiales (GAFE) and the Presidential Security Unit, and the Marines Special Forces, wore this grey dominant woodland variant pattern during the 1990s. Some special police units also wore this camouflage design. (*Private collection*)

Each is controlled by a separate secretariat within the government. Although Mexico has not been involved in a major international conflict since the nineteenth century, its armed forces have occasionally been utilized for internal security. Mexico sent its first international peacekeeping delegation to Haiti in 2016, and has also involved itself in disaster relief in Central America and

A copy of the US m81 woodland design was utilized by some units of the FAM from the 1980s onwards, although the primary combat uniform remained olive drab. (*Private collection*)

Selected units of the FAM such as Military Police, those serving in border areas and extremely arid regions in the 1990s wore a copy of the US tricolor desert pattern. (*Private collection*)

Indonesia. The Policía Federal (Federal Police) fall under the jurisdiction of the Secretariat of the Interior and are ostensibly responsible for all aspects of law enforcement, including internal security and counter-narcotics.

A digital camouflage design was adopted by the Army in 2008 and is now universally issued to all units, except those operating in arid environments. (*Private collection*)

The desert version of the Mexican Army's digital pattern is seen here. (*Private collection*)

The Mexican Naval Infantry adopted its own unique camouflage design in 2008, setting its troops apart from the Army and the rest of the Navy. (*Secretaría de la Defensa Nacional*)

Mexican Naval Infantry deploying to arid regions wear the desert version of their camouflage design, also issued in 2008. (*Secretaría de la Defensa Nacional*)

Also adopted by the Naval Infantry circa 2010, this urban variation is worn occasionally by personnel with special duties. (*Secretaría de la Defensa Nacional*)

A variation of the Army camouflage with a blue colorway was adopted by the Mexican Air Force in 2013. (*Private collection*)

Police Camouflage

The Police SWAT Unit of the Mexicali State and the Unete a los Defensores of the Jalisco State wear this grey-dominant digital pattern. (*Private collection*)

Multicam pattern uniforms are worn by Elite Police formations of the Sinaloa State Police. (*Private collection*)

The Universal Camouflage Pattern (UCP) originally worn by the US Army is in use with Unidad Especializada Antisecuestros (Special Anti-Kidnapping Unit) of the Sinaloa State Police. (*Private collection*)

A grey-dominant version of woodland pattern is in use with the Reacción Organizada Contra Asaltos or ROCA (Special Police Reaction) unit of the Yucatan State. (*Private collection*)

Newly formed in 2014, La Gendarmeria Nacional is issued with a digital camouflage pattern seen here. (*Private collection*)

As with most other countries in Central America, the United States provided considerable financial and military assistance to Nicaragua during the twentieth century, including support of the Somoza family hereditary dictatorship. Beginning in 1961, the Sandinista National Liberation Front (FSLN) gradually mounted an armed insurrection that took root in the 1970s and eventually wrested power away from the Somoza family. Both sides were guilty of human rights abuses during the revolution, including the use of torture, assassinations, kidnappings, and general intimidation of the civilian population. In July 1979 President Anastasio

The GN intermixed a number of combat uniforms, including m1948 ERDL pattern. (*Private collection*)

Some units of the GN also wore tiger striped pattern camouflage uniforms, both the horizontally-aligned as seen in this photo from 1978, and a unique vertically aligned variation. (*Private collection*)

The EPS obtained materiel from a number of sources, including 'leaf' type fatigues in green and brown-dominant patterns. (*Private collection*)

This unique and seldom-seen camouflage design has been attributed to the Brigadas Especiales contra Actos de Terrorismo (Special Counter-Terrorist Brigades) or BECAT, although its use is also documented during the Sandinista period. (*Author's Collection*)

This Bulgarian-produced camouflage design was provided to the ESN, presumably as war aid.

Somoza resigned and handed over control of Managua and the country to the FSLN.

Under President Ronald Reagan, the United States supported a strong anti-communist policy in Central America, and as a result it supplied covert military aid to the growing Contrarrevolución or 'Contra' movement consisting of former Somoza loyalists and indigenous Misurasata people who opposed the Sandinista government's nationalization of their land. War further ravaged the already devastated country for several years, ending with the Esquipulas II Accord of 1987. The country has slowly rebuilt itself since, instituting democratic reforms and improving relations with its neighbors and its people.

Many of the Contra units, particularly the ARDE, were documented wearing commercially available tiger stripe pattern camouflage uniforms.

Contra forces also made extensive use of both ERDL and woodland pattern uniforms, as they were made available. (*Private collection*)

The Miskito Indian MISURA units often wore this duck hunter camouflage pattern, which was probably obtained through sources in Honduras. (*Private collection*)

Both the Nicaraguan Army and Air Force have worn a copy of the US m81 woodland pattern since 1995. (*US DOD*)

Seen here with a US colleague, this Nicaraguan Navy officer wears the current issue blue woodland pattern that was adopted circa 1995. (*US Navy*)

Under the Somoza regime, the Nicaraguan military was known as the Guardia Nacional and received considerable war materiel from the United States. When the Sandinistas took over, a new Army was formed, the Ejército Popular Sandinista (EPS), which continued to exist under the early democratic government of President Chamorro. Constitutional reforms begun in 1995 again changed the structure and name of the armed forces to the Ejército de Nicaragua.

PANAMA

Panama was governed as a constitutional democracy until 1968, when a coup d'etat under Lieutenant Colonel Omar Torrijos put the country under military control. When Torrijos was killed in a mysterious plane crash, he was succeeded by General Manuel Noriega, who converted the National Guard into the Panamanian Defense Force (PDF) and declared himself commander in chief as well as president. Supported by the United States, the Panamanian government secretly fostered a criminal economy involved in international money laundering, drug smuggling, human trafficking, assassination of political dissidents and brutal suppression of civil rights activists. Noriega's regime also supplied war materiel to the Contra movement waging war against the Nicaraguan government at the time.

Responding to increased domestic crisis and an attack on the US Embassy in 1987, the US suspended economic and military aid to Panama. Noriega nullified the 1989

The Guardia National had its own version of m81 woodland, which remained in service with some units of the PDF after the reformation. A distinctive feature of this pattern is a small 'GNP' embedded into the design, over the black elements.

These soldiers of the 6th Mechanized Company are wearing a mixture of uniforms, including olive green and m81 woodland pattern. The latter was produced locally, but there were also US made BDUs intermixed within the PDF. (*Private collection*)

The PDF soldier seen behind General Noriega in this photograph wears the locally-produced copy of ERDL 'leaf' pattern camouflage that was still being worn at the time of the 1989 invasion. (*Private collection*)

election results, which contributed to an invasion of the country by US military forces in December 'to safeguard the lives of U.S. citizens in Panama, defend democracy and human rights, combat drug trafficking, and secure the neutrality of the Panama Canal'. Lasting five weeks, the campaign resulted in the complete defeat of the PDF and the removal of Noriega.

This special operations team of the Policia Nacional wear the US m81 woodland pattern that was retained by the police after the PDF was dismantled. (*US Army*)

The Servicio de Protección Institucional (SPI) wear this tiger stripe camouflage pattern with a very dark color palette. (*Private collection*)

This variation of the USMC temperate MARPAT camouflage pattern is in use with the Servicio Nacional Aeronaval and Servicio Nacional de Fronteras. (*Private collection*)

A slightly darker variation of the Universal Camouflage Pattern (UCP) has been in use with several units of the National Police, including the Unidad de Fuerzas Especiales (UFE), Grupo de Accion Policial (GAP), and the Grupo de Operaciones Especiales (GOE). (*Private collection*)

This unique bright orange camouflage design has been documented in use by some members of the Sistema Nacional de Proteccion Civil (National System of Civil Protection) or SINAPROC. (*Private collection*)

The National Police had been reformed into the Guardia Nacional de Panamá in the 1950s, which operated as a kind of gendarmerie. Noriega completely restructured this force into a much larger Fuerzas de Defensa de Panamá (Panamanian Defense Force), which included airborne, special operations, counter-terrorist, and elite infantry elements. Noriega further formed the so-called Dignity Battalions, loyal civilian paramilitary groups that were primarily utilized for political suppression. After Noriega was removed from office, the PDF was replaced with the Panamanian Public Forces (Fuerza Pública), which functions as an armed police and internal security force, but is not considered a military force in the conventional sense. The PPF includes the National Police, Aeronaval Service, the Border Service, and a presidential guard unit.

PARAGUAY

Paraguay has endured a succession of authoritarian governments, most notably that of Alfredo Stroessner who ruled from 1954 to 1989. His regime was finally toppled by an internal military coup which ushered in multi-party elections in 1993. The Armed Forces of Paraguay consist of the Army, Navy (including Marines) and Air Force. The country has largely followed the example of the United States with regards to military equipment, including the style of combat uniform. Law enforcement and internal security are overseen by the National Police.

A copy of the US m81 woodland pattern became standard issue for the Army and Marines in the late 1990s. (*Private collection*)

This photograph illustrates the use of 'duck hunter' pattern camouflage by members of the Brigada Aerotransportada during the 1980s, and possibly earlier. At least one version appears to be the same pattern worn in Brazil, with a darker model typically associated with Paraguay, and one more pattern of unknown origins. (*Private collection*)

In the late 1990s or early 2000s, some Army personnel were issued uniforms in the same tiger stripe pattern camouflage worn by the ROC Marine Corps.

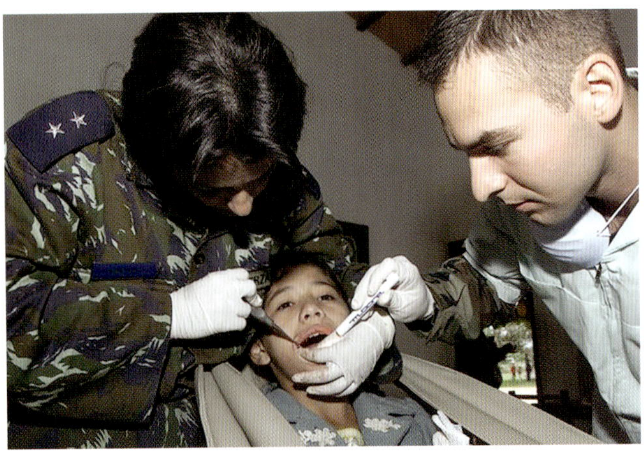

A version of the Brazilian Air Force 'lizard' pattern was issued to some personnel of the Paraguay AF in the 1980s. (*Private collection*)

Special units of the Policia Nacional, such as the Fuerzas de Operaciones Especiales (FOPE) have worn copies of both the six-color 'chocolate chip' and USMC desert MARPAT camouflage patterns. (*Private collection*)

A new digital camouflage pattern was adopted for the armed forces in 2014 and is now worn by all branches of service. (*Private collection*)

These members of Grupo Lince (Lynx Group) of the National Police wear a modified version of UCP with a darker color palette in 2017. (*Private collection*)

PERU

Shortly after the end of the Second World War, a military coup put General Manuel A. Odría in the president's seat. Although his regime was restrictive and corrupt, Odria himself was popular with the masses. A succession of military juntas followed throughout the 1960s and early 1970s, but in 1975 democracy was restored under Francisco Morales-Bermúdez.

In 1981, the country clashed with neighboring Ecuador over a border dispute, which ended after eight days of fighting. Conflict between the two nations erupted again in 1995, this time lasting over a month but without a clear resolution. The border was officially re-opened in 1998 when a treaty was signed clearly demarcating the boundary.

Some elements of the Armed Forces and Guardia Civil wore a camouflage pattern having splinter-like geometric shapes beginning in the late 1970s. (*Private collection*)

A later version, having completely different shapes, was adopted in 1980s for the Armed Forces, although still primarily worn by elite units. (*Private collection*)

The DINANDRO (Anti-Narcotics unit) of the National Police have worn a tiger stripe pattern camouflage since the 1980s. (*Private collection*)

This unique 'clouds and rain' camouflage pattern was worn by some paratroopers in 1970s.

These members of the 48 CGC 'Los Sinchis' unit of the Guardia Civil are wearing the South Korean-made 'waves' camouflage pattern in 1983. (*Private collection*)

Woodland camouflage was universally adopted by the armed forces and the national police in the late 1990s. Although some units wore more specialized camouflage designs, this was the standard operational pattern until 2007. (*Private collection*)

These commandos of the 48 CTC 'Los Sinchis' unit also have worn a copy of the US tricolor desert, as seen here during a parade.

A period of communist-inspired terrorism began in 1981, orchestrated by the 'Sendero Luminoso' or Shining Path. With an aim to establishing a communist dictatorship the group has engaged in bombing campaigns, sabotage, targeted assassinations and other human rights abuses. The Peruvian government has responded by utilizing kidnapping, torture, killings, and

The Peruvian Navy, including the Infanteria de Marina, introduced their own digital camouflage in 2008, a darker variation of the USMC temperate MARPAT design. (*Private collection*)

Two new digital camouflage patterns were adopted by the Army and Air Force in 2007 to replace woodland and desert patterns. The AMAPAT (Amazon Pattern) is now worn in heavily vegetated geographical regions, while the PACIPAT (Pacific Pattern) is for sandy beaches and desert regions. (*Private collection*)

Some elements of the Comandos Anfibios also wear the Universal Camouflage Pattern, although photos suggest it may only have been for public appearances. (*Private collection*)

even wholesale destruction of rural villages. Shining Path has continued its activities to the present day, despite the capture of several prominent leaders and the breakup of many of its training camps.

The Fuerzas Armadas del Perú consists of the Army, Navy and Air Force, all of which fall under the jurisdiction of the Joint Command. The Policía Nacional del Perú or National Police, formed in 1988, are tasked with law enforcement, internal security, counter-terrorism, and counter-narcotics operations, and fall under the Ministry of the Interior. The Police were preceded by the Guardia Civil, Guardia Republicana, and the Peruvian Investigative Police.

SAINT KITTS AND NEVIS

The Federation of Saint Kitts and Nevis is an island nation in the West Indies and a former British colony. Granted associated state status in 1967, it achieved full independence in 1983. The St Kitts and Nevis Defense Force is very small and consists of ground defense forces and a coast guard element.

The A-TACS® arid camouflage pattern is worn by both Infanteria de Marina (Naval Infantry) and Comandos Anfibios of the Navy. (*Private collection*)

There are also elements of the Peruvian Air Force wearing Multicam. (*Private collection*)

This Captain of the SKNDF wears the standard m81 woodland pattern camouflage uniform issued to all personnel. (*Private collection*)

SAINT LUCIA

A former British colonial possession in the Caribbean, Saint Lucia achieved full independence in 1979. It has no regular military force; internal and external security fall under the duties of the Royal Saint Lucia Police Force, which includes a Special Service Unit and Coast Guard.

Members of the SSU in this photo are clad in m81 woodland camouflage uniforms, worn by the unit until recently. (*Private collection*)

Since 2015, the SSU and some other units of the Police Force have worn this copy of the USMC temperate MARPAT design. (*Private collection*)

SAINT VINCENT AND THE GRENADINES

This small, island nation in the Caribbean was under British control until granted full independence in 1979. It has no standing armed force, internal and external security being tasks of the Royal Saint Vincent and the Grenadines Police Force. The United States provides training for this force.

These members of the Royal Saint Vincent and the Grenadines Police Force wear woodland camouflage utilities unique to the Special Services Unit (SSU). (*Private collection*)

SURINAME

A former constituent state of the Netherlands, the country remained under Dutch protection until 1975, after which it became a fully independent nation. Nearly a third of the population subsequently immigrated to the Netherlands, fearing economic collapse or worse. In 1980, a military coup led by several NCOs overthrew the government. Several counter coups were attempted between 1980 and 1982, but the perpetrators were all apprehended and executed. In 1986, responding to the massacre of a small village near the border with French Guiana, a group calling itself the Jungle Commando (Suriname National Liberation Army) – composed primarily of the ethnic Maroon population (those with African ancestry) – embarked on a guerilla war against the national army. Hoping to achieve equal rights for minorities, the war continued until 1992, interrupted by a ceasefire period in 1989. An agreement by the

Some elements of the Dutch Forces in Suriname wore old US issue camouflage coveralls in the 1940s.

A copy of US m18 woodland pattern camouflage was the standard combat uniform pattern from the 1980s onwards. (*US Army*)

government to embrace democratic reforms put an end to open hostilities. The current president, Dési Bouterse, elected in 2010, had previously been convicted of drug trafficking in a Dutch court and charged in the murder of fifteen political dissidents back in 1982. An amnesty was extended to Bouterse in 2012 for the murder charges.

Until 1975, the defense of Suriname was the responsibility of the Dutch Troepenmacht in Suriname (Forces in Suriname). The native elements of this force became the Suriname Armed Forces (Surinaamse Krijgsmacht) until the military junta in 1980 changed the name to Nationaal Leger (National Army). Although called an Army, it also includes an Air Force, Navy and Coast Guard elements. Law enforcement is overseen by the Korps Politie, Military Police, and by the Bureau of National Security.

A green-dominant digital camouflage pattern was adopted in 2015 for all branches of service. (*Private collection*)

TRINIDAD AND TOBAGO

This Caribbean state consists of two islands, Trinidad and Tobago, both former colonial possessions of Britain. Full independence was achieved in 1962. The Trinidad and Tobago Defense Force (TTDF) is comprised of the Trinidad and Tobago Regiment (Army), Air Guard, Coast Guard, Special Forces, and the Defense Force Reserves. Law enforcement and internal security is the province of the Police Service.

Seen here in 2017, DPM camouflage is worn by members of the TT Regiment, Coast Guard and tactical officers of the Police Service. (*US DOD*)

Although it remained somewhat isolationist up to the time of the Second World War, in the post-war years the United States became increasingly involved in military events around the world. Due to the buildup of the size of its armed forces, America has been considered a global 'superpower' into the present period. The list of US involvements in major (and minor) conflicts is far too lengthy and involved for this work, but a brief overview of major deployments will be included.

The first major deployment of post-war US personnel was to the Korean peninsula during the Korean War. More than 300,000 personnel were committed to the war, which resulted only in a stalemate or ceasefire agreement. Following this conflict, in 1958 more than 23,000 American personnel were deployed to the Dominican Republic in order to bolster the military junta that was in control at the time.

Beginning in the early 1960s, the US began sending advisory personnel to South Vietnam to assist the government there in resisting attack from the communist-supported North. The country ultimately became embroiled in the Vietnam War, which (for the USA) lasted from 1963 until 1975. At the end of the war, America had lost more than 58,000 troops. Although not officially sanctioned by the US government, US forces were also involved in a secret war in both Laos and Cambodia, combating North Vietnamese troops that were using these countries to move supplies into the South. The war in Vietnam was incredibly unpopular at home and for years to come the country would avoid large scale military involvement abroad.

A young Marine photographed in 1965 wears the 'USMC Standard' pattern camouflaged helmet cover and a rolled-up shelter-half in the same camouflage pattern attached to his pack. (*Private collection*)

Although it was primarily issued during the Second World War, surplus stocks of the M1942 'duck hunter/spot' pattern camouflage were issued to some personnel during the Korean War.

A series of relatively brief military operations marked the post-Vietnam years. In 1983, the installation of a communist-leaning government in Grenada prompted the United States to intervene militarily during

Originally developed by the US government in 1948, the ERDL (Engineer Research and Development Laboratory) or 'leaf' pattern, as it came to be known, was issued primarily to personnel in Vietnam engaged in reconnaissance and special operations. It would later gain favor with elite units such as the 82nd Airborne Division, Army Ranger Regiment, and the Army Special Forces, as well as units from the US Air Force, Navy and Marines, and was worn operationally as late as 1982.

Operation Urgent Fury, which lasted only three days. In addition to Grenadan forces, US personnel faced Cuban troops for the first time on foreign territory. During that same year, US Marines were deployed to Lebanon as part of a peacekeeping force, during which time their barracks were targeted by a car bomb that left 241 marines dead. In 1989 a longstanding feud with the leader of Panama resulted in the US invasion of that country (Operation Just Cause). After a month of fighting between Panamanian and US forces, Manuel Noriega was deposed.

America's first large-scale military deployment following the Vietnam War was during the Persian Gulf War (Operation Desert Storm) in 1990–91. As part of a coalition of allied nations, US military units pushed Iraqi forces out of Kuwait and inflicted considerable damage on the Iraqi military infrastructure, leaving the state crippled. Although the conflict lasted only six months, the US armed forces have retained a presence in the Persian Gulf among friendly nations such as Kuwait, Saudi Arabia, Bahrain and Turkey.

American forces also became involved in affairs in Somalia (Operation Restore Hope – 1992–93) and

Originally conceived in anticipation of future US involvement in the Middle East, the six-color or 'day desert' camouflage pattern, nicknamed 'chocolate chip,' began to enter service with the US armed forces in 1981 and would continue to be produced until 1991. This photograph of Generals Colin Powell and Norman Schwarzkopf in 1991 illustrates its appearance at that time, although the camouflage pattern was deemed too 'busy' for effective combat concealment and would rapidly be replaced by the three-color pattern. (*US DOD*)

UNOSOM II (1993–95), Haiti (Operation Uphold Democracy – 1994–95), and in the former Yugoslavia as part of the Implementation Force (IFOR – 1995–96), and multinational forces in Kosovo (KFOR – 1999–present).

The ERDL camouflage design was put through additional tests and evaluation towards the end of the 1970s and eventually found its way onto the transitional 'Hot Weather Uniform', which preceded the BDU. Although early versions of the uniform were made using surplus fabrics produced during the Vietnam War, a standardized coloration using a different color palette was eventually produced, which many collectors have termed 'transitional ERDL'. Although not universally distributed to any branch of service, this pattern saw extensive use with the USMC and other units attached to the Rapid Deployment Force, as well as special operations personnel such as US Army Rangers and Special Forces, and some US Air Force units.

The 'night desert' camouflage pattern was adopted in 1983 for use by personnel deployed to desert environments and issued as a hooded parka and over-trousers only. The pattern was reputedly created to thwart Soviet night-vision equipment in use at the time, but experience showed that night vision was considerably more sophisticated than initially believed and so the pattern fell into disuse shortly after Desert Storm in 1991.

The 'woodland' camouflage pattern was adapted from the ERDL design by enlarging the shapes approximately 60 per cent and using a modified color palette deemed more effective in generalized temperate conditions. Introduced for use by the US Army in 1981, this would eventually be the standard combat deployment pattern for all branches of service until the early part of the 2000s. These airmen are wearing the standard woodland BDU on exercise in Arizona in 2004. (*US Air Force*)

The limited effectiveness of the six-color desert pattern led to the development of the three-color pattern that eventually became the Desert Combat Uniform (DCU), which saw service with all branches of the US armed forces from 1991 until approximately 2005. These Navy personnel in Helmand Province, Afghanistan in 2012 are still wearing the design. (*US Navy*)

Developed in response to the highly effective Canadian CADPAT design, temperate MARPAT (Marines Pattern) was officially introduced in 2002 to replace the previously issued woodland BDU. Although there has been considerable debate as to the origins of MARPAT, evidence indicates it is really just a recoloration of the CADPAT design, with the addition of a USMC logo embedded into the design. (*US Marine Corps*)

A desert MARPAT version was also released at approximately the same time, for issue to personnel serving in arid geographical regions. (*US Marine Corps*)

Circa 2005, the USMC released a 'snow' pattern variation for use in arctic, sub-arctic and mountainous environments. (*US Marine Corps*)

Following a lengthy series of trials in which thirteen different camouflage patterns were tested by the US Army in an effort to find the most effective new design to replace the aging woodland and desert patterns, the pattern chosen was the so-called 'Universal Camouflage Pattern' or UCP. Although not included in any of the original evaluations that took place at various Army installations between 2003 and 2004, government officials insisted it satisfied the requirements set forth to provide an effective design for multiple environments and production began in 2005. Issued to US Army personnel for the next decade and a half (as well as to Air Force and Navy personnel attached to Army units), the camouflage design would prove to be universally disliked and almost totally ineffective in most environments. (*US Army*)

As a response to the 11 September 2001 terrorist attacks on American soil, the United States began its Global War on Terror (GWOT), a concerted effort to neutralize terrorist organizations and increase pressure on nations considered by the US to support terrorism. The most lengthy and expensive military operation involving US forces was Operation Enduring Freedom (2001–14) in which the Taliban government of Afghanistan was topped and attempts were made to democratize the region, as well as train and build up the Afghan armed forces and police. Under the pretense that Iraq was harboring weapons of mass destruction that could be used for terrorist purposes, the US launched a full scale invasion (the Iraq War, often called Operation Iraqi Freedom) in 2003 and retained a presence there with its handful of allies until late 2011. Although in theory Iraq is a democracy, the country remains unstable. US forces have also intervened in conflicts in Syria since 2014, and in Libya in 2011.

After the US Army adopted its UCP, the US Air Force decided to embrace a design unique to that service. The choice of pattern is a semi-pixelated design based on a 'tiger stripe' pattern created by the US firm Tiger Stripe Products© and utilizing essentially the same color palette as the Army's UCP. Although not adopted as an operational camouflage pattern, the USAF nevertheless has now elected to discontinue it in favor of the Operational Camouflage Pattern (OCP), which is a variation of Multicam. (*US Air Force*)

In 2008, the US Navy introduced the first version of its Navy Working Uniform (NWU-I), a blue-dominant digital pattern that is essentially a recoloration of the Army's UCP. The blue-grey color scheme is designed to hide stains and other soiling that are commonplace in a naval environment. Growing public concerns over the increasing production costs of so many different camouflage uniforms led the Navy to begin plans to discard the pattern, effective in 2019. (*US Navy*)

Two additional camouflage designs were developed for USN personnel serving in either temperate or arid operational environments, the NWU-II and NWU-III. These designs will be retained for the present. (*US Navy*)

A version of Multicam, commercially available and at one time tested by the US Army, was officially adopted for personnel deploying to Afghanistan in 2010. Known officially as Operation Enduring Freedom Camouflage Pattern (OEF-CP), the pattern had already gained favor with some US special operations personnel and would continue to be worn until US forces departed Afghanistan. (*US Army*)

In 2015, the US Army officially announced that it would adopt a modernized version of the Scorpion camouflage pattern (codeveloped with Crye Precision), previously tested during the 2003–04 Future Warrior trials. Officially named Operational Camouflage Pattern or OCP, this design replaced the Army's UCP in 2019 and has also been adopted by the US Air Force. (*US Army*)

In response to several attempts by an armed guerilla organization known as Tupamaros (Movimiento de Liberación Nacional-Tupamaros) to destabilize the country in the 1960s, a state of emergency was declared in 1968, followed by suspension of civil liberties in 1972, and establishment of a civic-military regime in 1973. Twelve years of civilian-military rule followed, during which a number of Uruguayans disappeared. Civilian rule was re-established in 1984.

Adopted in 1973 and used by FUSNA (Marines) as well as for general issue to ground forces. (*Private collection*)

A unique spot camouflage pattern was adopted for use by the Fusileros Navales (FUSNA) in the 1970s and continued in use until very recently. (*Private collection*)

A copy of the USMC 'standard' camouflage pattern entered service in the 1970s and was worn by the Air Force Batallòn de Seguridad Terrestre. (*Security Battalion*)

The Special Unit of the Coast Guard (UNAPO) was briefly issued this unique variation of the Marines pattern in the 1970s. (*Jorge Panuncio collection*)

The Army and Coast Guard (and some elements of the Police) adopted a copy of the US m81 woodland pattern in the 1980s. This was standard issue into the early 2000s and was obtained from a variety of sources, which explains the differences in color and shade. (*US Army*)

The Policía Aeronáutica and Batallòn de Seguridad Terrestre (Security Battalion) of the Uruguayan Air Force have worn two types of 'urban' camouflage, one with a blue colorway and the other with a more grey palette. (*Private collection*)

These Guardia de Grenaderos, part of the Grupos Operaciones Especiales (GEO) of the National Police, wear a blue 'leaf' type camouflage pattern. (*Private collection*)

Another 'brushstroke' type design for the Guardia de Granaderos can be seen here, with a blue-grey color palette. It is unknown whether these were created by dyeing the fabrics, or if the uniforms were specifically contracted for the unit. (*Private collection*)

Seen here in an old photo, these members of the Guardia de Grenaderos are wearing what appears to be a type of 'brushstroke' camouflage pattern, possibly copied from the Belgian version. (*Private collection*)

The Armada Nacional adopted this blue digital pattern in 2015, worn by most personnel except those serving in a ground combat or support role. (*Private collection*)

These officers of the Infanteria de Marina (Naval Infantry) wear the recently adopted digital pattern created for this service, incorporating the same color palette as was used historically on their old spot pattern. (*Private collection*)

A unique digital pattern was adopted by the Guardia Republicana of the National Police in 2015.

The Fuerzas armadas del Uruguay consist of the Army, Air Force and the Navy, which includes Marines and Coast Guard (Prefectura). Uruguay has been a participant in the Multinational Force and Observers (MFO) mission in the Sinai, and is a very active participant in United Nations peacekeeping missions around the world. The National Police are responsible for domestic law enforcement and internal security, and fall under the command of the Ministry of the Interior.

Circa 2016, the Exercito Nacional began to issue its own digital camouflage pattern, seen here. (*Private collection*)

Also in use with the Guardia Republicana since 2015, in particular with the Metropolitan Guard (Guardia Metropolitana), is a copy of the Universal Camouflage Pattern (UCP).

VENEZUELA

Following a brief, three-year period of post-war democracy, a military junta seized control of the government of Venezuela in 1948, ushering in a period of state capitalism and increased national debt under Pérez Jiménez. Inspired by the success of Cuba's communist revolution, a number of guerilla movements emerged in the 1960s hoping to foment a similar reaction in Venezuela. By 1968, however, most of these groups had been convinced to lay down their arms. A series of economic crises in the late 1980s led to the Caracazo riots – in which hundreds were killed – and two attempted coups d'etat (both failures) in 1992. Pardoned in 1994 for his role in the attempted coups, Hugo Chavez later went on to lead the leftist Bolivarian Revolution, which installed him as president from 1999 until his death in 2013.

The Fuerza Armada Nacional Bolivariana is the armed forces of Venezuela, consisting of the Army, Navy, Air Force, National Guard and the National Militia. Largely influenced and supplied by the United States from the 1950s to the 1970s, in the modern era the armed forces have depended more heavily on materiel from China and Russia.

An interesting tiger pattern camouflage was worn by the Guardia Nacional Bolivariana (GNB) from 1980s to 1994.

This group of Venezuelan Army officers (including future president Hugo Chavez) are wearing the 'leaf' type camouflage pattern that originated in the 1980s and saw use with most branches of service until 1994. (*Private collection*)

This digital pattern replaced the earlier woodland variants in 2017 for special units of the National Police. (*Private collection*)

In 1994 the government replaced earlier camouflage designs for a general copy of the m81 woodland pattern for all services. The pattern would be discontinued in 2005 and replaced by a solid green uniform, only to be revived once again towards the end of 2017. (*Private collection*)

The Milicia Nacional Bolivariana was formed in 2009 as a kind of national guard or civil defense organization. In 2017, the branch of service began appearing in this bright green tiger stripe camouflage pattern, which appears to be restricted to the MNB only. (*Private collection*)

These two variants of the woodland design were both issued to national police special units from 1994 onwards.

Chapter 3

ASIA

AFGHANISTAN

The region that comprises the Republic of Afghanistan has endured a long history of warfare, and unsuccessful attempts to colonize and control it. Following the Second World War, both the USSR and the United States made attempts to gain favor with the monarchy that had arisen here, with the Soviets funneling considerable infrastructure aid. In 1973, the monarchy was toppled in a bloodless coup d'etat that established a fragile secular government. However, in 1978 the People's Democratic Party of Afghanistan (PDPA) launched their own coup d'etat (the Saur Revolution) and set the course for the next ten years of Afghan history. The socialist ideals and radical modernization of traditional Islamic and tribal laws by the PDPA were unpopular with many segments of Afghan society; support and influence from the Soviet Union even more so. By spring of 1979 large portions of the country were in open rebellion against the government and significant numbers of Afghan soldiers deserted to fight with Afghan Mujahideen. At the request of the PDPA government, Soviet military units began entering Afghanistan in October 1979, leading to a ten-year occupation (the Soviet-Afghan War, 1979–89). Aided by several nations, particularly the United States, various Mujahideen factions waged a relentless guerilla war against the Soviets and the Democratic Republic of Afghanistan (DRA) armed forces. Suffering heavy losses, a demoralized Soviet Army ultimately withdrew from Afghanistan, leaving the government and infrastructure in shambles.

A period of civil war ensued from 1989 to 1992, pitting DRA forces against the Mujahideen. The Afghan government began to collapse in April 1992, and the nation became the Islamic State of Afghanistan for the next several years, but there was little stability as

A three-color camouflage design was worn by commando brigades in the late 1970s, 1980s, and into the early communist period. (*Private collection*)

This 'duck hunter' camouflage pattern was also worn by commando units in the 1980s and 90s. It was provided by the Soviet Union. (*Private collection*)

Provided to the country by Bulgaria, raw printed fabric in the 'splinter' camouflage pattern of that nation was made into locally-styled uniforms for the commando units from 1985 to mid-1990s.

This 'leaf' pattern, most likely obtained in Pakistan, was worn by elite units during the Taliban era.

Woodland camouflage designs of various types (most from Pakistan or Iran) can also be traced to the Taliban era, but were widely utilized by the Northern Alliance and during the early ANA period as well.

These Northern Alliance fighters are wearing a Chinese-made 'vertical lizard' camouflage design provided by coalition forces, and later worn in Mozambique. (*Private collection*)

the remaining Mujahideen factions (supported by Iran, Pakistan and Uzbekistan) continued to wage war in an effort to wrest complete control of the country.

The Taliban (طالبان) seized control of Kabul in September of 1996 (aided by Pakistan, Saudi Arabia and the assistance of independent Arab sources), creating the Taliban Emirate. In reaction, two former rival leaders combined their forces into the United Front (Northern

Another camouflage design from the same Chinese source is this duck hunter pattern, also worn by the Northern Alliance.

The newly formed Afghan National Army (ANA) was largely outfitted by coalition forces and included substantial amounts of surplus uniforms and equipment, as well as new issue uniforms supplied by Chinese factories. Once again m81 woodland pattern camouflage entered the supply system of Afghan forces and would continue to be the standard uniform of the Commando forces into the present era. (*US Marine Corps*)

Alliance), which waged its own guerilla war against the Taliban. Following the terrorist attacks in the United States on 11 September 2001, the United States enticed a coalition of nations to invade the country, ostensibly to hunt down Osama Bin Laden and destroy the Al-Qaeda training facilities believed to exist in Afghanistan. Working with the Northern Alliance, coalition forces toppled the Taliban regime, but have been embroiled in their own war since. Afghanistan is today officially known as the Islamic Republic of Afghanistan , and is in the process of being rebuilt along progressive, Western standards.

These Afghan special operations troops wear tricolor desert camouflage uniforms provided by the USA. Similar uniforms were worn by Ministry of Interior forces, as well as the ANP. (*Private collection*)

Seen here in a photo from 2010, these members of the National Interdiction Unit of the Afghan Police wear a copy of the USMC temperate MARPAT design. The pattern was initially worn by a unit called the National Security Force (NSF). (*Private collection*)

Members of the Afghan Border Police wear a grey version of the six-color 'chocolate chip' desert pattern, also seen in some Arab countries. (*Private collection*)

The 'desert tiger stripe' pattern has been worn by a number of small, specialist Afghan units since the early 2000s, but is most notably associated with National Directorate of Security (NDS). (*Private collection*)

A special anti-terrorist unit of the Afghan National Police as well as the NDS wear a dark version of tiger stripe camouflage as well. (*Private collection*)

The Afghan armed forces have experienced a number of changes since the monarchy period. While under control of the DPDA there was a strong Soviet influence in appearance and equipment, including the use of camouflage uniforms by elite units. During the Taliban era, uniforms were obtained via sources in Iran and Pakistan, with a wide number of camouflage patterns

Although it entered service relatively late in the war, Multicam pattern has been worn by special units of Afghan Police and the ANA. (*Private collection*)

Developed specifically for the ANA by Hyperstealth Industries© and officially called Spec4ce Afghan Forest pattern, this design has become the standard combat uniform of most conventional units of the Army. (*Private collection*)

Also designed by Hyperstealth Industries©, this arid camouflage design was developed specifically for the Afghanistan National Civil Police (ANCOP). (*Private collection*)

This brown digital camouflage design is issued to Public Protection Forces (PPF). (*Private collection*)

The Afghan NDS or Amaniyat also wear a brown leaf pattern camouflage uniform as seen here. (*Private collection*)

The Ghostex Kilo-1 camouflage design, also developed and marketed by Hyperstealth Industries©, is worn by members of the Afghan Partner Unit (APU). (*Private collection*)

being interspersed throughout the military. With the reformation of the armed forces into the Afghan National Army (ANA) came greater standardization and an entirely new array of combat uniforms, including some camouflage designs specifically created for Afghan units.

In addition to the Afghan National Army there is a small Afghan National Air Force. Law enforcement units include the Afghan National Police, Afghan Border Police, and various specialized units under the Ministry of the Interior.

ARMENIA

Armenia emerged from the Second World War as part of the Soviet Union (which it had been part of since 1936). During the 1970s, tensions built between Armenia and its neighboring Soviet republic, Azerbaijan, over the Nagorno-Karabakh region, which at the time was populated with nearly half a million Armenians. This led to the Sumgait pogrom of 1988. As the USSR began to split apart in 1990, the New Armenian Army (NAA) was created as a separate defense force; clashes with Soviet Ministry of Interior (MVD) forces ensued. The Baku pogrom in January 1990 resulted in nearly 200,000 Armenians from Azerbaijan fleeing the capital in a mass exodus to Armenia. By December 1991, the Soviet Union had completely collapsed and Armenia was officially recognized as an independent nation.

Tensions with Azerbaijan continued, however, over the Nagorno-Karabakh region. The two nations had essentially been in a state of undeclared war since 1984. In 1992, the conflict escalated into a full-scale war, with significant portions of the Karabakh region being captured by Armenian forces, establishing the Republic of Artsakh (Nagorno-Karabakh Republic), an unrecognized but de facto independent state. A ceasefire was announced in 1994, which has been largely observed, but tensions between the two nations continue.

The Armenian Armed Forces consist of the Land Forces, Air Force, Navy and Border Guards Service. As many as 20,000 personnel make up the armed forces of Nagorno-Karabakh, which relies exclusively on Armenian support.

The use of Soviet KLMK sunray or solnechnye zaychiki pattern camouflage by Armenian units dates back to the Soviet period. Large numbers of surplus stock were utilized by the Armenian National armed forces, as well as by paramilitary fighters such as these. (*Private collection*)

In service with Armenian forces since the Soviet era, a variant of the butane pattern with a strong darker brown element was worn by Armenian forces since around 1990.

This three color spot camouflage design was worn by some Armenian units in the mid-1990s; various types have been documented.

Another example of the Soviet-era TTsKO butane pattern being worn is seen here in this photo of Armenian Border Guards. (*Private collection*)

This solitary Armenian soldier wears two types of dubok pattern camouflage, carried over from the Soviet period and in use during the 1990s. (*Private collection*)

Surplus Greek 'lizard' pattern camouflage uniforms have been documented in use by Armenian troops, particularly with those serving in Kosovo and NATO. (*Private collection*)

Surplus US tricolor desert camouflage uniforms, provided by the USA, were worn by Armenian personnel serving in Iraq beginning in 2005. (*Private collection*)

The nation adopted its own version of m81 woodland pattern in the late 1990s, a design that would serve the country for nearly twenty years. Although variations have been noted, the unique coloration is distinctively Armenian. (*Private collection*)

These Armenian police photographed in 2007, wear a blue-dominant camouflage design also found in Belarus and Russia. (*Private collection*)

A number of other blue-dominant camouflage patterns are worn by various Armenian Ministry of the Interior units. The majority of these designs are unquestionably Russian in origin. (*Private collection*)

Armenian personnel serving in Afghanistan were documented wearing surplus German Army desert flecktarn pattern uniforms. (*Private collection*)

Developed exclusively for the Armenian Army, a digital camouflage design was adopted around 2016 and is largely replacing the earlier woodland design. (*Armenian Ministry of Defense*)

There has been an increased use of Multicam by some Armenian special operations troops of the MOD and MOI. (*Private collection*)

The same pattern worn by Russia's Border Guard has also appeared in use with some Armenian elite units. (*Private collection*)

This blue-dominant digital camouflage design was newly adopted by the Armenian police circa 2016–17. (*Private collection*)

This camouflage design of Chinese origins is worn by a special unit of MOI, and is also seen in some Arab countries. (*Private collection*)

Formerly the Azerbaijan Soviet Socialist Republic, the country proclaimed its independence from the USSR in August 1991. In a state of undeclared war with its neighbor, Armenia, over the Nagorno-Karabakh region since 1984, the nation lost control of that territory in 1994, but tensions have remained. In 1993, the democratic government was overthrown in a coup d'etat and former Soviet leader Heydar Aliyev was appointed president. Upon his death in 2003, Aliyev's son Ilham assumed the presidency and has retained that position into the present era.

The Azerbaijan Armed Forces consist of the Land Forces, Air Force and Navy, as well as a National Guard, Internal Troops (of the Ministry of the Interior), and the State Border Service. The country has strong ties to Turkey and receives military aid and training from that nation.

The Soviet KLMK sunray or solnechnye zaychiki pattern was in service with Azeri units during the Soviet era and its use continued well into the country's early independence. This Azeri border guard wears the modern berezhka pattern in 2014. (*Private collection*)

As in most other former Soviet countries, the use of TTsKO or butane camouflage patterns continued in Azerbaijan long after the fall of the USSR. The versions most commonly found here are dark brown dominant and green/brown variants. (*Private collection*)

The country's close relationship with Turkey has led to large quantities of military equipment being obtained. Here two Azeri Army officers wear a Turkish 'leaf' pattern camouflage circa 2001. (*Azerbaijan Ministry of Defense*)

This green tinted woodland pattern has been worn by the State Border Guards Service since the early part of the 2000s. (*Azerbaijan Ministry of Defense*)

These Azeri personnel are wearing an m81 woodland camouflage pattern almost certainly obtained from Turkish sources and seen throughout the 2000–12 period. (*Azerbaijan Ministry of Defense*)

The Azeri personnel that deployed to Iraq between 2002 and 2007 wore surplus US tricolor desert camouflage uniforms, as seen here. (*US Marines Corps*)

The Kobra Special Group of the Ministry of the Interior has appeared in public wearing the Universal Camouflage Pattern (UCP). (*Private collection*)

Both the Kobra Special Group of the Interior Troops, and the Rapid Response Unit of the State Border Service (seen here) have worn a modern copy of Multicam since approximately 2012. (*Private collection*)

The standard camouflage design of the armed forces since 2013 is the same design worn by Turkey. (*US Army*)

This member of the State Border Service Rapid Response Unit wears a copy of the A-TACS© AU design, probably procured from Russia. (*Private collection*)

This digital camouflage design has been worn by the special operations units of the Interior Ministry since 2014. (*Private collection*)

BAHRAIN

Formerly a protectorate of Britain, Bahrain declared its independence in 1971 and was considered an emirate until 2002. The government has withstood several attempts to topple it by violent means, including an attempted coup d'etat led by Shia fundamentalists in

Two spot type camouflage patterns were produced for the BDF during the 1970s, although little is known about their use.

Also in use with the BDF, and presumably supplied by Britain, DPM pattern uniforms saw use during the 1970s.

1981, and popular uprisings in 1994 and 2000. The nation is considered a constitutional monarchy today.

In 2001, Bahrain was marginally involved in the War in Afghanistan, but opposed the invasion of Iraq in 2003. A succession of protests by the Shia majority in 2011 led to military intervention from Saudi Arabia and a heavy crackdown on the protesters which continued into 2014.

Introduced in the late 1980s or early 1990s, these patterns were standard issue for conventional forces of the BDF for a number of years. (*Private collection*)

A variation of the old four-color DPM pattern was introduced in the late 1990s and worn by the four major combative services. Although at a distance the pattern appears to have only two colors, it is, in fact, composed of three. (*Bahrain Defense Force*)

The Bahrain Defense Force consists of the Army, Navy, Air Force, Royal Guard and the Royal Medical Services. The Special Security Force Command and Coast Guard are elements of the Ministry of Interior with paramilitary duties. The country has maintained strong ties to Britain, particularly in terms of military training and equipment. The majority of the nation's military camouflage uniforms have been supplied via British-owned companies.

Members of the Royal Special Forces in the late 1990s adopted this distinctive desert tiger stripe pattern. (*Bahrain Defense Force*)

The old DPM pattern was discarded in 2013, in favor of a new digital camouflage design, seen here. (*Bahrain Defense Force*)

A blue DPM variant pattern is in use with Bahrain Special Security Force Command. (*SSFC*)

This officer wears the latest, digital camouflage design worn by the Bahrain Navy, adopted in 2014. (*Bahrain Defense Force*)

Also adopted in 2013, the Royal Special Forces now wear a pixilated version of their classic 'tiger stripe' pattern. (*Bahrain Defense Force*)

In the aftermath of the Second World War, the former British province of Bengal was divided into East and West sections, with the East joining the newly established Dominion of Pakistan, and the West joining

The Bangladesh Rifles wore this duck hunter camouflage design until 2010, when the unit was restructured and became the Border Guard. (*US Marine Corps*)

Bangladesh adopted its own unique version of DPM in the 1980s, which became the standard camouflage pattern for the next twenty years.

Seen here with their Indian counterparts of the Border Security Force, these Bangladesh Border Guards wear the current brown dominant camouflage design of his service. (*Private collection*)

A woodland camouflage design was adopted in the 1990s, and this became the default deployment pattern for most Bangladesh Armed Forces personnel. Early incarnations had brighter greens. (*Private collection*)

The Bangladesh Ansar is frequently deployed abroad on peacekeeping missions, and has worn these two camouflage designs both at home and while on assignment. (*Private collection*)

The Navy's Special Warfare Diving and Salvage (SWADS) unit wear this leaf camouflage pattern, seen here in a photo from 2012. (*US Navy*)

the Dominion of India. A pattern of ethnic, linguistic and cultural discrimination ensued in Pakistan during the 1960s, culminating in calls for independence by East Pakistan. This led to the Bangladesh War of Liberation, an eight-month campaign pitting the armed forces of Pakistan against those of India and the provisional government of Bangladesh. The war was over by December 1971, with a peace accord signed and the establishment of Bangladesh as an independent state in 1972.

Not long after achieving independence, a one-party socialist government was installed in 1975, leading to three years under a military junta. Multiparty elections were held again in 1979 but civilian leadership only lasted until 1982, when another coup d'etat established army Adjutant General Hussain Muhammad Ershad as president, a position he retained by general election

There have been two types of camouflage worn by the Bangladesh Fire and Civil Defense Directorate. The earlier pattern has vertical orange stripes on a grey background, while the more recent pattern is busier and incorporates black and orange 'leaf' shapes into the design. (*Private collection*)

until 1991. Since this time the nation has been governed as a parliamentary republic.

The Bangladesh Armed Forces consist of the Army, Navy and Air Force, with the Coast Guard and Border Guard serving in a paramilitary capacity under the Ministry of the Interior. The Bangladesh Ansar is a paramilitary auxiliary force responsible for internal security and law enforcement. The country has never fought in a conflict outside its borders but has been one of the world's greatest contributors to United Nations peacekeeping operations since 1974.

BHUTAN

The Kingdom of Bhutan maintained neutrality through both world wars and has avoided external conflicts of any kind in the modern era. The country's strongest political, economic and military ties are with neighboring India, which maintains an ongoing Indian Military Training Team (IMTRAT) to assist in the instruction of the Royal Bhutan Army and Royal Body Guards. Equipment and arms likewise are of mixed Indian and Chinese origins. The Royal Bhutan Police are responsible for internal security and law enforcement.

A copy of US m81 woodland camouflage was in service with Army personnel for some time. (*Private collection*)

This 'leaf' type camouflage is in service with Royal Bhutan Police. (*Private collection*)

This photograph from 2015 shows the recently adopted digital camouflage pattern, chosen to replace previously issued clothing. (*Private collection*)

BRUNEI

Brunei remained a protectorate of Britain until 1984, having withstood a small armed insurrection against the monarchy in 1962, and attempts to lure it into the Malaysian Federation. The Royal Brunei Armed Forces consist of the Land Forces, Navy and Air Force. The Royal Brunei Police are responsible for law enforcement.

The Land Forces wore British DPM for years, obtained from a variety of sources. This photo from 2010 illustrates one variation worn at that time. (*Private collection*)

A digital camouflage pattern has replaced the previously issued design since around 2012, and is very similar to that worn by Singapore. (*US Army*)

CAMBODIA

Cambodia was formerly a part of French Indochina, but achieved full independence in 1953. The country was a monarchy until 1970, when a US-backed coup d'etat under Lon Nol wrested power from the royalists. During the Vietnam War, hostilities extended far into Cambodia, which was utilized as a refuge by the Vietnamese National Liberation Front (aka Việt Cộng). In 1975, the communist Khmer Rouge took control

The US-supported Khmer Serei ('Free Khmer') forces during Vietnam war have been documented wearing South Vietnamese-made National Police Field Force 'clouds' pattern uniforms.

A photo from approximately 1975 showing the mixture of camouflage worn by the Forces Armees Royales Khmere (FARK) airborne forces, including French leópard or 'lizard' pattern and a unique spot design found only in Cambodia. (*Private collection*)

The FANK Para-Commando Battalion trained at the Airborne Commando School at Batu Djadjar in Indonesia in 1975 and were issued Indonesian made 'blood vines' pattern uniforms.

Thai-made tiger stripe pattern uniforms were worn by the Khmer People's National Liberation Armed Forces (KPNLAF) in the 1980s.

of the country and changed its name to Democratic Kampuchea, embarking on a reign of terror against the educated and pro-Western members of Cambodian society in which over one million people died. Fueled by a fear of Vietnamese expansionism, in 1977 tensions with neighboring Vietnam began to rise. Small scale Khmer Rouge Army attacks into Vietnamese territory throughout 1978 led to a retaliatory invasion and the taking of Phnom Penh. In January 1979, the pro-Vietnamese People's Republic of Kampuchea was established, leading to ten years of occupation and insurgency. Among the belligerents fighting the PRK and Vietnamese forces were the National Army of Democratic Kampuchea (Khmer Rouge), the anti-communist Khmer People's National Liberation Armed Forces, the Armee Nationale Sihanoukiste (pro-royalist), and occasionally the armed forces of neighboring Thailand. Following Vietnamese withdrawal in 1989

Various 'tiger stripe' pattern camouflage uniforms were worn by Forces Armées Nationales Khmeres (FANK).between 1973 and 1975. Some of these were produced in South Vietnam, while others appear to have been locally made.

and the Paris Peace Accords of 1991, the country was governed briefly by United Nations mission (UNTAC) until the monarchy was restored in 1993.

Under French administration the Forces Armees Royales Khmere (FARK) were outfitted as were French troops of the period, with airborne and commando units receiving the lizard pattern tenue de saut camouflée. These remained in service with Cambodian units until around 1970, when the armed forces were renamed Forces Armées Nationales Khmeres (FANK). Several other camouflage patterns were in use among Cambodian forces during the Vietnam War, including some produced in South Vietnam and others unique to Cambodian units. The National Army of Democratic Kampuchea (NADK) did not issue camouflage uniforms to any of its personnel; however, the pro-democracy Khmer People's National Liberation Front (KPNLF) which waged an insurgency campaign against both the Khmer Rouge and Vietnamese communist governments, were supplied with Thai-made camouflage uniforms and military equipment.

The Royal Cambodian Armed Forces (RCAF) was created in 1993 by the merger of the Cambodian People's Armed Forces and two anti-communist resistance

This green woodland variant camouflage pattern was also produced in Thailand, specifically for the KPNLAF in the mid 1980s.

Thai-made ERDL pattern camouflage fatigues were also worn by the KPNLAF in the 1980s.

The RCAF's 911 Special Forces Regiment has had a long-standing relationship with the Indonesian Special Forces, and, as a result, is often outfitted by that country. Here, members of the unit wear both locally produced woodland and Indonesian-made DPM pattern camouflage uniforms. (*Private collection*)

These Cambodian troops serving as peacekeepers wear a variation of DPM, made locally, that has been in service since the mid-1990s. (*Private collection*)

A copy of the US m81 woodland camouflage pattern has been in use by conventional units of the RCAF since the 1990s and is still the standard combat uniform pattern. (*US Army National Guard*)

The Cambodian Navy, including its 31st (Marine) Brigade, wear a copy of US tricolor desert camouflage, as seen in this photograph from 2016. (*US Navy*)

Unlikely as it seems, this commercial-looking 'Green Leaf' camouflage pattern has been observed a number of times on Cambodian military personnel since the late 1990s.

These members of the 911 SF Regiment, photographed in 2010, are wearing Indonesian 'blood vine' pattern uniforms, which have continued to be used sporadically by this unit. (*Private collection*)

armies, the KPNLAF and the Armées Nationale pour Khmer Independent (ANKI). Since the mid-1990s, the RCAF has participated in some peacekeeping efforts as part of the United Nations. Today, camouflage uniforms are relatively standard issue to most conventional units. The RCAF consists of the Royal Army, Royal Navy, Royal Air Force, and the Royal Gendarmerie.

During the French Colonial period, elite units of the Forces Armees Royales Khmere (FARK) wore the same tenue du leópard pattern camouflage uniforms as regular French units. This tradition would continue for some years following independence, as surplus stocks were gradually used up. These camouflage designs are detailed in the section on France.

Circa 2016, the elite Cambodian Prime Minister's Bodyguard Unit (PMBU) adopted a digital camouflage pattern that is still in service. This pattern has also been observed on members of the 911 Special Forces Regiment. (*Private collection*)

CHINA

Following the Japanese surrender at the end of the Second World War, the Republic of China was immediately faced with a civil war between the Nationalist and Communist forces that had struck a tenuous ceasefire during the war. Hostilities continued until 1949, by which time the Communist Party was in control of most of the mainland and the Nationalists retreated to consolidate their power on the island of Formosa (which became the Republic of China). In October 1949, the new People's Republic of China was founded with Mao Zedong as its first Chairman.

The Sino-Vietnamese war lasted only three weeks and resulted in Chinese withdrawal, although border clashes would continue over the next ten years. China has also been involved in border disputes with India. In recent years, Chinese armed forces were involved in operations to curb piracy in the Indian Ocean, military operations against Al-Queda and ISIL, and the conflict in north Mali.

The Chinese armed forces are known collectively as the People's Liberation Army (中国人民解放军), the largest armed force in the world. The PLA consists of the People's

Reversible camouflage uniforms, printed on one side in a DPM-type pattern and on the opposite in a spot design, were first produced in the late 1970s and worn by some personnel in Sino-Vietnamese war. (*Private collection*)

One of the earliest documented camouflage designs produced in China is seen here – a woodland-type pattern reputedly produced in the 1970s.

A single-sided version of the 'duck hunter' pattern was issued to PLAF Airborne units in the 1980s.

Liberation Army Ground Forces, People's Liberation Army Navy or PLAN, People's Liberation Army Air Force or PLAAF, and the Second Artillery Corps (the PLA strategic missile forces). Special troops within the PLA include People's Liberation Army Special Forces (中国特种部队) as well as three complete Airborne Divisions under the Air Force. National law enforcement falls under the jurisdiction of the Chinese People's Armed Police Force (中国人民武装警察部队), or CAPF, with approximately 1.5 million personnel that include border security forces, special installation and national resource guard units, fire fighting units, and special operations forces.

This 'woodland-hybrid' camouflage design, introduced in 1987, would become the standard pattern of the PLAF and the Armed Police until approximately 2007. Although the design itself remained the same, uniform styles, dye combinations and even fabrics would fluctuate over the years. (*PRC Ministry of National Defense*)

While the remainder of the PLAF wore green-hued woodland-type camouflage, the Navy introduced a blue-dominant design for its personnel in the late 1980s and this would be worn into the 1990s. (*Private collection*)

These paratroops of the Chinese Air Force (PLAAF) wear a grey variation of the 'woodland' type camouflage, which was only used for public appearances. (*PRC Ministry of National Defense*)

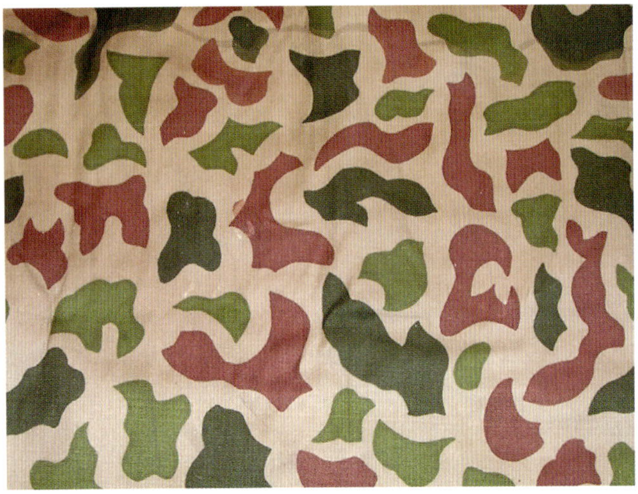

A later variation of the 'duck hunter' pattern issued to some PLA units in the 1990s.

Often referred to as a 'winter' pattern, this woodland variant also dates to the 1990s and was in circulation among some PLA units.

One of the last incarnations of the woodland-hybrid pattern, seen here in 2006, these Chinese Marines are training alongside US Marine colleagues in a rare exchange opportunity. (*US Marine Corps*)

Sources indicate this 'leaf' type camouflage design was worn by units in the Guangdong (广东省) region of China in the 1990s.

This photo from approximately 2004, shows Chinese Army special forces personnel wearing a copy of the US six-color desert camouflage. (*Private collection*)

This arid version of the flecktarn-derivative pattern was introduced in 2003 for issue to units serving in the occupied Tibet region, as well as Inner Mongolia and in other parts of the country. (*PRC Ministry of National Defense*)

A copy of the German Army's flecktarn pattern was adopted by some Chinese units as a training uniform, and also issued to Border Defense personnel such as this anti-aircraft unit. (*Private collection*)

Introduced in 2003, a true copy of the US m81 woodland pattern camouflage has been worn by some PLA personnel.

This photo of Chinese Armed Policewomen suggests at least limited use of a copy of tricolor desert pattern camouflage uniforms. It has also been suggested the pattern was tested by Chinese Army special forces. (*Private collection*)

This photograph from 2005 shows the then newly-adopted DPM pattern camouflage developed for the Special Forces. (*Private collection*)

In 2007, the Chinese Ministry of Defense adopted a new series of digital-type camouflage patterns for the various branches of service. The color palette seen here is considered the 'general service' pattern, with some units being issued more specialized or alternately colored patterns, depending on their duties. (*PRC Ministry of National Defense*)

This variation of the Type 07 camouflage replaced the one issued in mountainous regions such as Tibet. (*PRC Ministry of National Defense*)

These Chinese Marines wear the Navy-issue Type 07 camouflage pattern. (*PRC Ministry of National Defense*)

The green Type 07 camouflage design seen here is worn primarily by Strategic Artillery units of the PLA. (*PRC Ministry of National Defense*)

Seen in this photo is the version of the Type 07 camouflage that is issued to the PLAAF, including Airborne personnel. (*PRC Ministry of National Defense*)

China also embraced the use of Multicam pattern at some point after 2010. (*PRC Ministry of National Defense*)

These Chinese youths in 2012 are participating in a military-themed summer camp and have been issued a unique camouflage pattern with a brown-dominant theme. (*Private collection*)

A winter or snow-patterned coverall is also issued to PLA personnel serving in heavy snow conditions. (*PRC Ministry of National Defense*)

Adopted circa 2015 for wear by Opposing Forces (OPFOR), this pixelated design seen here has been documented in use by the PLA 195th Mechanized Infantry Brigade (aka 'Blue Force'). (*PRC Ministry of National Defense*)

The green-dominant pixelated design seen here has been adopted specifically for the 1st OPFOR Brigade (Wolves of Zhurihe) of the PLA, which is the current designation of the former 195th Mechanized Infantry Brigade. (*PRC Ministry of National Defense*)

The Special Forces of the PLA replaced their DPM camouflage pattern with a pixilated version. (*PRC Ministry of National Defense*)

CAPF Camouflage

In the late 1980s to early 1990s, the CAPF were also issued this vertical camouflage design.

A bright orange design has been issued to fire fighter units from 2005. (*Private collection*)

These Chinese Armed Policemen wear the first type digital pattern camouflage, issued in 2005. (*PRC Ministry of National Defense*)

A second type of pixelate camouflage, with much more arid color palette, was issued around 2014. (*PRC Ministry of National Defense*)

Elite SWAT units of the CAPF wear this pixilated tiger stripe pattern camouflage. (*PRC Ministry of National Defense*)

Control of this island nation has long been contested by the Greek and Turkish elements of its population, as well as by those nations themselves. This has led to periods of intercommunal violence that began in 1963 and lasted for eleven years, nearly sparking a war between Greece and Turkey. In July 1974, a coordinated coup d'etat between Greek Cypriot nationalists and the Greek military junta was aimed at achieving the unification of Cyprus and Greece. Turkey responded by invading the northern portion of the island and the region has remained thereafter in occupation, effectively dividing the country along old ethnic boundaries. A separate Turkish Cypriot political entity was officially established in 1983, and remains in control of north Cyprus. Today approximately 59 per cent of the island is under control of the officially recognized government of the Republic of Cyprus, with the remaining area (calling itself the Turkish Republic of Northern Cyprus)

Greek lizard pattern camouflage became the standard for most personnel in the 1980s and has been produced locally and procured from Greece and elsewhere. A number of variations have been documented, differing mostly in the color of the dyes used. The lizard patterns were worn well into the early 2000s.

The Cypriot NG Naval Commandos (OYK) wore a vertical stripe pattern uniform towards the end of the 1980s. (*Private collection*)

Air elements of the National Guard wear the same arid pattern, with blue replacing one of the brown tones in the design.

effectively controlling the remainder. The occupation of the northern part of the island by Turkey is considered illegal by the most of the international community.

The armed forces of the Republic of Cyprus are the Cypriot National Guard (Εθνική Φρουρά). Consisting of ground, air and naval elements, the Cypriot NG has traditionally been heavily based on the Greek model, with combat uniform traditions being no exception. For many years the majority of Cypriot guardsmen wore imported or locally-made copies of the standard

This National Guard general wears a brown 'arid' camouflage design adopted circa 2003. Secondary runs of the pattern were printed with a Cypriot national crest embedded into the design. (*Private collection*)

Special operations troops wear a variety of camouflage designs, including a copy of the USMC temperate MARPAT pattern seen here. (*Private collection*)

These Navy commandos wear a copy of US m81 woodland pattern, which is also worn by the Greek Navy SF. (*Private collection*)

Another pattern found within the Cypriot special operations community is the 'Universal Camouflage Pattern' of the US Army. (*Private collection*)

Multicam is currently being worn by Cypriot special operations personnel. (*Private collection*)

Greek military lizard pattern camouflage (with similar variability among the different manufacturers and years of production). It has only been recently that national patterns were adopted, setting the Cypriots somewhat apart from their Greek cousins.

The armed forces providing security for the northern part of Cyprus are called the Security Forces Command (Güvenlik Kuvvetleri Komutanlığı). Like the Cypriot National Guard, this is a combined force with land, naval and air elements, but using Turkish forces as a model. It is believed there are approximately 9,000 Turkish Cypriot men in the GKK, comprising fifteen battalions in two brigades. They are trained and supplied by the Turkish Armed Forces.

Camouflage of Northern Cyprus Forces

Turkish woodland pattern camouflage uniforms were formerly in use with GKK personnel.

These members of the GKK wear the current Turkish Army 'digital' camouflage pattern. (*Private collection*)

Formerly a part of the Soviet Union (USSR), Georgia is a sovereign country in the Caucasus region of Asia. Shortly after achieving independence, a coup d'etat orchestrated by the National Guards deposed the newly elected president and embroiled the country in a civil war lasting until late 1994. At nearly the same time, the region of South Ossetia declared its independence from Georgia and a seventeen-month military campaign ensued, ending in a Russian-brokered ceasefire and control of South Ossetia by the separatists. Meanwhile, in August 1992 separatists from the Abkhazia region (supported by Russia and other north Caucasian fighters) embarked on a military campaign for its independence lasting until late 1993 and resulting in the expulsion of nearly 250,000 Georgians from the region. The Abkhazian conflict was briefly rekindled in 1998 when ethnic Georgians unsuccessfully attempted to wrest control from the Abkhazian government.

Tensions with Russia came to a head in 2008, following accusations that Georgia had become involved in the Second Chechen War. In the resulting five-day war, Russia came to the aid of both the Abkhazian and South Ossetian separatists and Georgia lost what remaining control it had of those regions. Although both South Ossetia and Abkhazia are now de facto republics, the international community still recognizes these regions as Georgian territory.

This photo from 1993 shows two TTsKO derivative patterns being worn in Georgia during the conflict in the southern region. (*Private collection*)

These Georgian soldiers wear the Russian dubok (little oak) pattern camouflage in an undated photograph. (*Private collection*)

The Georgian Armed Forces consist of the Land Forces (including Air and Coast Guard elements), Special Operations Forces, and the paramilitary National Guard. As with most former Soviet republics, law enforcement is the responsibility of units attached

Another photograph from the conflict in Abkhazia shows a Georgian soldier wearing the Ukrainian-made 'swirl' design. (*Private collection*)

This photograph shows Georgian personnel wearing three different types of camouflage: a copy of US m81 woodland, a Chinese woodland-hybrid pattern, and the Turkish 'compressed leaf' design. (*US Air Force*)

The Georgian military contingents that deployed to Afghanistan and Iraq between 2005 and 2008 all wore surplus US tricolor desert pattern camouflage uniforms. (*US DOD*)

This Georgian interpreter wears the copy of USMC temperate MARPAT adopted by the armed forces in 2008 and still being worn by some personnel in 2017. (*US Army*)

A Georgian soldier on exercise wearing the copy of USMC desert MARPAT camouflage adopted circa 2014. (*Private collection*)

A copy of Multicam was initially adopted by Special Forces circa 2009, and by the rest of Armed Forces by 2014. (*US Army*)

These Border Protection troops wear a copy of the Italian Army's vegetato pattern. (*Private collection*)

to the Ministry of Internal Affairs. Soviet-designed camouflage patterns were employed until 1992, when variations unique to the region and the Georgian Armed Forces were introduced. Beginning in 2001, a variety of foreign-produced camouflage designs began to see short periods of service, including surplus uniforms from the USA, Germany and Turkey. Today the Georgian Armed Forces (საქართველოს შეიარაღებული ძალები, or Sak'art'velos Sheiaraghebuli Dzalebi) employ Asian-made copies of contemporary US patterns such as MARPAT and Multicam.

Camouflage of South Ossetian Forces

Ground Forces of South Ossetia wearing Russian flora pattern. (*Private collection*)

Russian tsifra pattern worn by Ground Forces. (*Private collection*)

Border Security personnel wearing the Russian FSB Border Guards pattern. (*Private collection*)

INDIA

The Republic of India was established in 1947 following a largely non-violent struggle for independence from Great Britain. When British India was dissolved it was partitioned into two separate territories, India and Pakistan (formed out of the Muslim majority provinces). In the resulting confusion, over 10 million displaced people were forced to migrate towards one or the other of the new nations.

India has fought three major conflicts with Pakistan (in 1947, 1965 and 1999) over the province of Kashmir, all of them ending essentially in stalemate. India also came to the aid of the Mukti Bahini during the Bangladesh War of Liberation (which ended in the creation of Bangladesh). Relations between India and Pakistan continue to be strained.

The Sino-Indian War broke out between India and China in 1962 under the pretext of a border dispute in the Himalayas. Although a ceasefire was announced in November of that year, it was not until 1993 that the two nations agreed to sign a peace agreement. In 1986, the Indian Navy helped avert a coup d'etat in the Seychelles. Indian forces later assisted the government of Maldives in averting a coup d'etat attempt in 1988, and also intervened during the Sri Lankan Civil War (1987–90) on the side of the Sri Lankan government.

India has been a frequent contributor to United Nations sanctioned peacekeeping efforts, participating in as many as forty-three different missions. Most recently Indian military personnel have been sent to Lebanon (UNIFIL), the Congo (MONUSCO), Sudan (UNMIS), the Golan Heights (UNDOF), Ivory Coast (UNOCI), Haiti (MINUSTAH) and Liberia (UNMIL).

India maintains the third-largest military force in the world. The Armed Forces of India include the Army, Navy and Air Force, the Coast Guard, the Strategic Forces Command (Nuclear Command) and the Paramilitary Forces of India (PFI). The latter consists of the Central Armed Police Forces (including the Border Security Force, Central Reserve Police Force, Indo-Tibetan Border Police, Central Industrial Security Force, and the Sashastra Seema Bal), the Central Reserve Police Forces (including Rapid Action Force and Cobra Commando Battalion), and other forces such as the Indian Home Guard, Civil Defense, Special Frontier Force, National Security Guard, Special Protection Group, Railway Protection Force, and several other agencies.

The majority of units of the Indian Armed Forces wear camouflage in one form or another, many having patterns specific to their particular Force or group. Some Regiments within the Army also employ their own unique patterns. The standard camouflage of the Indian Armed Forces is called Disruptive Pattern Material (DPM) although it has no relationship whatsoever to the British camouflage design of the same name. India has a very large textile and garment industry, supplying not only its own military needs but exporting fabric and uniforms to other nations as well.

The standard camouflage design of the Indian Armed Forces from the 1970s to mid-2000s, this 'palm frond' or Indian DPM pattern has quite a number of variations in color. (*Private collection*)

An Indian version of the 'brushstroke' design introduced by Britain in the Second World War has been in service with airborne and commando personnel since 1960s. This photo from 2010 shows the pattern is still being issued. (*Private collection*)

This copy of the Russian butane pattern appeared in the 1990s and was worn by some units.

A blue variant of the standard DPM pattern has been used by the Rapid Action Force and by the Civil Reserve Police Force. (*United Nations*)

These 'lizard' type camouflage patterns have been in service with units operating in the Maharashtra region, with some paramilitary units, and observed in the past with the National Security Guard. (NSG)

Various copies of US m81 woodland have been in service with a number of Indian units since the 1990s. The pattern has been worn during UN deployments, as well as by AF Security personnel and various federal agencies. (*Private collection*)

These patterns have both been worn in some capacity by the CRPF. (*Private collection*)

This three-color pattern has been worn by the BSF and internal security units since late 1990s. (*Private collection*)

This leaf pattern with similar arid coloration has been worn by the Sashastra Seema Bal (SSB) or Armed Border Force (previously known as the Special Service Bureau) since the late 1990s. (*Private collection*)

This vertical lizard pattern has been worn by the NSG.

The Indian Army adopted its own 'woodland' camouflage in 2006, which is now issued to most personnel of the Indian Armed Forces. (*United Nations*)

This flecktarn-like desert pattern was introduced in 2008 and is now worn by the BSF in some regions. (*Private collection*)

This orange 'spot' pattern camouflage smock has been observed on some Indian Army personnel on training exercises. (*US Army*)

This variant of the US tricolor desert pattern is in service with the Central Industrial Security Forces (CISF). (*Private collection*)

These Navy Marine Commandos wear a copy of UCP, which is also worn by the CRPF. (*Private collection*)

The Garud Commando Force of the Indian Air Force adopted this digital camouflage pattern in 2015. (*Private collection*)

Seen here are the former three-color design and the current digital camouflage pattern of the Indo-Tibetan Border Police; the latter was adopted in 2015. (*Private collection*)

Members of the seven India Reserve Battalions (IRB) of the Nagaland State Police wear a brushstroke type camouflage pattern. (*Private collection*)

This brushstroke type camouflage design is worn by units of the Central Reserve Police Force (CRPF) operating in Eastern and North-Eastern India.

Emerging from Japanese occupation following the Second World War, the former Dutch colony of Indonesia declared its independence in 1945. The Netherlands attempted to regain control, leading the nation into four years of armed conflict and eventual Dutch capitulation in December 1949. Newly elected president Sukarno began to move the country towards authoritarianism in the 1950s. Opposition to the formation of Malaysia (Konfrontasi) in 1963 led to an undeclared war in the region formerly known as British Borneo (now East Malaysia) lasting three years.

When the Army violently foiled an attempted coup d'etat in 1965, it followed up with large scale genocide against ethnic Chinese, communist sympathizers and alleged leftists. Three years later, the head of the military, General Suharto, assumed the presidency; his thirty-three year reign was marked by political oppression and corruption. In December 1975, Indonesian forces invaded East Timor, just a few months after the Frente Revolucionária de Timor-Leste Independente (FRETILIN) had declared its independence from Portugal. Indonesia occupied the region for twenty-four years, rebuffing the guerilla campaign being waged against it. Responding to international pressure, Indonesia finally relinquished control of East Timor in May 2002.

Two additional separatist movements arose during the 1970s. The Gerakan Aceh Merdeka (GAM) or Free Aceh Movement began its insurgency against the government in 1976, reaching a peace agreement with the Indonesian government only in 2005. In Western New Guinea (Papua), the Organisasi Papua Merdeka, (OPM) has been conducting a low-level guerilla campaign since 1969. A series of terrorist attacks orchestrated by Islamist movements have shaken several major cities and tourist spots in recent years.

The Indonesian National Armed Forces (Tentara Nasional Indonesia, or TNI) comprise the Army (TNI-AD), Air Force (TNI-AU), and Navy (TNI-AL). Formerly considered part of the military, the Indonesian National Police (Kepolisian Negara Republik Indonesia) or POLRI has been a separate branch of service since 1999 and is responsible for law enforcement and internal security, including anti-terrorism. Although not military organizations, Indonesia has a very long and varied list of political parties, many of whom adopted paramilitary uniforms. The country has embraced the use of camouflage uniforms like few other nations, some patterns having historical links to particular branches of service or specific units, while others were utilized as a unique identifier of political affiliations.

The Garuda Contingent has been Indonesia's contribution to United Nations peacekeeping efforts since 1956. It has been involved in more than twenty separate missions.

Military Camouflage

Original US M1942 spot pattern camouflage was employed by the Air Force Pasukan Gerak Tjepat (PGT), as well as the Army's Resimen Parakomando Angkatan Darat (RPKAD) or Special Forces, and airborne elements in the 1950s.

A copy of the British 'brushstroke' camouflage design was produced in Hong Kong for the RPKAD and the Combined Airborne Training Command (KOGABDIKPARA) from around 1962 until 1964.

These locally-made copies of M1942 pattern saw service with the PGT and RPKAD, as well as some infantry units into the 1970s.

Introduced in 1964, the Loreng Darah Mangalir ('flowing blood') was developed for use by RPKAD and saw service with the unit until 1986. (*Private collection*)

Indian-made camouflage smocks were worn by 454 Airborne Brigade from 1964 until the 1970s, and by the 18th Airborne Brigade from 1968 onwards.

A brightly colored brushstroke pattern was worn exclusively by the Army Jakarta Military Region (KODAM Jaya) Raider Battalion in the 1970s. This would be reintroduced for ceremonial purposes in 2012. (*Private collection*)

Another 'brushstroke' camouflage design was introduced for use by the KKO (Korps Komando Angkatan Laut) or Marine Commando Corps in 1965 and continued in service through the 1970s. The pattern was later reintroduced for ceremonial and training purposes beginning in the 1990s. (*Private collection*)

The unique jagged spot camouflage design was issued to Air Force KOPASGAT (Komando Pasukan Gerak Cepat) personnel from 1967 until 1976. (*Private collection*)

A vertical stripe pattern was worn by the Air Force KOPASGAT between 1969 and 1980, then again between 1983 and 84. Reintroduced unofficially in the 1990s, it was officially adopted in 2000 for ceremonial and training purposes. (*Private collection*)

This pattern was worn by Cavalry units of the Strategic Reserve for a short period in the late 1960s. (*Private collection*)

This 'spotted-stripe' design was issued between 1977 and 1979 to troops in the Tanjungpura Military Region (covering West Kalimantan).

A copy of the 'USMC Standard' (or 'wine leaf') camouflage pattern was issued to Airborne elements of the Army's KOSTRAD (Komando Cadangan Strategis Angkatan Darat) in 1975. It would later be revived for ceremonial purposes in the 1990s. (*Private collection*)

This vertical stripe pattern was issued to graduates of Raider Course between 1980 and 1983. (*Private collection*)

The Macan tutul or 'leopard' pattern was originally issued to Korps Marinir from 1983–84. The design would be revived for the Marines in 2011. (*Private collection*)

In 1984 it was mandated that the entire armed services would universally adopt a copy of the British DPM pattern. (*Private collection*)

Issued as coverall smock to Anti-Riot Troops of the Indonesian Army, the Pasukan anti huru-hara. (*PHH*)

A digital version of standard DPM was issued to the ten graduating Raider Battalions in December 2003. A second print run of this pattern had the Raider logo embedded into the design.

These medical personnel serving in Lebanon (Garuda Contingent) wear an arid DPM pattern that was originally released in 2010. (*United Nations*)

This pattern was issued to Navy Komando Pasukan Katak or KOPASKA (Special Operations) in 2006. (*Private collection*)

This blue stripe pattern was first issued to Indonesian Navy personnel in 2011. (*US Navy*)

The old Macan tutul pattern camouflage was reintroduced for the Indonesian Marine Corps in 2011. (*Private collection*)

Two members of the Brigif Lintas Udara 17 (17th Airborne Infantry Brigade) wearing the digital pattern adopted for airborne forces in 2012. (*Private collection*)

A bright blue camouflage design was adopted by the Air Force in 2015. (*Private collection*)

As of 2016, submarine crews of the Navy wear their own blue-dominant camouflage design, seen here. (*Private collection*)

Police Camouflage

This brushstroke design was adopted by the Police 32 Airborne Battalion and worn between 1967 and 1969.

The Police Mobile Brigade (Brimob) also wore a copy of the US M1942 spot pattern beginning in 1965. (*Private collection*)

A different kind of brushstroke design was worn by the Resimen Pelopor (Ranger Regiment) during 1960s.

Photographic evidence confirms the spot pattern seen here was worn sparingly by Brimob units in 1990s, and by some Brimob units serving in Timor-Leste.

A vertical stripe design was initially adopted by the National Police Resimen Pelopor (MENPOR) in 1966. In 2000, it was reissued for ceremonial use with the unit. (*Private collection*)

IRAN

Iran emerged from the Second World War an independent state and a constitutional monarchy. In 1953, the democratically elected prime minister was deposed in a coup d'etat that placed additional power in the historical Pahlavi monarchy. Coup leader general Fazlollah Zahedi was installed as prime minister. Under Shah Pahlavi, Iran became modernized and secular, but his reign was also marred by autocratic abuses of power, political oppression and draconian human rights abuses by the secret police. Hit by a recession in the 1970s, the

Two of the earliest Iranian camouflage designs, vertical 'brushstroke' designs that were worn by elite Imperial Guards and Imperial Marine Commandos during the Shah period. (*Amin Allah Shakeri collection*)

A copy of British DPM was reproduced in Iran and worn by Imperial Marines and Marine Commandos, as seen here. (*Private collection*)

monarchy fell into increasing disfavor with working-class Iranians. What began as public disapproval led to civil resistance, demonstrations and, ultimately the Iranian Revolution of 1979, in which the Shah was deposed and sent into exile. The Islamic Republic in Iran was thereafter established.

(*Private collection*)

The new government was immediately faced with a series of ethnic uprisings in various parts of the country, including Kurdistan, Kuzestan in the west, and Sistan and Baluchestan in the southwest. Fighting with government forces went on for several years, but by 1983 the insurgencies had been quelled. Meanwhile, in September 1980, the Kuzestan region was invaded by neighboring Iraq in an attempt to gain control of the oil fields there. This sparked a bloody eight-year war that claimed as many as half-a-million lives and included the use of chemical weapons, child soldiers and suicide troops. Relations between the two countries remained tense until Saddam Hussein's regime was toppled.

These vertical stripe or 'brushstroke' designs can be traced to the Imperial period. Additional variations of this pattern would continue to be worn throughout the Iran-Iraq War and beyond, particularly by Basij volunteer units. (*Amin Allah Shakeri collection*)

(*Private collection*)

Iran has remained overtly disengaged from military operations for the past twenty years, but the country has provided covert military assistance to numerous Islamic fundamentalist organizations around the world, most notably Hezbollah in Lebanon, Shi'a militias in Iraq, and recently the government forces of Syria.

The Armed Forces of the Islamic Republic of Iran include the Army (Artesh) the Iranian Revolutionary Guard Corps (Sepāh) or IRGC, and the Law Enforcement Forces. The army includes ground forces, air defense forces, air forces, and naval forces. The IRGC consists of the Ground Force, Aerospace Force, IRGC Navy, the Quds Force (special operations troops), and the Basij Mobilization Force – a kind of paramilitary militia.

The Imperial Marines also wore early incarnations of what came to be called the 'panther' pattern, most likely copied from the Second World War era M1942 spot pattern of the American Marines. Use of these designs has continued nearly unaltered into the present day, although now they are mostly worn by Army Commando units and experts in desert and mountain warfare.

Another panther spot variation is seen here, worn by a Basij volunteer of the IRGC. (*Private collection*)

These two 'puzzle' patterns have been linked with IRGC ground and Basij units during Iran-Iraq war, although they may have been produced earlier than this. (*Amin Allah Shakeri collection*)

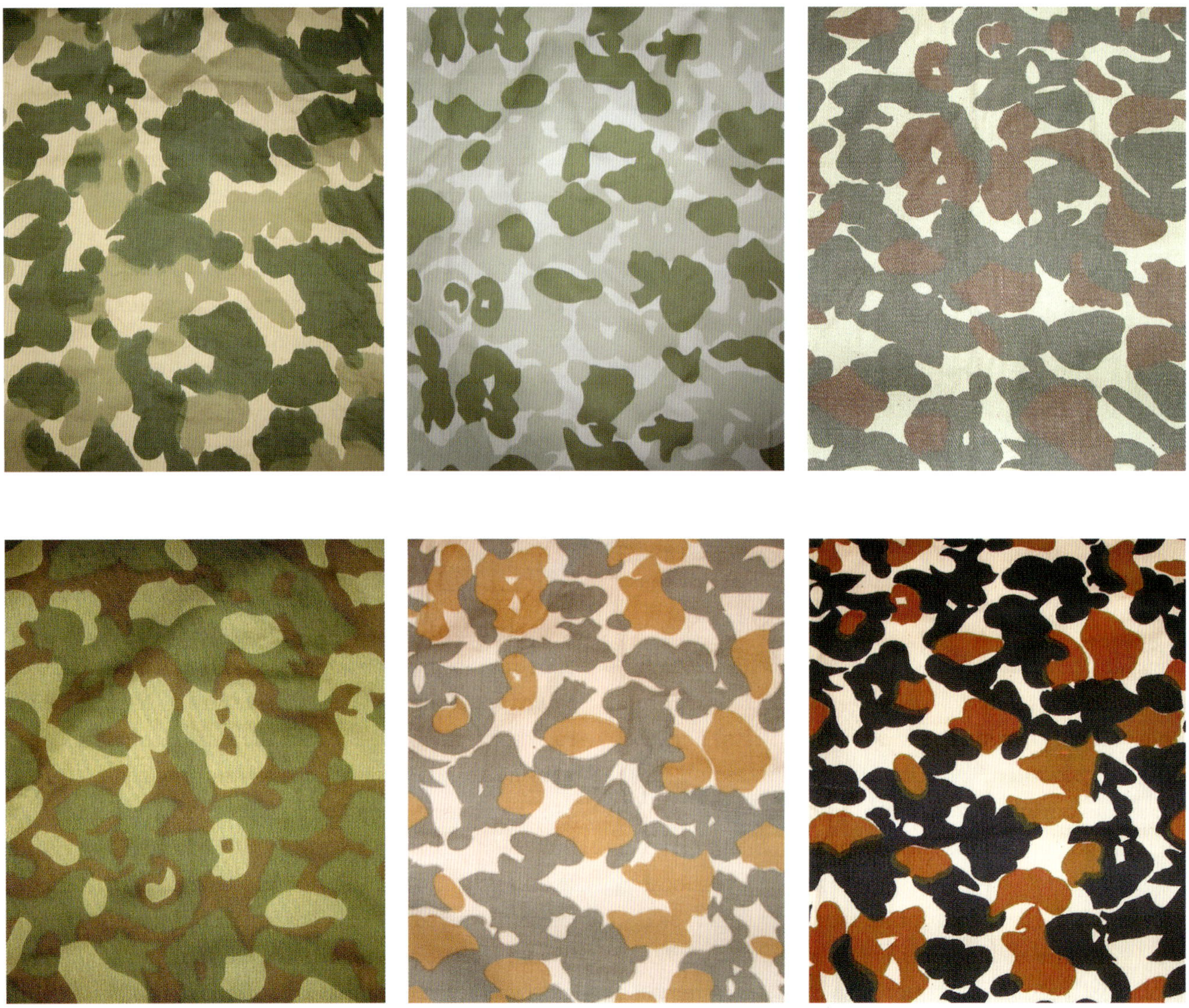

Some additional panther patterns are documented here. These have been worn by Army Special Forces and Basij units from 1979 to the present. (*Amin Allah Shakeri collection*)

A child soldier of the Iran-Iraq War here wears the vertical stripe pattern that has come to be most strongly associated with the Basij units. (*Private collection*)

Another similar design is seen here, again worn by a Basij volunteer during the war. (*Private collection*)

This arid DPM pattern was adopted by NOHED or Niroe Vije Hava Bord (Special Air Service) Brigade 65, also known as the Iranian Rangers or Special Forces in the 1990s. (*Private collection*)

A camouflage design in use with installation and prison guards.

The Iranian Marines (including Commandos) began using this camouflage pattern loosely based on US six-color desert in the 1990s. (*Private collection*)

These patterns were used by Basij and IRGC special operations units in late 1990s. (*Amin Allah Shakeri collection*)

Introduced in the 1980s, both the Army and the IRGC have made extensive use of woodland camouflage, although today it has largely been phased out. (*Private collection*)

A woodland variant with blue color palette was also in use with Air Force units.

These personnel of the Air Defense Artillery branch wear a 'leaf' type camouflage pattern with a multi-colored pathway. (*Private collection*)

Another woodland variant, utilizing mostly shades of brown, was adopted in the 1990s by the Emergency Brigade (Yegane Emdad) of the Iranian Police and by Border Guard units.

These IRGC Sepah Commandos wear copies of two US designs, the chocolate chip six-color and later tricolor desert patterns. The latter pattern was also worn by Iranian Police Border Guard units. (*Private collection*)

This unusual variation of the six-color desert pattern was issued to Iranian Military Police and Base Guards.

These Iranian generals are wearing the arid DPM pattern originally introduced for use by the Special Operations Brigade 23, but later adopted by many army units. (*Private collection*)

Assigned specifically to protect the nation's nuclear power facilities, this unique 'water spots' pattern is worn by personnel of the Iranian Atomic Energy Organization Guards. (*Private collection*)

A copy of the UCP is being worn by Iranian Marine Commandos and some Basij special operations units. (*Private collection*)

These Sepah commandos of the Iranian IRGC wear two types of digital desert camouflage based on the USMC temperate MARPAT design. This pattern, adopted in 2009, is also worn by some Airborne units of the Army. (*Private collection*)

The digital pattern worn by this officer replaced the former 'leaf' design in 2010 and is now worn by the Air Defense Artillery Forces. (*Private collection*)

Members of the NOHED (Special Air Service) Brigade 65 wear the new, pixilated version of their old DPM pattern. (*Private collection*)

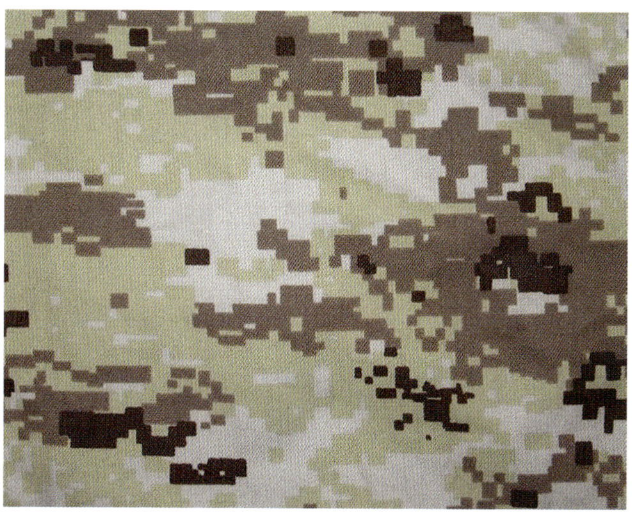

This digital pattern has been adopted by the Iranian Marines to replace their previous six-color derivative design.

This DPM-based desert camouflage pattern was introduced 2010–11 for use by IRGC.

These digital patterns, introduced in 2013, are now being worn by the Basij units of the IRGC.

IRAQ

This rare photo from 1969 shows Iraqi airborne troops wearing late issue Denison smocks provided by the British officers that trained them. (*Private collection*)

The 'ragged leaf' design is one of the few truly unique designs associated with Iraq. This pattern can be traced at least as far back as the Iran-Iraq War and was issued to commandos and paratroops.

Following the end of the Second World War, the old Hashemite Kingdom of Iraq was reinstated, but in a 1958 coup d'etat known as the 14 July Revolution it was replaced with military rule. The Ba'ath Party usurped control of the government in 1968, paving the way for leadership under Saddam Hussein, who assumed control of the presidency and leadership of the Revolutionary Command Council in July 1979. Hussein declared war against neighboring Iran in 1980, but after eight years and some minor exchanges of territory, the war ended in stalemate, having cost the two nations more than half-a-million lives. Iraq employed chemical weapons both against Iran and during the Al-Anfal Campaign targeting the Kurdish population in Iraq.

In August 1990, Iraq invaded and attempted to annex Kuwait, leading to military response from a US-led coalition of Arab and non-Arab states (the Persian Gulf War). Iraqi forces were severely reduced during this conflict and were ultimately expelled from Kuwait. As a result, a series of armed uprisings among the Shia and Kurdish population took place, but were severely repressed by the remaining elements of the Iraqi security forces, which again employed chemical weapons. The United Nations attempted to compel destruction of the

A copy of the West German sumpftarnmuster was certainly used among Iraqi officers in the 1970s and 1980s. The officer in this photograph appears to wear a custom-made jacket of some sort. (*Private collection*)

The pattern here was produced in Germany and saw limited distribution to Iraqi personnel in the 1980s.

remaining chemical and biological weapon stores; failed compliance resulted in sanctions lasting until 2003.

In March 2003, the United States again led a small coalition of forces (with support from Kurdish Peshmerga) in an invasion of Iraq (Operation Iraqi Freedom), ostensibly to rid the country of its chemical, biological and (non-existent) nuclear arsenal, and depose president Hussein. Although the Iraqi Armed Forces were theoretically defeated after less than five weeks of open warfare, subsequent hostilities against both Iraqi and outside insurgents have continued into the present era. A new Iraqi government and restructured Iraqi Armed Forces were created with assistance from allied forces, while opposition to what is considered a foreign occupation was taken up on many fronts by former supporters of Hussein, Shia militias, Sunni insurgents, and foreign fighters under the banner of Al-Qaeda and the Islamic State of Iraq (ISI). The Iraq War itself is officially considered to have ended with US withdrawal

Another brushstroke-type design favored by Iraqi officers in the 1980s is derived from the Belgian pattern. (*Private collection*)

Of undetermined origins and only sparsely documented, this pattern was found in Iraq during the First Gulf War. (*Private collection*)

These officer candidates are all wearing the South Korean-made 'waves' pattern, a design that was also worn by Ba'ath Party Talia Youth. (*Private collection*)

The only documented use of this pattern in Iraq has been by Ba'ath Party Talia Youth, although it is possible some military personnel also obtained quantities of it.

These young children are members of the Ba'ath Party Talia Youth organization. Evidence suggests the organization was broken into age groups, for each of which a camouflage pattern was assigned. (*Private collection*)

in 2011, but fighting continues presently with no end in sight.

The Iraqi Armed Forces under Saddam Hussein were divided into the regular forces (Army, Navy, Air Force and Republican Guards) and the loyalist forces (the Popular Army, and the paramilitary Fedayeen Saddam). For the most part, only elite or specialized units were issued camouflage uniforms, this often being an indication of their status. The Republican Guards were considered the most well-trained and well-equipped of the Iraqi forces, although commando and paratroop units likewise benefited from higher quality training and equipment.

Restructured in 2003, the Iraqi Armed Forces are reorganized and have eliminated loyalist elements. They consist of the Army, Navy, Air Force, Air Defense Forces, and a separate Special Operations Command. Most Iraqi units now wear camouflage uniforms in a variety of patterns, some copied from those of other nations and others obtained through foreign contracts.

Copies of French 'lizard' camouflage saw extensive use with elite units and officers from the late 1980s and into the 1990s. (*Private collection*)

A rare photo showing an Iraqi wearing the 'oakleaf' pattern (based on Second World War eichlaubmuster) which is likely to have been Kuwaiti in origin, and brought back in small quantities to Iraq following the 1991 Gulf War. (*Private collection*)

These members of the 66th Special Forces Brigade are wearing a combination of British-made and locally procured four-color desert DPM pattern uniforms in the late 1980s. (*Private collection*)

Another brushstroke variation seen here was supplied by Asian manufacturers and saw use with paratroops and commando units.

Predating the First Gulf War, this photo illustrates nicely the heavy use of desert DPM pattern camouflage among Iraqi Forces. (*Private collection*)

The use of British DPM pattern uniforms was extensive in the pre-Gulf War period. They were supplied in large quantities to Iraqi elite units as well as many Iraqi officers and officer candidates. (*Private collection*)

A nice photo giving a clear view of the leaf pattern camouflage uniform supplied to the Popular Army as well as Republican Guard and commando units during the pre-1991 era. (*Private collection*)

Large quantities of captured uniforms were brought back from Kuwait after the First Gulf War and ended up as supply stocks for a multitude of Iraqi units.

A crudely-printed version of DPM or brushstroke camouflage was locally-produced after the First Gulf War and supplied to elite units. A number of color variations have been documented. (*Private collection*)

Although it saw service with some Iraqi elite units prior to 2003, the spot pattern seen in this photograph was also worn by re-formed Iraqi units (including ICDC and ING). (*Private collection*)

A locally produced copy of m81 woodland that appeared very late in Saddam Hussein's regime.

The Free Iraqi Forces (FIF) was an anti-government unit equipped by coalition forces during the early stages of the Iraq War. These troops were primarily outfitted with surplus US six-color desert uniforms, and appropriate badges. (*Private collection*)

The restructured Iraqi Armed Forces saw extensive use of m81 woodland pattern camouflage; obtained through various sources (including Jordan and Iran) these have seen use particularly in Baghdad and Kurdish regions. (*Private collection*)

In this photo from the 2001–02 period, Iraqi military students are outfitted in a variety of new and older camouflage designs, including the 'leaf' pattern that was later pressed into service with new Iraqi units following the 2003 invasion. (*Private collection*)

The most widely seen camouflage design within the new Iraqi Forces has been a copy of the six-color desert pattern. This was the standard pattern of most conventional forces from around 2004 until it was replaced by digital designs. (*Private collection*)

This six-color desert variant, with pink and mint green elements, was primarily worn by the Iraqi Training Brigade and its new recruits, although it has also been documented in use with the Coastal Defense Service as late as 2008. (*Private collection*)

Large quantities of the Kuwaiti National Guard camouflage were obtained and issued to various units, including ICDC and Police.

Commonly found throughout the region, elements of Iraqi Police have worn blue or purple-dominant DPM variant camouflage since at least 2005. (*Private collection*)

Many other blue-dominant camouflage designs have been documented in use with Iraqi Police units, including the woodland pattern worn by this member of the TSU. (*Private collection*)

Initially provided in some quantity by US forces and later obtained from Asian manufacturers, the US tricolor desert pattern has seen extensive use with Iraqi Army and Police units. (*Private collection*)

These members of the 36th Commando Brigade wear a unique camouflage design originally produced in Lithuania; this design was also used by the Iraqi Counter-Terrorist Forces. (*US DOD*)

Two officers of the Iraqi Special Operations Forces (ISOF) wear a copy of British desert DPM that has been worn by several Iraqi units, including the 36th Commandos. (*US DOD*)

Seen here are a variety of camouflage designs, including the desert tiger stripe pattern. (*US Army*)

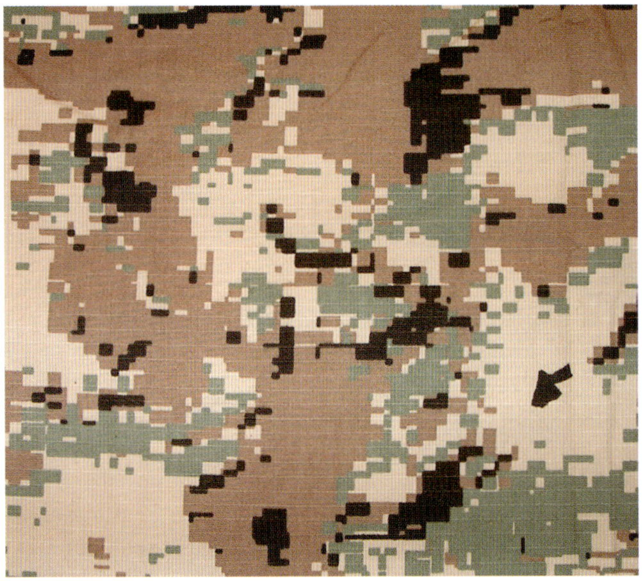

The Jordanian Army's KA2 digital camouflage pattern was also pressed into service with some units of the Iraqi Armed Forces for a short period of time.

The Iraqi Police Force have worn a couple of digital patterns, some having a lighter color base and some a much darker one. The latter seems to be much less common and may be privately sourced. (*Private collection*)

This soldier wears a copy of the USMC temperate MARPAT design, which was reproduced both with and without the EGA symbol. (*Private collection*)

This photograph from 2014 illustrates the use of USMC desert MARPAT camouflage by Iraqi forces. The pattern was also produced both with and without the EGA symbol and another version with the Iraqi flag embedded. (*Private collection*)

The desert pattern seen here, of Chinese origin, has been documented in use by regular Iraqi military personnel as well as Shi'ite militia such as the Jihad Brigade.

The strange black-gray camouflage design here, also of Chinese origin, is used by Ministry of Interior SWAT teams, and possibly other federal units. (*Private collection*)

Various specialized Iraqi units, such as that seen here, have adopted Multicam. (*Private collection*)

These two operators are wearing a Chinese copy of the A-TACS© Arid Urban (AU) camouflage design. (*Private collection*)

Seen here on an officer of the Iraqi Police unit that protects oil facilities, this blue design appears to be based loosely on Multicam. (*Private collection*)

Some additional camouflage designs seen sporadically in Iraqi are shown here, including a brown design also likely based on Multicam. (*Private collection*)

ISRAEL

The State of Israel was created in 1948 out of the British Mandate of Palestine, to provide a permanent Jewish homeland following the Second World War. The establishment of Israel was met with immediate antagonism by neighboring Arab states, thus sparking the 1948 Arab-Israeli War. The nation was drawn into the Suez Crisis of 1956, fighting alongside France and Great Britain against Egypt. Ten years later Israel was attacked by Egypt, Jordan and Syria during the Six-Day War (1967), but soundly defeated its attackers and captured several pieces of key territory in the process (including the Golan Heights and Sinai Peninsula). Attempts to retake the territory in 1973 (Yom Kippur War) were initially successful, but the land was retaken and Israel again achieved victory.

In 1964 the Palestine Liberation Organization (منظمة التحرير الفلسطينية – PLO) was founded as a political and paramilitary organization aimed to liberate Palestine through armed struggle. Throughout the course of its existence, numerous factions came into existence (many aligned with and/or supported by outside entities, including Syria, Iran, et al). The nation was drawn into the Suez Crisis of 1956, fighting alongside France and Great Britain against Egypt. In 1988 a Palestinian Declaration of Independence was issued, resulting in the establishment of the Palestinian National Authority in 1994, which governs the Palestinian territories within the State of Israel.

First worn by the IDF during the Six-Day War in 1967, surplus French lizard camouflage uniforms of various designs would see sporadic use for the next 10–20 years.

The Israeli Defense Forces were actively engaged during the Lebanese Civil War, and invaded South Lebanon in 1982 (what became known as the Lebanon War). Forces were withdrawn in 1983. Between July and August 2006, however, the nation again moved troops into Southern Lebanon, this time moving against Hezbollah.

The standard combat uniform of the IDF has always been khaki or olive green. Camouflage uniforms have been employed from time to time, as needed, by various units but are not considered to be standard issue. The

The IDF began using some ex-US BDUs beginning in the 1980s and continued to employ woodland camouflage unofficially or many years to come. (*Private collection*)

Some use has been made (again, unofficially) of US six-color 'chocolate chip' camouflage uniforms and equipment by IDF personnel.

The Israeli soldiers here were all engaged in the OPFOR role, and most are clad in US tricolor desert pattern uniforms. (*Private collection*)

These IDF troops employ Mit'znefet camouflage headnets in a six-color desert camouflage pattern. (*Private collection*)

(*Private collection*)

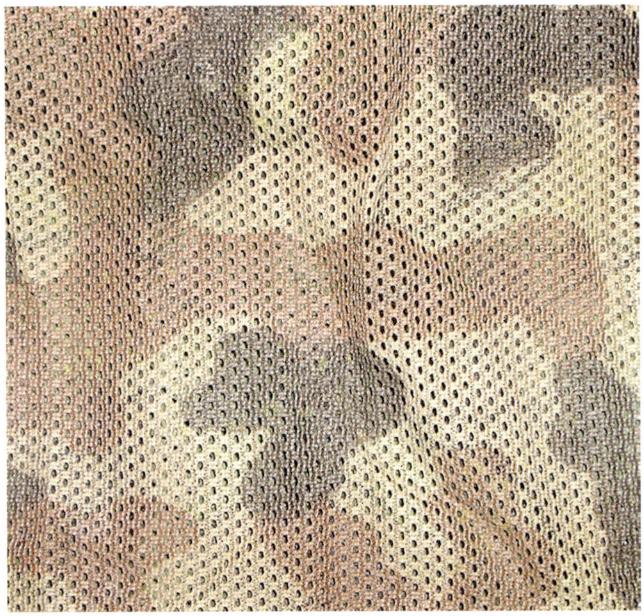

Related to the Mit'znefet, a reversible fully-body oversuit was also produced for the IDF in the 1990s.

earliest camouflage uniforms of the IDF were donated by France and worn by airborne troops during the Six-Day War. American-made combat uniforms have also long been in the IDF inventory, frequently worn for training and operational purposes.

JAPAN

Japan renounced its right to declare war in the aftermath of the Second World War, but nevertheless maintains a sizeable and well-trained self-defense force. Although the nation has not been involved in any direct hostilities in the modern era, since 1992 the National Diet has permitted deployment of Japanese military personnel to some theaters of war as observers, peacekeepers, or to provide non-combat support such as medical services, etc.

Japan introduced its first camouflage design in the 1980s, initially for use by the 1st Airborne Brigade. It was later issued to conventional units. (*US Army*)

Personnel of the Japanese Air Self-Defense Force wear the recolored version of the old JSDF pattern, introduced circa 1988. (*US Air Force*)

Introduced in 1991 and based on the German Army's flecktarn design, this remains the standard combat uniform pattern of the Ground Forces. (*US Army*)

A copy of US tricolor desert, reduced slightly in size, is worn here by two Japanese military personnel that have deployed to Iraq in 2008. (*Private collection*)

This photo of a Japanese airman, taken in 2014, shows the digital design that replaced the earlier pattern of the JASDF in 2009. (*US Air Force*)

A Japanese officer working with a US Navy counterpart wears the desert version of the JNSDF camouflage design, now being worn by personnel deploying to arid regions of the world. (*US Navy*)

This NCO of the Japanese Maritime Self-Defense Force (JMSDF) wears the blue digital camouflage design currently being worn by that branch of service. (*US Navy*)

Formed in 1954 from elements of a National Security Force, the Japanese Self Defense Forces (JSDF) consist of Ground, Maritime, and Air Elements. In recent years, JSDF personnel have deployed to Cambodia, Iraq, Somalia, and Haiti. Solid color olive green uniforms were standard issue in the Japanese Self Defense Force until the early 1990s.

The Hashemite Kingdom of Jordan was formed in 1948 from elements of the British Mandate of Palestine and Transjordan. Jordan fought alongside Egypt, Syria and Iraq during the Six-Day War (June 1967) against Israel, and took part in the War of Attrition (with Egypt and the PLO) from July 1967 to 1970. As Palestinian groups operating within Jordan gained favor and recognition within the Arab world, increased fedayeen activities threatened the Jordanian monarchy's control of the country. A resulting military campaign known as Black September (mostly fought between 16 to 27 September 1970) resulted in the PLO being forced out of Jordan and into neighboring Lebanon. In 1973, Jordan sent a brigade to Syria during the Yom Kippur War, but did not engage Israel directly from its territory. It subsequently recognized the PLO as the legitimate representative of the Palestinian people. In 1994, it signed a peace treaty with Israel. The country presently makes great efforts to remain at peace with all of its neighbors and promotes diplomatic solutions to regional problems. Nevertheless, Jordan experienced three terrorist attacks against civilians in 2005, orchestrated by Al-Qaeda in retaliation for its peace agreement with Israel.

The Jordanian Armed Forces (JAF) were formed out of the old Arab Legion in 1956, and today consist of the Royal Jordanian Army, Air Force and Navy, as well as combined elements that fall under the Joint Special Operations Command. The JAF has been a long-standing and frequent contributor to United Nations peacekeeping missions, and has also supplied military and police training to a number of Arab Gulf States.

These Jordanian Special Forces personnel are wearing a copy of the US ERDL or 'leaf' pattern camouflage that was in use during the late 1970s and early 1980s. (*Private collection*)

Two Jordanian peacekeepers deployed with UNPROFOR wear a copy of US m81 woodland pattern camouflage that was adopted by the Jordanian Armed Forces in the late 1980s. (*Henrik Clausen*)

Camouflage Denison smocks were supplied by the UK and worn by the Special Service Group, a predecessor to the modern Jordanian special operations forces in the 1960s.

A derivative of the brushstroke design, this pattern was produced in South Korea and saw use with early Jordanian special forces units in the 1970s.

These Jordanian personnel serving with the UN are wearing the six-color 'chocolate chip' camouflage design also adopted by Jordan in the late 1980s. (*Private collection*)

The camouflage design seen here was issued primarily to Jordanian Air Force personnel. (*US Air Force*)

This DPM derivative pattern was worn by elements of the Public Security Directorate beginning in the early 1990s.

Adopted in 2005, the KA2 digital desert pattern (developed by Hyperstealth Industries ©) is now the standard operational uniform of the Jordanian Air and Land forces. (*US Army*)

A version of the KA2 design, adopted for Special Forces, is seen here. (*Private collection*)

This variation of the KA2 was developed for use by the Jordanian Royal Guards.

Wearing full riot gear in 2012, these members of the Public Security Directorate (PSD) wear an urban version of the KA2 pattern. (*Private collection*)

These marines of the 77th Marine Battalion wear the version of KA2 developed for the Royal Jordanian Navy. (*Private collection*)

A version of the KA2 developed for the Civil Defense Directorate.

Multicam was briefly adopted by Special Operations Command personnel (2012–14). (*Private collection*)

Adopted for the Joint Special Operations Command (JSOC) in 2015, the design seen here is highly derivative of Multicam but has some distinctive features of its own. (*US Air Force*)

Also adopted in 2015 and replacing the previous KA2 design, this variation of Multicam is now being worn by the PSD. (*Private collection*)

One of the former Soviet Republics that declared independence following the collapse of the USSR in 1991, the Republic of Kazakhstan has continued to exist under authoritarian rule into the present era. The president is commander in chief of all the armed forces and has full veto power over any legislation passed by the bicameral parliament.

The Armed forces of Kazakhstan were initially inherited from the Soviet units of the old Turkestan district. Presently it consists of the Ground Forces, Air Force, Air Defense Forces, Naval Forces (operating on the Caspian Sea), the Republican Guard, and the National Guard. The National Security Committee

This early photograph of Kazakh personnel shows the use of both surplus East German strichtarn pattern uniforms, and the continued use of Soviet-era KLMK berezhka pattern coveralls. (*Private collection*)

Seen here during an exchange with US counterparts, Kazakh soldiers wear a variation of the Soviet butane pattern generally associated with Uzbekistan. (*US Marine Corps*)

This photo of a Kazakh paratrooper shows the use of woodland camouflage, adopted in the mid-1990s. (*Private collection*)

Variations of 'leaf' camouflage patterns, many incorporating bright green and yellow hues, emerged in the early 2000s and are still in use by personnel of the Forest Guards. (*Private collection*)

This unique variation of the six-color 'chocolate chip' pattern was first observed on Kazakh personnel that deployed to Iraq circa 2003–04. The pattern saw service for a number of years but has now fallen into disuse. (*Private collection*)

(UQK) operates its own Internal Security Troops, Border Guards, Military Counterintelligence, the Foreign Intelligence Bureau and a number of special operations units. Kazakhstan is a founding member of Collective Security Treaty Organization (CSTO) and the Shanghai Cooperative Organization (SC), has an Individual Partnership Action Plan with NATO and a strategic cooperation agreement with the Turkish Armed Forces. In 2013, the country announced it would begin sending officers to support peacekeeping efforts.

An officer of the Kazakhstan National Guards here wears a large pixilated design that originally came out of Russia. This has seen extensive use with personnel of the NG. (*Kazakhstan Ministry of Defense*)

This blue variation of the 'leaf' pattern has been worn by some units of the National Security Committee and the National Guards. (*Private collection*)

The country adopted its own digital pattern, based around the UCP of the US Army, circa 2008–09. This photo illustrates the wide range of variations that are in circulation, with different shades of brown, grey and green. This pattern is now standard issue to the armed forces. (*Kazakhstan Ministry of Defense*)

These members of the special operations forces wear the Russian 'SS-Leto' design. (*Private collection*)

Kazakh special forces have also made extensive use of Multicam in recent years. (*Kazakhstan Ministry of Defense*)

This digital desert pattern is also in use with some special operations troops and may also be worn by conventional peacekeeping forces. (*Kazakhstan Ministry of Defense*)

KUWAIT

Kuwait achieved independence in 1961 after Britain ended its protectorate status. The country supported Iraq during the Iran-Iraq War, but refused to forgive the debt incurred by Iraq, thus creating tensions between the two nations. In August 1990, Iraq invaded Kuwait, alleging the country had been stealing oil from a field near its border by slant drilling. Although Kuwait forces put up a stiff resistance, they were quickly overwhelmed by the Iraqis, with those units that had not been overrun retreating into neighboring Saudi Arabia. The Iraqi occupation was universally condemned, and when Iraqi forces refused to withdraw at the end of 1990, the United States and a coalition of Arab and other states led its own assault on Iraqi forces (Persian Gulf War) and pushed them back into Iraq. The country was declared liberated on 25 February 1991.

Kuwait rebuilt its military with the assistance of the United States, Britain and France, all of whom signed defense cooperation agreements. Although it did not send any military personnel into Iraq during the Iraq War, the country was used as a staging point for coalition forces. Thousands of US military personnel continue to be hosted here.

The Kuwaiti Armed Forces consist of the Land Forces, Naval Forces, and Air Forces, as well as the Emiri Guard, Military Police, and the independent Kuwaiti National Guard. Falling under the jurisdiction of the Ministry of the Interior are the Kuwaiti Police, Land Border Force, and the Coast Guard.

This two-color camouflage pattern (probably Egyptian in origin) was in use with some Kuwaiti units by 1962, and possibly earlier.

This four-color desert DPM pattern was in use with the Kuwaiti Army prior to the 1990 invasion by Iraq.

A variation of the DPM pattern with blue colorway was worn by the Ministry of the Interior during the same time period.

Although it was in service prior to the 1990 invasion, this two color camouflage pattern has remained in service with the 25th Commando brigade into the modern era.

This variation of six-color 'chocolate chip' camouflage is believed to have been worn by the Kuwaiti Marines prior to the First Gulf War.

Another pattern in use with Kuwait prior to the war is this blue-dominant variation of six-color desert, although it is not known which service wore it.

Taken in 1991, this photo shows an officer of the Kuwaiti Security Forces wearing standard six-color desert camouflage fatigues (probably Saudi in origin), while behind him a guard is wearing the unique 'barbed wire' variant of that pattern that pre-dates the Gulf War. (*Private collection*)

Kuwaiti Navy personnel, alongside American counterparts, wear the tricolor desert camouflage pattern adopted by the Armed Forces after 1991. (*US Navy*)

This unique pattern was adopted by the Kuwait National Guard after the 1991 invasion, and can be seen in this photo in two slightly different color variations. (*US Army*)

The Kuwaiti Police have continued to wear a blue-dominant version of DPM, but with a slightly darker color scheme. (*Private collection*)

Cadets of the Kuwaiti Police Academy wear a two-color variation of the DPM design. (*Private collection*)

Adopted circa 2002–03, this pattern is worn by the Royal Emiri Guard. (*Private collection*)

A variation of the British desert DPM pattern is worn by the Land Border Forces. (*Kuwaiti Ministry of Defense*)

These Kuwaiti Army officers wear the desert digital pattern adopted by Kuwaiti Armed Forces in 2006. (*US Army*)

This Kuwaiti Commando wears a version of an old design that is likely to have been in the Kuwaiti supply system prior to the First Gulf War. Circa 2017 the camouflage design was reintroduced into service with Kuwaiti SF personnel. (*Kuwaiti Ministry of Defense*)

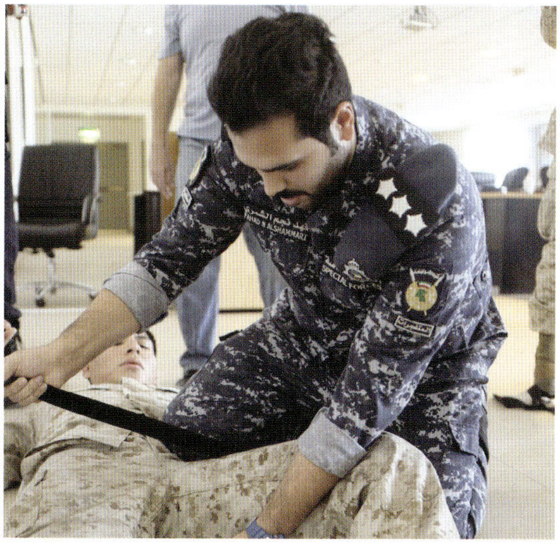

A Kuwaiti Ministry of Interior EOD technician is seen here in the blue-dominant digital pattern now issued to that branch of service. (*US Marine Corps*)

Two more digital patterns, both introduced in 2017 for the Kuwaiti National Guard. The design on the right is simply a pixilated version of the old amoeba pattern. (*Kuwaiti Ministry of Defense*)

KYRGYZSTAN

A former Soviet republic, Kyrgyzstan became an independent nation state on 25 December 1991, one day before the Soviet Union dissolved. The nation is officially known as the Kyrgyz Republic. In the new millennium, the country has experienced political instability, including the assassination of four members of parliament in 2005 and 2006. In April 2010, civil unrest over corruption and increased living expenses escalated into violent clashes with police that left at least eighty people dead and several hundred hospitalized.

Clashes between ethnic Kyrgyz and Uzbeks in June 2010 sparked fear of a civil war, with a state of emergency being declared in the Jalal-Abad region. As

This TTsKO variant pattern was worn during the formative period into the mid-1990s by many Kyrgyz troops. (*Private collection*)

Surplus East German strichtarn pattern uniforms were also in use during the 1990s.

Russian-made flora pattern camouflage was worn between 1998 and 2006.

This leaf type camouflage design has also been documented in use with Kyrgyz military personnel.

These young Army soldiers wear a copy of US m81 woodland, variations of which have been in use since the late 1990s. (*US DOD*)

These troops from the 25th Special Forces Brigade wear the pixilated version of Russian skol pattern, worn by units of the Armed Forces since 2012. The normal version has also been documented in use. (*Private collection*)

Additional personnel of the 25th Special Forces Brigade are seen here wearing the Russian berezhka camouflage design. (*Private collection*)

Taken in 2012, this photo shows the use of an Asian-made copy of German flecktarn now being worn by many Kyrgyz personnel. (*Private collection*)

This digital camouflage design was adopted in 2016 and is very similar to the one used by neighboring Kazakhstan. (*Private collection*)

Various blue-dominant camouflage designs are worn by Ministry of Interior personnel. (*Private collection*)

many as 30,000 Uzbeks fled to neighboring Uzbekistan to escape the violence, which claimed more than 100 lives. An international commission reported in January 2011 that the clashes were part of an organized effort to split the nation along ethnic lines.

Originally formed from units of the former Soviet Military District of Turkestan, the Armed Forces consist of the Army, Air Force, and National Guard, as well units controlled by the Ministry of the Interior (Internal Troops and Frontier Forces).

LAOS

Following the Second World War, the status of Laos was uncertain, with Lao nationalists initially declaring independence, but French troops reoccupying and resuming control in early 1946. The communist Pathet Lao arose in 1950 as a resistance movement to the French occupation. The resulting insurgency, at the height of the First Indochina War, put pressure on France to grant the country semi-autonomy, and, later, full independence as a constitutional monarchy in 1953. Meanwhile, the Pathet Lao continued to vie for control of the country as a communist state, receiving assistance from North Vietnam and the Soviet Union, as the Royal Lao Army and indigenous tribal groups were supported by the United States. By 1962, the country had descended into

Laotian airborne and commando formations used French tenue de leópard uniforms during the colonial period, and these were also worn by FAR elite units. (*Private collection*)

Members of the 1er Bataillon de Parachutistes wear surplus US M1942 frogskin pattern camouflage uniforms. (*Private collection*)

Surplus British Army camouflage uniforms were worn by elements of the 2e Bataillon de Parachutistes from 1954–57.

The US-supplied SGUs frequently wore civilian duck hunter pattern camouflage fatigues, or South Vietnamese-made beo-gam and ERDL/leaf pattern uniforms.

full scale civil war, with part of the country occupied by North Vietnamese troops, and US forces providing clandestine support of anti-communist forces, while at the same time waging a bombing campaign across the border from South Vietnam. With the assistance of North Vietnamese forces, the Pathet Lao won a strategic victory in 1968, leaving the remnants of the Royal Lao Army scattered and in disarray, although the US bombing campaign continued into 1974 and curtailed a full takeover of the government. When the United States pulled out of Southeast Asia in 1975, the royalist Lao government was overthrown by the Pathet Lao (assisted by the Vietnamese People's Army and the Soviet Union). The country then changed its name to the Lao People's Democratic Republic, which it retains.

Under the Laotian monarchy the armed forces were known as the Forces Armées du Royaume (FAR), and consisted of Land, Air and Maritime elements modeled after French formations. These included a number of airborne, commando and special guerilla units (SGUs). All of these elements were eradicated or disbanded following the establishment of the communist government. Formed in 1975, the current Lao People's Armed Forces consist of the Army (including a small naval force) and Air Force. It receives military assistance from neighboring Vietnam, and has continued to wage a counter-insurgency campaign against ethnic Hmong and anti-communist Lao forces into the present era.

This Laotian Army soldier wears a distinctive yellowish woodland-leaf pattern camouflage uniform. It was not until 2009 that the Laotian People's Armed Forces adopted the use of camouflage. (*Private collection*)

Use of camouflage by Laotian forces was almost entirely a practice of the pre-communist era. Indeed, until quite recently, the LPAF wore only solid color uniforms and had no camouflage at all in its inventory.

Lebanon emerged from the Second World War an already established free and independent state, but an unwritten national pact had placed key government positions in the hands of specific religious and/or ethnic groups, with slight favor to Christians over others. This would affect Lebanese politics for many years to come. Although Lebanon supported the coalition forces during the Arab-Israeli War by supplying logistics and war materiel, Lebanese forces did not cross over into Israel. In the aftermath, more than 100,000 Palestinians that had fled the conflict were refused re-entry into Israel and forced to remain in Lebanon, many of them in refugee camps. The Palestine Liberation Organization (PLO) emerged out of this poverty and homelessness. In 1970, when Jordan ousted thousands of Palestinians (including many fedayeen), most fled into Lebanon. The border with Israel became a lawless area from which PLO factions mounted their operations. The Palestinian situation only compounded already existing political and ethnic rivalries, leading the country down the road to a civil war that lasted from 1975 to 1990.

As many as fifty different militias and paramilitary organizations have operated out of Lebanon at one time.

Camouflage of Lebanese Armed Forces

The vertical stripe or brushstroke pattern worn here by an officer of the Magaweer commandos, was probably derived from designs that emerged during the civil war period. (*Private collection*)

A kind of 'brushstroke' design was adopted by special units during civil war and later by Moukafaha Regiment, seen in this photograph. (*Private collection*)

Woodland pattern camouflage has been worn by LAF units since the mid-1980s, when it was provided by the US as part of a military training program. The pattern remains the standard for conventional units. (*US Army*)

The two DPM-derivative patterns seen in this photo are worn by the General Security Directorate (GSD) and the Internal Security Forces (ISF), respectively. The former first appeared in late 1980s. (*Lebanon General Directorate of Security*)

Another DPM derivative is worn here by the Civil Defense Directorate in 2012. (*Private collection*)

This brown digital pattern was adopted in 2007 for use by the Airborne Regiment, but was soon discontinued. (*Private collection*)

By 2012, the Magaweer Commando Regiment had begun to wear this copy of USMC temperate MARPAT. (*Private collection*)

Adopted by the Lebanese Navy Marine Commandos, the UCP design is now being worn. (*Private collection*)

Two additional digital patterns adopted by the GSD/ISF in 2011, are seen here. The brown pattern is associated with the Al-Fouhoud (Black Panthers) unit. (*Lebanon General Directorate of Security*)

The Moujawkal Airborne Regiment adopted a copy of the USMC desert MARPAT camouflage in 2011, replacing its earlier brown digital design. (*Private collection*)

A pixilated version of the old DPM pattern has now been adopted by the GSD, seen here being worn by its commanding officer. (*Lebanon General Directorate of Security*)

This unusual black-grey digital pattern is now being worn by a special unit of the GSD. (*Lebanon General Directorate of Security*)

First observed in 2017, some units of the Lebanese Armed Forces are now wearing Multicam. (*Private collection*)

A member of the Druze Progressive Socialist Party (PSP) seen here wears a strange brushstroke pattern of undetermined origins. (*Private collection*)

At various points, the country was completely split along factional lines, with specific regions under the control of particularly strong paramilitary units. Although a complete list of such organizations is unfeasible to reproduce due to space considerations, some of the major players in the civil war were the Lebanese Front (Christian coalition), Lebanese National Movement, Palestine Liberation Organization (including a dozen or more factions), Palestine Liberation Army (supported by Egypt/Syria), Amal, Hezbollah, Islamic Jihad, and the Tawheed. In addition to the militias, both Israel and Syria played major parts in the civil war, which also involved the Lebanese Armed Forces, and the intervention of the United Nations from 1978 to 1990.

The Republic of Lebanon has remained largely stable since the end of the civil war. The Lebanese Armed Forces today consist of the Ground Forces, Air Force, and Naval Forces. The Special Operations Command is a joint command including elite units from all services. The Internal Security Forces are a gendarmerie type organization tasked with internal security, law enforcement, intelligence and counter-terrorism, and includes its own special operations unit.

Camouflage of Paramilitary Forces

A vast majority of the camouflage patterns worn by paramilitary factions are detailed in the section on Palestine and will not be repeated here. However, some units that were active solely within the borders of Lebanon did have their own designs as well.

The Phalange Lebanese Forces primarily wore solid color uniforms, but there was some use of this South Korean duck hunter pattern. (*Private collection*)

These members of the PSP wear Pakistani brushstroke uniforms. (*Private collection*)

Two PSP militiamen wearing surplus German Army splittermuster pattern camouflage field jackets in 1984. (*Private collection*)

MALAYSIA

Malaysia initially came into being in 1948, when the short-lived Malayan Union (a British crown colony) was dissolved and replaced by the Federation of Malaya, a confederation of protectorates that restored autonomy to the traditional symbolic rulers of the Malaysian states. Under the Malayan Union, all ethnic groups had equal rights, but this was opposed by many traditional Malays and one of the reasons the Union was dissolved. Ethnic Chinese in particular viewed this as a betrayal, and many saw communist ideals as a means of achieving fair treatment. The Malayan National Liberation Army (MNLA), already experienced in guerilla warfare against the Japanese during the Second World War, and comprised mostly of Chinese communists, eventually brought about an armed revolt (the Malayan Emergency) that lasted until 1960. This conflict was largely a guerilla campaign, pitting British and Commonwealth forces against the communist-supported MNLA.

The Celoreng Harimau Kumbang (panther camouflage) design seen here was tested to replace brushstroke between 1993 and 1994 only and was never officially adopted.

A distinctive Malaysian brushstroke pattern was introduced in the 1970s and worn until 1994 by the Armed Forces. Seen here in a photo from 2014, it is still being worn by the Johor Defense Forces. (*Private collection*)

A replacement for the brushstroke pattern was introduced in 1994 and became the standard camouflage design of the armed services until 2003. (*Ministry of Defense – Malaysia*)

The Navy's elite PASKAL commando unit has worn a copy of US m81 woodland pattern since 2000. (*Private collection*)

The Bomba dan Penyelamat (BOMBA), or National Fire and Rescue Service, wear this orange and black patterned camouflage operational uniform. (*Private collection*)

This pattern was worn by the Royal Malaysian Police General Operations Forces (Pasukan Gerakan Am) – formerly the Police Field Force (PFF) – from 1990–2005.

A garish, blue and white striped pattern is worn by those completing the National Service program and was first adopted in 2003. (*Private collection*)

Introduced in 2005, the pattern seen here was chosen to replace the old bright blue General Operations Forces design. (*Royal Malaysia Police*)

Members of MALBATT 4 deploying to Lebanon with the UN wear the desert camouflage pattern introduced in 2006. (*United Nations*)

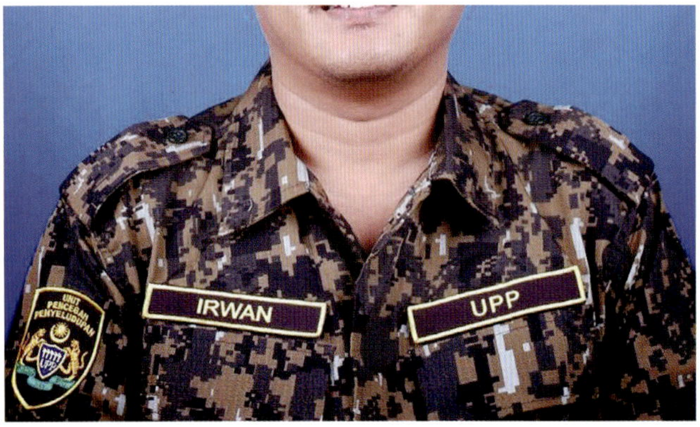

A pixilated pattern worn by the Anti-smuggling Unit (UPP) of the Malaysian Maritime Force. (*Private collection*)

Both the Navy PASKAL and the MMEA Special Tasks and Rescue (STAR) unit wear the Universal Camouflage Pattern (UCP) in some capacities. (*Private collection*)

A digital version of the old PDRM (Royal Malaysian Police Force) design has been in service since 2012. (*Private collection*)

This two-tone grey dominant pattern is worn by the Jabatan Imigresen Malaysia (Malaysian Immigration Service). (*Private collection*)

Members of the 15th Royal Malaysian Regiment wearing the pixilated camouflage design adopted for the Army in 2013. (*Ministry of Defense – Malaysia*)

Personnel deploying for service overseas wear a desert version of the current design. (*Private collection*)

A distinctive digital pattern for the Royal Malaysian Navy was adopted in 2016. (*US DOD*)

A pattern for the Air Force was also adopted in 2016. (*Private collection*)

In 1957 Malaysia became an independent member of the British Commonwealth. In September 1963, federation was extended to North Borneo (Sabah), Sarawak, and Singapore. This federation was opposed by communists in Sarawak, leading to another insurgency that lasted from 1962 until 1990. Meanwhile, tensions heightened with Indonesia over the Sabah region, resulting in an armed confrontation stretching through to 1966, when the federation was ultimately accepted by Indonesia. Although the guerilla war with the MNLA had formally ceased in 1960, the paramilitary group had been training for a future offensive, which they resumed in 1968. Lasting twenty-one years, a peace accord was finally reached in December 1989, under which the Malaysian Communist Party was dissolved.

The Malaysian Armed Forces are known as Angkatan Tentera Malaysia (ATM) and consist of the Army, Navy and Air Force. A national service program was implemented in 2004. The Polis Diraja Malaysia (PDRM) or Royal Malaysian Police are a centralized federal police force.

The Republic of Maldives is a chain of atolls lying in the Indian Ocean to the southwest of the subcontinent. It remained a British protectorate until achieving full political independence in 1965. In the 1980s, the country experienced three separate attempts to wrest control from the republic via coup d'etat. The third attempt in 1988 met with initial success after the airport was seized, but intervention by paratroops from India restored control during Operation Cactus. In the modern era, growing political and social unrest fueled by pro-Islamic sentiments led to a mutiny by elements of the army and police in February 2012. The president was arrested, convicted of terrorism, and sentenced to prison. Subsequent elections in 2013 were annulled by the Supreme Court and rerun with a different result and the appointment of Abdulla Yameen as president. His anti-West, pro-Islam policies were popular with some, but resulted in a botched assassination attempt in 2015 and subsequent crackdown against political dissent.

The Maldives National Defense Force (MNDF) was formed in 2006 after the National Security Service was divided into branches for domestic law enforcement and national defense. The MNDF consists of the Coast Guard, Marine Corps, Special Forces, Service Corps, and the Corps of Engineers. The Maldives Police Service is responsible for domestic and internal security.

Members of the MNDF photographed in 2014 wear the leaf pattern camouflage that was in service with this country for years. (*US Navy*)

A very bright, blue design is in use with the Emergency Response Team of the National Police Service. (*Private collection*)

Members of the Special Forces Team of the MNDF wearing Multicam. (*Private collection*)

An officer of the MNDF wearing a newly adopted digital camouflage design in 2015. (*Private collection*)

Mongolia emerged from the Second World War divided into an independent socialist state (outer Mongolia) and an autonomous region (inner Mongolia) within the Republic of China. Both Russia and China exercised political pressure to prevent the two Mongolias from reuniting, which remains an issue today. The Mongolian People's Republic maintained close relations with the USSR and permitted the stationing of Soviet troops on its soil until they began to withdraw in 1987. Its political system began to loosen following the collapse of the Soviet Union. After a series of peaceful demonstrations and hunger strikes in 1990, the authoritarian government resigned without protest and a multi-party system and new constitution were instated in 1992.

The Mongolian Armed Forces consist of the General Purpose Force, Air Force, Border Defense Force and the Internal Security Force. Mongolia contributed military personnel to the Iraq War as part of the Multinational Force. It has been an active participant in peacekeeping efforts in recent years, participating in missions to Sierra Leone, Ethiopia, Congo, Eritrea, Western Sahara and Liberia, as well as the ongoing ISAF effort in Afghanistan.

This brown camouflage design was the standard pattern of the General Purpose Force for many years. (*Private collection*)

A contingent of Mongolian personnel deployed to Iraq in 2005–06 wore US tricolor desert pattern camouflage uniforms. (*Private collection*)

The first camouflage design of the Border Defense Force was adopted in the 1990s and worn until 2007.

The second pattern of the Border Defense Force was adopted in 2007. (*Private collection*)

A digital version of the old GPF pattern was adopted in 2011. (*United Nations*)

A digital version of the Border Defense Force camouflage pattern was adopted in 2012. (*Ben Playford collection*)

These heavyweight, extreme cold weather parkas in use with the Border Guards are printed in a woodland-type camouflage design with grey colorway. (*Private collection*)

Members of the GPF 84th Airborne Brigade are now wearing a copy of the USMC temperate MARPAT design. (*Ministry of Defense of Mongolia*)

MYANMAR

Officially the Republic of the Union of Myanmar, this nation was known as Burma from the imperial period until 1989. In the aftermath of the Second World War, Burma became a British protectorate, but it was granted independence just three years later. In March of 1962, a military coup d'etat led by General Ne Win wrested control of the nation from the legitimate government and installed a one-party socialist state that remained in power until 1987. A collective series of protests, demonstrations and riots in 1988, known as the 8888 Uprising, resulted in thousands of civilian deaths and the installation of a new government under military junta calling itself the State Law and Order Restoration Council. In 1989 the name of the country was officially changed to Myanmar.

Renamed the State Peace and Development Council (SPDC) in 1997, the military junta retained control of the nation for years, nullifying election results, suppressing political dissent, and fending off insurgency movements. Although the junta was dissolved in 2011, it was not until 2016 that the first civilian since 1962 was installed as president.

Myanmar has been in a virtually constant state of civil war since 1948, mostly reflecting the struggle of ethnic and religious minorities to gain fair representation or some degree of autonomy. More

This woodland variant pattern first appeared in 2005, worn by Army personnel. It is believed the pattern was for public appearances only. A tan version for Air Force and a blue version for Navy were also observed. (*Private collection*)

This copy of m81 woodland camouflage appeared in the early 2000s, first as a field jacket worn by officers, and later as a full uniform worn by the Special Operations Task Force. By 2009 the pattern was being worn by conventional units as well. (*Private collection*)

Seen in this photo only as a helmet cover, this camouflage design was also worn as a full uniform by some elements of the People's Police Force. (*Private collection*)

First observed in 2016, a digital woodland camouflage design is now being worn by the Army. (*Private collection*)

Also introduced in 2016, this blue digital pattern is issued to the Myanmar Navy. (*Private collection*)

Air Force pattern, introduced alongside the Army and Navy in 2016. (*Private collection*)

This camouflage design is worn by the Myanmar Border Guard Police. (*Private collection*)

These soldiers of the Democratic Karen Buddhist Army are wearing tiger stripe pattern uniforms, presumably imported from Thailand. (*Private collection*)

Camouflage in Use with Insurgent Forces

Thai-made tiger stripe pattern uniforms were in service with the Shan State Army in the 1980s.

Members of the Shan State Army here wear a camouflage design featuring a tiger motif embedded into the pattern. (*Private collection*)

The KNLA have worn Thai-made ERDL and 'oakleaf' camouflage since mid-1980s.

Another camouflage design worn the KNLA in 1990s is this green woodland pattern, reputedly made in Cambodia.

Several types of camouflage worn by the Ta'ang National Liberation Army (TNLA), including woodland and a strange dark olive/black pattern. (*Private collection*)

Fighters of the Arakan Army have been documented wearing this digital camouflage design of unknown origins. (*Private collection*)

Another camouflage design worn by Arakan Army fighters is this digital tiger stripe pattern of Chinese origins. (*Private collection*)

These Arakan Army leaders are wearing Chinese PLA Type 07 pattern uniforms. (*Private collection*)

The Kachin Independence Army has worn old-pattern Chinese Army woodland uniforms for many years. (*Private collection*)

Members of the Kachin Independence Army here wear a DPM-like camouflage design, presumably the same one observed in the Arakan Army. (*Private collection*)

than sixteen different insurgent groups have been in conflict with the government of Myanmar since 1949, including the Karenni Army (KNPP), Karen National Liberation Army (KNU), Mon National Liberation Army, Kachin Independence Army, Shan State Army (North and South), All Burma Student's Democratic Front, Myanmar National Democratic Alliance Army, National Democratic Alliance Army, United Wa State Army, Ta'ang National Liberation Army, Arakan Army, and the Arakan Rohingya Salvation Army. Funding and assistance for the groups has been through various sources, with considerable materiel coming from China and Thailand.

The Burmese Armed Forces are known as the Tatmadaw, and consist of the Myanmar Army, Navy, Air Force and Police Force. People's Militia units also exist, as well as Frontier Units called Na Sa Kha. Historically, the Armed Forces of this nation have not worn any type of camouflage uniform. Circa 2005, a series of three patterns emerged during public military parades, and since that time quite a few additional designs have been documented in used by units of the Tatmadaw. By contrast, the insurgent movements have traditionally adopted many camouflage patterns imported from Thailand, China and other sources.

NEPAL

Unlike many of its neighbors, Nepal has retained its sovereignty throughout the modern era. The country has experimented with several forms of government since the 1950s, including a traditional self-governing 'partyless' Panchayat system that lasted from 1960 until 1990, when a people's movement pressured the monarchy to accept constitutional reforms and adopt a multi-party system. Between 1996 and 2006, the Communist Party of Nepal waged a civil war against the government in an attempt to establish a people's republic. By the end of the war, the Maoist movement had agreed to renounce violence in exchange for democratic reforms. In 2012, the remnants of the People's Liberation Army (armed wing of the CPN) integrated with the Nepalese Army.

The Nepalese Armed Forces consist of the Nepalese Army and the much smaller Nepalese Army Air Service. Nepal has been involved with United Nations peacekeeping efforts since 1958 and has deployed personnel to Lebanon, Somalia, Haiti, Sierra Leone, Sudan and East Timor. The Nepalese Armed Police Force is a paramilitary agency responsible for law enforcement, internal security and counter-insurgency duties.

The earliest camouflage pattern of Nepal is seen here; it was copied from the Japanese design and utilized by the Airborne Battalion in the 1980s.

Another variation of the Japanese pattern is seen here, produced on thinner material with poorly matched dyes.

The third incarnation of this camouflage design saw a brighter color scheme that was utilized in the 1990s.

The current camouflage design of the Nepalese Army was introduced around 2000 and is still being worn. (*US Marine Corps*)

Seen here with an Indian counterpart, this Nepalese UN peacekeeper wears the first pattern camouflage of the Police. (*United Nations*)

A blue DPM variant is also worn by the Nepal Police. (*Private collection*)

NORTH KOREA

Following the Second World War, the Korean peninsula was divided in two zones along the 38th parallel, with the northern half occupied by the Soviet Union and the southern half occupied by the United States. Land reforms were immediately instituted in the North, and many fled to the south to escape retaliation. The Democratic People's Republic of Korea was officially established in 1948. At Soviet urging, and with an eye to unifying Korea under socialism, North Korea invaded and quickly overran the south in June 1950, ushering in the Korean War. In response, a United Nations force led by the United States intervened, pushed the DPRK forces out of the south and swiftly advanced towards the border with China. When Chinese forces stepped in to support the North, allied forces were pushed back again. By July 1953, an armistice was signed by all sides and the original boundaries of the two nations were restored, with a heavily guarded Demilitarized Zone imposed as a buffer to ease tensions. In subsequent years, relations with South Korea have been marked by subterfuge, political intrigue, border skirmishes and saber rattling. An attempt at establishing discussions to work towards peaceful reunification failed in 1973.

The country has been headed by a member of the Kim family since it became a Democratic Republic. Efforts by both the USSR and China to replace Kim Il-sun were resisted, although the country maintained alignment with both nations for years. His successor Kim Jong-il adopted a policy of Songun (military

The earliest use of camouflage by this country was Soviet M1944 TTsMKK by reconnaissance and special operations units during 1960s and 70s. (*Private collection*)

first), which greatly increased the country's military resources, strengthened state security, restricted travel and may have been responsible for the country's inability to avoid famine in the late 1990s. Upon his death in 2011 he was succeeded by his son Kim Jong-un, who has continued the Songun policy, to include ballistic missile and nuclear weapons development programs.

The Korean People's Army (KPA) is the term for the complete military forces of North Korea, including the Ground Force, Naval Force, Air & Air Defense Force, Strategic Rocket Force, Special Operations Force, and the Red Guards.

The vertical stripe pattern seen in this photograph from 2005 is probably of Chinese origin. (*Private collection*)

A duck hunter camouflage pattern has been documented in use by North Korean personnel, although most of the photos appear to be propagandistic in nature. (*Private collection*)

A camouflage design with arid coloration, possibly for troops deployed to desert or mountainous regions. (*Private collection*)

A dark leaf camouflage design from 2012. (*Private collection*)

Snow camouflage issued to North Korean winter warfare troops. (*Private collection*)

Special Forces personnel wearing woodland camouflage uniforms with body armor vests in a pixilated camouflage design similar to UCP. (*Private collection*)

First observed in 2016–17, a blue-dominant camouflage pattern is also worn by some North Korean units, possibly Navy or Air Force personnel. (*Private collection*)

OMAN

The Sultanate of Oman is an absolute monarchy under hereditary leader Sultan Qaboos bin Said al Said, who deposed his father, Said bin Taimur, in 1970. With the assistance of British forces, Sultan bin Taimur (at the time, Sultan of Muscat) wrested control of the Imamate of Oman from the Ibadi rulers in 1959, solidifying his rule over the entire region. Although the Arab League and United Nations were both petitioned for recognition of the old Imamate of Oman, the cause was dropped in the 1970s. Between 1962 and 1976 a rebellion surged in the Dhofar region, pitting leftist insurgents against the Sultan's Armed Forces (supported by Iran and the UK). On 23 July 1970, Sultan bin Taimur was deposed by his son in a bloodless coup, which would bring about a number of social, educational and military reforms. Although the insurgency continued for several years, ultimately the rebels were defeated.

In the 1980s a DPM variation was designed specifically for Oman Ground Forces, having elements of black, orange-brown, very light olive green and khaki. A number of variations were produced, but the pattern remained consistent until the very late 1990s. (*Private collection*)

British DPM uniforms were introduced to the country via British military advisors in the 1970s. This photo from 1976 shows Sultan bin Qaboos himself and several of his personal guard wearing what are probably still British-sourced uniforms. (*Private collection*)

The Sultan's Armed Forces (SAF) follow a British model and have historically relied heavily on British training and military assistance. The SAF consist of the Royal Army, Royal Air Force, Royal Navy, Royal

The current version of the Ground Forces pattern now has stronger orange elements that have replaced the earlier green color. (*US Army*)

The Royal Guard has continued to wear standard UK DPM pattern, but with a distinctive coloration seen here. (*Sultan of Oman Ministry of Defense*)

Members of the Royal Air Force band wear the yellow-tinted DPM version worn by that branch since the early 2000s. (*Private collection*)

Photographed alongside colleagues from Bahrain, these three soldiers of the Royal Oman Special Forces wear the distinctive DPM pattern of that service. (*Sultan of Oman Ministry of Defense*)

A Royal Oman Navy EOD technician wearing the unique brown-ochre DPM pattern adopted in the early 2000s. (*US DOD*)

This distinctive purple DPM pattern is worn by the Royal Oman Police. (*Private collection*)

Civilian technicians, mechanics and other expert employees of the Ministry of Defense, wear a DPM variation with light brown background. (*Sultan of Oman Ministry of Defense*)

The pipe band of the Royal Court Affairs here wears their green-tinted DPM pattern. (*Sultan of Oman Ministry of Defense*)

Guard, and the Sultan's Special Force. A number of additional branches serve paramilitary and support functions. The Royal Oman Police are responsible for internal security and law enforcement. Although a wide number of camouflage patterns have been worn by the Armed Forces and paramilitary units of Oman, they are all based around the original British Disruptive Pattern Material (DPM) design from the 1960s.

PAKISTAN

Following the Second World War, a popular movement pressured the British government into granting independence to India, and forcing the breakup of the old British Raj. Under terms agreed to by the British government and representatives of India's nationalists, the state of Pakistan was created as a homeland for India's Muslim population, comprising the provinces of Balochistan, East Bengal, West Punjab, Sindh, and the Northwest Frontier. A period of religious persecution and genocide followed in both India and Pakistan, resulting in hundreds of thousands of deaths, and as many as 10 million individuals displaced during a mass migration.

Pakistan has engaged India militarily on three separate occasions (1947, 1965 and 1999) in a land dispute over the Kashmir region, all without any resolution. During the 1960s, a pattern of ethnic, linguistic and cultural discrimination had developed in Pakistan, resulting in calls for independence by East Pakistan (East Bengal). The subsequent Bangladesh War of Liberation lasted eight months and again brought India into conflict with Pakistani forces on the side of the provisional government of Bangladesh. By December 1971 the war had come to an end, and Bangladesh was declared an independent state in 1972. Nevertheless, the peace existing between India and Pakistan is tenuous at best.

A period of democracy embraced under Zulfikar Ali Bhutto came to an end with a military coup d'etat in July 1977, replacing Bhutto with Army General Muhammad Zia-ul-Haq. This change in government heralded in a much more conservative, pro-Islamist, anti-communist regime. Control of the government shifted back and forth throughout the late 1980s and 1990s, but during the Kargil War with India in 1999 another bloodless coup put General Pervez Musharraf in power, a position he retained until 2008.

The Armed Forces of Pakistan are the eighth largest in the world, comprising the Army, Navy and Air Force. Although the government of Pakistan has maintained a strong anti-terrorist policy, many of the tribal areas are believed to provide a base for Muslim extremists (particularly those bordering Afghanistan). The Pakistani MOD has shifted troop placements since 2004 to help address this issue. Military personnel also have a strong presence overseas as part of peacekeeping missions, military training teams, and mutual defense agreements, particularly in Arab countries. Pakistan has deployed with the United Nations in the modern era to the Congo (DRC), Liberia, Burundi, Côte d'Ivoire and the Sudan. The use of camouflage by Pakistan Armed Forces has been widespread and varied, much like its neighbor India.

Adopted in the 1970s during the Bhutto regime, this brushstroke camouflage pattern saw widespread usage by PAF and also has been exported to several nations.

The elite Special Service Group (SSG) has worn a copy of the British DPM pattern since the late 1980s or early 1990s. (*Private collection*)

Initially worn by the SSG, woodland camouflage was later integrated into the armed services and has been worn by conventional personnel serving abroad as well as some units within Pakistan such as these Air Force Security personnel. (*Private collection*)

These Pakistan Navy personnel wear a blue-green camouflage design, adopted in 2000s for this branch of service. (*Private collection*)

This arid design has been in use with the Army since 2004. (*Ministry of Defense*)

Various 'leaf' camouflage designs have been worn by Pakistani personnel since the late 1990s. (*US Army*)

A copy of the US six-color desert pattern is generally associated with the Sindh Rangers Regiment (Border Security), but has also been worn by elements of the SSG. (*Private collection*)

A variation of the six-color design is worn by Pakistan Air Force personnel.

This arid design is worn by the Frontier Corps serving in the Baluchistan region. (*Private collection*)

A woodland variant pattern with grey color palette is also worn by some Pakistan Navy personnel. (*Private collection*)

A digital version of the earlier Pakistan Army arid design was adopted in late 2012 and is now the standard operational and working uniform pattern. (*Private collection*)

Personnel of the Pakistan Air Force now wear a copy of the US Air Force digital tiger stripe design. (*Private collection*)

This digital camouflage design is worn by the Airport Security Force. (*Private collection*)

Members of the Strategic Plans Division Force (SPDF) wearing the copy of USMC temperate MARPAT unique to that agency.

This general of the Frontier Force wears the latest digital camouflage design of that Regiment. (*Private collection*)

The name Palestine historically refers to a region lying between the Mediterranean sea and the River Jordan. It can also refer to the British Mandate of Palestine, established by the League of Nations in 1922, which became the State of Israel in 1948, and sparked a decades-long struggle between Jews and Palestinians (as well as neighboring Arab states) for control of the region. Although Israel retains absolute authority over its territory, the establishment of the Palestinian National Authority (السلطة الوطنية الفلسطينية) in 1994 to administer the Palestinian territories within Israel, is considered a positive step towards addressing Palestinian rights of self-determination.

The Arabic term fedayeen (فدائيين), meaning 'men of sacrifice' or 'redeemers,' was first applied to Palestinian fighters by Egyptian President Gamal Abdel Nasser, who began arming and organizing small units for his own purposes beginning in 1955. Founded in 1964, the Palestine Liberation Organization was established as a political and paramilitary organization with the stated goal of the liberation of Palestine. Since 1974 it has considered the establishment of an independent Palestinian state of the highest priority. Paramilitary factions of the PLO have employed guerilla warfare tactics from bases in Jordan, Syria, Lebanon, and within Israel to attack Israeli military and civilian targets. Some ultra-militant groups are responsible for terrorist practices, including kidnappings, assassinations, bombings and the like. Although a Charter exists, there is no governing mechanism within the PLO, and a number of factions claiming membership have arisen since inception, many of them with incongruent goals and methods. The following list identifies some of the former and current member factions of the PLO: Al-Fatah, Popular Front for the Liberation of Palestine (PFLP), Democratic Front for the Liberation of Palestine (DFLP), Palestinian People's Party (PPP), Palestinian Liberation Front (PLF), Arab Liberation Front (ALF), As-Saiqa (al-Saika), Al-Fatah Revolutionary Council, Palestinian Popular Struggle Front (PPSF), Palestine Democratic Union, and the Palestinian Arab Front (PAF).

The Palestine Liberation Army (PLA) was formed in 1964 by Egyptian President Nasser but served primarily as a proxy force supporting its host governments. A substantial number of PLA members formed the core of the Palestinian National Security Forces in 1994.

Palestinian guerrilla units have always operated using whatever uniforms and equipment were available and

Both the Egyptian 'rocks' and two-color desert patterns were worn by the PLA and some PLO units from the 1960s to 1970s.

Al-Fatah fighters in 1968 wearing French lizard pattern camouflage uniforms. This pattern was also provided to PNSF in 1970s. (*Private collection*)

Dark lizard pattern variant worn by a Palestinian fighter during the withdrawal from Beirut in 1982.

Czechoslovakian-made mlok or 'salamander' camouflage uniforms were worn by various Palestinian groups from the 1970s to the 1990s.

This 'lizard' variant pattern, probably made in Syria, was worn by the PNSF and As-Saiqa commandos.

best suited to the environment, although it is worth noting that the PLO was one of the most well-financed guerrilla organizations in history. Although impossible to document every type of camouflage uniform utilized at one time by groups claiming to represent Palestinian causes, some factions and individual units did adopt particular camouflage designs for operational or impressionistic purposes.

Vertical 'lizard' patterns such as these were most commonly seen among PLO El-Fatah units.

Special units of the Palestine Civil Police are seen here wearing a blue DPM pattern seen commonly throughout the region. (*Private collection*)

Other woodland variants have been worn at different times by the PNSF. These include copies of the French CE woodland.

South Korean-made 'waves' camouflage was often worn by PLFP units.

This unique 'brushstroke' design was used by Palestinian forces and probably sourced from the PSP in Lebanon.

Seen here in use by Palestinian National Security Forces personnel, m81 woodland camouflage had been used at various times by the PLO as well. (*Private collection*)

Obtained through sources in Iraq, this 'leaf' or ERDL-type camouflage design was worn by the Arab Liberation Front.

Palestinian Forces, during 1982 withdrawal from Beirut, wearing full South-Korean made 'turtle shell' pattern camouflage uniforms. This pattern was also worn by As-Saiqa commando units.

PFLP troops in 2003 appeared during a parade wearing this unusual arid-woodland camouflage design. (*Private collection*)

This blue 'leaf' camouflage pattern was also worn by some Palestine Civil Police units for a period of time, although it appears to no longer be in service. (*Private collection*)

Some elements of the PNSF briefly wore the Jordanian KA2 digital camouflage design seen here.

Masked member of the Al-Quds Brigade wearing a digital camouflage design of undetermined origins. (*Private collection*)

PHILIPPINES

The Republic of the Philippines was officially recognized as an independent nation through the Treaty of Manila, signed 4 July 1946. At least nineteen regional languages are spoken on the more than 7,000 islands, with Filipino (based on Tagalog) and English being the two official languages. Under President Ferdinand Marcos, martial law was declared in 1972, followed by political repression, corruption, censorship, and human rights violations. In 1983, Marcos' political rival Benigno Acquino Jr. was assassinated. Democracy was restored in 1986 when Marcos fled to the United States, but parts of the country have remained unstable.

An ongoing communist-supported insurgency has been waged since 1969 in the mostly central and southern parts of the islands. The Communist Party of the Philippines (CPA), New People's Army (NPA) and National Democratic Front (NDF) have been supported by China and, more recently, North Korea. The Mindinao region has also undergone a separatist conflict with the Moro National Liberation Front (MNLF) as well as several splinter groups, since 1969. In March 2000 the government announced it would be intensifying its military campaign against the Moro Islamic Liberation Front (MILF); subsequently the headquarters and a number of rebel camps were neutralized.

The Armed Forces of the Philippines (AFP) have used the United States Armed Forces as a strong model. The three branches are the Philippine Army, Navy (including Marine Corps) and Air Force. The Philippine Constabulary (PC) was a paramilitary law enforcement branch that existed until 1991; it has been replaced by the Philippine National Police (PNP), which is responsible for all domestic land-based law enforcement tasks. The Philippine Coast Guard, created in 1967, conducts maritime law enforcement and safety, but can be mobilized in time of war.

Army and Constabulary Patterns

This rare photo shows a duck hunter type camouflage design worn by two Philippine Constabulary Rangers in the 1960s or 1970s. (*Private collection*)

(*Private collection*)

A number of domestically-produced tiger stripe camouflage patterns were worn by various elite units in the 1960s and 1970s, including the PC Rangers, Special Forces, and Navy special operations. By the late 1980s it was only being worn by Navy SWAG.

Modeled after the South Vietnamese Airborne 'pinks' camouflage pattern, this design was introduced in 1977 and was popular with the HDFG, Army SF and Scout Rangers.

A domestic woodland-type 'puzzle' pattern was worn by Army and PC units from the 1970s until the late 1980s.

Variations of the 'puzzle' design came from different factories, producing a wide range of shapes due to mis-aligned screens and the different colored dyes used.

In the mid or late 1980s, both the Army and PC adopted a copy of the US ERDL 'leaf' pattern camouflage.

This Marine photographed during the 1986 revolution is wearing a surplus US m81 woodland BDU with appropriate insignia. These were scattered throughout the services for many years; however, locally-produced copies were also worn. (*Private collection*)

The Army and Air Force standardized their combat uniform to a version of DPM in the 1990s, although as with other patterns several color variations were produced. (*US Army*)

The Air Force did adopt its own variation of DPM for issue to some personnel. (*Private collection*)

These members of the 1st Special Forces Battalion wear the tiger stripe pattern camouflage uniform adopted for the SF Regiment in the mid-2000s. (*Dept of National Defense*)

This digital design was adopted in 2009 for use by the Special Operations Command personnel. (*Dept of National Defense*)

Three members of the 1st Scout Rangers Regiment wear the distinctive black-grey digital pattern adopted by this unit in 2009. (*Private collection*)

The Light Reaction Regiment (LRR) also has its own distinctive digipat design. (*Dept of National Defense*)

Originally created in 2016 for the Philippines Army by Hyperstealth Industries©, this pattern was initially just referred to as Camopat™. The pattern was later changed slightly to avoid copyright infringement and is produced by the Philippine Government under the name PHILARPAT. (*US Army*)

Navy and Marine Patterns

A distinctive camouflage design for the Philippine Marine Corps called Malunggay was implemented in the early 1980s and continued in use well into the early 2000s with few changes.

Another pattern worn by some elements of the PMC is this 'leaf and twigs' design, possibly of Thai origin and adopted in the 1980s.

Some additional variations of the Malungay camouflage of the PMC, dating from the late 1980s to the early 2000s.

This vertical tiger stripe pattern was worn for a period by the Navy Seabees.

The Navy Special Warfare Group (SWAG) is the only unit that has continued to wear tiger stripe patterned fatigues since the 1970s. This photo shows a number of variants being worn by members of the same unit. (*Private collection*)

A new camouflage design was introduced for the Marine Corps in 2008 and has replaced earlier designs. (*Private collection*)

A variation of the Camopat™ design is now being worn by the Philippines Navy. (*Private collection*)

Coast Guard Patterns

This DPM variant was previously issued to the PCG, although primarily to K-9 units.

A recoloration of the US six-color desert camouflage pattern, this was previously worn by the Philippine Coast Guard.

The blue digital camouflage design currently worn by the PCG. (*US Coast Guard*)

National Police Patterns

A recolored version of the standard Army pattern became a general issue design for units of the PNP.

A different version of the US six-color desert pattern was worn by the Special Action Force (SAF) of the PNP between 1995 and 1997.

The third SAF pattern seen here, issued between 2001 and 2006 (although in practice worn by some units until 2014) is worn by Regional Director Robert Guzman Quenery. (*DILG*)

The second pattern of the SAF was issued between 1997 and 2000. (*Private collection*)

Members of the Rescue Battalion of the Metro Manila Development Authority (MMDA) wear these red woodland patterned camouflage jackets. (*Private collection*)

The digital camouflage design seen here was introduced for the SAF in 2006 and is still being worn. (*Private collection*)

A unique 'bricks' camouflage design has been worn by the Presidential Security Group since the late 1990s. (*Private collection*)

This bright orange design is worn by the Special Reaction Unit (SRU) of the Department of the Interior and Local Government's Bureau of Fire Protection since 2012. (*US Army*)

A blue dominant pixilated design is now worn by Bureau of Jail Management and Penology personnel. (*BJMP*)

Fighters of the Moro Islamic Liberation Front (MILF) clad in a mixed assortment of tiger stripe patterned uniforms. (*Private collection*)

Women of the MILF wearing identical Islamic-style tiger stripe patterned suits. (*Private collection*)

MILF troops clad in brown digital pattern uniform from 2015. (*Private collection*)

QATAR

Formerly a British protectorate, the country achieved independence in 1971 and is ruled as a hereditary monarchy. Qatar played an important role in the Persian Gulf War (1991), particularly during the battle of Khafji. In 2003, it was one of the primary launching sites for coalition troops moving into Iraq. The country supported NATO operations in Libya, and funded armaments for both Libyan and Syrian paramilitary opposition groups. It has also supported the intervention in Yemen against loyalists.

The Qatar Armed Forces are small and well-trained, following the British model very closely. They consist of the Land Forces, Emiri Guard, Navy, Air Force, and the Internal Security Forces. Historically the QAF have been outfitted with a variation of DPM, but this changed recently when new patterns were introduced unique to Qatar.

Several variations of a four-color desert DPM pattern have been worn by this country since the late 1980s. Later versions feature much darker yellow hues. (*Private collection*)

A blue DPM variant pattern is used by the Internal Security Force (ISF), or 'Lekhwiya Force'. (*Private collection*)

These Qatari personnel deploying to Lebanon in 2006 are wearing camouflage uniforms in the French CE woodland pattern. (*United Nations*)

These members of the Qatar Special Operations Command wear the DPM variant pattern of this service. (*US Army*)

This camouflage design of fractured shapes was introduced in 2015 for Qatari forces. (*US Marine Corps*)

A variation of the splinter pattern is worn by National Servicemen. (*Qatar Ministry of Defense*)

SAUDI ARABIA

The Kingdom of Saudi Arabia is an absolute monarchy and the largest producer of oil in the world. Although its monarchs have been deposed through both peaceful and violent means, the country has always been tight-fisted with regards to human rights and personal freedoms. It is one of the few countries in the world that observes pure Sharia law. Anti-government uprisings such as the Qatif Uprising and seizure of the Grand Mosque (both in 1979) were dealt with using a very heavy hand.

Saudi Arabia condemned the Iraqi invasion of Kuwait in 1990 and was part of the coalition of military forces that retook the country during the Gulf War. The country has also intervened militarily in Yemen since 2015, supporting the government of President Abdrabbuh Mansour Hadi.

The Royal Saudi Arabian Armed Forces consist of the Royal Army, Royal Navy, Royal Air Force, Royal Air Defense Forces, and the Royal Strategic Missile Forces. The Saudi Arabia National Guard (SANG) is a separate military force, in effect a private army of the monarchy which exists to prevent an overthrow of the government by military means. Paramilitary forces administered by the Ministry of the Interior include the Emergency Force, Border Guards, Civil Defense Forces, and the National Police.

Presumably the very first camouflage design worn by this country, four color desert DPM was worn by both the Saudi Arabia National Guard (SANG) and the regular Armed Forces.

A variant of the SANG design dating to the 1980s, this version was used by the National Security Council.

These members of the SANG wear the early DPM variant pattern associated with this branch of service. (*US Army*)

Seen here with an American Special Forces instructor, these Saudi Special Forces troops are wearing m81 woodland camouflage. Woodland camouflage was also worn by Air Force security personnel. (*US Army*)

This photograph of two Saudi officers from 1991 shows the recently adopted copy of US six-color desert camouflage that became the standard camouflage pattern of the armed forces at that time. (*Private collection*)

A grey-dominant variation of the six-color desert pattern was adopted by the Royal Saudi Border Guards in the 1990s and is still current. (*Private collection*)

Most of the Armed Forces replaced the earlier camouflage patterns with a copy of US tricolor desert in the early 2000s. (*US Army*)

A unique design resembling the cracked earth of a dried up wadi is worn by the Saudi Mujahideen. (*Private collection*)

Another variation of six-color desert pattern is worn by the Emergency Force of the Ministry of the Interior. (*Private collection*)

This camouflage design was worn for a period of time the Royal Saudi Air Defense Forces.

A two-color camouflage design that is worn by the Public Security Directorate.

A grey DPM variant has been worn by the MOI Special Security Force for the Hajj and Umrah since 2008. (*Private collection*)

This design was worn at the King Fahd Security College until 2010.

These SANG officers wear the copy of USMC desert MARPAT camouflage that was replaced the earlier tricolor desert pattern for this service. (*Ministry of Defense*)

A variation of the standard tricolor desert pattern, with a slightly different color palette, is worn by the General Directorate of Narcotics Control.

These MOI Special Security Force personnel wear a DPM-derivative pattern issued since 2005. (*Private collection*)

A general of the Saudi Arabian Army here wears the current issue desert pattern (also based on USMC desert MARPAT) of the Armed Forces. (*US Army*)

The elite Saudi Guards Regiment wears a distinctive digital camouflage design with sparse green elements.

A copy of the UCP with somewhat darker color palette was introduced for the Royal Saudi Air Force personnel circa 2014.

This digital design is used by the Diplomatic Security branch of the Saudi National Security Council.

These agents of the Royal Saudi Directorate of Passports wear a digital design with an olive green colorway. (*Private collection*)

This desert camouflage design composed of very large pixels is worn by the Installations Security Forces (Critical Structure Security). (*Private collection*)

An officer of the Facilities Security Forces wearing a grey-dominant camouflage design from that unit. (*Private collection*)

The commanding general of the King Fahd Security College here wears the pixilated camouflage design worn since 2014. (*Private collection*)

A colorful grey-blue digital pattern worn by MOI General Directorate of Prisons. (*Private collection*)

This pattern based on the USMC temperate MARPAT design is currently worn by the Agency for Regiment Affairs. (*Private collection*)

SINGAPORE

Singapore emerged from the Second World War a Crown Colony. With the exception of several incidents of rioting it largely escaped the warfare of the Malayan Emergency, and became a self-governing state within the British Commonwealth in 1959. A referendum held in 1962 led to a merger including Singapore in the Federation of Malaya, but the union only lasted three years, with Singapore being expelled in 1965 for political reasons.

The Singapore Armed Forces (SAF) were formed in 1966, initially from two infantry regiments commanded by British officers. A British military presence remained in the country until approximately 1976, but the country was also assisted by Israel in the formation of a modern and efficient military force. The SAF today consists of the Army, Navy and Air Force. The country has deployed military personnel abroad only to render humanitarian assistance in places like Kosovo, Iraq, East Timor, Afghanistan and Haiti. The Singapore Police Force is responsible for domestic law enforcement and internal security.

A vertical stripe design, seen here, was issued to the Commandos from 1976 until the mid-1980s.

Influenced by the US ERDL camouflage pattern of the 1960s, the 'leaf' design here was adopted as standard battledress by the SAF in the mid-1980s. (*Private collection*)

DPM camouflage has been worn by the Singapore Police Force Gurkha Contingent. (*Private collection*)

These two members of the small contingent deployed to Afghanistan in 2006–07 are wearing desert tiger stripe™ pattern uniforms. (*Private collection*)

A new green digital camouflage pattern was adopted in 2009, replacing the earlier ERDL design. (*US Marine Corps*)

The Singapore soldier on the left is wearing the newly adopted digital desert camouflage pattern while serving with ISAF in Afghanistan. (*Private collection*)

These Navy Lieutenant is wearing the Navy camouflage design adopted in 2012. (*US Marine Corps*)

Two Singapore Air Force officers wearing the design of this service, also adopted in 2012. (*US Air Force*)

At the end of the Second World War, the Korean peninsula was divided along the 38th parallel into northern and southern zones, with the United States Military Government in Korea (USAMGIK) controlling the southern part. The First Korean Republic was established in 1948 when the US relinquished control, and was noted for its brutal repression of communist sympathizers. North Korea subsequently invaded the south in the hopes of unifying the entire peninsula under one government, which instigated the Korean War. Supported by the United States and a coalition of allied nations, South Korea continued the war with the north until a 1953 armistice was signed, restoring the original borders of the two countries, with a Demilitarized Zone between them. Although relations between North and South Korea have remained tense, at times even heated, a resumption of open hostilities has been avoided.

In May 1960, General Park Chung-hee assumed control of the government in a coup d'etat. Described by many as a military dictator, he was assassinated in 1979 and replaced by General Chun Doo-hwan in another coup. The entire country was subsequently placed under martial law, and pro-democracy protests were suppressed with violence. Under increasing political pressure to institute more democratic reforms, direct election of the president was instituted in 1987.

A copy of the US M1942 spot design, 'duck hunter' patterns were introduced in the 1960s and only issued to Marines and special forces, but were later utilized by reserve forces and even high school military programs. (*Private collection*)

This camouflage design incorporating 'jigsaw' shapes was adopted in the 1970s by the ROK Marines. (*Private collection*)

The Republic of Korea Armed Forces consists of the Army (ROKA), Navy (ROKN) and Air Force (ROKAF) and is one of the largest standing forces in the world. Tasked primarily with domestic defense against invasion, South Korea did send several hundred thousands of personnel to fight in the Vietnam War, both as advisors and combatants. Military personnel have also participated in the Persian Gulf War (1991), Afghanistan, and the Iraq War. The country is also very active in United Nations-sponsored peacekeeping operations, with deployments all over the world since the 1990s. The use of camouflage by South Korean forces has historically mirrored that of the United States, with some exceptions.

ROK Special Forces NCOs wearing the 'waves' pattern that was introduced in the late 1960s. (*Private collection*)

A copy of the US ERDL camouflage was worn by Navy units such as UDT/SEALs and other diving units in the 1980s. (*Private collection*)

Between 1980 and 1991, the ROK MC wore this 'turtleshell' design. (*Private collection*)

A South Korean soldier deployed with the United Nations in Europe wearing the woodland-hybrid camouflage design adopted by the ROKA and AF units beginning in 1992. (*United Nations*)

Two South Korean soldiers deployed to Afghanistan wearing a copy of six-color desert camouflage that was issued to ROK forces deployed to arid regions between 1991 and 2001. (*Private collection*)

Introduced in 2004, this desert camouflage design replaced the earlier one for personnel deployed overseas. (*Private collection*)

A variation of the USMC temperate MARPAT design was introduced in 2006 for use by the ROK Army's Special Warfare Command. (*US Army Special Operations Command – Korea*)

A new camouflage design was developed for the major branches of the ROK Armed Forces and introduced in 2010. (*Ministry of National Defense*)

This South Korean marine wears the digital tiger stripe pattern introduced in 2010 for that service. (*Ministry of National Defense*)

This digital desert pattern was introduced in 2016 for use by personnel deployed on foreign assignments. (*Private collection*)

South Korean Navy UDT/SEAL personnel wearing contemporary Multicam uniforms. (*Ministry of National Defense*)

The Korean Army Augmentation to the US Army (KATUSA) personnel wear standard US Army camouflage. Seen here are two soldiers wearing the old (UCP) and current (OCP) camouflage designs. (*US DOD*)

SOUTH VIETNAM

A former French colony, South Vietnam originally came into being in June 1949 through cooperation between anti-communist Vietnamese and the French government. The Democratic Republic of Vietnam (North Vietnam) had previously been declared following the Japanese surrender in 1945, but was not recognized by the French government. A battle for control of all of Vietnam ensued, pitting French forces and the Vietnamese National Army against the communist Viet Minh and the People's Army of Vietnam. When the war ended in 1954, it was stipulated at the Geneva Conference that the State of (South) Vietnam would exist from the 17th parallel south, and the DRV from that point north. As many as one million North Vietnamese subsequently fled to the south. The Republic of Vietnam was created a year later, when emperor Bảo Đại was deposed by Ngô Đình Diệm, who became the country's first president.

As France withdrew support from Vietnam in 1956, the United States offered financial, political and military aid to the fledgling Vietnamese government. President Diệm's refusal to enter negotiations with North Vietnam and hold elections for control over all of Vietnam led to gradual disintegration of diplomatic relations between the two countries. This was one of the leading causes of the Second Indochina War (1959 to 1975), aka the Vietnam War. From 1955 to 1975, a state of war existed between North and South Vietnam, which also faced insurgency from the largely rural National Liberation Front (aka Việt Cộng) movement. Faced with decreasing popular support for the war, the United States eventually withdrew all military personnel from the country, which fell to the north shortly thereafter in April 1975.

The Army of the Republic of Vietnam (ARVN) was the name for all ground forces during the Second Indochina War. Army units were organized into four Corps (I through IV), each covering a geographical region of South Vietnam. Primary combat units included eleven Infantry Divisions, one Airborne Division (Nhẩy Dù), the ARVN Rangers (Biệt Động Quân), and the ARVN Special Forces (Lực Lượng Đặc Biệt or LLDB). The Vietnam Air Force and Republic of Vietnam Navy (including the Republic of Vietnam Marine Corps or Thủy Quân Lục Chiến) made up the remainder of the South Vietnamese armed forces. Other combatant units during the Vietnam War included the National Police Field Force and the Civilian Irregular Defense Group (CIDG) units, the latter composed of minority tribal people, trained by the US Army Special Forces and funded primarily by the CIA (from 1961 until 1970).

South Vietnam was innovative in its design and use of camouflage clothing. Indeed the Second Indochina War was probably the first major international conflict in which camouflage clothing played a significant role. The most notable patterns to emerge from this war are the tiger stripe designs, influenced by the French lizard designs but deserving categorization all to itself. Tiger stripe began in South Vietnam, and spread across the world.

British-made 'windproof' camouflage uniforms were worn by some Vietnamese airborne and commando units during the First Indochina War.

Also worn by some Vietnamese airborne units during the First Indochina War was the US M1942 duck hunter/spot pattern.

French camouflage uniforms were commonly worn by airborne and commando units during the colonial period, and leftover stocks were worn by Vietnamese units from 1952 until depleted.

These officers of the Airborne Division wear the early 'pinks' pattern based on British brushstroke designs of the Second World War. (*Private collection*)

Loosely-based on commercial 'duck hunter' designs brought over by US military advisors, the Beo Gam (leopard) pattern was used primarily by CIDG units. (*Private collection*)

Vietnamese Marines from the South Vietnamese Marines Division, or Sư Đoàn Thủy Quân Lục Chiến, clad in their own distinctive tiger striped pattern uniforms. (*Private collection*)

Another ERDL variation is seen here, worn by these ARVN Rangers. (*Private collection*)

Two officers of the South Vietnamese Airborne Division wearing slightly different ERDL patterned uniforms. (*Private collection*)

A young policeman of the National Police Field Force (NPFF) wearing the indigenous 'clouds' pattern derived from the US 'Mitchell' design. (*Private collection*)

Tiger stripe pattern uniforms worn by officers of the Lực Lượng đặc biệt, or Vietnamese Special Forces. (*Private collection*)

SRI LANKA

The country was known as Ceylon during its British colonial period, but chose to become an independent republic in 1972 and renamed itself Sri Lanka. A secessionist insurgency waged by militant groups representing the Tamil population lasted twenty-five years (1983–2009), but ultimately ended in resounding defeat by the Sri Lankan armed forces. The most prominent militant group was the Liberation Tigers of Tamil Eelam (LTTE). For much of the war, most of the northern and eastern region of the island was under the control of the LTTE. Between 1987 and 1990 the Indian Peace Keeping Force (IPKF) was deployed to Sri Lanka, with the primary objective of disarming the militant groups. The IPKF was eventually drawn into hostilities when the LTTE refused to disarm.

The Armed Forces of Sri Lanka consists of the Army, Navy and Air Force under command of the Ministry of Defense. Also falling under this jurisdiction is the Coast Guard (although this branch is largely staffed with civilians), the Sri Lanka Police and the Sri Lanka Civil Security Force.

Members of the Police Special Task Force wearing British DPM pattern uniforms, in service since the unit was founded in 1983. (*Private collection*)

Sri Lanka Army Commandos wearing early woodland pattern camouflage uniforms. (*Private collection*)

This woodland-derivative pattern was previously worn by some units of the Sri Lankan Air Force. (*Private collection*)

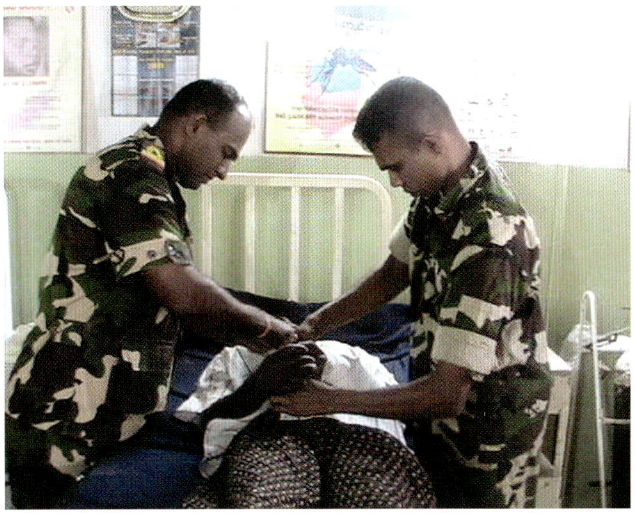

Navy personnel wearing a woodland pattern worn by this service for a short period of time. (*Private collection*)

A Sri Lankan Air Force Chief Marshal and a Navy Rear Admiral wearing the respective camouflage patterns of their services. (*US Marine Corps*)

The camouflage pattern seen here was originally adopted by the Commando Regiment, but later became the official pattern of the Sri Lankan Army in 2010. (*Isuru Wakkumbura*)

This copy of US tricolor desert pattern has been used by the Civil Security Force since 2013. (*Private collection*)

The current pattern of the Sri Lankan Marines, adopted in 2016. (*US Marine Corps*)

These Sri Lankan military personnel serving with the United Nations in Mali (2017) are wearing a newly adopted desert camouflage design. (*United Nations*)

Tamil Tiger Patterns

During the Civil War the military wing of the LTTE consisted of at least eleven divisions including conventional forces, the Sea Tigers naval wing, Air Tigers aviation wing, LTTE leadership personal security detachments, a suicide wing called the Black Tigers, and several independent units. The LTTE had its own series of camouflage uniforms.

A unique pattern worn by the Liberation Tigers of Tamil Eelam (LTTE) is seen here in a rare formation photograph. A variation with a bright blue color palette was worn by the air element of this organization. (*Private collection*)

A similar grey hued design was worn by the so-called 'Black Tigers' unit, who often launched suicide attacks against civilian and military targets. (*Private collection*)

SYRIA

The Syrian Republic was established and recognized in 1946. The country promptly allied itself with the other Arab nations during the Arab-Israeli War of 1948, and its subsequent defeat led to a period of instability lasting throughout the 1950s. Historically aligned with the USSR and Egypt, Syria merged with the latter in 1958 forming the United Arab Republic (1958–1961). However, a military seizure of power in September of 1961 dissolved the union and led to the establishment of the Syrian Arab Republic, the name that the nation retains today.

Syria fought Israel again in the Six Day War (1967), during which the Golan Heights were lost. The territory was regained briefly during the Yom Kippur War (1973), but retaken by Israel, which has retained possession ever since. Syria was heavily involved during the Lebanese Civil War, sending troops into Lebanon itself to support insurgent forces (particularly the Amal Movement) and plausibly to seek control over the entire territory. Syrian military forces remained in Lebanon long after the war ended, but were forced to withdraw finally in 2005 under international pressure.

Some Syrian units in the 1970s wore brushstroke camouflage, identical to or very similar to that initially produced in Pakistan.

The Syrian government has long been supportive of Palestinian efforts to establish sovereign territory within the boundaries of the present state of Israel. Various factions of the PLO have received direct military aid from Syria (including Syrian-made camouflage uniforms). Syrians have also harbored mixed views about neighboring Lebanon, with a strong percentage hoping to establish a pro-Syrian government or even outright unification, with complete Syrian control. Certain paramilitary groups operating within Lebanese territory have historically been trained and funded completely by Syrian government sources. A list of groups operating outside Syria but with political and military allegiance to the Syrian government include: the Syrian National Socialist Party (SSNP), Al-Mourabitoun ('the Guardians'), aka the Independent Nasserite Movement, Popular Front for the Liberation of Palestine, General Command (PFLP-GC), As-Sa'iqa or al-Saika, the Palestine Liberation Army (PLA), and The Amal Movement.

Sparked by political unrest and regime change in other parts of Western Asia and North Africa (collectively referred to as the 'Arab Spring' Movement), Syrian dissidents began demonstrating against President Bashar al-Assad and his Ba'ath party, which has maintained strict one-party control over the nation for nearly fifty years, in March 2011. Heavy-handed and violently oppressive measures against the protesters, and lack of international involvement, eventually spawned a full-scale civil war, which continues to rage across the nation.

A series of vertical stripe patterns were reputedly worn by Syrian commando or paratroop units, and also by Palestinian As-Saika units during the 1970s and 80s. (*Private collection*)

Brightly colored red 'lizard' designs were produced and worn by Syrian elite units from the 1970s through to the 1990s and beyond. (*Private collection*)

This Syrian Commando wears a vertically-aligned red lizard design. The orientation of the stripes may have reflected the unit status or purpose. (*Private collection*)

Also worn were other lizard variations such as this one with an almost purple coloration.

A 'leaf' type camouflage design was introduced in 1980s, but restricted to use by elite units.

This variant of the 'leaf' pattern, in bright red-pink color palette, was produced for elite formations, military police or security forces.

Syrian generals wearing a variety of woodland-type camouflage patterns that were introduced between the late 1990s and 2000s. (*Private collection*)

These members of the Ministry of Interior's Special Mission Force wear a blue woodland camouflage pattern, in use since 2012. (*Private collection*)

Three members of the pro-Assad Slavonic Corps wearing US tricolor desert, a two-color black-grey camouflage often seen in Iraq, and a copy of British desert DPM. (*Private collection*)

Camouflage of Non-government Forces

Members of the Pro-Assad STK militia clad in a mixture of Iranian digital and woodland camouflage uniforms. (*Private collection*)

FSA fighters wearing a mixture of clothing and equipment, including Turkish Army arid nano pattern. (*Private collection*)

A group of Free Syrian Army fighters wearing a mixture of indigenous woodland, US tricolor desert and Turkish Air Force digital pattern camouflage. (*Private collection*)

An Liwa'a al-Imam al-Hasan al-Mujtaba fighter wearing a copy of USMC desert MARPAT camouflage. (*Private collection*)

Fighters of the Islamic Liwa'a Zulfigar (Zulfigar Battalion) wearing a copy of British desert DPM. (*Private collection*)

The Republic of China was re-established in 1949 on the island of Taiwan (previously known as Formosa) after the government of Chiang Kai-shek was defeated by the communists, and his supporters forced to evacuate the mainland. The political status of the nation is contentious due to the fact that the People's Republic of China insists the island is a historical part of their nation, and that the government of Taiwan is illegal. The ROC considers itself a sovereign nation, but it is unrecognized by the United Nations.

The Chinese National Armed Forces (CNAF) consists of the Army, Navy (including Marine Corps), Air Force, Military Police, Joint Logistics Command, and the Armed Forces Reserve. The United States had a military presence in Taiwan until 1979 when it formally recognized the PRC and withdrew its military from the island. Nevertheless, the USA continues to provide military assistance and conducts joint exercises with the CNAF. Taiwan's military forces also have a good working relationship with those of Singapore.

This tiger stripe pattern was introduced around 1979 for use by the ROC Marine Corps.

A camouflage helmet cover indicative of the earliest tiger pattern designs produced in Taiwan. (*Private collection*)

A promotional photo showing another tiger stripe variant adopted in the mid-1980s by Airborne and Special Forces Command personnel only. (*Private collection*)

Members of a Marine Corps reconnaissance unit wearing the standardized tiger stripe pattern adopted in the mid-1980s for that branch. (*Private collection*)

An Army machine gun crew clad in the copy of US ERDL 'leaf' camouflage introduced for general use by ROC Armed Forces circa 1991–92. (*Private collection*)

These members of the Army's elite Airborne Special Service Company are wearing an urban woodland type camouflage uniform. (*Private collection*)

This digital camouflage pattern was introduced for general use by the Army and Air Force in 2013. (*Private collection*)

This digitized 'tiger stripe' pattern uniform was tested by the Marines in 2017 and began to enter service in 2018. (*Private collection*)

UCP worn by members of the Airborne Special Service Company. This unit has also been observed wearing Multicam. (*Private collection*)

TAJIKISTAN

Tajik nationalists had begun to clamor for increased rights while still a republic within the Soviet Union, but the country did not declare itself independent until the collapse of the USSR in 1991. Almost immediately the nation descended into a civil war pitting clan-based factions from the Garm and Gorno-Badakhshan regions against the government of President Rahmon Nabiyev, which was dominated by people from the Khujand and Kulyab regions. The conflict ended with an armistice in 1997, followed by a comprehensive peace agreement promising fair representation to the United Tajik Opposition representing a combination of democratic, nationalist and Islamic interests. It is estimated between 20,000 and 100,000 people were killed during the civil war, and over one million displaced. The country has served as a base to support air operations for the ISAF force in Afghanistan and often hosts joint military exercises both with the United States and Russia.

The Armed Forces consist of the Mobile Forces, Air Force, Presidential National Guard, Internal Troops, and Border Troops. Unlike most other former Soviet republics, the Tajik forces were not formed out of former Soviet units but created from the ground up.

A photo from 1997 shows three Tajik soldiers wearing Soviet era dubok pattern camouflage uniforms. (*Private collection*)

Russian flora pattern camouflage uniforms have been in service with the Tajik Armed forces since around 1999.

Tajik Ministry of Internal Affairs soldier in 2007 wearing a woodland pattern uniform. (*US Army*)

Riot police of the Ministry of Internal Affairs wearing blue woodland type camouflage. Other special units wear blue tiger pattern uniforms. (*Private collection*)

Airborne officer wearing current issue Multicam pattern uniform. (*US Army*)

Berezhka pattern camouflage uniforms in use with Tajik Border Guards. (*Private collection*)

Two Tajik members of a Peacekeeping Battalion wearing Russian tsifra pattern camouflage. (*US Army National Guard*)

THAILAND

Historically known as Siam, the Kingdom of Thailand is a constitutional monarchy in Southeast Asia. It has never been occupied or colonized by another nation. In the years following the Second World War, Thailand developed a friendship with the United States and was a reliable ally of the USA and South Vietnam during the Vietnam War. It became a signatory of the Southeast Asian Treaty Organization (SEATO)

These early tiger stripe patterns were based on South Vietnamese design, but produced in Thailand during the Vietnam War period.

in 1954. Thailand has experienced periods of military rule, the most recent of which occurred in September 2006 when a military junta overthrew the government and declared martial law, appointing its own prime minister and writing an abbreviated constitution. Although martial law was partially revoked in 2007 and a new constitution approved, another military coup took control in 2014.

The Royal Thai Armed Forces consists of the Army, Navy (including Marine Corps), and the Air Force. Paramilitary forces include the Thahan Phran and the Territorial Defense Students, both auxiliaries of the Army. Law enforcement is the jurisdiction of the Royal Thai Police, which also includes the Border Patrol Police. Thai military personnel were deployed to fight in the Korean War and the Vietnam War, while back home they were faced with a communist insurgency from 1976 to the 1980s as well as incursions from Vietnamese troops entering through Cambodia (1979–88). The country engaged in a small border war with Laos from 1987–88, and has dealt with another insurgency in the south since 2001. In recent history, Thai military personnel have deployed as part of United Nations peacekeeping efforts to East Timor and Sudan.

The Armed Forces have largely looked to the United States with regards to trends in camouflage and combat uniform development. Many of the designs worn by military and paramilitary personnel are copies of those developed in South Vietnam or the USA.

Royal Thai Army Special Forces soldiers wearing the copy of ERDL 'leaf' pattern camouflage in service with most branches from the 1970s onwards. (*US Air Force*)

Based on the USMC Standard or 'vine leaf' pattern, Thailand produced full uniforms in this pattern in the 1970s and 80s.

Tiger stripes continued to be produced in the 1980s and 1990s, worn primarily by elite units such as the Special Forces, Rangers, SEALs, and Marine Recon.

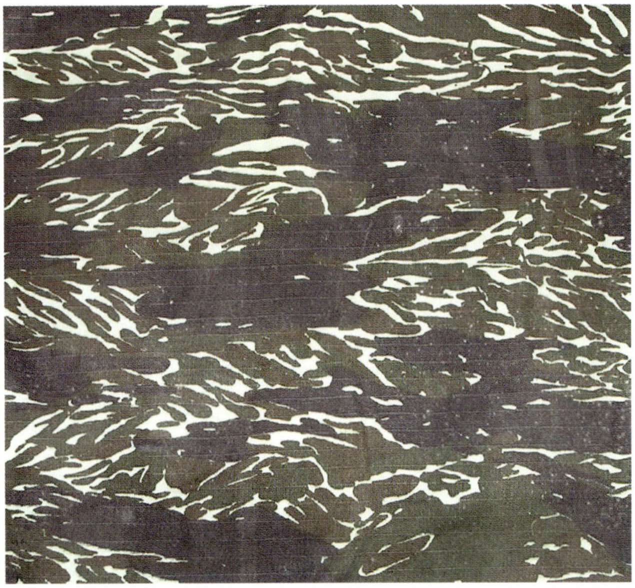

A variation of the tiger stripe pattern unique to Thailand is characterized by the use of dark dyes with a single, very pale background color, nicknamed 'Shadowtiger'.

This photo from 1996 illustrates the variation of ERDL that was being worn in Thailand at the time, and for 10-15 years before this. (*US Army*)

This variation of the leaf pattern was worn by some Air Force security units during the 1990s.

Woodland camouflage became standardized for use in the Royal Thai Navy and Marines during the 1990s. (*Private collection*)

An unusual camouflage design worn by the Royal Thai Navy Air and Coastal Defense Command.

This unique pattern was worn by Forest Rangers of the Thai Dept of National Parks. (*Private collection*)

Tiger stripe camouflage still being worn by Border Patrol Police personnel in 2013. (*Private collection*)

These Thai Army Rangers wear the digitized version of the old leaf pattern camouflage adopted in 2008 by the Army. (*US Army*)

This pixilated design was adopted by the Royal Thai Air Force in 2009. (*US Air Force*)

A digital version of woodland camouflage was adopted by the Royal Thai Marine Corps in 2009-10. (*USMC*)

Thai peacekeepers in Sudan in 2013 wearing the pixilated desert pattern now worn by all personnel deployed to arid regions. (*United Nations*)

The Forest Rangers of the Thai Department of National Parks now wear this digital camouflage pattern, adopted in 2013. (*Private collection*)

Members of the Volunteer Defense Corps wear a copy of US tricolor desert. (*Private collection*)

Two Navy officers here wearing the grey-dominant pattern adopted by that service in 2016. (*US Navy*)

TIMOR-LESTE

The Democratic Republic of Timor-Leste (Repúblika Demokrátika Timór-Leste) or East Timor comprises the eastern-half of the island of Timor in Southeast Asia. The Frente Revolucionária de Timor-Leste Independente (FRETILIN) declared the region's independence from Portugal in 1975, but only a few months later East Timor was invaded by Indonesia and incorporated into that nation as a 27th province. From 1975 until 1999 FRETILIN waged a guerilla campaign against the Indonesian occupying force, which eventually came to an end with the assistance of an Australian-led UN peacekeeping force. Indonesia relinquished control and the sovereign nation of East Timor was declared on 20 May 2002.

Organized in 2001 from elements of the Forças Armadas de Libertação de Timor-Leste (Armed Forces for the Liberation of East Timor) or FALINTIL, the armed forces of East Timor are known as the Forças de Defesa de Timor Leste or FDTL. With approximately 1,500 active duty personnel (as of 2010), the FDTL are primarily a ground-defense force comprised of two light infantry battalions, with a small naval component

East German strichtarn pattern uniforms were worn by FALINTIL during the war of independence.

FALINTIL commander Alfredo Reinado giving an interview, clad in the Portuguese m63 pattern camouflage that saw extensive use by his forces during the war; other Portuguese camouflage, such as the Air Force lizard, was also documented. (*Private collection*)

A photo from 1999 showing the transitional forces wearing a mixture of Portuguese lizard and DPM pattern uniforms. (*Private collection*)

for coastal defense. Also formed in 2001, the Policia Nacional de Timor-Leste (National Police of East Timor) provides law enforcement and internal security services to the nation.

The region's close historical and political ties to Portugal have influenced both the insignia and the camouflage dress of its combat services.

The first pattern to become standardized issue with the FDTL was this Chinese copy of French 'lizard' pattern, first seen around 2004. (*Private collection*)

Another early pattern used by the FDTL is this copy of USMC temperate MARPAT.

In 2014 a pixilated version of the lizard pattern was officially adopted by the FDTL. (*Private collection*)

These officers of the Polícia Nacional de Timor-Leste (National Police) wear two vertical stripe designs and a woodland variant. (*Private collection*)

TURKEY

The Republic of Turkey was a charter member of the United Nations and has been a member of NATO since 1952. Although multiparty elections were instituted in 1946, several coups d'etat (1960, 1971 and 1980) have put the country temporarily under the control of the military.

Responding to a coup d'etat by Greek nationalists on the island of Cyprus in 1974, Turkey invaded the northern part of the island and it has remained under Turkish occupation ever since.

The Kurdish population in the south of Turkey has long been a target of suppression and forced assimilation, giving rise to a separatist movement since the early part of the twentieth century. The militant Kurdistan Workers Party (PKK) emerged in 1978 and launched a guerilla war against the Turkish government from 1983 until the 1990s. The conflict claimed more than 37,000 lives and resulted in destruction of Kurdish villages and the exodus of thousands from their homes. With an increase in acceptance of Kurdish culture, violence in the region has eased in recent years, although pockets of armed resistance continue to operate from mountain enclaves.

Although considered a part of Asia by the United Nations, Turkey has many long-standing cultural and

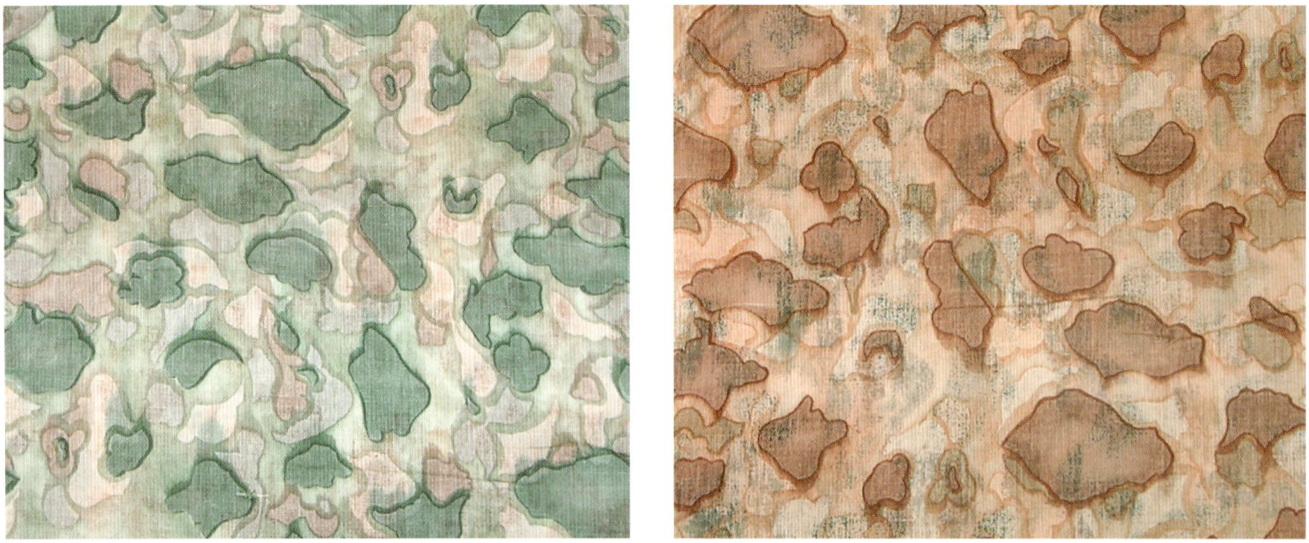

The earliest camouflage designs were copied from the US M1942 spot pattern of the Second World War. Several variations have been documented, the earliest emerging in the 1970s. Issue was generally limited to units with elite status, although some conventional units did use shelters, ponchos and tailor-fabricated helmet covers.

geographical links to Europe. The region of Eastern Thrace is in fact part of what is considered continental Europe. The Turkish Armed Forces (Türk Silahlı Kuvvetleri) consist of the Land Forces, Air Force, and Navy, all falling under command of the Ministry of Defense. The Ministry of the Interior operates the Gendarmerie General Command (Jandarma Genel Komutanlığı) and the Coast Guard. National law enforcement is under the control of the General Directorate of Security, which oversees regional units as well as a number of specialized sub-units. Turkey has been a member of the Eurocorps since 2002. The Turkish Gendarmerie has also been an observational member of the European Gendarmerie Force (EUGENDFOR) since 2009. Turkey has contributed military personnel to Bosnia, Kosovo, Afghanistan (ISAF) and Somalia.

A Turkish commando bazooka team wearing the 'Aegean spot' pattern camouflage uniform so often associated with airborne and commando troops. (*Private collection*)

A 'compressed' or 'elongated' style of leaf design, adopted in the mid-1990s, is seen here worn by Turkish Marines in 2005. This pattern was worn by the armed forces and the Gendarmerie. (*Private collection*)

This more faithful copy of m81 woodland was also issued from the late 1990s to late 2000s, seen here on these two Turkish generals. (*Private collection*)

These locally produced copies of US M1948 ERDL (with darker color palette) were adopted in the 1980s.

Based on the US m81 woodland drawings, the Turkish woodland introduced in 1989 has a slightly different color palette.

This variant of woodland with blue-grey colorway was worn by the Turkish Air Force beginning in the early 2000s. (*Private collection*)

This brown/black woodland pattern was worn by the Polis Özel Harekât (Police Special Action) unit or PÖH of the General Directorate of Security until recently. (*Private collection*)

A new camouflage design was introduced for the Armed Forces in 2008. These Turkish Marines are still wearing the pattern in 2015. (*US Marine Corps*)

A digital pattern adopted by the Turkish Air Force, introduced around 2010.

Turkish troops serving in Qatar wear a lighter-colored version of the standard digital camouflage design.

Another variation for winter/snow operations is primarily issued to special operations personnel.

A local copy of Multicam has been worn by the Navy's Amfibi Komando and by the Su Altı Taarruz (SAT – the Navy Special Warfare unit) since 2013. (*Private collection*)

Operational units of the Jandarma were presented with a new camouflage design in 2016, seen here. (*Private collection*)

Members of the Police Special Action unit in 2016 wearing a recently adopted camouflage design. (*Private collection*)

Introduced late in 2017, this three color pattern is believed to be under consideration for the entire Army in the future. (*Private collection*)

TURKMENISTAN

Formerly the Turkmen Soviet Socialist Republic, this country reluctantly accepted independence in 1991 following the dissolution of the USSR, although it retained communist leader Saparmyrat Nyýazow until 2006. A border dispute with neighboring Uzbekistan arose between 2002 and 2004, ending in a series of bilateral treaties. Nyýazow was only replaced as president following his death.

Turkmenistan retains an essentially neutral foreign policy, eschewing membership in any international defense organizations. The country has a history of human rights abuses and discrimination against minorities.

The Armed Forces include the Ground Forces, Air Force & Air Defense Forces, Naval Forces, National Guard, Internal Troops, Border Troops and the Ministry of Emergency Situations.

Introduced late in 2017, this three color pattern is now being fielded by some Turkish Army units. (*Private collection*)

Airborne troops on parade wearing old Soviet era dubok pattern uniforms, in service with Ground Forces and State Border Guards. (*Private collection*)

This Turkmen soldier wears a copy of the US six-color desert camouflage design, in service with some units. (*Private collection*)

The desert design seen here was also adopted within the 2012–13 time frame. (*Private collection*)

Young troops, possibly cadets, wearing woodland patterned heavy winter uniforms. This pattern has also been observed on airborne personnel. (*Private collection*)

This camouflage design was adopted between 2012–13, and reflects the first truly national pattern adopted specifically for Turkmenistan. (*Private collection*)

The design on the far left is also known to be worn in this country by units of the Ministry of Internal Affairs. (*Private collection*)

From another military parade, these vehicle crewmembers appear to be wearing a copy of the Croatian Army's desert camouflage. (*Private collection*)

Troops of the Ministry of National Security (MNB) clad in a blue digital camouflage pattern. (*Private collection*)

Infantry personnel on parade wearing the Russian Spectre pattern. (*Private collection*)

These special operations personnel appeared in 2017 wearing complete Multicam camouflage kit. (*Private collection*)

UNITED ARAB EMIRATES

The UAE is a federation of seven Arab emirates (formerly known as the Trucial States) which came under the protection of the United Kingdom in the post-war years. Bahrain and Qatar were also part of the original protectorate, from which Britain withdrew in 1968. After Bahrain and Qatar became independent states in their own right, the remaining sheikhdoms agreed to form the United Arab Emirates in December 1971. The previously independent defense forces also pulled together to form the Union Defense Force (UDF), the present armed forces of the UAE. These consist of the Army, Air Force, Air Defense Forces, Navy and the paramilitary forces (Federal Police Force and Special Security Force of the MOI).

The UAE sent personnel to Kuwait during the Gulf War in 1991, many of whom advanced into Kuwait City. Personnel also deployed to Somalia in 1993 (as part of UNOSOM II) and to Kosovo. Some UAE forces have also intervened on the part of the Hadi government of Yemen during its civil war.

This British DPM pattern was in use with the 'Desert Wolves' Commando unit of the Abu Dhabi Defense Force as early as 1971.

This camouflage design was utilized to some degree in at least one of the Emirates (possibly Abu Dhabi) in the 1980s or 1990s.

An example of the desert DPM pattern in service with the UDF during the 1990s.

British DPM was also worn by some UDF personnel in the early 1990s.

Special Security Forces of the Ministry of Interior wear the purple-blue DPM variant pattern associated with that service. (*Private collection*)

Two types of six-color desert pattern were adopted in 1990s for the UDF, a standard copy and one without any black elements. (*Private collection*)

UAE members of the contingent sent to Kosovo in 2001 wearing French CE woodland pattern uniforms. On other deployments, the UAE has worn a copy of the Daguet desert pattern. (*Private collection*)

A variation of the six-color pattern in grey was issued to UAE Marines during the 1990s. (*Private collection*)

The US tricolor desert pattern was adopted in the late 1990s, replacing the earlier chocolate chip design. (*Private collection*)

Similar to the USMC desert MARPAT design, the camouflage seen here was adopted mid-2000s for the entire armed forces. (*Private collection*)

Members of the Critical National Infrastructure Authority (CNIA) in Abu Dhabi wear a true copy of the desert MARPAT. (*Private collection*)

The armed forces introduced a new digital pattern in 2015–16 to replace the MARPAT copy, seen here. (*US Army*)

The Republic of Uzbekistan came into being as an independent state in August 1991, following a failed coup attempt in Moscow. The collapse of the Soviet Union followed. The first president of the country, Islam Karimov, remained in power until his death in 2016. The country has a very poor human rights record, perhaps best illustrated by an incident in the city of Andijan in 2005 in which protestors were fired upon by Ministry of Interior and National Security Service personnel, leaving hundreds dead.

The Armed Forces of Uzbekistan (O'zbekiston Respublikasi Qurolli Kuchlari) include the Ground Forces, Air and Air Defense Forces, Naval Forces, and the National Guard. The State Security Service (national intelligence agency) also operates the Frontier Service (border protection). The Ministry of Internal Affairs is responsible for national law enforcement, internal security, and counter-terrorism, and includes Internal Troops.

Variations of the Soviet dubok pattern were worn by the National Security Service beginning in the late 1990s.

Issued in 1994 and nicknamed 'mountain desert', this pattern is based on the Soviet butane design and saw service until 2009. (*US Army*)

Both grey and bright blue copies of Russian 'reed' camouflage (nicknamed 'shadow') have been worn by units of the Ministry of Internal Affairs since the 1990s. (*Private collection*)

This unique camouflage design was issued to the Border Guards from 2001 to 2014.

This grey DPM variant, nicknamed 'mountain stone', was worn by some special units beginning in 2006.

East German strichtarn pattern camouflage uniforms were issued to Airborne and Special Task Force personnel between 2002–06.

This variation of the 'reed' pattern was worn by Ministry of Internal Affairs and National Firefighter units since 2004. (*Private collection*)

These Uzbek soldiers are wearing the digital pattern introduced in 2009 for the armed forces. (*Private collection*)

It would appear the Frontier Service is now wearing a digital pattern similar to UCP. (*Private collection*)

The Ministry of Internal Affairs has changed its pattern to a pixilated design since 2012. (*Private collection*)

A digital version of the old brown reeds pattern is now issued to the MIA, NSS, and Firefighter units. (*Private collection*)

This digital desert pattern is of recent introduction. It is unknown what particular units are wearing the design. (*Private collection*)

An officer of the Armed Forces wearing the newly issued Multicam-type pattern. (*USA Centcom*)

VIETNAM

After the Japanese occupation of the Second World War ended, the communist Việt Minh strongly opposed French reoccupation of the country, which rapidly ushered in the First Indochina War. Following ten years of fighting, the Geneva Accords of 1954 effectively ended the war by declaring Indochina's independence, and establishing two nations out of the Vietnamese territory, the Democratic Republic of Vietnam in the north, and the State of Vietnam (later South Vietnam) in the south. South Vietnamese president Ngô Đình Diệm's refusal to enter into negotiations with North Vietnam over unification brought about gradual deterioration of relations between the two countries, and ultimately led to the Second Indochina War (1959 to 1975). Vietnam was unified in 1975 when the United States and its allies withdrew all forces from South Vietnam, which was rapidly overrun by North Vietnamese troops shortly thereafter. The country is now the Socialist Republic of Vietnam.

In 1978, Vietnam invaded Cambodia and overthrew the Khmer Rouge, leading to tense relations with China and ultimately sparking the brief Sino-Vietnamese war between February and March 1979. Vietnamese troops remained in Cambodia until 1989.

During the Vietnam War, the People's Army of Vietnam (PAVN) was often referred to as the North Vietnamese Army (NVA). The Vietnam People's Army (Quân Đội Nhân Dân Việt Nam) consists of the Ground Forces, Navy, Air Force, Coast Guard and the Border Defense Force. The Vietnam People's Public Security (Công an Nhân dân Việt Nam) includes the People's Security Force, People's Police Force, and the Dân quân (People's Militia) which cooperatively handle law enforcement, intelligence gathering, internal security, firefighting, disaster response, and civil defense. The VPA were approved to join the United Nations peacekeeping force in 2014, and have since deployed to South Sudan. Both military and civil agencies utilize camouflage patterns as a means of identification as well as combat concealment. Some of these designs are derived from foreign sources but many are of indigenous origin.

Early Vietnamese Special Forces or đặc công and airborne forces in the 1980s wore this camouflage design.

The design was retained in the 1990s era and has been worn into the present era by elite units. (*Private collection*)

A similar spot pattern with blue colorway was worn by the Vietnamese Navy (Hải quân Nhân dân Việt Nam), including special forces (đặc công hải quân or đặc công nước) and security personnel. (*Private collection*)

One of several leaf prints introduced by the quân đội (Army) around 1994 for general issue. (*Private collection*)

Another leaf pattern of the Army. (*Private collection*)

A pattern of Chinese origin worn during the 1990s.

A copy of the South Vietnamese ERDL camouflage was issued to special units in the mid-1990s and probably made from bolts of original cloth leftover from the Vietnam War.

The K94 'tiger stripe' pattern was introduced in 1994 for general use and was in service until approximately 2007. (*Private collection*)

This 'yellow leaf' pattern entered service in the late 1990s, but a variation with much lighter coloration has also been documented in service. (*Private collection*)

A pattern based on US woodland, with a brighter colorway, was introduced in 2007 (called K07) for general issue to ground personnel and the Border Guards. (*Private collection*)

This brightly colored blue variant has been worn by Coast Guard and Navy personnel since 2007. (*Private collection*)

Another woodland variation is worn by Air Force personnel with ground defense duties.

Vietnamese Naval Infantry Brigade personnel wearing a true copy of m81 woodland pattern camouflage. (*Private collection*)

YEMEN ARAB REPUBLIC

Also known as North Yemen, the Yemen Arab Republic was established in 1962 when King Muhammad al-Badr was deposed by revolutionaries inspired by the Arab nationalism of Egyptian president Abdel Nasser. This incited a civil war in which royalists supported by Saudi Arabia and Jordan fought the newly established Yemeni republican government (supported by Egypt). Following Egyptian withdrawal from Yemen in 1967, a final attempt was made by the royalists to seize control of Sana'a, lingering until February 1968. The new republic was recognized by Saudi Arabia and the war officially ended in 1970. A brief war was fought with South Yemen in 1972, ending in negotiations through the Arab League and a tentative agreement on unification which went nowhere. Fighting was renewed in 1979 for a short time.

During the civil war period, Egypt provided its own camouflage uniforms to troops with elite status in the YAR.

These Egyptian camouflage patterns were worn by some units of the YAR into the 1970s.

SOUTH YEMEN

The State of South Yemen arose in 1967 by the merging of the Protectorate of Saudi Arabia with the Federation of South Arabia. Three years later it declared itself a Marxist socialist republic, the People's Democratic Republic of Yemen (PDRY). Although by this time relations with its northern neighbor remained friendly, a failed coup attempt in January 1986 led to twelve days of fighting between two factions of the Yemeni Socialist Party. Several thousand were killed during the brief civil war, including key members of the YSP's leadership. The country began to lose its support from the Soviet Union in the mid-1980s. This prompted discussions in 1988 between North and South Yemen over the possibility of unification. Following two years of negotiations, the two states agreed to merge into one country in 1990.

Fabric produced in Czechoslovakia was made into localized combat uniforms for special units of the PDRY.

REPUBLIC OF YEMEN

Shortly after the unification of North and South Yemen, the Iraqi invasion of Kuwait pulled together a coalition of Arab nations that took part in the Gulf War. Yemen opposed military intervention from non-Arab states and was punished by being forced to receive 800,000 Yemeni refugees expelled from Saudi Arabia. The coalition government formed by merging northern and southern Yemeni political parties was at this time relatively fragile. The south had become more prosperous and had better relations with western nations, causing resentment and accusations of violence against the Yemeni Socialist Party. As tensions mounted in 1994, the as yet non-integrated armies of both regions took up defensive positions. Although a peace accord was signed by politicians, it was ineffective in preventing civil war. South Yemen declared itself the Democratic Republic of Yemen on 21 May and a civil war correspondingly raged for two months, resulting in thousands of deaths and the defeat of the south. Once hostilities had ended, a general amnesty was declared and the country was again unified.

In June 2004, the northern part of Yemen again erupted into violence when the government attempted to arrest Zaidi religious leader Hussein Badreddin al-Houthi. The tribal Houthis were in turn accused of trying to overthrow the Yemeni government and implement Zaidi religious law. A de facto state of insurgency has existed in the north since, marked by brief periods of violence and occasional ceasefire periods. Throughout this time the Republican government has been assisted by Saudi Arabia, while the Houthis are believed to be clandestinely supported by Iran. Al Qaeda began to involve itself in Yemeni affairs in 2009 and has claimed responsibility for several bombings. A series of drone strikes sponsored by the United States have targeted Al Qaeda training camps, but many have gone astray and killed civilians.

A pro-democracy uprising arose in January 2011, similar to that sparked by the Arab Spring in other parts of the world. When it ended in February 2012, the Saleh government had been overthrown and the military was restructured, but the central power remained weak as increased territorial control of much of Yemen transferred to both Houthi and Al-Qaeda insurgents taking advantage of the chaos of the revolution. By September 2014, Houthi insurgents and opposition leaders loyal to former president Saleh mounted a coup d'etat and wrested control of the government. This seizure of power was condemned by the United Nations and resulted in a number of nations closing their embassies. The Yemeni parliament has been dissolved and the government is now run by a Revolutionary Committee essentially under control of the Zaidiyya Shia movement. Yemen has been in a full state of civil war since March 2015, with various regions of the country being under the control of different factions, including the Houthi, forces loyal to former president Hadi, Southern Transitional Council, Al-Qaeda in the Arabian Peninsula (AQAP), Islamic State of Iraq and the Levant (ISIL), and non-aligned entities. Much of the Arab world supports the pro-Hadi security forces and many have contributed military personnel and materiel to influence the outcome of the war.

The Armed Forces of Yemen consist of the Army (including the Republican Guard – now called the Presidential Defense Forces), the Navy and the Air Force. Both the Army and the Republican Guard include special operations and mountain units in addition to conventional infantry, armor and support units. The Ministry of the Interior also maintains approximately 50,000 paramilitary troops, concentrated primarily in the Special Security Forces (known as the Central Security Organization until 2013); they also administer a small Coast Guard contingent. The SSF functions as a kind of Gendarmerie, and has a wide range of infantry materiel and light armor in its arsenal. In addition the Central Security Forces (CSF), the primary internal security element of the CSO, there is also a Counter-Terrorist Unit under its command.

The Egyptian two-color 'sand' pattern came into service in 1990, and variations are still being worn today within Army and CSO units.

A DPM variant pattern that was general issue for Army units and some units of the National Police. (*Private collection*)

These soldiers of the 1st Armored Division wear a six-color desert camouflage design that has been general issue to Army personnel. (*Private collection*)

This desert-colored camouflage design was issued to Special Forces and Republican Guards during the 1990s and early 2000s. (*Private collection*)

A Yemeni officer, possibly of the Central Security Force, wearing a copy of m81 woodland pattern. (*Private collection*)

Yemeni soldiers, circa 2011, wearing a three-color pixilated desert design. (*Private collection*)

An officer of the Yemen Coast Guard wearing the grey six-color camouflage design of this service. (*Private collection*)

A blue-purple DPM variant was previously worn by some Yemen Police units.

This three-color pattern, similar to the old Finnish M70 design, was issued to some units of Republican Guards. (*Private collection*)

An officer of the Special Security Forces wearing the pixilated camouflage design now issued to this service. (*Private collection*)

This soldier wears a copy of the USMC desert MARPAT design, in service with Military Police and other units since 2013. (*Private collection*)

Digital version of the old Egyptian two-color pattern now used by the Special Security Forces. (*Private collection*)

The pattern seen here is believed to be a variation of the Special Security Forces digital design, but having a very different colorway. (*Private collection*)

Unidentified personnel wearing a copy of USMC temperate MARPAT, which has also been worn by Houthi rebel forces. (*Private collection*)

Houthi rebels wearing blue woodland and digital pattern uniforms, the latter possibly the same design issued in Jordan. (*Private collection*)

Chapter 4

Europe

ALBANIA

In the aftermath of the Second World War, nationalist forces were defeated by the numerically superior communist forces, which created the People's Republic of Albania. Although allied to the Soviet Union for many years, the country was never a member of the Warsaw Pact. The People's Republic was officially dissolved in 1991 and the Fourth Albanian Republic established. The country faced a serious crisis in 1997 when peaceful protests over collapsing pyramid-banking schemes became violent. Both the Police and Republican Guards deserted their posts, leaving armories open for pillaging by militia and criminal gangs. A six-month period of civil war followed, resulting in more than 2,000 deaths. Stability was restored with the assistance of UN peacekeeping forces, mostly from Europe.

The armed forces followed a Soviet-Chinese model during the Cold War period, and retained this structure even after the collapse of the Eastern Bloc. Much of the armed forces disintegrated during the 1997 civil war, prompting a complete restructuring which continued for many years. The modern armed forces consist of the Land Forces, Air Force, Naval Force and the Military Police. Albania became a member of NATO in 2014 and has participated in several multinational operations.

The Soviet M1944 TTsMKK tricolor deceptive pattern was used by some Albanian troops from the 1970s until the 1990s.

This unique vertical stripe pattern was introduced in mid-1990s but saw only limited distribution, and may even have been experimental. (*Private collection*)

The two soldiers in this photo wear a mixture of surplus US m81 military kit and uniforms made from Chinese 'woodland-hybrid' pattern camouflage in use since 1995. (*Private collection*)

These Albanian officers are clad in uniforms of a different woodland type pattern, possibly locally-made. (*Private collection*)

More of a 'leaf' type design, this brown pattern was introduced mid-1990s. (*Private collection*)

Commandos from the Albanian Special Forces Battalion preparing for deployment to Afghanistan are wearing surplus US tricolor desert camouflage uniforms. (*Private collection*)

Multicam uniforms were also worn by Albanian personnel serving in Afghanistan, and, as seen here, continue to serve with the Special Forces Battalion. (*US DOD*)

A new camouflage pattern, similar at a distance to German flecktarn, was introduced in 2012 for the armed forces. (*US Marine Corps*)

These Commandos model a light-colored fleck camouflage also adopted in 2012. Originally designed for use in snow-conditions, it was also deemed appropriate for issue to personnel deploying to desert regions abroad. (*Private collection*)

This blue woodland type camouflage is in use with the Forzat e Nderhyrjes se Shpejte (FNSH) of the State Police. (*Private collection*)

A copy of USMC temperate MARPAT is here worn by the Reparti i Eleminimit dhe Neutralizimit te Elementit te Armatosur (Department of Neutralization of Armed Elements) of the MOI. (*Private collection*)

US and Turkish Gendarmerie woodland patterns also in use with the RENEA unit of the MOI. (*Private collection*)

AUSTRIA

Following a period of post-war occupation by Allied Forces, Austria regained its full independence in 1955 and at the same time declared it would remain in a state of 'perpetual neutrality'. The country remained non-partisan throughout the Cold War and has avoided any international conflicts with its neighbors, although it has been a member of the United Nations since independence.

The Austrian armed forces are known as the Bundesheer and consist of Land and Air Forces, as well as Special Forces (Jagdkommando), which are primarily concerned with counter-terrorism and counter-insurgency. For most of its history, the Bundesheer did not issue camouflage uniforms, retaining instead an olive green working uniform until very recently.

Nicknamed 'steintarn' (stone pattern) this 'splinter' design was printed only on the reversible zeltbahn issued to individual soldiers.

Loosely based on German Erbsenmuster and introduced in 1957, the Austrian 'pea' pattern was in general service until 1976. (*Private collection*)

These Austrian personnel serving in Sri Lanka wore modified US tricolor desert camouflage uniforms, also issued to personnel serving in Iraq. (*Private collection*)

A new camouflage pattern was introduced in 2017 for general issue to the Bundesheer. (*Austrian MOD*)

BELARUS

With the collapse of the Soviet Union in 1990, the former Byelorussian SSR became a sovereign state and changed its name to the Republic of Belarus in August 1991. The country remained very strongly under the influence of neighboring Russia until President Alexander Lukashenko revived an interest in Belarussian national identity. The present administration is considered severely authoritarian and has received numerous accusations of human rights violations, particularly against non-governmental organizations. Belarus remains a member of the Commonwealth of Independent States (CIS) and the Collective Security Treaty Organization (CSTO), as well as the United Nations.

The armed forces were largely inherited from those of the old Soviet Belorussian Military District. Presently they consist of the Ground and Air Forces. Additionally, the Ministry of the Interior has its own Internal Troops, as well as The Federal Police, Presidential Security Service, and State Security Agency.

The Soviet era solnechnye zaychiki (sunshine rays) pattern continued in use with Belarussian airborne and special forces personnel long after the country became independent. Both KZS and KLMK type uniforms have been used.

Also carried over from the Soviet era were variations of the TTsKO butane pattern. These were also used for many years primarily by airborne and special operations personnel. (*Private collection*)

Other versions of the three-color design, referred to as 'hoptoad' by some sources, were used by airborne/SF personnel in Belarus from 1991 to 1995 or so.

These internal troops wear a very light-colored variation of dubok that was in use from the mid-1990s to early 2000s. (*Private collection*)

A two-color desert camouflage design, based on the TTsKO, was introduced for peacekeeping personnel in 2003–4.

The Russian flora design came into general use with the armed forces and interior troops around 2000. (*Private collection*)

These paratroopers of the 38th Airmobile Brigade are wearing the Russian tsifra pattern that was introduced for general service in 2008 for the armed forces and interior troops. (*US Army*)

As a member of the Collective Security Treaty Organization (Организация Договора о Коллективной Безопасности) or CSTO, Belarussian personnel wear the distinctive desert camouflage pattern seen here. (*Private collection*)

These troops from an undetermined unit (possibly Internal Troops) are wearing the Russian-produced SS-Leto camouflage design. (*Private collection*)

The OMON unit of the Ministry of the Interior wear this interesting pattern of brown, black and grey. (*Private collection*)

These personnel from the special unit Almaz of the MVD wear the Russian Border Service camouflage. (*Private collection*)

This blue-grey four color camouflage scheme was in service with regular Police and special police units during the early period of independence.

Spetsnaz personnel of the Ministry of the Interior often wear a woodland-variant pattern as seen here. (*Private collection*)

Although attired for a public appearance, these Border Guards still wear the berezhka pattern commonly associated with the old Soviet KGB units. (*Private collection*)

A unique design, known colloquially as Kamysh (reeds) or Podlesok (undergrowth) pattern was used previously by the Border Guards.

This officer of the Forest Guard wears a pixilated camouflage design, which is the same pattern worn by the Ukrainian Border Service. (*Private collection*)

BELGIUM

As the country was rebuilt in the aftermath of the Second World War, Belgium also faced an obligation to its colonial possessions in Africa, notably the Congo and Ruanda-Urundi. Nationalist sentiments, which had arisen in parts of Africa during the 1950s, came to a head in the Congo with a series of riots in the 1960s calling for an end to colonialism. This was granted in June of that year, followed two years later by Belgium's other colonial possession, separated into the nations of

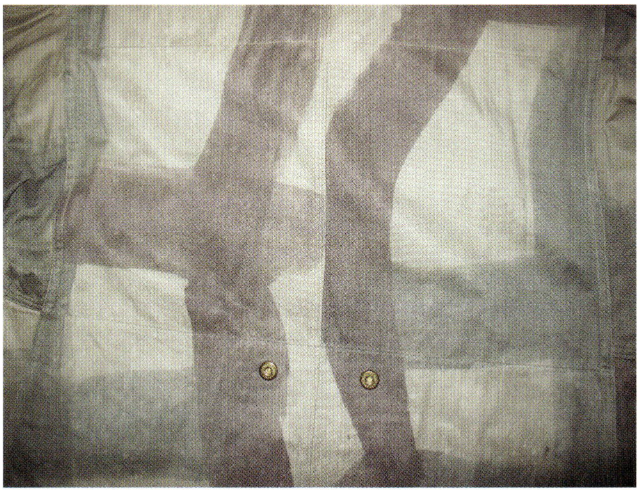

The first effort at a locally-produced camouflage design is seen here. This was an effort in the late 1940s to copy the Second World War era Denison pattern. The results are fairly crude.

A two-color 'waves' design was introduced in 1951 and worn in conjunction with the earlier Denison copy pattern by the Belgian United Nations Command (Volunteer Corps) in Korea. (*Private collection*)

A second version of Belgian 'brushstroke' camouflage was produced between 1952 and 1956, but worn into the 1970s by airborne and commando formations.

Rwanda and Burundi. Belgian military officers continued to train and advise all three countries for a number of years. A founding member of NATO, Belgium sent a battalion-sized unit to support the allied effort during the Korean War, participated in the International Security Assistance Force in Afghanistan, and has been a frequent contributor of peacekeeping forces to United Nations efforts, particularly in Africa.

The armed forces of Belgium are comprised of four elements, Land, Air, Naval and Medical.

A third variation of 'brushstroke' pattern introduced in 1954 continued in production until the 1970s. (*Private collection*)

A 'jigsaw' camouflage design, indigenous to Belgium, was introduced in 1956 and restricted to elite units as was most camouflage of the period. This Para-Commando, photographed in 1989, wears a later version of the pattern as a combination airborne smock and combat trousers. (*Henrik Clausen*)

The Belgian Air Force was given its own camouflage design in 1989 for use primarily by the ground defense and security personnel such as this anti-aircraft team. (*Private collection*)

The jigsaw pattern was universally adopted by the Belgian armed forces in 1999. (*US Air Force*)

Belgian military personnel deployed to Afghanistan wear the desert jigsaw design introduced in 2004. (*Private collection*)

This Belgian Special Forces Group operator is fully-outfitted in a combat uniform of Multicam, in service with special operations since 2016. (*Private collection*)

BOSNIA AND HERZEGOVINA

This region was formerly a constituent state within the Socialist Federal Republic of Yugoslavia, created in 1946. With the breakup of the Soviet Union came an emerging desire to shake off communism and embrace ethnic nationalism, which sparked widespread violence in Yugoslavia. In November 1990, multi-party elections initially established a coalition government incorporating the three primary ethnicity-based parties (representing Bosniaks, Serbs and Croats) but the coalition was short-lived when it became clear the Serbian element wished to remain a part of Yugoslavia, while the other two segments of the population did not. A state of war erupted as a result, lasting from 1992 to 1995 and resulting in thousands of deaths, including substantial numbers of civilians who died as a result of ethnic cleansing. Three principal belligerents took part in the war: the HVO (Bosnian Croats), Army of BiH (primarily Bosniak Muslims), and the Bosnian Serb Army (BSA). However, the war also included a number of paramilitary, volunteer units, foreign fighters and the involvement of NATO air strikes against the BSA.

Peace talks in late 1995 resulted in the Dayton Peace Agreement, followed by the deployment of a NATO-led Implementation Force (IFOR) to monitor the peace process.

Between 1995 and 2005 the armed forces of Bosnia and Herzegovina consisted of two separate entities, the Army of the Federation of Bosnia and Herzegovina (incorporating Croat and Muslim elements) and the Army of the Republika Srpska (Bosnian Serbs). In 2005 the elements merged into a single entity, although retaining cultural/ethnic elements as part of their distinctions. The present armed forces consist of the Ground Forces, and the Air Force and Air Defense Forces. Since 2007, the AFBiH have deployed personnel to Afghanistan, Iraq and the Democratic Republic of Congo. With the assistance of the European Union Police Mission (EUPM) the country has also consolidated and restructured its national law enforcement agencies to include the Bosnian State Investigation and Protection Agency (SIPA), the Ministry of Security (MoS), and the State Border Service (SBS).

Two Bosnian soldiers, probably from a unit with elite status, wear the old JNA 'branch' pattern which has been field-crafted into load bearing vests. The soldier on the left is also wearing a locally-produced copy of the JNA issue M89 oakleaf design. (*Private collection*)

Locally produced woodland camouflage, such as that seen in this photo from 1993, was worn by Croatian HVO and Bosnian BiH elements during the civil war, and also by Federation Forces during the interim period. (*Private collection*)

This unique 'frogskin' pattern was worn primarily by Bosnian units operating in the Bihac Pocket region, and is likely to have originated from a single factory. (*Private collection*)

A strange amoeba-type pattern, also probably locally produced, did see limited use with some Bosnian units.

A copy of the USMC temperate MARPAT design was introduced in 2005 for the confederated AFBiH forces. (*US Army*)

These members of the Bosnian contingent leaving Afghanistan in 2014 wear the US tricolor desert pattern camouflage. (*US Marine Corps*)

This two-color olive/black design is worn by Special Units of the Republika Srpska police. (*Private collection*)

These two Federal Ministry of Interior Police men deployed on a peacekeeping operation wear a combination of Slovakian desert camouflage and UCP. (*Private collection*)

Another Bosnian FMI Policeman on a mission in Africa is wearing Multicam pattern fatigues, also worn domestically by special police units. (*Private collection*)

Members of the Federalno ministarstvo unutrasnjih poslova (FMUP) of the Federal Police Administration here wear a unique urban camouflage pattern. (*Private collection*)

The Bosnian Serb Interior Ministry Specijalna jedinica policije or SJP wearing their camouflage pattern. (*Private collection*)

BULGARIA

Bulgaria emerged from the Second World War as a one-party, Communist People's Republic under the influence of the Soviet Union. It became a member of the Warsaw Pact in 1955 and sent military advisors to various regions in Africa and the Middle East during the 1970s and 1980s. In 1989, responding to the collapse of the Eastern Bloc, the Bulgarian Communist Party relinquished its political monopoly and in 1990 free elections were held. The country was invited to join NATO in 2004 and deployed military personnel to Afghanistan as part of ISAF.

The Bulgarian People's Army was an active member of the Eastern Bloc. The country produced considerable war materiel which were exported or supplied as war aid to friendly governments and sympathetic Marxist guerilla movements. In addition to Land, Air and Naval Forces, the military included Labor Forces, Rocket Forces, Transport Troops, and Signals personnel. The Ministry of the Interior forces included the Border Guards, Interior Troops, and the People's Militia (armed police). Early Bulgarian camouflage patterns were heavily influenced by those of the German

An early splinter camouflage pattern was developed during the Second World War and its use was extended into the communist era.

A second splinter design was introduced between 1951 and 1952 for reconnaissance personnel. This is a variation of the earlier pattern in which the splinter shapes are more densely situated.

Wehrmacht, particularly the splittermuster or 'splinter patterns'.

The Bulgarian armed forces have been significantly reduced in size in the modern era, although it retains Land, Air and Naval Forces. The Ministry of the Interior continues to hold responsibility for internal security and law enforcement duties.

The pattern seen here was introduced in 1953, crudely printed, and issued primarily to airborne and recon personnel – this was the first Bulgarian pattern to incorporate 'rain straits' and is more faithful to the wartime German original, at least in concept.

The жабежка кожа or 'frogskin' pattern was introduced in 1968. It was issued primarily to airborne, reconnaissance and chemical troops, and later adopted by the Federal Border Guards. (*Private collection*)

A third version of the splinter pattern was introduced in 1959 and produced until 1968; this design had much more well-defined shapes. (*Private collection*)

Seen here with Serbian, American and Moldovan colleagues, a Bulgarian paratrooper (in the foreground) wears the last version of the splinter pattern, adopted in 1991 and still being used by some personnel in the 2000s. (*Private collection*)

A 'desert lizard' pattern camouflage uniform was produced in the 1980s or 1990s, reputedly for issue to military personnel serving in advisory roles.

This 'green lizard' design was also produced during the 1990s, supposedly for special operations personnel.

A series of camouflage designs, based loosely on British DPM, were adopted in 2003 when the country became a member of NATO. The first incarnation of a woodland or temperate pattern is seen here.

A Bulgarian Army sniper wearing the second incarnation of the temperate DPM pattern adopted for general issue. (*US Army*)

Bulgarian personnel deployed to Afghanistan in 2005 wearing the recently adopted desert DPM variant pattern. (*Private collection*)

Air Force personnel undergoing medical training in the grey DPM variant pattern worn by that branch of service. (*US Air Force*)

Bulgarian Army personnel in Afghanistan are wearing a copy of US tricolor desert camouflage in 2014. (*US Army*)

CROATIA

Responding to the dissolution of two neighboring states within the Federation of Yugoslavia, Croatian nationalists began calling for looser federation in 1990, while Croatian Serbs maintained their desire to remain a part of the union. A full declaration of independence was issued in June 1991, followed in December by the establishment of an unrecognized Republic of Serbian Krajina in the Serb regions. Tensions eventually escalated into full civil war. The conflict lasted four years, involving the Croatian armed forces on one side (assisted from 1994–95 by the Bosnian Army), and the forces of Serbian Krajina (heavily supported by the Yugoslavian People's Army until 1992) on the opposing side. An independent Croatia was officially recognized in 1992, after which a United Nations Protection Force (UNPROFOR) was deployed. Hostilities were largely intermittent thereafter, and by the end of 1995 the conflict was essentially over, with Croatian victory.

At the beginning of the civil war, the Croatian Police took the brunt of the fighting from Serbian militia units. A National Guard Corps (Zbor narodne garde – ZNG) was rapidly formed in 1991 to provide increased military capability, supplied in large part by purchases of war materiel made from ex-Warsaw Pact countries like East Germany and Hungary. The ZNG eventually were incorporated into a new Croatian Army (Hrvatska vojska). The armed forces today consist of Naval and Air Forces, in addition to the Army. Croatia was invited to join NATO in 2013, and has participated in a number of United Nations peacekeeping missions as well as deploying personnel to Afghanistan as part of ISAF.

Surplus East German strichtarn pattern winter uniforms were initially worn by the ZNG during early months of the war, and by a few units of the HV until stocks were depleted.

A member of the ZNG during the war clad in locally-produced 'tiger stripe' pattern fatigues. (*Private collection*)

Taken in Karlovac in 1992, these two photos show Croatian soldiers wearing two different copies of US m81 woodland pattern in use with Croatian forces during the war. There were, in fact, many variations in circulation, most produced locally. (*Henrik Clausen*)

A copy of the Soviet butane pattern was produced in small numbers during the war.

A desert pattern based on US tricolor was adopted by Croatian personnel deployed to Afghanistan in the early rotations. (*Private collection*)

Two additional 'tiger stripe' patterns that continued in service after independence with Ministry of Internal Affairs units.

This photo from 2005 shows the two newly adopted pixilated camouflage designs (desert and woodland) next to the outgoing m81 woodland pattern that was current at the time. (*Croatia Ministry of Defense*)

Croatian Navy personnel wearing the blue digital pattern adopted in later years. (*Croatia Ministry of Defense*)

CZECHOSLOVAKIA

Like much of Eastern Europe, Czechoslovakia was absorbed into the Eastern Bloc following the end of the Second World War. Although Slovakia had supported a Democratic party in the 1946 elections, the Communist party seized control of the entire country in 1948, entering Czechoslovakia into the Warsaw Pact in 1955. In January 1968, a short period of political liberalization was attempted under the leadership of Alexander Dubček. Facing mixed reactions from other Warsaw Pact nations, the Soviet Union initially tried to limit democratic changes through negotiation, but when talks proved unsatisfactory the Soviets invaded with 200,000 troops supported by 2,000 armored vehicles. Scattered resistance was quelled and the country was returned to its former state under a new first secretary. In the following year, the country became a federation of two states, the Czech and the Slovak Socialist Republics. Transition away from communism eventually took place during the so-called Velvet Revolution in late 1989. Long-time dissident leader Václav Havel subsequently became the first president of a Federal Republic of Czechoslovakia. Two years later, the federation of the two states was dissolved and on 1 January 1993 the Czech Republic and Slovak Republic came into being.

The Czechoslovak People's Army (Československá lidová armada) consisted of Ground Forces, Air Force, and the Air Defense Forces. There is some evidence to suggest that German machinery for printing camouflage fabric had been moved to Czechoslovakia during the later stages of the Second World War, where it continued to produce material for the Wehrmacht war effort. These machines appear to have produced some of the earliest camouflage patterns worn by the new Socialist Republic of Czechoslovakia. By the 1950s, however, these older designs faded away in favor of patterns seemingly designed for use in specific terrain or perhaps even during certain seasons. In 1963, the Czech Army fell into line with the drab trends of the rest of the Warsaw Pact, adopting a 'rain' pattern design barely distinguishable at a distance as anything but a solid color. A plain khaki uniform was also introduced in 1975, but by the mid-1980s experiments with new camouflage designs began anew, producing a 'leaf' pattern based on the US M1948 ERDL, and a two-color desert pattern.

The first Czech airborne units in 1948 wore smocks made from surplus Italian M1929 fabric leftover from the Second World War. (*Private collection*)

Two scouts or reconnaissance personnel wearing the mrácky ('clouds') pattern with the grey side out. The uniforms were reversible, with the opposite side being primarily green. (*Private collection*)

Two early Czechoslovak designs based on the German sumpfmuster (marsh) pattern, it is likely these were in fact printed on war era German equipment. (*Henrik Clausen collection*)

A variation of the sumpfmuster design, using brighter colors was introduced in 1948 and printed mostly on shelter material. (*Henrik Clausen collection*)

This sniper wears the third pattern utilized on the reversible uniforms, the duby ('oaks') design. Similarities to the German Leibermuster pattern from the Second World War are easily apparent. (*Private collection*)

An infantryman wearing the jehlicí (needles) or oblaky (clouds) pattern, introduced in 1963. (*Private collection*)

Introduced in 1960 the vz 60 mlok (salamander) pattern featured a bright yellow base color and was worn by conventional as well as special operations personnel. (*Private collection*)

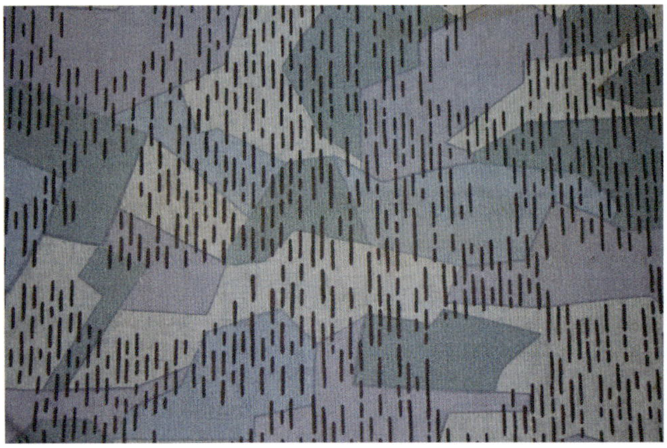

This pattern was produced in the late 1980s and worn by the Lidové milice (People's Militia). The design had similarities to one produced in Poland. (*Henrik Clausen collection*)

The Svaz pro spolupráci s armádou (Union for Cooperation with the Army) or SVAZARM was a paramilitary youth organization established in 1951 and given its own splinter type camouflage design. (*Henrik Clausen collection*)

CZECH REPUBLIC

The Czech Republic was invited to join NATO in 1999 and is also a member of the Organization for Security and Co-operation in Europe (OSCE). The armed forces, consisting of Land and Air elements with support services, have been completely transformed from those of the Warsaw Pact era into a very professional military force. In addition to its role with NATO, military personnel from the Czech Republic are actively involved in rescue and humanitarian operations, and international peacekeeping through the United Nations. Czech forces deployed to Afghanistan and Iraq, were involved with IFOR and SFOR, and participated in operations in Bosnia, Turkey, Kosovo and Albania.

The vz 85 or 'leaf' pattern was actually introduced prior to the dissolution of Czechoslovakia, but its use carried over to personnel from the Czech Republic in the early stages of its independence.

Adopted purely as a working uniform, the Vz. 92 uniforme pracovni (work uniform) nevertheless features a camouflage design intended to 'mask' oil smears, stains, and other blemishes.

Seen here in 2014, the two color desert was first issued to Czech military personnel operating in arid regions in 1991. (*Private collection*)

The Vz. 95 pattern was adopted for the armed forces in 1995 and has remained in service with most units into the present day. (*Ministry of Defense*)

British Army issue 'windproof' camouflage tank crew uniforms were put into service in the 1950s by Danish vehicle crews, where they were designated the Kampvognsdragt M/1952. (*Henrik Clausen*)

DENMARK

The Kingdom of Denmark was a founding member of NATO and its armed forces have been involved with international peacekeeping for many years. The term Forsvaret is used for the armed forces, and roughly translates as 'Danish Defense'. This unified force consists of the Royal Army, Royal Navy, Royal Air Force, and the Home Guard. Danish military personnel deployed in support of NATO efforts during the Kosovo War and the war effort in Afghanistan. Several hundred Danish personnel were also sent to Iraq between 2003 and 2007.

As with most European nations, Danish military personnel wore solid olive colored uniforms for much of the Cold War period. The first experiment with camouflage, the Truppenversuch 76, was based on German Army trials, but not universally adopted until 1984.

These Danish personnel wear the desert version of M/84, introduced in 2000 for Danish personnel deployed to Eritrea and Ethiopia. (*Private collection*)

These soldiers wear the Multicam pattern uniforms adopted by the Danish Armed Forces in 2013. (*Private collection*)

This curious camouflage design was printed only on fabric made into issue scarves, worn with the M/58 olive green combat uniform between 1977 and 1985. The same design was later adopted by the Norwegian Air Force.

Danish soldiers on exercise wearing the standard issue M/84 camouflage pattern uniform, introduced in 1984 and loosely based on German drawings but with a unique color scheme. (*Henrik Clausen*)

EAST GERMANY

Officially the German Democratic Republic (Deutsche Demokratische Republik) the country came into existence in 1949 from the Soviet portion of the post-war division of Germany. Issues such as the status of Berlin and construction of the Berlin Wall in 1961 contributed to deepening the tensions of the Cold War. Both East and West Germany claimed they were the only legitimate government of the German state, although the claims were ultimately relinquished by a series of treaties signed in the early 1970s. The DDR had its own armed forces, but nevertheless Soviet troops occupied the country for its entire existence.

In 1989, public outcry over contentious election results brought about a mass exodus of East German citizens crossing the borders into Czechoslovakia and then into the west. Following this, a series of demonstrations against the government resulted in the opening of several sections of the Berlin Wall, new elections in 1990 and, eventually, reunification with West Germany. Although the full process took a number of years, East Germany officially ceased to exist on 3 October 1990.

The National People's Army, or Nationale Volksarmee (NVA), was the armed forces of the DDR from 1956 to 1990. It consisted of the Land Forces (Landstreitkräfte), Naval Forces (Volksmarine), Air Forces (Luftstreitkräfte) and the Border Troops (Grenztruppen). Additionally, state security was supplemented by the Volkspolizei-Bereitschaften (VPB) of the Ministry of the Interior, the Staatssicherheitsdienst (State Security Service) or Stasi, and the auxiliary Kampfgruppen der Arbeiterklasse (Workers Party Combat Groups). In addition to its membership in the Warsaw Pact, East Germany deployed military advisors to a number of sympathetic regimes, particularly in Africa, and also provided war materiel to Marxist insurgent movements in places like Southwest Africa. Early East German camouflage was heavily influenced by Soviet war-era designs, but later followed in the footsteps of other East Bloc nations and became quite drab.

Heavily influenced by Soviet camouflage from the Second World War era, the earliest East German pattern put into use was known as M49 sowjetische tarnbekleidung or Russisches tarnmuster (Russian camouflage). (*Private collection*)

Issued between 1956 and 1967 to units of the NVA and Ministry of the Interior, M58 Flachtarnenmuster has also been called Kartoffelmuster (potato camouflage) or Blumentarn (flower camouflage). (*Private collection*)

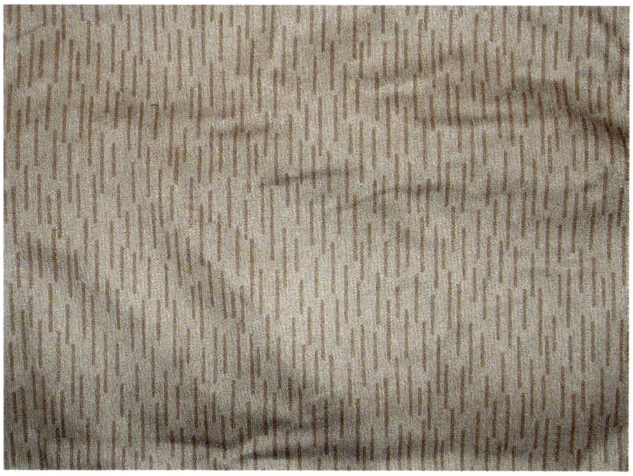

A good photo of the early Strichmuster (line pattern) uniforms, which became the general issue camouflage design for all NVA forces in 1965. (*Private collection*)

Estonia had been incorporated into the Soviet Union prior to the end of the Second World War and remained the Estonian Soviet Socialist Republic until 1991. During the late 1940s, heavy resistance to Soviet occupation brought about the formation of the Forest Brothers (metsavennad), a partisan movement involving as many as 15,000 combatants. By 1953 the movement had essentially died out through attrition. The country became heavily militarized, with hundreds of thousands of ethnic Russians being resettled there. The era of perestroika brought about renewed feelings of national pride in the Baltics and a desire for increased autonomy. A mass demonstration in August 1989 united more than two million people in a human chain across all three Baltic states. A referendum in 1991 showed 71 per cent in favor of independence, which was officially declared in August of that year. The last Russian military units left Estonia in 1994. Estonia was invited to join NATO in 2004.

The armed forces of Estonia consist of the Estonian Defense Forces (Land, Naval and Air Forces) and the Estonian Defense League (unified paramilitary forces). In addition to its role in NATO, Estonian troops participated in the War in Afghanistan and also deployed to Iraq. As part of peacekeeping efforts with the United Nations, Estonian personnel have deployed to Lebanon, Mali and several other countries.

Two Estonian Border Guards circa 1991 show the use of old Soviet-era TTsKO uniforms during the formative years of the armed services. (*Private collection*)

An Estonian soldier wearing the green variation of Soviet TTsKO, which entered service in the very late 1980s. (*Private collection*)

Early production runs of locally-produced TTsKO camouflage were inconsistent and often had lighter-colorations, as seen in this photo. (*Private collection*)

When the Eesti Kaitseliit or Estonian Defense League was re-formed in 1990, many personnel received surplus East German camouflage uniforms that were cheaply available in Europe at the time. (*Private collection*)

Some Estonian units wore surplus US m81 woodland pattern camouflaged uniforms, including during a deployment to Bosnia (SFOR) in 1996. (*US DOD*)

This short-lived uniform was issued to the Border Guards between 1993 and 1998. (*Private collection*)

The Estonian contingent to Bosnia (SFOR) between 1996 and 1998 also wore Danish M/84 fleck pattern uniforms.

A three-color desert variation of the standard TTsKO design was between 2001 and 2004 for personnel serving in Iraq and Afghanistan. (*Private collection*)

Estonian personnel deploying to Iraq and Afghanistan during the initial stages were issued a mixture of US six-color and tricolor desert camouflage. (*Private collection*)

Soldiers on exercise wearing the Estonian Digital Combat Uniforms or ESTDCU adopted in 2006. (*US Marine Corps*)

Estonian officer modeling the ESTDCU for desert deployments in 2009. (*Private collection*)

FINLAND

Despite pressures from the West and the Soviet Union, Finland remained largely neutral in the post-war years. Its focus was on becoming a productive, industrialized nation. Relations with the USSR were friendly, although Finland retained a market economy and trade with the west. When the Soviet Union finally collapsed in 1990, the country was free to integrate further with the rest of Europe.

The Finnish Defense Forces (Puolustusvoimat) consists of a cadre of professional soldiers (about 25 per cent) and the remainder national servicemen. The Army, Navy and Air Force fall under the Ministry of Defense, while the Border Guard is under the authority of the Ministry of the Interior. All former conscripts remain on reserve status until they reach the age of 50 or 60.

Finnish military personnel have participated in peacekeeping operations as part of the United Nations since 1956. Recent deployments include Afghanistan, Kurdistan, and Lebanon, in addition to missions in Africa and Europe. The armed forces did not embrace the concept of camouflage until the 1960s, although Finnish personnel have traditionally worn snow camouflage since the Winter War (1939-40). Finnish camouflage has retained a unique flavor and has even been copied or modified by other nations.

The M/62 pattern camouflage was introduced in the early 1960s and is nicknamed kurkkusalaatti (cucumber relish) by some soldiers. Many color variations were produced, and the uniforms remained in service with reserve units well into the 2000s. (*Henrik Clausen, 1992*)

The M/91 pattern was an updated version of the M62 (retaining the same drawings) that was primarily worn as barracks dress until the early 2000s. (*Private collection*)

These soldiers are wearing solid white oversuits for operations in heavy snow. (*Private collection*)

The first digital design was released with the M04 Hellepuku uniform for issue to Finnish personnel deploying to desert regions. (*Private collection*)

The M05 Maastokuvio (Landscape pattern) followed shortly after and is the standard operational and deployment uniform for the Armed Forces. (*Finnish Ministry of Defense*)

Seen here, the M05 Pakkaskuvio (Frost pattern) uniform is an additional layer for cold and inclement weather, providing warmth and repellency. (*Private collection*)

Lastly, the M05 Lumikuvio or snow pattern uniform is issued as overwear in snow conditions. (*Private collection*)

These Finnish Jaegers are wearing Multicam, which has been in use with special operations since around 2015. (*Private collection*)

FRANCE

In the aftermath of the Second World War, France struggled to maintain control of its former colonial possessions, with mixed success. Weakened by the war, the country faced a monumental task of rebuilding its domestic armed forces, while at the same time retaining colonial units in sufficient strength to stave off insurrection and maintain internal security. French control of Indochina (Cambodia, Laos and Vietnam) was never truly regained, as a communist government in north Vietnam had already been established, and a movement was afoot in 1946 to end colonialism in the south (Cochinchina). The resulting conflict, known as the First Indochina War (1946–54) resulted in French withdrawal from Southeast Asia and independence granted to its former colonial possessions. Just months later, another anti-colonial conflict erupted in Algeria. Members of the National Liberation Front (ALN) waged a bloody, seven-year war against French colonial forces which spilled over onto the French mainland in the form of terrorist attacks, perpetrated by supporters of both sides. Although French forces retained the upper hand militarily, political pressure and instability within the Fourth Republic resulted in capitulation by 1963. In Africa, France granted independence to the majority of its former possessions largely without conflict.

Although it was a founding member of NATO, France limited its participation in the organization beginning in 1959, ostensibly so that it might achieve an independent peace with the Eastern Bloc in the event of war. This relationship lasted until renewal of full participation in 2009. France also remains a supporter of the OSCE. The country retains a few overseas possessions, which it garrisons with moderate forces to provide security and training opportunities for its armed forces. The Forces armées françaises consist of the Army, Navy and Air Force. The Ministry of the Interior operates two police agencies, the Gendarmerie nationale and the National Police. Additionally, France recreated its historical formation – the National Guard (la Garde nationale) – in response to a series of terrorist attacks in 2016.

France was one of the coalition forces that fought Iraq during the Persian Gulf War (Opération Daguet), but did not participate in the later Iraq War. French personnel deployed to Afghanistan in support of operations there but had withdrawn the majority by the end of 2014. France has been a major contributor of peacekeeping forces to the Balkans, Africa and the Middle East.

This copy of the German Wehrmacht splittermuster pattern was produced for troops during the Indochina war as a shelter.

Another splinter type pattern produced around 1950 for individual troop shelters.

A section of French-made Luceber parachute in a wavy camouflage design produced in the 1950s.

This photograph shows Captain (later General) Marcel Bigeard wearing a Second World War vintage M1942 windproof pattern camouflage smock, which saw extensive use with French and Vietnamese colonial troops during the First Indochina War. (*Private collection*)

A photo from 1950 showing French forces wearing surplus US M1942 'spot' pattern camouflage uniforms and custom-made headgear during the First Indochina War.

'Lizard' pattern camouflage was introduced in 1951, and was loosely based on brushstroke patterns developed by the British in the Second World War. The term 'lizard' was actually a nickname given to French paratroopers during the Algerian war, whereas the camouflage itself was generally called camouflee de leópard (leopard camouflage). Variations were produced from 1951 into the 1970s, although for the most part the use of camouflage was discontinued in the 1960s due to its association with the airborne units, some of whom attempted a coup d'etat during the Algerian War. Although some experimentation with camouflage designs did occur in the 1980s, French armed forces would not adopt its own unique design until the Persian Gulf War in 1990.

A well-known photograph of Capitaine Vial and Commandant Masselot just after the battle of Dien Bien Phu, wearing crisp early pattern Troupes Aeroport.es (TAP) model uniforms in one of the early 'lizard' designs. (*Private collection*)

A section of French-made Luceber parachute in a wavy camouflage design produced in the 1950s. (*Private collection*)

A Vietnamese officer of the 3e Bataillon de Parachutistes Vietnamiens wearing the TAP model 'lizard' camouflage uniform of his unit, with examples of early lizard camouflage designs. (*Private collection*)

Members of the Commando Georges unit during the Algerian War wear later pattern, custom-tailored tenue du leópard fatigues and matching soft caps. (*Private collection*)

A legionnaire of the 2e Régiment Etranger de Parachutistes (2 REP) in Algeria wearing a Troupes Aeroportées (TAP) pattern lizard uniform. (*Private collection*)

French sailor of the Groupement des Commandos-Marine (Marine Commando Group) during the 1st Indochina War wearing the unique 'frogskin' design created for that unit and worn from 1951 to 1959. (*Private collection*)

French Legionnaires during Op Serval (Mali) wearing the tricolor desert pattern introduced during the First Gulf War. The Daguet desert pattern has remained in use with French forces into the present period, although the pattern has been slightly modified in recent years. (*ECPAD*)

These French Legionnaires wear the camouflee Centre Europe (CE woodland) pattern introduced shortly after the desert pattern. (*ECPAD*)

This Legionnaire of the 3e Régiment étranger d'infanterie (3 REI) wears commercially-procured 'tiger stripe' pattern camouflage utilities, worn by cadre of the Army Jungle Warfare School in French Guiana. (*Private collection*)

Operators from the Groupes d'Intervention de la Police Nationale (National Police Intervention Group) or GIPN wearing the standard CE woodland design with grey colorway. (*Private collection*)

Soldiers at the Centre d'Entraînement aux Actions en Zone Urbaine (CENZUB), or Urban Zone Combat Training Center of the French Armed Forces in OPFOR role wearing a blue-dominant woodland pattern. (*ECPAD*)

Also worn by OPFOR personnel at the CENZUB is this unique blue flecktarn type design. (*ECPAD*)

This three-color winter/snow pattern is worn by units of the Commandement des Operations Speciales (Special Operations Command) operating in mountainous regions. (*ECPAD*)

GERMANY

The Federal Republic of Germany (Bundesrepublik Deutschland) was formed in May 1949 by merging the three western sectors of occupied post-war Germany into a single state. Although it fell within the Soviet-controlled territory that was to become East Germany, the city of Berlin was also partitioned into East and West sections, with the latter becoming part of the Federal Republic. Germany re-formed its own military along western European lines in late 1955 and immediately joined NATO. This added to already mounting tensions with the Eastern Bloc, and contributed to the building of the Berlin Wall in 1961, which further isolated West Berlin. A series of events in 1989 and 1990, however, led to the dismantling of the wall, allowing thousands of East Germans to travel and even emigrate from the DDR. As the world watched the Iron Curtain crumble, the two Germanys engaged in discussions about reunification, which were finalized in October 1990.

The Bundesgrenzschutz (Federal Border Guard) or BGS was actually the first paramilitary organization permitted to form by the occupying allied forces. Formed in 1951, the name of the agency was changed to the Bundezpolizei in 2005. The Federal Defense Forces, or Bundeswehr, were formed in 1955, consisting of the Army, Navy, Air Force and Medical Services. At the time of reunification, approximately 50,000 members of the East German Volksarmee were integrated into the German Army. Mandatory conscription ceased to exist in 2011 and was followed by a reduction in the overall size of the Bundeswehr. German forces have taken part in a number of international operations, including those in Afghanistan, Kosovo, Lebanon, Mali and Iraq. Both the BGS and Bundeswehr inherited much of the camouflage tradition of war era Germany, but the use of camouflage was discouraged by NATO and fell into disuse in the 1960s and 1970s in favor of olive drab. With a renewed interest in camouflage expressed by other NATO countries in the mid-1970s, Germany embarked upon its own series of trials (Truppenversuch 76), which eventually led to the adoption of flecktarn that is still in use today.

The Bundesgrenzschutz (Federal Border Guard) were the first service created in post-war Germany, and also the first to utilize camouflage. The individual here wears the first pattern splittermuster (splinter pattern) adopted by the BGS in the early 1950s and based strongly on original Wehrmacht designs. (*Private collection*)

The Bundeswehr (German Army) adopted its own variation of splittermuster camouflage in 1956, although it saw only limited distribution to infantry and airborne units and was discontinued in 1960. (*Private collection*)

A variation of the splittertarnmuster pattern that appeared during the same time frame is seen here; this version appears to have had much more limited fielding.

A soldier from Gebirgsjägerbataillon 231 (Mountain Infantry battalion) wearing the schneetarnmuster or 'snow pattern' camouflage introduced in the 1960s and worn by units operating in snow-covered terrain well into the 1980s. (*Private collection*)

Three members of the Bundesgrenzschutz wearing the second camouflage design of this federal branch, introduced in the late 1950s. A variation of the wartime sumpfmuster (marsh pattern), the design would continue to be worn sporadically into the 1970s. (*Private collection*)

Produced only as a reversible shelter half (zeltbahn), these were issued to German ground troops in the 1950s. (*Private collection*)

These mechanized infantry personnel are wearing flecktarn camouflage, adopted by the German Armed Forces in the late 1980s and continuing to serve the military today. (*US Army*)

German military personnel wearing the Tropentarn pattern, officially adopted in 1998 for all German armed forces deploying to arid regions of the world. (*US Army*)

Members of the elite Kommando Spezialkräfte (KSK) or Special Forces Command here wear the Multicam pattern uniforms adopted by this unit in 2014. (*Private collection*)

A new type of snow camouflage based on the flecktarn drawings was adopted in 2015. (*Private collection*)

Immediately following the end of the Second World War, Greece was plunged into a civil war between communist KKE forces (supported by neighboring Albania, Bulgaria and Yugoslavia) and the armed forces of the Greek Monarchy (supported by the UK and USA). After three years of fighting, the war ended with the defeat of the KKE. Shortly thereafter, in 1952, Greece was accepted into NATO. Following his dismissal of the centrist government in 1965, King Constantine II was ousted in a coup d'etat in April 1967, replacing the government with a military junta. The next seven years were marked by political suppression and severe human rights abuses, culminating in the death of forty civilians during the Athens Polytechnic uprising.

An attempted coup d'etat on the island of Cyprus, sponsored by the Greek junta, resulted in an invasion of the island by Turkish forces, which seized control of the Turkish-dominated north portion of the island and have kept it under occupation. As a result of the failed coup attempt, the junta collapsed and a democratic constitution was adopted in June 1975. The Greek monarchy was never restored.

The Greek Armed Forces consist of the Army, Navy, Air Force and Coast Guard. The country has been an active participant in NATO exercises since rejoining the organization in 1980. Greek peacekeeping efforts with the United Nations have primarily revolved around regions closest to home such as the Middle East and the Balkans. Camouflage developments were mostly influenced by those of France and the United States.

Essentially copied from the French leópard or 'lizard' pattern, the first Greek camouflage design was introduced in the 1970s.

Officers of the Special Forces Brigade wearing a later camouflage pattern with slightly different color palette. (*Private collection*)

A Greek marine wearing the vertically aligned 'seaweed' camouflage pattern that remained in service until the end of the 1980s. (*Private collection*)

Security personnel of the Greek Air Force wearing the blue variation of the lizard pattern adopted by that branch in the 1990s. (*Private collection*)

These members of the Greek contingent serving with ISAF in Afghanistan wear the desert variation of the standard lizard pattern adopted in the late 1990s. (*Private collection*)

These members of the HAF special operations are wearing British DPM pattern camouflage uniforms. (*Private collection*)

A Greek Air Force Warrant Officer serving with ISAF in Afghanistan in 2015 here wears US tricolor desert pattern. (*US Air Force*)

Operators from the Greek Navy Special Forces have often deployed using US m81 woodland pattern.

Since 2007, the Army Special Forces have also worn a copy of UCP.

As the Second World War came to an end, Hungary was occupied by the Soviet Union and quickly became a satellite state, the Hungarian People's Republic. Seeking to rid the country of intellectuals, democrats, free-thinkers, and former officials, hundreds of thousands were subsequently purged by the regime between 1948 and 1956, many ending up dead or imprisoned. Hungary became a member of the Warsaw Pact in 1955, an unpopular move that contributed to an armed uprising in 1956 in which a few thousand revolutionaries faced the tanks and heavy weapons of the Soviet army. The insurgency was quelled after thirty days of fighting and the loss of more than 20,000 Hungarian lives. With the decline of communism and the USSR in 1989 came a renewed interest in shaking off Soviet influence. The country experienced a very peaceful transition to democracy culminating in free elections in May 1990. Although beset by economic recession, Hungary continued to embrace integrationist policy, joining NATO in 1999 and the EU in 2004.

Under communism the Hungarian armed forces were known as Magyar Néphadsereg, the Hungarian People's Army. Consisting primarily of Ground and Air Defense forces, they were supplemented by the State Border Guard, People's Security Police, National Police and the Worker's Guard Corps. In addition, the entire Soviet Southern Group of Forces was stationed in Hungary between 1947 and 1989. Today the armed forces are called the Magyar Honvédség or Hungarian Defense Force (HDF), consisting of the Hungarian Army and Air Force. Hungarian personnel deployed to Afghanistan in support of ISAF, and also sent personnel to Iraq, Bosnia and Kosovo. Additionally, the country has been an active participant in United Nations-sponsored peacekeeping and observer missions. The use of camouflage by Hungarian forces was carried over from the Second World War, although initially only as printed shelter material. Hungary has prided itself on showing national identity in its camouflage, a tradition that carried through until the early 2000s.

The 1949 M háromszínü sátorlap-esögallér or M1949 was initially produced as combination poncho/shelter, but later as a one-piece coverall for Border Troops and in 1982 as a uniform for airborne personnel.

Although it was introduced in the late 1930s, the M38 pattern camouflage was utilized in the post-war period as a combination poncho/shelter half until 1949. (*Private collection*)

Hungarian reconnaissance personnel wearing an M1951 one-piece coverall, produced between 1951 and 1953 in two color schemes – one in a green-dominant version for lowlands and open terrain, and one in a brown-dominant version for highlands and forested areas. (*Private collection*)

This 'leaf' type camouflage was introduced in the 1970s and utilized primarily by the Border Guards, Worker's Militia and as NBC gear into the late 1980s.

A 'leaf' variation with green colorway from around the same period was issued only to the Border Guards as a coverall. (*Private collection*)

A second 'leaf' variation with green colorway was produced in smock & trousers combination uniform for the Worker's Militia into the 1980s and also as combination poncho/shelter. (*Private collection*)

A largely experimental design, this pattern was printed on NBC gear and vehicle tarpaulins that were issued to the HDF. (*Private collection*)

The M49/82 pattern is a reissued version of the M49, distributed between 1982 and 2000 and worn by Hungarian Army, Border Guards, Air Force ground crew, and the National Police CT unit. (*Private collection*)

Two Hungarian officers, one dressed in the tropical Hurrikán camouflage pattern, and the other in the re-issued M49/82 pattern. (*Private collection*)

These Hungarian troops serving in Iraq in 2008 are mostly wearing locally made uniforms in US tricolor desert pattern, which was originally issued in 2003. (*United Nations*)

This pattern, nicknamed Pakisztáni (Pakistani), was first worn by Hungarian personnel deployed to Iraq during the First Gulf War, but was discontinued in 1999.

This photo, taken in 2005, shows Hungarian Air Force personnel wearing the four-color camouflage design adopted in 1994 as a universal pattern for the HDF, the color scheme chosen to keep in line with NATO. (*Henrik Clausen*)

This 'amoeba' type camouflage pattern was issued in 2001 to MVB (County Defense Committee) personnel.

Two Hungarian soldiers stationed in Afghanistan as part of ISAF wearing the four-color desert camouflage design adopted in 2004 for arid environments. (*Private collection*)

These soldiers in Kosovo 2017 are wearing newly issued 'HUNPAT' camouflage uniforms, based around a Multicam color palette, adopted by the HDF 2016. (*Private collection*)

The Hungarian elite Terrorelhárítási Központ (TEK) or Counter-Terrorism Center has deployed operationally in several camouflage patterns, including UCP, Multicam and a commercially-available digital design. (*Private collection*)

ICELAND

Iceland has no standing Army and has never been in a war with another country in the modern era. National security is the responsibility of the Coast Guard, the Air Defense System, and the Iceland Crisis Response Unit (ICRU), created in the 1990s to participate in international peacekeeping missions. The ICRU also has a paramilitary role, in the event of national crisis. Iceland was a founding member of NATO. Members of the Coast Guard deployed to Iraq in 2003, although they were later replaced by members of the ICRU. Iceland was also a participant in the conflict in Afghanistan and supported the bombing of Yugoslavia in 1999. Iceland does not have its own camouflage design, so its personnel have utilized those of other countries on some deployments.

Two members of the ICRU personnel attached to ISAF wearing Norwegian desert camouflage. (*Private collection*)

During deployments to both Bosnia and Kosovo, members of the ICRU wore British DPM camouflage.

These ICRU personnel wear Norwegian M98 pattern field jackets. (*Private collection*)

IRELAND

The Republic of Ireland has retained its neutrality since the end of the Second World War. Although not a full member of NATO, the country has joined the Partnership for Peace program and is active in peacekeeping operations in Europe and around the world. Members of the Defense Force have deployed to Kosovo, Bosnia, Somalia, East Timor and Afghanistan.

The Irish Defense Forces (Óglaigh na hÉireann) consist of the Army, Naval Service and Air Corps, including reserves. Ireland retained solid color combat uniforms long after many countries had adopted their own camouflage uniforms, and only in 1999 did the country introduce its own unique design.

British DPM clothing was worn by members of the Army Ranger Wing from the 1980s until the mid-1990s.

A small Irish contingent that deployed to Somalia in 1993 wore US 'chocolate chip' desert pattern uniforms.

An Irish Army Captain here wears the Irish Disruptive Pattern (DPM) introduced in 2000 and universally issued to members of the Defense Forces. (*US Army*)

These members of the Irish contingent to Afghanistan wear the desert variation of the DPM pattern developed for personnel serving in arid regions. (*Private collection*)

ITALY

Italy became a republic shortly after the end of the Second World War. Under the 1947 Peace Treaty it relinquished all of its wartime and colonial possessions, including Libya, Eritrea, Somaliland, and territory that would become parts of Albania, Yugoslavia, and France. Unlike Germany and Japan, the Italian Armed Forces were not disbanded in the post-war years, although their size and capacity were initially reduced. Italy became a member of NATO in 1949 and has been an active participant in training maneuvers and peacekeeping operations since. In 1982, Italian troops deployed to Lebanon as part of the multinational effort to enforce the ceasefire between Israel and the PLO. Italian Naval vessels were part of the coalition forces during the Gulf War; although no ground troops took part in combat operations, Italian personnel did deploy in the aftermath to provide humanitarian assistance to Kurdish refugees in northern Iraq. Italian personnel have also deployed to Afghanistan as part of ISAF, the NATO force and the provisional reconstruction team. Between 2004 and 2011, Italy provided training and assistance to Iraq in the aftermath of the Iraq War. The country has been active in peacekeeping efforts with the United Nations since 1951, participating in missions to Bosnia, Cyprus, Georgia, Kosovo, Somalia, Niger, Mali, Libya and the Central African Republic.

These Paracadutisti (paratroops) serving in Lebanon in 1982 wear a variation of the original M1929 telo mimetico issued primarily to Army units from 1950 into the 1980s. (*Private collection*)

Marines of the Battaglione San Marco in a third variation of the three-color pattern, with a strong grey element. (*Private collection*)

The Italian Armed Forces consist of four branches: the Army, Navy, Air Force, and the Carabinieri (national Gendarmerie). Italy was the first country to develop a distinctive camouflage pattern of its own, which can be traced to 1929. Modified versions of the pattern were still in use with Italian forces as late as the 1970s. This design would later be discarded in favor of a pattern more in line with NATO standards, although the Marines would be issued their own distinctive designs from the 1990s onwards. By 2004, a new series of camouflage designs were developed for all services.

Navy divers wearing the color variations associated with the Battaglione San Marco Naval Infantry unit and special forces. (*Private collection*)

Italian Army Alpini (mountain warfare troops) wearing the German Army schneetarn camouflage pattern initially seen in the 1990s. (*Private collection*)

These Italian Marines wear a camouflage pattern issued to the BSM and Italian Navy COMSUBIN (Comando Raggruppamento Subacquei e Incursori Teseo Tesei) beginning in 1991. (*Private collection*)

The four-color desert camouflage design seen here was introduced in 1991, and first worn by Italian troops deploying to Somalia. (*Private collection*)

Soldiers from one of the Bersaglieri battalions deployed to Bosnia wearing the roma 90 woodland camouflage that was implemented in 1990 and remained with the Italian Army until 2005. (*Private collection*)

The first of several variations of the standard BSM camouflage pattern was tested in 1993 but never fully implemented. Only a handful of uniforms were ever issued, but oddly enough flak vest covers in this pattern turned up among paratroops deployed to Somalia.

The second variation, with a very orange colorway, was issued primarily to Navy special forces (COMSUBIN) and trialed around 1994.

This COMSUBIN operator wears the last desert incarnation of this design, with strong pinkish tones, while serving in Afghanistan. (*Private collection*)

A close-up photo of an Italian soldier pulling urban security duty. He wears the mimetico Vegetata (vegetated pattern) design introduced in 2004 as a replacement for the earlier woodland design. (*Private collection*)

This Italian paratrooper wears the desert version of the mimetico Vegetata while serving in Iraq. (*Private collection*)

An air gunner of the Italian Air Force here wears the desert variant of the Vegetata pattern adopted by that branch of service. (*Private collection*)

These Italian Marines wear the new Vegetata design that replaced their older patterns, incorporating a different color palette than the Army and AF version. (*Private collection*)

The Vegetata variant pattern here was developed for the COMSUBIN when deploying to desert regions.

A Navy special operator here wears the commercially available 'Vegecam' or 'Multiland' design that was adopted by Italian special forces and worn during deployments to Afghanistan from 2012. (*Private collection*)

Kosovo was formerly a constituent state of Yugoslavia with a high percentage of ethnic Albanians. In the late 1960s, power in Yugoslavia became somewhat decentralized, and the Albanian population took greater control of administrative and law enforcement positions. Additional autonomy was granted to the region by the 1974 Constitution, giving rise to increased Albanian nationalism, although in the wake of public protests in 1981, territorial defense units were called up to quell the disorder. This resulted in the federal government rescinding a number of special provisions that had previously been granted to the Albanian population. Ethnic tensions and continued calls for Kosovar autonomy deepened throughout the 1980s, with the government relying on violent suppression as its only means of dealing with the issue.

In July 1990, the Albanian population established the Republic of Kosova, and confirmed its independent status in September 1992. Albania was the only country to officially recognize the existence of Kosova. When the Bosnian war ended in 1995 and the status of Kosovo was not resolved, the Kosovo Liberation Army (Ushtria Çlirimtare e Kosovës – UÇK), a paramilitary organization made up of ex-JNA veterans, émigrés and a percentage of Islamic fighters from around the world, embarked on a military campaign against the Yugoslav Army and police. The UCK smuggled vast amounts of war materiel into the country via Albania during the 1997 civil war there, thus increasing the overall effectiveness of its war effort. A ceasefire brought about in 1998 lasted only a few months, and a subsequent draft resolution sponsored by NATO was refused by Yugoslavia. NATO forces intervened by bombing Serbian installations in an attempt to force withdrawal. The war resulted in tens of thousands of deaths and disappearances, and as many as a million ethnic Albanians displaced. When the Yugoslav Army finally withdrew, tens of thousands of ethnic Serbs were subsequently expelled from Kosovo or abused by the remaining Albanian population. Kosovo was placed under transitional UN administration in June 1999, under which the Kosovo Force (KFOR) was established. Under the resolution, Kosovo remained a part of Yugoslavia with increased autonomy.

Following the 2007 parliamentary elections a coalition government voiced its intention to work towards full independence, which was declared on 17 February 2008. The majority of United Nations member states officially recognize the Republic of Kosovo; however, Serbia does not.

The Kosovo Protection Force (Trupat e Mbrojtjes se Kosoves or TMK) was a civilian emergency services/paramilitary organization established via UNMIK from 1999 to 2009. Established in January 2009, the Kosovo Security Force (Forca e Sigurisë së Kosovës – FSK*)* was a transitional paramilitary organization designed to perform a number of duties including law enforcement, internal security, search and rescue, and EOD. In 2014, it was announced that the FSK would transform into the Kosovo Armed Forces (Forcat e Armatosura të Kosovës, FAK*)* by 2019.

Newly adopted in 2012, these FSK personnel wear a pixilated camouflage design that incorporates the Kosovo coat of arms. (*US Army*)

This photo from the war of independence period shows the wide number of camouflage designs worn by the UCK, including Turkish woodland, m81 woodland, German flecktarn and Swiss alpenflage. In addition, older Yugoslavian patterns were also observed. (*Private collection*)

Latvia was forcibly collectivized and became a part of the Soviet Union as the Second World War in Europe was drawing to a close. During this time period, tens of thousands of Latvians fled to neighboring countries to avoid Soviet dominion. Between 1945 and 1952, tens of thousands more were imprisoned or exiled to Siberia. In the 1950s, a mass immigration of ethnic Russians to Latvia and the other Baltic states significantly decreased the percentage of ethnic Latvians residing in their native home. Demonstrations supporting political and economic reforms which began in the summer of 1987 led to the formation of the Popular Front of Latvia (Latvijas Tautas fronte). A brief period followed in which the nation was granted greater autonomy within the USSR. By 1989 the Soviet Union was crumbling and the supreme Soviet granted each of the Baltic states the right to hold democratic elections. In May 1990 a resolution was adopted restoring independence to the Republic of Latvia; however, transition was not immediate. An attempt was made in January 1991 by

Early Latvian camouflage was based on the Soviet three-color TTsKO concept, but generally using an alternative set of screens and varying color palettes. Most of these patterns date to the early 1990s.

From 1995, this design was adopted by Ministry of Interior units. (*Private collection*)

An early pattern associated with the Border Guards. (*Private collection*)

Soviet military and police to usurp the authority of the transitional Latvian government, which failed. Full independence was officially declared in August 1991, with full Soviet withdrawal of military forces completed in 1994.

The Nacionālie Bruņotie Spēki are the Latvian National Armed Forces, consisting of the Land, Naval and Air Forces, and the National Guard. Following Soviet withdrawal of its forces, the nation restructured and rebuilt its military along more contemporary European lines. In 2007 conscription was dissolved and the nation adopted a professional army. Latvia joined NATO in 2004 and has a joint-cooperative agreement with neighboring Estonia and Lithuania (Baltic Battalion/BALTBAT and Baltic Naval Squadron/BALTRON) to serve in peacekeeping roles. Latvian personnel have participated in military operations in Iraq and Afghanistan, as well as peacekeeping efforts in Somalia and Mali.

In use with Latvian special operations personnel as early as 1992, a copy of m81 woodland pattern was later adopted by the Land Forces as general service pattern until 2008. (*Private collection*)

Swedish M90 pattern camouflage was worn by Latvian troops attached to SFOR in 1996.

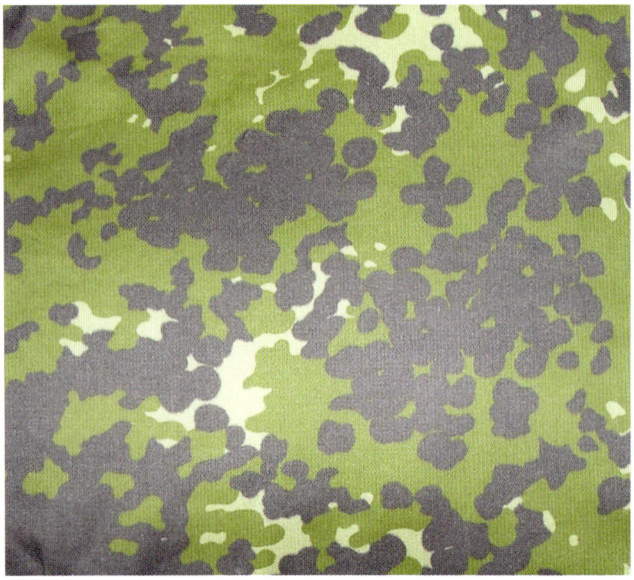

The Danish M84 pattern was worn by the Latvian contingent to Bosnia in 1998.

These Latvian personnel are wearing US three-color desert camouflage pattern uniforms in 2007 while on a deployment. (*Private collection*)

A unique tricolor desert camouflage design was adopted by Latvia in 2004, to be issued on foreign deployments to arid regions. These men in Afghanistan with ISAF all wear the pattern, except for the individual on the far left. (*Private collection*)

This Army officer wears the Latvian Camouflage Pattern (LatPat) designed by Barracuda of Sweden and adopted as a general issue pattern in 2007. (*Private collection*)

An improved design, seen here, was implemented in 2016 for use in summer and foreign deployments to tropical regions. (*Private collection*)

LITHUANIA

Lithuania was annexed by the Soviet Union in 1944 and it became the Lithuanian Soviet Socialist Republic once the war ended. As happened in other Baltic states, tens of thousands of ethnic Lithuanians were imprisoned or forcibly exiled to Siberia to make room for massive Russian immigration. An armed resistance was ignited and primarily took the form of guerilla warfare, but this was inevitably defeated by 1953. Nevertheless, the spirit of independence continued as an underground movement within Lithuania for subsequent decades. Sąjūdis (movement) or the Reform Movement for Lithuania emerged in 1988 and can be credited with helping organize the 'Baltic Way' human chain

Seen here with a Polish colleague, these Lithuanian troops wear a copy of the US m81 woodland pattern adopted by the Ground Forces and Ministry of interior in 1998. (*Private collection*)

involving 2 million people across the three Baltic States, among other things. In March 1990, Lithuania became the first Soviet republic to announce its secession from the USSR. The Soviets responded first by imposing an economic blockade, and in January 1991 by an attempted coup d'etat involving the Army, KGB and Ministry of the Interior, which was met entirely with unarmed resistance. Ultimately the USSR backed down and in September of that year the country was admitted to the United Nations. When a new constitution was adopted in 1992, the Soviet withdrawal of military forces began, and was completed by August 1993.

The Lietuvos ginkluotosios pajėgos (Lithuanian Armed Forces) was formed in April 1990, and consists of Land, Air and Naval elements, as well as the National Defense Volunteer Force and the Special Operations Force. Lithuania has gradually built up and restructured its armed forces along European lines. Conscription was continued until 2008. The country was admitted to NATO in 2004 and contributes personnel to the BALTBAT and BALTRON. Lithuanian personnel deployed to Afghanistan as part of ISAF and to Iraq as part of the Combined Joint Task Force. They have also been present in Somalia, Mali and Libya.

Some of the earliest military units formed following independence from the USSR wore dubok camouflage patterns.

Lithuanian Infantry clad in the M05 misko (forest) pattern introduced in 2002 for all armed services; the design features the cross of Lorraine embedded into the pattern. (*Private collection*)

The first truly native camouflage design emerged 1991 and was loosely based on Soviet TTsKO designs with a grey base color. The pattern would later by discarded by SKAT but adopted by the Border Guards. (*Private collection*)

These personnel in the OPFOR role wear desert fatigues overdyed black, which produces a new grey-brown colorway. (*Private collection*)

Members of the Lietuvos Viešojo Saugumo Tarnyba (VST) or Lithuanian Public Security Service wearing the 'Polygon' pattern adopted by the agency in 2010. (*Private collection*)

A rifleman modeling the desert camouflage pattern introduced in 2003 and worn in Afghanistan; the early version of this pattern had much more yellow in it. (*Private collection*)

Soldier modeling the variegated camouflage design original adopted by the Special Operations Force in 2011, but later approved for the entire ground forces. (*Ministry of Defense*)

A blue dominant camouflage design worn by the Lithuanian Navy, beginning in 2015. (*Ministry of Defense*)

Luxembourg was a founding member of the United Nations and initially declared its neutrality, but this ended in 1949 when it joined NATO. The Luxembourg Army was formed in 1945 and consisted of two infantry battalions, plus the Grand Ducal Guard Corps. Part of the French Zone in Germany was placed under the care of one battalion. The Ducal Guard later became integrated into the territorial command, but ultimately was disbanded in 1966. Troops from Luxembourg served alongside those of Belgium during the Korean War. The country has been part of the Eurocorps since 1994 and has contributed personnel to operations in the former Yugoslavia (UNPROFOR, IFOR, and SFOR), as well as the ISAF (again alongside Belgian personnel) in Afghanistan. The army has provided humanitarian relief to efforts in Rwanda and Albania.

Historically Luxembourg has utilized the camouflage combat uniforms of other nations, namely the United States and France. This changed in 2011 when a unique design was implemented for the Army.

The small Luxembourg Army issued surplus US m81 woodland pattern camouflage uniforms from 1985 until around 2004. (*Private collection*)

Army personnel serving with ISAF (Afghanistan) in 2004 wearing Belgian jigsaw pattern camouflage uniforms. (*Private collection*)

These personnel also serving in Afghanistan are wearing Belgian desert jigsaw pattern uniforms. (*Private collection*)

These young soldiers are wearing the temperate version of a new camouflage pattern introduced in 2011. (*Ministry of Defense*)

Two members of the UN mission in Lebanon (FINUL) wearing the desert version of Luxpat camouflage. (*United Nations*)

MACEDONIA

Formerly one of the six republics within the Socialist Federal Republic of Yugoslavia – within which it was known as the Socialist Republic of Macedonia – the country passed a referendum endorsing independence in September 1991. Shortly thereafter the Republic of Macedonia peacefully came into being. The country maintained neutrality throughout the series of wars that split up the remainder of Yugoslavia, although it was forced to deal with several hundred thousands of ethnic Albanian refugees during the conflict in Kosovo. Between February and August 2001, Albanian nationalists in the north and west regions took up arms against Macedonian forces. The conflict ended in an agreement for increased political rights for ethnic Albanians in exchange for disarmament.

The Army of the Republic of Macedonia (Армија на Република Македонија) or ARM consists of the Ground Force and Air Force, as well as a Special Operations Regiment. The armed forces have been a professional service since 2005. Although it has applied for membership, the country has not yet been accepted into NATO. Nevertheless, Macedonia has contributed military personnel to ISAF, and took part in Operation Iraqi Freedom alongside American allies. Macedonians also deployed to UNIFIL. Although initially outfitted in combat uniforms of the Yugoslavian National Army (JNA), the ARM shortly introduced its own distinctive camouflage uniform in 1992. Some units have also worn surplus US military uniforms.

The old Yugoslavian 'mountain' pattern was pressed into service by the earliest Macedonian units and utilized by special units for years to come.

During the formative years of the ARM, surplus stocks of Yugoslavian M89 'oakleaf' pattern uniforms were used, most of which were phased out by 1992. (*Private collection*)

A unique four-color camouflage design was adopted by Macedonia in 1992, with several variations noted using different color palettes. (*Private collection*)

Special elements of the Macedonian Federal Police initially wore Yugoslavian-era 'lizard' pattern uniforms.

Use of surplus US m81 woodland uniforms was seen by some ARM units, followed by procurement of the locally-produced copies seen here. (*Private collection*)

ARM special operations troops serving in Afghanistan here wear surplus US tricolor desert camouflage uniforms with Macedonian national insignia in 2005. (*Private collection*)

A mixture of grey woodland and UCP pattern uniforms worn here by the Rapid Deployment Unit (EMR) or Единица за брзо распоредување of the National Police; the Special Operations Unit 'Tiger' (Единица за специјални задачи) also has worn these patterns. (*Private collection*)

The USMC temperate MARPAT design is worn by the Special Support Unit or Посебна Единица за Поддршка of the National Police. (*Private collection*)

New camouflage designs for the ARM were adopted in 2009; seen here in the green/temperate version. (*Private collection*)

Macedonian personnel serving with ISAF in 2010 wearing the newly adopted national desert camouflage design. (*Private collection*)

MALTA

Malta achieved its independence from Britain in September 1964. It was declared a republic in 1974, but remains a member of the British Commonwealth. Since 1980 it has maintained a policy of strict neutrality. The Armed Forces of Malta (AFM) or Forzi Armati ta' Malta, is the combined defense service of this nation, including ground, naval and air elements, and traces its origins to the King's Own Malta Regiment. At several points in its history, the AFM has received technical assistance from the Italian government in the form of an Italian Military Mission to Malta.

The Italian vegetata camouflage designs were briefly worn by the AFM during the period 2011–12. (*AFM Press*)

These soldiers of C (Special Duties) Company are wearing US tricolor desert pattern camouflage uniforms. (*Private collection*)

The Italian patterns were quickly dropped in favor of Multicam, which is now the current camouflage design of the AFM. (*Private collection*)

US m81 woodland pattern uniforms were worn by the AFM until 2012. (*AFM Press*)

The historical region of Moldavia has long-standing ties to Romania, with which it shares a common language and many cultural similarities. It became a part of the Soviet Union in 1940, within which it was known as the Moldavian Soviet Socialist Republic. In the aftermath of the war, a great many ethnic Moldavians were deported to the Urals and Siberia, which contributed to the formation of a number of anti-Soviet resistance groups. By 1955 most of these dissidents had been arrested or executed by the Soviet government. Between 1969 and 1971 the National Patriotic Front was formed with the goal of establishing a Moldavian Democratic Republic and eventual union with Romania, but most of its leaders were eventually imprisoned. By the 1980s, however, the new period of openness inspired by Mikhail Gorbachev led to the formation of the Democratic Movement of Moldova, which in 1989 became the Popular Front of Moldova. The FPM organized a mass demonstration in August (the Grand National Assembly) and inspired anti-communist rioting in November. National elections held in February and March 1990 resulted in a declaration of sovereignty in June of that year. In August 1991, the Republic of Moldova declared itself an independent state. Although it became a member of the Commonwealth of Independent States (CIS), Moldova remained politically neutral and did not join the military branch. The United Nations officially recognized Moldova as an independent state in March 1992.

Trouble arose in the eastern region of Transnistria (where approximately 54 per cent ethnic Slavs resided) beginning in August 1990, stemming in large part from a rise in Moldovan nationalism and fear of union with Romania. The Pridnestrovian Moldavian Soviet Socialist Republic declared its independence and by the winter of 1991–92 there were clashes between Moldovan police and the Transnistrian militia (supported by elements of the Russian 14th Army). By July of 1992, Transnistria had become a de facto independent state, although it remains internationally recognized as a part of Moldova.

The Armed Forces of Moldova were formed out of the Garda Republicană (Republican Guard) established in 1990. Its two primary elements are the Ground Forces and Air Force. Moldova joined the NATO Partnership for Peace in March 1994, and has signed a defense agreement with Romania to strengthen regional security. Since 1991, Moldovan peacekeeping personnel have deployed to Liberia, Côte d'Ivoire, Sudan and Georgia. The Moldovan Armed Forces have received considerable military assistance and training from the United States in recent years, which has influenced its choice of camouflage.

This Moldovan soldier is wearing a Ukrainian-made three-color design loosely based on the Soviet butane but with unique 'whorl' shapes, worn by Moldovan forces between 1991 and 1995. (*Private collection*)

Another pattern found among the Moldovan forces between 1991 and 1995 is this three-color 'swirl' design, also sourced from Ukraine. (*Private collection*)

A recent photo showing the use of older Soviet and Ukrainian butane pattern uniforms, in the supply system since the country gained independence and now primarily utilized by OPFOR during training exercises. (*Private collection*)

These Moldovan paratroopers wear US m81 woodland patterned BDUs with local insignia, which were adopted in 1996. (*US Army*)

Moldovan paratroops in 2017 wearing a copy of US tricolor desert. (*Private collection*)

Police containing a demonstration outfitted in several types of blue-dominant camouflage, most based on woodland designs. (*Private collection*)

This border guard of the Poliția de Frontieră is wearing a Soviet era KLMK camouflage coverall, still in use presently. (*Private collection*)

Transnistrian Ground Forces personnel wearing a woodland variant. (*Private collection*)

Internal security personnel clad in a blue-woodland variant pattern. (*Private collection*)

Special operations personnel wearing a copy of USMC temperate MARPAT. (*Private collection*)

Soldiers of the Transnistrian Armed Forces wearing recently adopted Russian tsifra pattern camouflage uniforms. (*Private collection*)

MONTENEGRO

This region was one of the six republics within the Socialist Federal Republic of Yugoslavia and remained a part of the Federal Republic after its dissolution. The only two remaining states by 1992 were Montenegro and Serbia. In 2002, the two states signed the Belgrade Agreement which decentralized the Federal Republic and established the state of Serbia and Montenegro. In May 2006 a referendum monitored by the OSCE on the independence of Montenegro narrowly passed; the results were confirmed in June that year and a formal declaration was issued, without protest from Serbia.

The Armed Forces of Montenegro consist of the Ground Forces, Navy and Air Force. They have been a professional force since 2006. The nation became a member of NATO in 2016. Personnel have deployed in support of ISAF and Resolute Support Mission (RSM) in Afghanistan, and observers have also been sent to Liberia, Cyprus and Somalia. In 2009, Montenegro adopted its own camouflage design based on Multicam.

Old stocks of the M89 'oakleaf' pattern uniforms remained in service with Montenegrin forces until depleted. (*Private collection*)

A variation of Multicam was adopted by the VCG in 2009, incorporating an outline of the country into the design. (US Marine Corps)

Members of the Posebna Jedinica Policije (Special Police Unit) or PJP of the Ministry of Interior and Public Administration practise hand-to-hand combat dressed in the urban woodland pattern of this unit. The PJP also uses standard m81 woodland and UCP patterns. (*Private collection*)

The M89 was replaced by the M03 'oakleaf' variant in 2006 and worn until 2009.

This grey digital pattern is worn by other units of the Public Administration Police, including the riot control forces seen here. (*Private collection*)

A new pattern was issued in 2013 to Navy personnel, being essentially a recoloration of the existing Multicam-derivative. (*Private collection*)

These Military Police personnel wear the desert coloration of the national camouflage design while serving with ISAF in Afghanistan. (*Private collection*)

Shortly after the end of the Second World War, the newly restored Dutch government became embroiled in a military struggle against nationalists to retain its colonial possessions throughout the Indonesian archipelago. Although largely successful from a military perspective, international pressure and an inability to wrest control over much of the countryside from the Republican forces forced the Dutch government to capitulate in December 1949 and recognize the United States of Indonesia. Along with Belgium, France, Luxembourg and the United Kingdom, the Netherlands signed the Treaty of Brussels in 1948, a mutual defense treaty and the precursor to NATO. The creation of NATO led to some standardization of allied military technology, which would be integrated into the Dutch armed forces.

The Dutch Armed Forces (Nederlandse krijgsmacht) consist of the Royal Dutch Army, Royal Dutch Navy, Royal Dutch Air Force and the Royal Military Constabulary.

Dutch military personnel served with the US 2nd Infantry Division during the Korean War, and also deployed to Bosnia and Kosovo during the wars there. Between 2003 and 2005 Dutch personnel served in Iraq as part of the Multi-National Force. The Netherlands also supported the military effort in Afghanistan and was part of ISAF between 2006 and 2010. Since the late 1940s, the country has employed a wide range of camouflage designs, including some borrowed or copied from other nations, and many of local manufacture. In 2011 it was announced that a completely new series of fractal designs would be adopted by the Dutch Army in 2017, although this has yet to be fully implemented.

These men of the Korps Commandotroepen (Army Commandos) are wearing a combination of surplus US WW2 frogskin and experimental 'large blotch' shape uniforms on Curacao in 1951. (*Private collection*)

This rifleman serving in Indonesia circa 1947–48 is clad in a US-made M1942 'spot' pattern camouflage uniform. (*Private collection*)

Members of the Regiment Speciale Troepen fighting in Indonesia are wearing uniforms made from experimental camouflage designed in the United States and donated to the Netherlands in the post-war years. (*Private collection*)

The locally-produced spot pattern here was influenced by the US M1942 design, and began production in 1951.

These Dutch Marines wear a 'jigsaw' camouflage design produced by the Belgian firm Seyntex in the 1980s, and used by the Dutch Army and Marines for a few years. (*Private collection*)

British-made DPM was adopted by the Royal Dutch Marine Corps (Korps Marinirs) in the early 1980s, before the pattern was being produced locally.

For a short period of time, from 1986 until the early 1990s, the Dutch Marines wore its own DPM pattern camouflage.

Dutch-made DPM camouflage (referred to as woodland in the Dutch Army) was adopted by most of the armed forces in 1993 and has continued into the present period although it will shortly be phased out. (*Private collection*)

Dutch military personnel serving with ISAF in Afghanistan wearing a desert-pattern based on the US tricolor desert design. (*Private collection*)

A Dutch Army officer wearing the tropical or 'jungle' pattern introduced in 1993 for personnel serving in warm weather climates. (*Private collection*)

Royal Dutch Marines here wear a copy of US m81 woodland adopted by that service in 1993. (*Private collection*)

A Dutch Marine NCO wearing US-made tricolor desert pattern modified for use by RNMC. (*Private collection*)

Multicam operational uniforms have been worn by the Korps Commando Troepen (KCT) in Afghanistan, 11 Luchtmobiele Brigade (11th Airmobile Brigade) serving in Mali circa 2014, and by the Maritime Special Forces (MARSOF) of the Royal Dutch Marines. (*Private collection*)

Introduced in 2011, the Netherlands Fractal Pattern (NFP) has been produced in three variants – temperate/ woodland, arid/ desert, and transitional for field equipment. Uniform pieces began to enter service in 2020. (*Private collection*)

The commercial A-TACS® desert camouflage design has been worn by members of the Army Special Forces Regiment.

A variation of the NFP was introduced in 2016 for special operations personnel and produced by the Israeli firm Fibrotex. (*Private collection*)

NORWAY

Norway was a founding member of NATO in 1949. The Norwegian Armed Forces, or Forsvaret, consist of the Army, Royal Navy (including Coast Guard), Royal Air Force, and the Home Guard. Military service is a civic duty and, since 2013, has included women. Norwegian military personnel deployed to Afghanistan in support of ISAF and have frequently contributed to peacekeeping efforts with NATO and the United Nations. Norway's military use of camouflage stretches back to the 1950s, where it was employed on individual shelters. There has been a remarkable consistency to Norwegian designs despite changes in color palettes and usage.

This camouflage design was implemented as a combination poncho/shelter in 1950s and was used well into the 1970s.

An alternative camouflage design, also printed on shelters in the 1950s and 1960s.

A unique puzzle-type design that was issued to Norwegian Air Force ground crew and air defense personnel from the early 1980s until 1996.

The Feltuniform M/75 modeled here consisted of an olive green ensemble with camouflaged field jacket. (*Norwegian Army*)

These infantry personnel wear the Feltuniform M/98, issued from 1998 onwards as a full ensemble that would eventually include Goretex gear, field equipment, and other sundries. (*Norwegian Army*)

These Norwegian military personnel wear the desert camouflage pattern adopted in 2003 for personnel serving in arid environments such as Afghanistan. (*Norwegian Army*)

Navy special forces personnel serving in Afghanistan here wear Multicam patterned camouflage uniforms and field equipment, popular with Norwegian special operations. (*Private collection*)

POLAND

Although a legitimate Polish government had survived the Second World War in exile, the Soviets refused to recognize or include it in the Yalta conference. Stalin soon reneged on a promise to maintain Polish sovereignty and established a communist government in Poland, which was met with armed resistance (the Żołnierze wyklęci or 'cursed soldiers'). More than 50,000 armed insurgents waged a guerilla campaign against the Soviet-sponsored government from 1945 into the 1950s, most of whom were hunted down and executed by the Ministry of Public Security and the NKVD. The People's Republic of Poland was officially proclaimed in 1952.

The Solidarity Movement (Solidarność) began in Poland in the 1980s and, despite suppression and the imposition of martial law in 1981, developed into a powerful political force. Elections held in 1989 reflected this popularity and resulted in a Polish transformation to democracy, culminating in the election of Solidarity leader Lech Wałęsa, and the establishment of the Third Polish Republic. Poland became one of the first former Warsaw Pact nations to join NATO (in 1999).

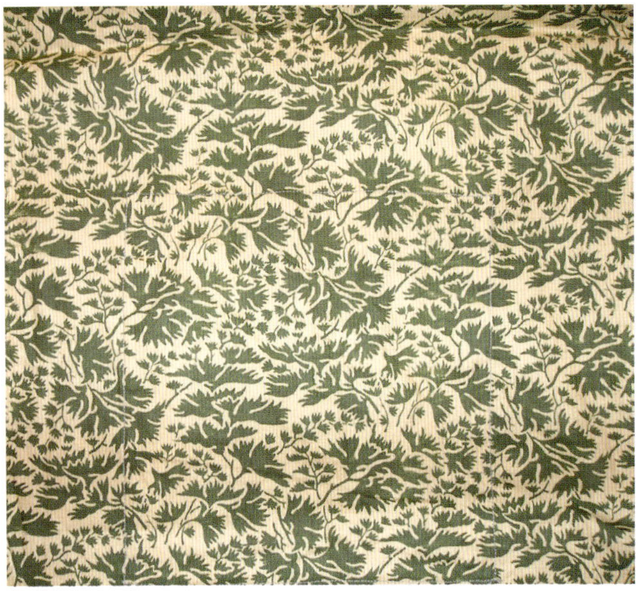

A Soviet-style camouflage uniform was adopted in 1952, nicknamed Pietruszka or 'parsley,' that saw service only with reconnaissance and special operations personnel.

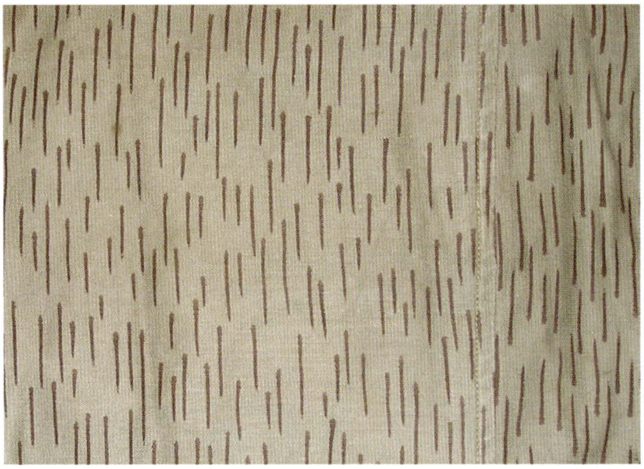

These paratroops are clad in the wz58 Deszczyk or 'raindrop' design, adopted circa 1958 and the first of the so-called 'rain patterns' to emerge out of the Warsaw Pact. These uniforms were worn by conventional troops as well as special operations personnel. (*Private collection*)

The Polish Armed Forces consist of the Land Forces, Navy, Air Force, Special Forces, and the Territorial Defense Force. Already heavily active in NATO cooperative exercises, Poland was part of the Coalition Force that deployed to Afghanistan as part of ISAF in 2002, maintaining a presence there until 2012. Poland also joined the small coalition of allied forces that invaded Iraq

This paratrooper wears the wz56 'splinter' pattern design, adopted in 1954 for use by reconnaissance and airborne personnel. (*Private collection*)

Polish military parachute shrouds were printed in a camouflage design adopted in the 1960s, the Żaba or 'frog' pattern. This fabric, in turn, was adopted by airborne and special operations personnel for use as custom made overall uniforms and field equipment.

The wz68 Moro Wojsk Lotniczych i Marynarki Wojennej, or 'black Moro' camouflage, worn by Naval Infantry and Air Force personnel in the 1970s and also by the Komenda Główna Policji (Chief Police Command) in the 1990s.

in 2003. Polish troops continued to serve with the Multi-National Force in Iraq until 2008. Additionally, Polish military personnel have participated in peacekeeping operations in Western Sahara (MINURSO), Democratic Republic of Congo (MONUC), Côte d'Ivoire (UNOCI), Lebanon (UNIFIL), Ethiopia/Eritrea (UNMEE), Kosovo (UNMIK), Liberia (UNMIL), and Georgia (UNOMIG). Since the 1950s, Poland has embraced a wide variety of camouflage designs, initially for special operations troops, but increasingly for conventional personnel as well.

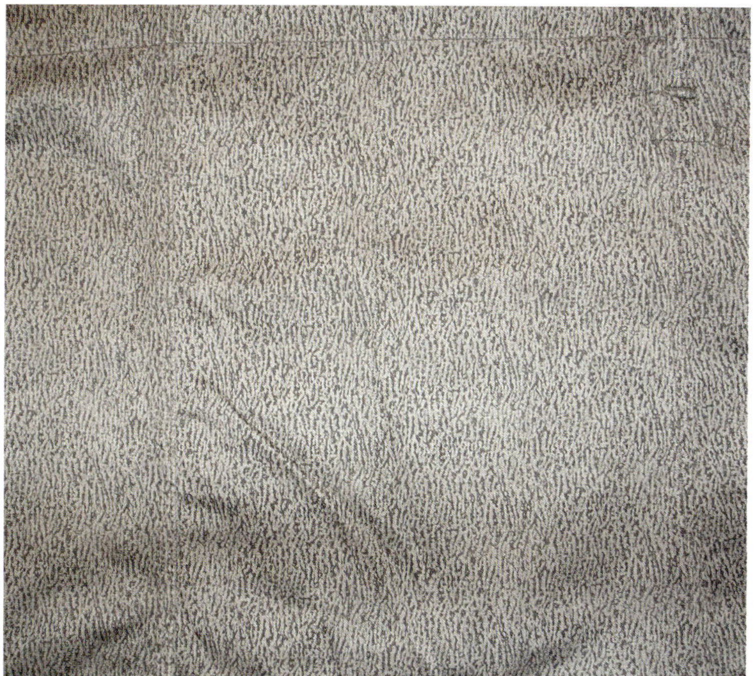

This Polish Airborne officer attached to UNPROFOR in 1992 is wearing the Army version of the wz68 Moro Ludowe Wojsko Polskie (LWP) pattern, introduced in 1968. Elements of the Ministry of Internal Affairs (Ministerstwo Spraw Wewnętrznych or MSW) such as the Border Guards (Wojska Ochrony Pogranicza) and the Motorized Riot Police (Zmotoryzowane Odwody Milicji Obywatelskiej) wore the same design into the early 1990s. (Henrik Clausen)

Universally adopted for the Army, Marines and Air Force personnel in 1989, the wz89 Żaba or 'frog' pattern (also called Puma) was worn until 1993.

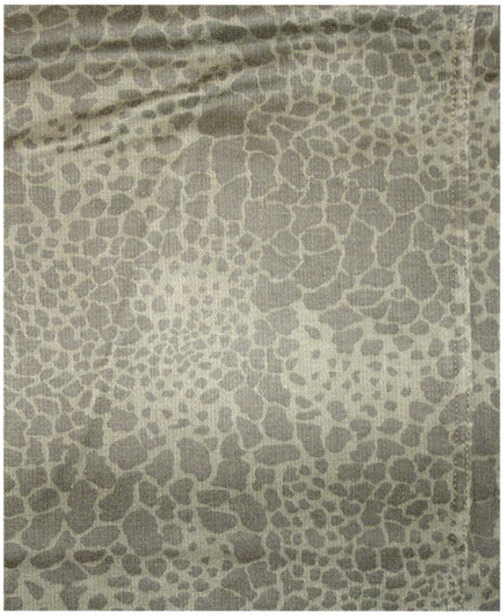

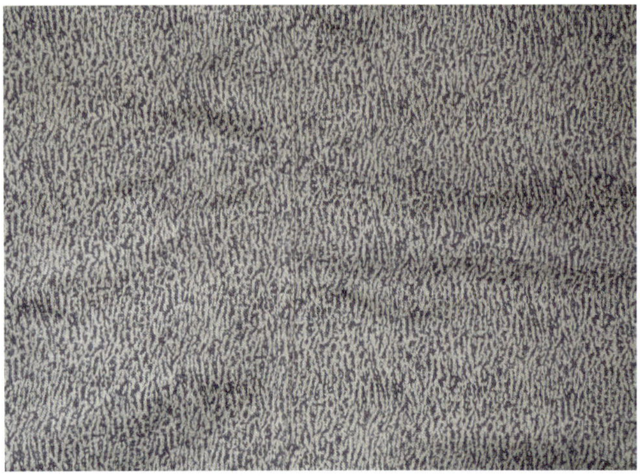

Another Moro pattern variation with more blue coloration worn by Polish Police (Milicja Obywatelska) of the Ministry of Internal Affairs (Ministerstwo Spraw Wewnętrznych or MSW) from 1970s to 1990s.

Introduced in 1993, the wz93 Pantera replaced the communist era patterns for general service with the armed forces and the Ministry of the Interior. (*Private collection*)

Members of the National Police Samodzielny Pododdzial Antyterrorystyczny Policji (SPAP) anti-terrorist unit here wearing the wz AT 1 PLAMIAK or Metro pattern, based on the German flecktarn design but with a grey colorway. (*Private collection*)

Two members of the Agencja Bezpieczenstwa Wewnetrznego (ABW), the Polish Internal Security Agency, clad in a darker green flecktarn variant pattern. (*Private collection*)

The Oddział Wart Cywilnych (Department of Civil Guards) and the Straż Ochrony Kolei (Railway Guards) have both worn this grey woodland variant pattern since the late 1990s. (*Private collection*)

Adopted in 2003 for personnel serving in desert and arid climates, the wz2000 Snajper or Pantera Pustynna (desert Panther) pattern saw extensive use with Polish troops serving in Iraq and Afghanistan, as well as on missions with the United Nations. (*Ministry of Defense*)

Polish Army Special Forces began using a Multicam-derivative design called Suez in 2008. (*Private collection*)

A flecktarn variant produced by the Polish firm Kama has been fielded by the Wydział Realizacyjny, Komenda Stołeczna Policji (WR KSP) or Implementation Department, Metropolitan Police Command of the Warsaw Police since 2012. (*Warsaw Police*)

This border guard is wearing a Multicam variant adopted by the Straż Graniczna (Border Guards) in 2015. (*Private collection*)

Portugal remained neutral during the Second World War, but began to experience difficulties within its overseas possessions in the 1950s. In 1954, the territories of Dadra and Nagar Haveli were annexed by India following a brief clash between Indian forces and colonial paramilitaries. This was followed in 1961 by the annexation of the small fort of São João Baptista de Ajudá by Dahomey. Later that year, Indian military forces again mounted a military operation against the Portuguese territories in Goa, Daman and Diu, ending in victory for India. Meanwhile, independence movements in Africa began to take root in the Portuguese colonies of Angola, Guinea-Bissau, and Mozambique. Between 1961 and 1974, Portuguese European and colonial forces were embattled on three separate fronts against a number of African liberation movements, some of whom were also in opposition to each other. The colonial war came to an abrupt end when a military coup d'etat – known as the 'Carnation Revolution' – moved against the authoritarian Estado Novo government and replaced it with the Junta de Salvação Nacional (National Salvation Junta). By 1975, all of its former colonies except East Timor and Macau were granted independence as Portugal tottered on the edge of civil war between right- and left-wing political movements. Nearly one million Portuguese citizens (refornados) would leave the former African colonies between 1975 and 1976.

Portugal was one of the founding members of NATO. Its armed forces (Forças Armadas) consist of the Army, Navy and Air Force. Although not part of the armed forces, the National Republican Guard (Guarda Nacional Republicana) is a paramilitary force that has internal security responsibilities. Until 1974, the Legião Portuguesa (Portuguese Legion) and the Brigada Naval (Naval Brigade) were right-wing paramilitary organizations responsible for organizing civil defense in territorial possessions. Additionally, during the colonial period the armed forces also included native African troops, as well as the Organização Provincial de Voluntários e Defesa Civil (OPVDC) or Provisional Organization of Volunteers and Civil Defense, which were localized auxiliary internal security forces. The latter were supplemented by native African militia

The Páraquedistas (paratroops) of the Portuguese Air Force (FAP) were the first troops to receive an operational camouflage pattern. Loosely based on French designs, this pattern emerged around 1955 and was also worn by elite Caçadores serving in Africa. (*Private collection*)

The M1964 'vertical lizard' pattern was worn extensively by troops serving in Africa and varied considerably in color, ranging from dark purple to reddish orange stripes dominating. (*Private collection*)

The Fuzileiros Navais (Portuguese Marines) continued to utilize lizard camouflage long after the remainder of the services switched to alternative patterns. In later years, the coloration became even darker. (*Private collection*)

Portuguese Air Force personnel wearing m81 woodland pattern uniforms, which entered service in the 1990s and ended around 2010. (*Private collection*)

known as Grupos Especiais (GE) and Grupos Especiais Paraquedistas (GEP), as well as the Flechas ('arrows'), small counter-insurgency specialist units attached to the armed forces and the secret police (PIDE). All of these latter units ceased to exist when the former colonies gained their independence.

Portuguese forces have deployed in a peacekeeping role to East Timor, Bosnia, Kosovo, Afghanistan (as part of the Resolute Support Mission), Somalia, Mali, Lebanon, the Central African Republic, and to Iraq (as part of the Combined Joint Task Force – Operation Inherent Resolve) since 2014.

Portuguese camouflage was strongly influenced by the French camoufleé du leópard or lizard designs of the 1950s, which continued in use with the Portuguese armed forces long after they were discarded by France. The main difference being that the stripes of Portuguese lizard camouflage are consistently oriented vertically and not horizontally. In the 1990s, the country began moving away from its traditional use of lizard camouflage in favor of a copy of British DPM.

A copy of British DPM was adopted by the armed forces in the 1990s. Even the Marines (seen here in 2016) eventually embraced DPM after discarding their beloved lizard pattern. (*Ministry of National Defense*)

A desert version of the DPM pattern was introduced around 2005 for Portuguese personnel deploying to Afghanistan. (*Private collection*)

A second version of the desert DPM was adopted around 2008 and is primarily worn by Air Force personnel serving in arid regions. (*Private collection*)

A third type of desert DPM, lacking the black elements, came into service around 2008 as well and is now worn by Army elements serving abroad. (*Private collection*)

ROMANIA

As the Second World War drew to a close, Romania was firmly under Soviet occupation and this was confirmed by the Treaty of Paris in 1947. A fraudulent election held in 1946 created a communist government, following which Romania was soon proclaimed a People's Republic. A Romanian anti-communist resistance movement was one of the longest living in all of the Eastern Bloc, with the last major resistance groups being crushed by the Securitate (Romanian secret police) in 1962. As many as 2 million Romanians were victimized.

Romania refused to participate in the 1968 Soviet invasion of Czechoslovakia, and further maintained open relations with both Israel and various Arab countries during the 1960s and 70s. By the late 1980s, the cult of personality surrounding Nicolae Ceausescu, coupled with increased repressive actions of the secret police, culminated in a popular overthrow of the communist government in December 1989. Among the violent acts of retribution were the arrest and execution of Ceausescu and his wife. Thereafter Romania began a slow movement toward a more democratic society. The country was invited to join NATO in 2004.

The leaf-type pattern seen here, nicknamed persilla (parsley), was also adopted in the 1960s and worn into the 1990s.

The Romanian Armed Forces (Forţele Armate Române) consist of the Land Forces, Air Force and Naval Forces. A number of paramilitary agencies also exist, including the Jandarmeria Română (Gendarmerie), Romanian Intelligence Service, Foreign Intelligence Service, and the Protection and Guard Service. Romanian personnel deployed to Iraq as part of the coalition forces in 2003 and withdrew in 2009. Romanian Special Forces personnel have also worked closely with US Army Special Forces in Afghanistan as part of ISAF. Romania initially adopted Russian post-war camouflage that was issued only to special operations and reconnaissance personnel. Only in the 1990s did the country develop its own unique camouflage designs.

A Romanian version of the Russian M1941 'leaf' design was worn from 1960s into the 1990s by reconnaissance personnel in a number of variations. (*Private collection*)

This Romanian officer serving in Kosovo wears the M1990 'leaf' pattern, introduced in the same year for all personnel of the Armed Forces. A number of variations exist, including one in which the black and brown colors are reversed, and others with a much lighter color palette. (*Private collection*)

These Gendarmerie personnel wear a purple/blue variation of the M1990 that was issued to this branch of service. (*Private collection*)

Romanian personnel wearing the M2002 copy of British DPM that replaced the earlier designs for all services. (*US Army*)

The 'fleck' pattern was introduced in 1994 (designated M1994) and was used interchangeably and often concurrently with the M1990.

A desert version of the DPM pattern was also issued from 2002 onwards, and saw service with Romanian personnel operating in arid regions such as Afghanistan. (*Ministry of National Defense*)

This odd 'seaweed' pattern was adopted by the Grupul Special de Protecție și Intervenție (Special Group for Protection and Intervention) or GSPI, but fell out of service when the unit was disbanded. (*Private collection*)

The Gendarmerie Brigada Specială de Intervenție a Jandarmeriei (BSIJ), a special operations unit, at one time wore this darker grey version of the UCP. (*Private collection*)

This operator of the Serviciul Independent pentru Intervenții și Acțiuni Speciale (Independent Service of Special Interventions and Operations) unit wears an alternative type of urban digital pattern, also used by Rapid Reaction Units of the Romanian County Police Inspectorates and the Bucharest Police. (*Private collection*)

A series of 'fractal' type camouflage designs were adopted by the armed forces in 2016, and included variants for the Army, Navy and Air Force. (*Ministry of National Defense*)

The history of Russia is also the history of the Soviet Union, which will be detailed in a separate section. In 1991, a referendum on the future of the Soviet Union was held, in which the vast majority of voters showed support for a different kind of federation allowing increased independence for many of the Soviet republics. In August of that year, a failed attempt to overthrow the progressive government of Mikhail Gorbachev by major supporters of the Communist Party (as well as a handful of republics such as Byelorussia, Tajikistan and Azerbaijan) led to the dissolution of the USSR and the Communist Party. The Russian Federation came into being shortly thereafter, and is now the largest country in the world by land mass. Although an attempt was made to retain control over the former Soviet Army and transform it into a unified armed force of the new Commonwealth of Independent States (CIS), this idea was ultimately rejected by most of the former Soviet republics resulting in the division of assets and the formulation of a new Armed Forces of the Russian Federation (Вооружённые Силы Российской Федерации).

Russian forces deployed to the Northern Caucasus region of Chechnya twice in the 1990s. The First Chechen War (December 1994 to August 1996) was largely a guerilla campaign pitting Russian federal forces against the heavily armed militia of the separatist Chechen government, and resulting in the withdrawal of Russian forces and de facto establishment of an (unrecognized) independent Chechen Republic. A Second Chechen War (August 1999 to May 2000) reversed the results of the first campaign, establishing a pro-Russian Chechen government but sparking a low-intensity insurgency which continues into the present. Several international human rights organizations have said both sides were guilty of numerous war crimes, including executions, rape, kidnapping, hostage taking, looting, and bombings.

In 2014, Russia involved itself in the crisis in neighboring Ukraine, throwing its support behind pro-Russian separatists in the Crimea and ultimately annexing the region in March of that year. This was opposed by a majority of the members of the United Nations.

In September 2015, Russia intervened on behalf of the Syrian government of Bashar al-Assad in the ongoing Syrian Civil War. As a result, pro-government forces have increased the amount of territory under their control.

Unlike many of the former Soviet states, the new Russian Armed Forces retained some symbology of the Soviet Army and continued wearing Soviet uniforms for a number of years. With regards to combat uniforms, changes had already been implemented prior to the breakup of the USSR to introduce a durable and practical camouflage uniform that would be standard issue for all military personnel. By 1990 a plan was already in place to issue a completely new camouflage pattern for conventional forces, which was implemented in 1994. The dubok or 3-TsV pattern became the first camouflage design to be universally issued to Russian military personnel. The pattern was also adopted by a number of ex-Soviet republics, including Azerbaijan, Belarus, Georgia and Kazakhstan. Within a few years, another general purpose camouflage design would be issued, the Flora pattern (introduced in 1998), which also populated the armed forces of several former Soviet republics.

Beyond the issue of general purpose camouflage, Russia has in fact been one of the most innovative nations in terms of camouflage design, producing a wide variety of unique patterns since 1991, many of which are associated with special units of the VSR or the Ministry of Internal Affairs (MVD). Some of these camouflage designs saw only limited production and distribution, whilst others continue to be worn in one form or another into the present era. This is particularly true of spetsnaz (special operations) units of the Army and Ministry of Internal Affairs. Russia has also copied or reproduced a number of camouflage designs created in or used by other nations, including the USA, Great Britain, Germany, and Finland.

The dubok (little oak) pattern was adopted in 1991 as a universal pattern for the armed forces and internal troops. Like its Soviet predecessor, the butane pattern, this pattern was produced in a multitude of color palettes that are too numerous to document in a publication of this nature. (*Private collection*)

Issued specifically to special units of the Министерство по чрезвычайным ситуациям or Ministry of Extreme Situations (MYC), particularly Unit Fakel, this variation of dubok has a bright orange colorway.

Introduced in 1998, the Flora or arbuz (watermelon) pattern was created by enlarging the dubok designs and rotating the pattern horizontally. This too has been issued in a number of color variants. (*Private collection*)

Developed during the Soviet era, this series of camouflage designs were issued primarily as lightweight KLMK suits and worn by Special Designation Brigades of the MVD in the early 1990s.

Three woodland-type patterns worn primarily by MVD Special Purpose Brigades (BONVV) and Spetsnaz (Vitiaz) units during the 1990s.

MVD special operations wearing a combination Les (woodland) pattern camoufage uniform with Tigr (tiger) patterned load-bearing equipment vest. (*Private collection*)

A classic photo showing MVD special operations personnel wearing a variety of camouflage designs, including the Gorod or 'city' woodland-type pattern and two variations of the green Tigr (tiger stripe) pattern. (*Private collection*)

Russian Police officer wearing a blue woodland type camouflage pattern, of which many variations have been produced. (*Private collection*)

These special operators serving in Chechnya wear a more literal copy of the m81 woodland pattern, often referred to colloquially as NATO pattern. (*Private collection*)

Another photo showing use of multiple patterns. Here an OMON special police constable wears two different types of Ten (shadow tiger) patterns, while standing next to him is another MVD operator wearing a full suit of Rastr (reed figure) camouflage. (*Private collection*)

This series of mottled camouflage designs are found on the spetsial'nyi maskirovochnyi komplekt (SMK) uniforms favored by special operations personnel of the MVD.

The modern incarnation of Берёзка (Berezhka) or 'birch tree' pattern from the 1960s continues to see use among special operations personnel from all branches of service. (*Private collection*)

Based on German Second World War designs, the SS-Leto or 'SS Summer' camouflage pattern is quite popular with spetsnaz units of the Army, MVD, and the FSB. (*Private collection*)

The камышовый рисунок (Kamyshovy risunok) or 'reed figure' patterns entered service around 1995 with MVD Internal Troops Divisions, RUOP & Opnaz units.

Popular with MVD special operations units like Vitiaz, as well as with some VDV units, the Смог (Smog,) or Кукла (kukla) (doll) camouflage pattern is based on British DPM. (*Private collection*)

Members of the FSIN Federal Penitentiary Service wearing a DPM variant with strong blue coloration. (*Private collection*)

Elements of the 45th Airborne Reconnaissance Regiment in 2008 wearing Излом or izlom (meaning 'fracture' or 'fissure') pattern camouflage fatigues. (*Private collection*)

A paratrooper of the VDV wears the skol camouflage design, also popular with reconnaissance and special operations units. (*Private collection*)

MVD spetsnaz personnel on training exercise wearing Flectar-D pattern camouflage, known variously as Ryaska (duckweed), Sever (North) and Tochka (dots/points). Obviously based on the Danish M-84 pattern. (*Private collection*)

These rapid-response personnel of the FSB wear a literal copy of German flecktarn, simply referred to locally as Flectar. (*Private collection*)

Personnel of the FSB Vympel unit here wear a couple variations of the Kamush (cane) pattern based on tiger stripe designs. (*Private collection*)

A member of the 45th Guards Special Forces Regiment wearing the digital version of flecktarn adopted by some airborne units. (*Private collection*)

The диная маскировочная расцветка (Edinaya maskirovochnaya rascvetka) or EMR camouflage design, nicknamed tsifra or tetris, was adopted by the armed forces in 2008 as a universal pattern to replace the flora and other previous designs. (*Private collection*)

The desert pattern seen here was adopted specifically for the Коллективные силы оперативного реагирования (KSOR, or Collective Rapid Reaction Force) and is worn by all participating nations. (*Private collection*)

Variations of tsifra are worn by some units in varying geographical settings, including autumn, arid, desert and arctic. (*Private collection*)

The Russian Border Service of the FSB adopted its own series of digital camouflage designs beginning in 2008. (*Private collection*)

The Federal Penitentiary Service (Федеральная служба исполнения наказаний – ФСИН) or FSIN in recent years adopted its own series of digital camouflage designs, including a green-dominant design for its Special Purpose Units (отряд специального назначения) or OSN. (*Private collection*)

This operator of the Federal Drug Control Service (FSKN) GROM unit wears the SURPAT design, also used by units attached to the Federal Protective Service (FSO), and special units of the MVD. (*Private collection*)

Special Forces operator wearing the Russian copy of Kryptek Mandrake® pattern. (*Private collection*)

This Russian Policeman attached to the United Nations in 2013 wears a digital desert camouflage design reminiscent of the old MVD KLMK patterns. (*Private collection*)

The Russian Ministry of Natural Resources and Environment issues its own camouflage design seen here. (*Private collection*)

MVD special operators from the SOBR unit here wear a copy of the A-TACS AU® (Arid Urban) pattern. (*Private collection*)

MVD units also wear a copy of the A-TACS FG® (Forest Green) camouflage design. (*Private collection*)

A copy of the German Army's old schneetarn design has been reproduced in Russia as Klyaksa or Клякса (ink blotch) and is worn by some military personnel. (*Private collection*)

MVD OMON personnel here wear locally made Multicam pattern, which has become increasingly popular with a number of Russian special units. (*Private collection*)

A recently adopted pattern of some Russian Police units is this blue-dominant design, also based on the A-TACS®. (*Private collection*)

Here we see a Russian special forces operator wearing the рябь (Ryab) or 'ripple' pattern. (*Private collection*)

These MVD special forces personnel wear a copy of the German sumpfmuster camouflage design, known as Сумрак (Sumrak), or Sumrak M2 BARS. (*Private collection*)

The Ягель (Yeger) camouflage design is based on the Finnish Army's M-05 pattern, and is also worn by a number of special operations units of the MVD. (*Private collection*)

A modern version of the old Soviet TTsMKK three color 'stair step' pattern is seen here, recolored and marketed as 'Palma-Spring'. (*Private collection*)

Russian MVD special forces personnel here can be seen wearing two versions of the Spekter-S pattern camouflage. (*Private collection*)

Serbia was one of the six republics within the Socialist Federal Republic of Yugoslavia. It remained a part of the Federal Republic after the dissolution of the SFRY. By 1992, the only two remaining states were Serbia and Montenegro. In 2002, the two states signed the Belgrade Agreement which decentralized the Federal Republic and established the state of Serbia and Montenegro. In May 2006 a referendum monitored by the OSCE on the independence of Montenegro narrowly passed, leaving Serbia to declare itself the legal successor to the former state union. In February 2008 the Assembly of Kosovo declared its independence, which was immediately condemned by Serbia. Although it has not taken any military action, Serbia refuses to acknowledge the statehood of Kosovo.

While still federated with Montenegro, the armed forces were known as Vojska Srbije i Crna Gore (Army of Serbia and Montenegro) or VSCG. The Serbian Armed Forces (Vojska Srbije) today consist of the Army and the Air Force, plus a small River Flotilla that patrols the Danube. Serbian military forces have deployed with several multinational peacekeeping operations, including those to Cyprus, Central African Republic, DR Congo, Lebanon, and Somalia. The Ministry of Internal Affairs (Министарство унутрашњих послова) or MUP have traditionally held responsibility for internal security and

These paratroops of the 63rd Airborne Brigade wear the 2002 incarnation of the original Yugoslavian M93 'oakleaf' pattern with color palette adjusted to be more in line with NATO countries. (*US Army*)

A copy of British DPM camouflage was worn for a period by the Специјална антитерористичка јединица (SAJ) or Special Anti-terrorist Unit of the Serbian Police. (*Private collection*)

Members of the Special Brigade's Counter-Terrorist Battalion wearing 'Dragon Flight' digital camouflage in 2009, tested by special operations but never officially adopted by the MOD. (*Private collection*)

Special operators of the UBPOK unit of the Жандармерија or Žandarmerija – part of the Serbian Federal Police – in 2007 can be seen wearing a locally-produced copy of German schneetarn as well as a woodland-type design with black/grey colorway. (*Private collection*)

The Јединица за специјалне операције or JSO unit of the Federal State Security Service wore a number of camouflage designs, including this copy of m81 woodland, until the unit's disbandment in 2003. (*Private collection*)

The Противтерористичка јединица or PTJ unit of the Serbian Police also wore a number of camouflage designs, including this one based on USMC temperate MARPAT. (*Private collection*)

law enforcement duties, as well as counter-terrorism and other specialized services. Both branches of service have made heavy use of camouflage since the days of the Yugoslavian Republic. The VSCG retained a larger number of traditional camouflage designs worn by the SFRY, but Serbian Forces have since adopted their own distinctive pixilated designs.

In the interests of space, I have purposely left out many of the camouflage patterns carried over from the Yugoslavia period, although old stocks of uniforms were certainly worn for many years, particularly among units of the MUP. Additionally, the Army continued to use old stocks of M89 and M93 pattern clothing, until it was officially replaced or upgraded, depending on the unit.

Seen here is the desert variation of the M-10 digital pattern, in service primarily with troops serving with the UN. (*Ministry of Defense*)

The Serbian Army adopted its own digital version of the old M02 'oakleaf' pattern camouflage in 2010. (*Ministry of Defense*)

Operators from the SAJ unit here wear the so-called Universal Camouflage Pattern (UCP). (*Private collection*)

These UN peacekeepers serving in Chad in 2013 wear Bulgarian desert DPM pattern camouflage uniforms. (*Private collection*)

During a deployment to Mali, Serbian peacekeepers wore German desert flecktarn pattern camouflage uniforms. (*Private collection*)

Serbian Police

The old Yugoslavian 'blue tiger stripe' pattern was worn by MUP until 2001.

This locally produced copy of US m81 woodland pattern was worn by JSO operators.

Yugoslavian grey and green 'tiger stripe' patterns were also worn by units of the MUP.

The Republic of Serbian Krajina (Република Српска Крајина, or *Republika Srpska Krajina*) existed from 1991 to 1995 within the borders of present day Croatia. Its goal was to retain Serbian identity and connection to the Socialist Federal Republic of Yugoslavia, which supported its efforts during the Croatian War of Independence. The unrecognized state ceased to exist after Croatian forces overran the majority of its territory and the Republic of Croatia was created.

Aside from the Yugoslavian National Army (JNA), there were two primary Serbian Krajina forces opposing the Croatian bid for independence: the Serbian Army of the Republic of Serbian Krajina (Srpska vojska Republike Srpske Krajine – SVRSK) – aka the Krajina Serb Army – and the Krajina Police (Milicija Krajine – MK), the latter of which included Special Police units (Specijalne jedinice milicije – SJM). Although Serbian Krajina units wore distinctive insignia, they were outfitted by Yugoslavia and used the same equipment as the JNA and Yugoslavian Police. This extended to the use of camouflage uniforms, nearly all of which were Yugoslavian in origin.

The 'lizard' patterns were popular with the Krajina Territorial Defense Force as well as later units of the SVRSK. (*Private collection*)

A rare photo of SVK soldiers wearing the same uniforms, in this case the M89 JNA 'oakleaf' design. (*Private collection*)

The elite Kninjas unit under Kapetan Dragan wore one-piece coveralls made from m82 TTsKO butane pattern three-color camouflage fabric. (*Private collection*)

These 'blue lizard' patterns were often worn by Krajina Police units.

Also worn by the Krajina Police was the blue version of the M89 pattern.

SLOVAKIA

Slovakia was a part of the Czechoslovak Socialist Republic (Československá socialistická republika) or CSSR from 1948 until 1990. Although a popular vote supported democracy in the aftermath of the Second World War, the Communist Party seized power in a coup d'etat and a Soviet supported government was installed. Following a Warsaw Pact invasion in 1968 to quell the Prague Spring movement, a moderate federalization occurred within Czechoslovakia, creating the Czech Socialist Republic and the Slovak Socialist Republic (Slovenská socialistická republika) or SSR, although control was still maintained by the Communist Party.

Beginning in November 1989, the 'Velvet Revolution' brought about the rapid collapse of communist rule and the breakup of Czechoslovakia. Socialism was scrapped, and in July 1992 Slovakia declared itself an independent state – the Slovak Republic (Slovenská republika), which was finalized on January of the following year. It was immediately recognized by the United Nations, and in 2004 became a member of NATO. The Slovak Armed Forces consist of the Ground Forces and the Air Force, as well as the 5th Special Forces Regiment, which is attached to the Operational Reconnaissance Bureau. Slovakia has deployed small numbers of military personnel to Cyprus, Bosnia, Kosovo and Afghanistan. Although in the immediate period following the dissolution of the Czechoslovakian Armed Forces, Slovakia did issue the same camouflage uniforms as its Czech neighbors, the country was quick to adopt its own designs with a national flavor and similarity to those of other NATO countries.

Both the vz85 and vz95 Czech patterns were worn initially by Slovakia until around 1995. This member of the 5th Special Purpose Regiment (5. Pluk špeciálneho určenia) is still wearing the vz95 pattern uniform several years later. (*Private collection*)

These two members of the Slovakian contingent serving in Kosovo (2005) wear the vz 97 woodland camouflage design adopted in 1995 to replace the 'leaf' patterns. (*Private collection*)

These UN-assigned personnel wear the locally-produced copy of the Czech desert pattern that was adopted in 1995. (*United Nations*)

The desert variation – vz 2007 Pust (desert). (*Private collection*)

A light machine gunner wearing the vz 2007 Les or 'forest' pattern, a pixilated design that replaced the woodland. (*Private collection*)

During the post-war period, Slovenia was one of the six republics within the Socialist Federal Republic of Yugoslavia (SFRY). Beginning in 1987, a popular movement for independence started gaining ground and led to a number of democratic reforms being enacted. Parliamentary democracy was adopted in September 1989, followed by an official name change to the Republic of Slovenia in March 1990. In June of the following year, parliament legalized a declaration of independence, which was met with military resistance from the Yugoslavian People's Army (JNA). Following a brief period of hostilities (the Ten Day War) Yugoslavia reluctantly recognized the independence of Slovenia and its soldiers departed Slovenian territory. The nation became a member of NATO in 2004.

The Slovenian Armed Forces (Slovenska vojska) are a standing, professional Army consisting of Ground Forces, Air Force, and Navy. Since 1997, Slovenian military personnel have deployed to various parts of the world to join in peace operations and humanitarian activities. Most notable have been deployments to Kosovo (KFOR), Afghanistan, Iraq, Cyprus, and Latvia (as part of NATO Enhanced Forward Presence).

This Slovenian soldier on exercise in Norway is wearing a camouflage design adopted by the Armed Forces in 2013 and heavily influenced by Multicam. (*Ministry of Defense*)

Above: Members of the 1st Special Brigade MORiS wearing surplus British Army DPM pattern uniforms. (*Private collection*)

Left: A recoilless rifle team of the Slovenian Territorial forces, who wore Bulgarian 'splinter' pattern camouflage from around 1990–92. (*Private collection*)

US m81 woodland pattern uniforms were also worn by members of the 1st Special Brigade MORiS, even when the remainder of the armed forces had adopted the 'oakleaf' design. (*Private collection*)

The Slovenian m91 pattern seen here is based on the Yugoslavian m87 'small oakleaf' design, but utilizes a different color palette. (*Ministry of Defense*)

Slovenian personnel serving with ISAF in Afghanistan in 2004 wear surplus US tricolor desert pattern camouflage uniforms. (*Ministry of Defense*)

Seen here in 2007, these UN personnel wear the desert variation of the m91 design, in use since 2005. (*United Nations*)

SPAIN

As the Second World War raged in Europe, Spain was embroiled in its own Civil War at home, which ended with victory for General Francisco Franco in 1939. Supported by both Germany and Italy, Spain became politically isolated when the war ended and was prevented from joining the United Nations when it was formed. Diplomatic relations loosened in the mid-1950s with the emerging Soviet threat, leading to its admission in 1955. The country remained under the authoritarian leadership of Franco until his death in December 1975, at which time Juan Carlos I succeeded to the Spanish throne and became head of state. Gradually the country began transitioning to democracy.

The Basque population of Spain has pushed heavily for independence since the formation of the ETA (Euskadi Ta Askatasuna) in 1959. The ETA have been classified as a terrorist organization, while members have countered that the Spanish government is guilty of many human rights violations against the Basque population.

Spain was a latecomer to NATO, joining only in 1982, but has since been a supporter of international security endeavors. The Spanish Armed Forces (Fuerzas Armadas Españolas) consist of the Army, Air Force, and Navy, as well as the Royal Guard, Military Emergencies Unit (UME), and the Common Corps which provide support services to all branches of the armed forces. The Guardia Civil is a gendarmerie-like national law enforcement agency with numerous paramilitary duties. Spain joined the US-led coalition during the Iraq War, and later participated in the offensive against Moammar Gaddafi in Libya. Spanish military personnel have served in numerous international peacekeeping, monitoring,

Introduced in 1959 or 1960, the rocoso (rocks) pattern was only issued to elite units such as the Spanish Legion, paratroops, and commando companies. It would remain in service until the 1980s. (*Private collection*)

A green variation, the m60 boscosos (woodland), was introduced in the 1960s and also issued primarily to special operations and paratrooper units into the 1970s.

The M75 lagarto (lizard) pattern was a desert version of the earlier designs first introduced in 1973, primarily for use by the Spanish Legion operating in the Sahara, although it also saw service with at least one Army commando company.

A later variation of the rocoso pattern was produced in the 1970s, and saw service with the Legion, Army commandos, and Army & AF paratroops. (*Private collection*)

These camouflage designs were produced as Traje de Lanzamiento Camuflado (camouflage jumpsuits) for special operations personnel, and were issued to the Air Force paratroops (Zapadores) and Army commando companies into the 1970s. (*Private collection*)

This three-color 'frogskin' pattern camouflage first emerged in 1970 as a field tent and later as a poncho, helmet cover, and on field equipment, with some articles of clothing also being produced.

Adopted in 1982, the Spanish 'woodland' pattern is a hybrid of the US ERDL and woodland designs. This became the standard combat uniform for most of the armed forces in 1986. (*Private collection*)

The Legion were the last unit to utilize a camouflage pattern based on the old M-60 designs. This boscoso or 'woodland' design was adopted in 1986 and could still be found in some units as late as the early 2000s.

Air Force personnel from the Escuadrón de Zapadores Paracaidistas (EZPAC) or Parachute Squadron wear the copy of six-color 'chocolate chip' desert camouflage introduced 1990 and used by the Spanish Air Force, Army, and Legion when serving abroad. (*Private collection*)

The Infantería de Marina or Spanish Marines adopted a faithful copy of the US m81 woodland design in the late 1990s, which continued in service until very recently. (*Private collection*)

Two types of 'leaf' camouflage are worn by the Grupo Especial de Operaciones (GEO) of the National Police Corps – one having a brown colorway, and the other a blue one. (*Private collection*)

Spanish troops in Iraq wearing the M09 Ejercito pixelado árido digital design, adopted in 2009. (*US Army*)

The Spanish Marines adopted its own desert design in 2003. (*Private collection*)

Two Spanish Army medical officers wearing the M09 Ejercito pixelado boscoso (woodland) camouflage pattern adopted in 2009. (US Army)

and humanitarian missions, including those to Mali, Lebanon, Senegal, Albania, Mozambique, Haiti, Indonesia, Sudan, and the Congo, as well as numerous exercises and operations with NATO allies.

Spain has traditionally been very innovative with regards to its military camouflage designs, setting its own trends and developing its own unique design features. After joining NATO this trend eased quite a lot with the universal adoption of a woodland-derivative pattern, followed by a slightly modified version of the US-designed six-color desert pattern.

SRPSKA REPUBLIC

The Bosnian Serb Republic, or Republika Srpska was a breakaway region of the Republic of Bosnia and Herzegovina during the Civil War period (January 1992–December 1995) which contended it would remain a part of the Republic of Yugoslavia. Supported by the government of Yugoslavia, the Bosnian Serb Army (Vojska Republike Srpske or VRS) was one of three native military organizations that were in contention for territory, the others being the Croatian Defense Council and the Army of the Republic of Bosnia and Herzegovina. The territory of the Bosnian Serb Republic comprised a

A typical photograph showing the wide mixture of camouflage designs worn within the same unit of the VRS – in this case, M93 'oakleaf', m81 woodland, and several types of tiger stripe camouflage. (*Private collection*)

Rare photo of a VRS unit all clad in Yugoslavian M93 'oakleaf' camouflage, generally seen throughout the war interspersed with other uniforms. (*Private collection*)

Two members of the elite White Wolves unit wearing Russian butane pattern camouflage coveralls, also worn by some units in Serbian Krajina (Croatia). (*Private collection*)

The dark green tiger stripe pattern was probably the most widely used during the war by VRS units, although many color variations were produced. (*Private collection*)

Blue and purple tiger pattern uniforms were worn by the Special Police detachments during the war.

large portion of the north and most of the eastern region of the present state of Bosnia & Herzegovina. By 1993 this territory had been expanded to cover nearly 70 per cent of the territory, but at the end of the war this was reduced to approximately 49 per cent under Bosnian Serb control. The General Framework Agreement for Peace in Bosnia and Herzegovina, usually referred to as the Dayton Agreement, was a peace accord between the belligerents of the civil war that ended the conflict, and established areas of control for both the Bosnian and Serbian elements of the population at the end of 1995. By terms of the agreement, the Republika Srpska is recognized as a political sub-entity within the Republic of Bosnia and Herzegovina.

The VRS made heavy use of camouflage uniforms, most of which were obtained from existing stocks for regional militias, or supplied directly by the government of Yugoslavia. The VRS was particularly well-supplied with several variations of 'tiger' pattern, but also wore the more conventional designs of the JNA.

SWEDEN

The Kingdom of Sweden has officially been a neutral country since the Second World War. This neutrality extends to non-membership in any military alliance, although it has entered into partnerships with other countries for purposes of peacekeeping missions and in the sharing of defense technologies. During the Congo

Swedish Jägare from an Amphibious Battalion wear the M90 'splinter' camouflage design, adopted in 1989. The pattern has remained in service with the Swedish Armed Forces into the present era. (*US Marine Corps*)

The M90K is the issue uniform for desert deployments, modeled here by personnel completing a rotation in Afghanistan with ISAF. (*Försvarsmakten*)

A four-color camouflage regnskyddet (rain cover) was introduced for general use in the 1960s, both as poncho and for creating shelter tents. These items saw service well into the 1980s and possibly later. (*Henrik Clausen collection*)

Seen here is the winter/snow version, printed on oversuits and worn by personnel serving in the sub-arctic regions of Sweden. (*Private collection*)

Crisis, as many as nine battalions of Swedish forces were deployed between 1960 and 1964. Swedish armed forces have participated in joint military exercises with NATO, and also came under NATO command when deploying to Afghanistan. Swedish personnel deployed as peacekeepers to EU-sponsored missions in Bosnia, Kosovo, and Cyprus, and as observers to Georgia, Lebanon, Israel, and Sri Lanka. Within the European Union, Sweden belongs to the Nordic Battle Group.

The Swedish Armed Forces are known as Försvarsmakten, and consist of the Army, Air Force, Navy, and the Home Guard (a military reserve force). Compulsory military service for eligible males was reduced in the 1990s as part of a reduction in the size of the armed forces. An all-volunteer system is scheduled to take over in 2019. Sweden has utilized camouflage since the 1940s, despite the fact that the armed forces have seen minimal combat service.

SWITZERLAND

The Swiss Confederation is another country that has maintained strict neutrality since the Second World War. Switzerland is not part of any military alliance and does not participate in joint military exercises, although it has joined some peacekeeping missions around the world. The Swiss Armed Forces consists of the Army and Air Force, and is almost entirely composed of conscripts with just a small cadre of professional soldiers.

Swiss camouflage designs have largely been influenced by those of Second World War Germany.

Based on the German Leibermuster design of the Second World War, the Swiss Alpentarn or Alpenflage (aka Vierfruchtpyama) was adopted in 1955 and printed on fabrics made into full uniforms, shelters, ponchos, rain gear and helmet covers. The pattern would remain relatively unchanged until dropped in 1990. (*Private collection*)

Originally adopted in 1938, the Zelteinheiten 1901 pattern reflects a strong influence from the German Wehrmacht splittertarn. Printed only as a shelter pattern, this saw service until 1955.

A reversible 'splinter' design adopted in 1944 for helmet covers, and worn well into the 1960s and possibly later.

A green tinted version printed on helmet covers from 1957 until the late 1960s.

A Swiss officer wearing the TAZ90 uniform, the pattern for which is essentially a recoloration of the original design utilizing dyes that suit the natural surroundings in Switzerland. (*US DOD*)

These Swiss personnel serving in Kosovo wear an arid camouflage pattern adopted in 2007-8, and known colloquially as Südtarn or Wüstetarn. (*Private collection*)

Ukraine was part of the Soviet Union during the Second World War and throughout the Cold War era. In the post-war years, as much as 20 per cent of the population was ethnically cleansed under policies set by Stalin. Ukraine was a major source of industrial production for the Soviet Union, and many of its factories were dedicated to the manufacture of combat uniforms, including camouflage suits. In July 1990, a new parliament adopted the 'Declaration of State Sovereignty of Ukraine', which created an atmosphere of confrontation with Soviet authorities. Following the failed attempt to remove Soviet leader Mikhail Gorbachev in August 1991, a full Act of Independence was adopted by the Ukrainian parliament, which ultimately was supported by more than 90 per cent of the electorate when voted on in December. When the Soviet Union was dissolved at the end of 1991, Ukraine became one of the first members of the Commonwealth

Two different types of locally-made butane pattern camouflage, derived from the Soviet 1988 TTsKO pattern. (*Private collection*)

Old stocks of Soviet era berezhka (birch) pattern camouflage uniforms have remained in service with many Ukrainian units well into the present period. (*Private collection*)

The Бе́ркут (Golden Eagle) unit of the Ministry of Internal Affairs (MVS) wore a variety of blue-colored camouflage designs, including DPM, butane, and tiger stripe. The unit was disbanded in 2014. (*Private collection*)

This blue woodland pattern is also worn by special police units of the MVS

This particular version of m81 woodland was adopted by the State Border Guards service in the 1990s.

Officers of the State Border Guards modeling two slightly different variations of the digital camouflage design adopted in 2013. (*Private collection*)

Ukrainian Air Force cadets wearing a variety of camouflage designs, including butane, Russian dubok, and several types of woodland. (*Private collection*)

Two types of desert camouflage employed by Ukrainian personnel when serving abroad: a copy of the US tricolor, and the more commonly seen variation of butane pattern adopted in 2003. (*Private collection*)

Ukrainian Army officers in 2014 modeling the recently adopted digital camouflage design now being issued to most of the Armed Forces. (*Private collection*)

These officers wear a lighter-colored variation of the digital pattern, also adopted by the Armed Forces in 2014; note also the officer wearing a copy of the A-TACS® AU camouflage design, seen in some Ukrainian units like the special rapid reaction unit (KORD) of the Ukrainian National Police. (*Private collection*)

Circa 2014–15 the Internal Troops of the Ministry of Internal Affairs introduced its own digital camouflage design with a strong grey colorway. (*Private collection*)

A member of the Spetsgruppa Alpha, the counter-terrorist unit of the Служба Безпеки України, Ukraine's Security Service, wearing special Multicam-patterned assault gear. (*Private collection*)

These soldiers in 2014 are wearing a privately-produced camouflage design, nicknamed 'toad' or zhaba. (*Private collection*)

Ukrainian soldier in 2014 wearing the arid coloration of the zhaba camouflage pattern. (*Private collection*)

Originally issued to the 79th Mobile Brigade in 2015, the ВАРАН ВСУ (Varan VSU) or Varan pattern of the Ukrainian Military Forces, is a textured design that is now being fielded to some Ukrainian units. (*Private collection*)

This member of a Navy special operations unit wears a locally-made copy of the A-TACS FG® pattern. (*US Navy*)

These Ukrainian Police officers wear a hybrid pattern combining elements of German flecktarn and traditional TTsKO, adopted in 2016. (*Private collection*)

Ukrainian personnel clad in what appears to be a mixture of solid white and German Army issue schneetarn camouflage for cold weather operations. (*Private collection*)

This Ukrainian Navy officer wears an American Universal Camouflage Pattern uniform. (*Private collection*)

Ukrainian MVD soldier wearing the commercial pattern known as 'Predator,' in use by some units since 2014. (*Private collection*)

The Ukrainian Navy adopted its own camouflage design in 2017, featuring a blue color palette. (*Private collection*)

of Independent States (CIS), along with Russia and Belarus.

Following its independence Ukraine was declared a neutral state, despite its membership in the CIS. A limited partnership with NATO was adopted in 1994, but full membership has not yet been extended. In November 2013, a series of public protests and demonstrations known as Euromaidan were sparked by the Ukrainian government's refusal to sign an association agreement with the European Union, choosing instead to publicly voice a desire for closer relations with Russia. In what became known as the Ukrainian Revolution, public demonstrations and blockades extended into February 2014 and were met with violent suppression by federal riot police and pro-government vigilantes, resulting in a number of deaths and thousands of injured.

While disorder was occurring in Kiev, the Russian-speaking region of Crimea experienced its own unrest as Ukrainian military and police forces clashed with pro-Russian militias and volunteers. Russian intelligence operatives and military personnel were covertly inserted into Ukraine to assist in the defeat of Ukrainian forces, leading to a self-proclaimed Republic of Crimea and a mutual treaty of accession signed with Russia. Meanwhile in the Donetsk and Luhansk regions of Ukraine (historically known as Donbass), local pro-Russian militias seized control of government buildings and police stations in several cities. This escalated into full-scale warfare involving Russian military personnel, separatists, and the Ukrainian security forces, which has ended thus far in stalemate. Ukraine withdrew its military forces from Crimea in late March 2014; by July 2015, Russia declared that Crimea had been 'fully integrated'.

The Armed Forces of Ukraine consist of the Ground Forces, Air Force and Naval Forces, as well as the National Guard (newly re-formed) which provides the main reserve component to the armed forces. Paramilitary forces include the State Border Guards and Coast Guard, Internal Troops and State Police units of the Interior Ministry, the Civil Defense Forces, and the various units of the Security Service of Ukraine (SBU). Like its neighbor Russia, Ukrainian forces have adopted a multitude of camouflage uniforms for both military and paramilitary units, some with historical connections to the Soviet era but many of modern design and manufacture.

During the internal conflict of early 2014, widespread use of surplus camouflage clothing articles was observed on many of the civilian protesters, pro-Ukraine militia, and a number of Ukrainian military personnel including special operations, airborne forces and air force personnel. These included German flecktarn, British temperate and desert DPM, US MARPAT and UCP. Use of these patterns has largely discontinued now that the country is stabilized.

UNITED KINGDOM

The UK saw a gradual lessening of its colonial holdings in the twenty years that followed the end of the Second World War. In certain parts of the former British Empire, this brought the armed forces into conflict with local movements working towards independence, although not always towards a democratic government. The first major portion of the old Empire to achieve independence was the British Raj, which was partitioned into two dominions, India and Pakistan. This was followed in 1948 by the independence of Burma and Ceylon. What had been the British mandate in Palestine eventually became the state of Israel, which was created by a decision of the United Nations. Britain retained its hold on Malaya until 1957, although British forces continued to fight against Chinese-supported communist insurgents during the Malayan Emergency, which did not reach conclusion until 1960.

During the Suez Crisis in 1956, Britain joined forces with Israel and France in an attempt to regain control of the canal from Egypt, which ultimately failed despite a military victory. This was followed by British withdrawal from Aden in 1967, Bahrain in 1971, and the Maldives in 1976. Most of the British Caribbean territories were granted independence in the 1960s, excepting Belize, which remained a provisional part of the UK until 1981.

Meanwhile, at home in Northern Ireland, British forces attempted to maintain a peace between Catholic and Protestant paramilitaries beginning in the 1960s.

This peacekeeping role largely became adversarial as ultimately both sides in the conflict came to see the British as occupiers. 'The Troubles', as they were known colloquially, continued until 1998, when the vast majority of British forces were withdrawn and the paramilitaries agreed to a ceasefire.

Decolonization in Africa began in the 1950s with the independence of the Sudan and the Gold Coast (Ghana). The Mau Mau rebellion in Kenya had begun in 1952 when the largely Kikuyu-dominated insurgency movement waged open warfare against the British Army and soldiers of the colonial Kenya Regiment. Although most of the fighting was over by 1956, it would not be until 1960 that independence was ultimately achieved for Kenya. Southern

The 'brushstroke' design implemented during the Second World War continued to see use by elite troops well into the 1950s, most especially within the Parachute Regiment.

Second World War era 'windproof' camouflage remained very popular with British Special Forces, and surplus stocks would be proudly worn on training exercises into the 1960s, as well as on operations such as here in Dhofar. (*Private collection*)

The Parachute Regiment was the only British unit to continue using the 'brushstroke' Denison design well into the 1970s. Although changed markedly from the war-era design, the Paras were reluctant to give up their Denisons, which remained in production until 1969–70. (*Private collection*)

This group of Royal Marines from 42 Commando, photographed right after the capture of South Georgia in the Falklands, wears the 1968 pattern DPM kit that was in service at that time. (*Private collection*)

Some examples of DPM color variations from the 84-85 series of clothing, which was printed on the same cotton modal fabric used for 68 pattern clothing. Parachute smocks, sniper smocks, windproof and arctic issue clothing and a host of other specialized items were also issued.

Rhodesia issued its famous Unilateral Declaration of Independence (UDI) in 1965, ending British rule and severing the decades-long relationship it had with Britain. The remaining British colonies in Africa were all granted independence by 1968 without major conflict.

The British Armed Forces consist of the Royal Army, Royal Air Force (RAF) and the Royal Navy (which includes the Royal Marines). Britain maintains a number of overseas garrisons, and military facilities in many of its former colonies. A founding and active member of NATO, British forces have seen a gradual reduction since the end of the Second World War. During the Dhofar Rebellion (1963–76) in Oman, British personnel assisted the Sultan's forces in defeating the insurgents, as well as modernizing the Royal Oman Armed Forces. When the Argentine military junta seized control of the Falkland Islands in 1982, British forces were deployed thousands of miles away with little advance preparation in order to reclaim them. The British Armed Forces have also participated in a number of recent military campaigns and peacekeeping operations, including the intervention in Sierra Leone (2000), operations in Kosovo and Bosnia, the war in Afghanistan (2001–present), the Iraq War (2003–09), and military operations against ISIL (2014–present).

British ground troops have employed camouflage since before the First World War. However, the tradition of employing wide 'brushstrokes' to create a disruptive pattern of several colors on a drab background has remained with HM Armed Forces since the end of the Second World War. Airborne and Special Forces troops continued to utilize old stocks of wartime camouflage and were supplied with freshly manufactured ones well into the 1960s, by which time the government had developed its own Disruptive Pattern Material (DPM) for general issue. Although Britain has embraced the concept of a 'multi-terrain pattern' in the twenty-first century like many countries, the design currently worn by British personnel still shows an influence of the earlier DPM and brushstroke patterns.

British Army DPM tropical clothing historically had a different coloration to that issued for wear in temperate climes. A distinctive feature was the use of brighter colors, particularly the yellows and greens, at least into the late 1980s.

The Soldier 95 pattern series of clothing DPM patterns. Although colors were mostly standardized by this time, the type of fabric utilized did produce some variation in texture and appearance, particularly the ripstop material.

British Army personnel during Operation Granby (Persian Gulf War) wearing examples of the mixture of desert DPM clothing that was in circulation at the time. (*Private collection*)

An example of the 'sparse' version of desert DPM, also issued during Operation Granby.

Royal Marines wearing later (1995) series desert DPM combat clothing, but still using standard subdued insignia. (*Private collection*)

Soldiers from the Prince of Wales Royal Regiment in the OPFOR role wearing a blue-dominant variation of DPM utilized by the British Army Training Unit Suffield (BATUS). (*Private collection*)

The British Armed Forces adopted 'Multi-Terrain Pattern' (MTP) in 2010, which utilizes the palette developed in the United States for Multicam on a distinctly British layout. (*US Army*)

Despite a loss of nearly 27 million people during the Second World War, the Soviet Union emerged as a 'super power' in the war's aftermath and continued to expand its control of territory in Europe and Asia. As the USSR rebuilt its economy and recovered from the mass destruction inflicted by the Axis during the war, it effectively took over control of most of Eastern Europe, imposing communism on Bulgaria, Czechoslovakia, East Germany, Hungary, Poland and Romania. When the United Nations was formed in 1945, the Soviet Union became one of only five permanent Security Council members. Nevertheless, a combination of fear and resistance to Soviet expansion turned erstwhile war-era allies such as Great Britain and the United States into ideological foes. A Cold War existed between East and West from 1947 until the collapse of the USSR in 1991.

The Soviets used force to suppress a number of post-war independence movements, notably uprisings in Poland and Hungary (both in 1956) and later in Czechoslovakia (1968). Soviet influence was extended into other parts of the world as well, particularly to the budding independence movements in parts of Asia, Africa and Latin America. An attempt to provide Cuba with nuclear missiles in 1962 led to the Cuban Missile Crisis, the closest that the USA and the Soviet Union ever came to a nuclear confrontation. Soviet assistance in Africa propped up governments in Angola and Mozambique, as well as pro-Marxist movements in Rhodesia, South Africa, and Namibia, all of which led to eventual capitulation by pro-Western governments.

The USSR became embroiled it its own counter-insurgency campaign when it became involved in Afghan politics following a takeover by the People's Democratic Party of Afghanistan (PDPA) in 1978. Unable to retain control over the entire country, the Afghan government enlisted the assistance of its Soviet allies, who began moving troops across the borders in June 1979. The resulting Soviet-Afghan War lasted until the Soviet pullout in February 1989.

Under the leadership of Mikhail Gorbachev the USSR entered a more progressive era in the 1980s and 1990s. This era was marked by the perestroika movement of political reform, as well as the policy of glasnost or 'openness'. These policies brought about increased cooperation with the west and also contributed to the political movements of the late 1980s and early 1990s that ultimately brought about the dissolution of the Warsaw Pact and the Soviet Union. In December of 1991, following a failed military coup d'etat, the USSR was dissolved into fifteen independent states: Russia, Ukraine, Belarus, Armenia, Azerbaijan, Estonia, Latvia, Lithuania, Georgia, Moldova, Kazakhstan, Kyrgyzstan, Uzbekistan, Turkmenistan, and Tajikistan.

Soviet and Russian contributions to camouflage development began in the late 1930s and continued well into the Cold War era. During the immediate post-war period, Soviet military designers continued to work with existing concepts (such as the disruptive 'stair step' design) to create more practical camouflaged combat clothing for specialized troops. The early Soviet uniforms were lightweight, cheaply produced and not particularly robust, but in 1981 a much more durable combat uniform was introduced that incorporated many of the features of American and NATO field uniforms. The six-pocket khaki airborne uniform, widely distributed to Soviet personnel operating in Afghanistan, was soon manufactured in a newly-designed three-color camouflage pattern (nicknamed 'woodland', although having no relationship to the US pattern of the same name) and initially distributed to Soviet airborne and special forces personnel. The six-pocket combat uniform in a tricolor camouflage pattern would eventually become the standard combat uniform of the Soviet Union and the post-war republics, remaining essentially unchanged until the early years of the twenty-first century. Soviet camouflage designs, although not terribly sophisticated, were nevertheless effective for their time and have been reproduced in a multitude of variations by most countries of the former USSR. They have seen service with numerous Marxist and pro-Soviet insurgent movements, particularly in Africa, and constitute an important chapter in the history of camouflage development.

Soviet scouts operating in Lithuania in 1947 wearing the makirovochnyi kamuflirovannyi kostium or MKK uniform in letniy kamuflyazh (summer camouflage), introduced in 1941 and worn into the 1960s. (*Private collection*)

Soviet troops circa late 1970s wearing the tritsvetnyi makirovochnyi kamuflirovannyi kostium or TTsMKK, introduced in 1944. (*Private collection*)

A hybrid-pattern, combining elements of both the wartime 'amoeba' and 'leaf' patterns, was introduced towards the end of the Second World War, and saw limited use into the 1950s.

Nicknamed listopad kamuflyazh,(falling leaves camouflage), this design was introduced in the post-war period but remained in service for years.

This leaf pattern design was introduced in 1948 and utilized on the first of the one-piece coveralls. (*KLMK*)

This 'blotch' pattern was introduced in 1960 and reversible to a pattern thought to thwart night vision technology of that period; it was issued primarily to airborne, reconnaissance, and GRU spetsnaz units.

Soviet Naval Infantry wearing the solnechnye zaychiki (sunshine rays) camouflage design worn well into the 1990s and beyond. (*Private collection*)

Essentially the same camouflage design, also termed berezhka or 'birch' was printed on very loose-weave fabric, but with much greater variety of dye combinations.

These Soviet Border Guards are wearing the berezhka pattern printed on heavy cotton for use with spetsodezhda (special purpose) uniforms beginning in 1981. (*Private collection*)

The tritsvetnaia kamuflirovannaia odezhda (three color camouflage) was introduced in 1981 and is generally called Бутан (butane) or butan in Russian. Many dye combinations have been documented, of which perhaps half a dozen were probably intentional, for use in various geographical regions. (*Private collection*)

Soviet advisors to Angola in the 1980s wearing Cuban-made 'grey lizard' pattern camouflage uniforms. (*Private collection*)

Soviet advisors to Mozambique wore the Portuguese-style vertical camouflage typical of Frelimo and the FADM.

YUGOSLAVIA

The Federal People's Republic of Yugoslavia was established by the Communist National Front in 1946 as a confederation of six different entities – Bosnia and Herzegovina, Croatia, Macedonia, Montenegro, Slovenia, and Serbia, plus the autonomous provinces of Kosovo and Vojvodina. Former Partisan leader Marshal Josip Broz Tito became, in effect, supreme leader of the country once King Philip II was deposed. Although initially friendly with other communist nations of Eastern Europe, a political rift arose with the Soviet Union in 1947, when Stalin vetoed a plan by Yugoslavia to ally itself militarily with Bulgaria and Albania in order to plot a civil war in neighboring Greece. From 1948 onwards, the country began to diverge from the Soviet model and formulate its own brand of socialism. Between 1949 and 1953 Yugoslavia received aid from the United States, although this relationship stopped short of any kind of alliance. Beginning in 1961, and in response to the emerging Cold War, Yugoslavia helped form the Non-Aligned Movement, which has continued to exist in various forms into the present period. The nation was renamed the Socialist Federal Republic of Yugoslavia (SFRY) in 1963, with Marshal Tito being named President for Life.

Following the death of Tito in 1980, the centralized authority that had heretofore been solidified by his presence began to disintegrate, fueled by ethnic tensions. Minorities began to call for increased independence, but it took nearly ten years and the crumbling of the Eastern Bloc to bring about real change. In 1990, disagreement over whether more power should be granted to the republics within the SFRY resulted in the Slovenian and Croatian delegations leaving Congress and the dissolution of the Communist Party. Multi-party elections were held later that year in each of the republics, with Croatia and Slovenia both electing to peacefully secede from Yugoslavia. Resistance to this decision by ethnic Serbian elements living in each of the republics resulted in armed conflict, and the establishment of the Republic of Serbian Krajina in Croatia. One year later, Bosnia and Herzegovina erupted into its own civil war, and in September 1991 Macedonia declared itself an independent republic, but was spared any violence with the federal government. Meanwhile, United Nations peacekeeping forces began to deploy to regions of the former Yugoslavia in an attempt to curb the ethnic violence that had spread into the civilian population. By January 1992 both Slovenia and Croatia had achieved international recognition as independent states; that same month the SFRY was officially dissolved and replaced by the Federal Republic of Yugoslavia, consisting of Serbia and Montenegro as well as the autonomous region of Kosovo. Although Bosnia and Herzegovina were officially recognized by the UN in 1993, the internal war continued until the Dayton Agreement in December 1995. In 2003 Yugoslavia changed its name to the State Union of Serbia and Montenegro.

In June 2006 the republic of Montenegro became an independent nation following a referendum, and the Federal Republic of Yugoslavia ceased to exist. The successor to the Federal Republic now established itself as the Republic of Serbia.

Camouflage has been widely worn by Yugoslavian forces only since the late 1980s. Prior to that the standard working uniform of military personnel was olive green, and camouflage was reserved for use by special operations personnel, such as airborne forces, snipers, reconnaissance troops, etc.

Yugoslavian engineers wearing Soviet-produced MKK letniy kamuflyazh (summer camouflage) uniforms, circa 1947. (*Private collection*)

These JNA soldiers wear the first locally-produced camouflage pattern, introduced in the 1960s, and intended for wear over the normal combat clothing. The fabric was extremely lightweight, like early Soviet camouflage uniforms. (*Private collection*)

The M68 Maskirno Odelo Letnje or MOL summer camouflage pattern was first issued in 1968 as a recon/sniper oversuit, then later as shelter and body armor covers. Widely cannibalized during the civil war period and made into a number of uniform items as well as field equipment. (*Private collection*)

The M87 'small oak' was early camouflage design for ground troops was tested by airborne units, reconnaissance troops, and military police between 1986 and 1988, but never fully implemented.

The Uniforme M-89 entered into service with JNA in 1990 using the same drawings as the 'small oak' but enlarged; this design remained in common service with units until 2003. (*Private collection*)

This VJ officer wears the Uniforme M-93; the name change primarily reflected an alteration in uniform design although some color changes were also noted in newly issued fabrics. (*Private collection*)

A 'tiger stripe' pattern with a grey background color was introduced in the late 1980s for the the MUP (Ministarstvo Unutrašnjih Poslova), or Ministry of Internal Affairs, and also embraced by special operations units such as the 63rd Airborne Battalion and the 72nd Special Battalion. (*Private collection*)

A blue-dominant version of the 'oakleaf' pattern was adopted in 1992 for use by MUP special police, but only saw two series of production before being phased out. (*Private collection*)

The blue 'tiger stripe' patterns were adopted around 1992 by Yugoslavian police (MUP) personnel. Phased out in 2001, some color variations are more blue and others more purple.

Chapter 5

Oceania

AUSTRALIA

Following the end of the Second World War, Australia adopted a policy of 'forward defense', in which the military began to cooperate heavily with its allies in order to counter what were seen as threats to the safety and security of Australia and its neighbors. The nation joined the South East Asia Treaty Organization (SEATO) in 1954, attempting to block communist expansion in Asia. Australian troops (Australian Army Training Team Vietnam/AATTV) were first sent to Vietnam in 1962 as advisors, but involvement increased in 1965 with the commitment of additional infantry, air force and special forces (SASR) personnel, which remained in country until 1972.

Australia became somewhat more self-reliant in the mid-1970s, but continued to participate in regional and international peacekeeping efforts. Large peacekeeping deployments were sent to Namibia in 1989, Cambodia in 1992–93, Somalia in 1993, Rwanda in 1994–95, and to the Bougainville region of Papua New Guinea in 1994, and again in 1997. Australian participation in the Persian Gulf War in 1991 was mostly limited to Air Force and Navy units, but a large contingent deployed to East Timor beginning in 1999.

Australian personnel had a significant involvement in Afghanistan from 2001 to 2014 (known as Operation Slipper) and again in 2015 during Operation Highroad. The Australian commitment included a Special Forces Task Group, ground combat personnel, mentoring teams, and a significant number of RAAF and RAN units. In 2003, an Australian Special Forces Task Group and elements of the RAAF also joined the United States sponsored invasion of Iraq, retaining a presence there until 2009.

The US ERDL or 'leaf' camouflage pattern was worn extensively in Vietnam by members of the Special Air Service Regiment, as well as by Australian Advisory Training Team Vietnam (AATTV) personnel.

AATTV soldier wearing Vietnamese-made tiger stripe pattern fatigues, also used by SASR in Vietnam. (*Private collection*)

The 'Smock, Psychological' was a plastic rain jacket first issued in 1971, and worn by some Australian personnel in Vietnam. The camouflage design is black on olive green.

Locally produced, this copy of US tricolor desert pattern was initially tested by the SASR, but was primarily worn by OPFOR personnel in the mid-1990s.

The Australian Defense Forces (ADF) consists of the Australian Army, Royal Australian Navy (RAN) and the Royal Australian Air Force (RAAF). The Army is subdivided into the Forces Command, 1st Division, and the Special Operations Command. The ADF has been an all-volunteer force since conscription was abolished in 1972. The widespread use of camouflage by the ADF began during its involvement in Vietnam, where covert operations by the Special Air Service Regiment (SASR) necessitated being able to disappear in the dense jungle environment. At the time, localized camouflage and uniforms obtained from its US allies were most commonly worn. It was not until the early 1980s that Australia developed its own unique camouflage design.

The Disruptive Camouflage Pattern (DCP) was first introduced in 1982, and remained in general service with the ADF until the adoption of Australian Multicam in 2010 (although it would continue to be worn by personnel in training, such as those seen here). (*Private collection*)

Incorporating a unique color palette, the 'Red Auscam' pattern was adopted in 1997–98 as a replacement for the tricolor desert pattern, to be used by OPFOR personnel.

A variation of the DCP (Desert Pattern Disruptive Uniform/DPDU) pattern was issued to the SASR in 1998 and tested in Afghanistan between 2001 and 2002, although never officially adopted. (*Private collection*)

A second version of the DPDU was tested by SASR and RAAF support personnel between 2002 and 2003 but also not officially adopted. This pattern can be distinguished by the mint green color incorporated into the design.

These Australian Navy personnel wear the Disruptive Pattern Navy Uniform (DPNU) issued from 2008 until 2018. (*Department of Defense*)

The third version of the DPDU was approved and issued from 2003 onwards to Australian military personnel deployed to desert regions around the world. Seen here, a soldier serving with ISAF in Afghanistan in 2008 wears the latest desert uniform. (*Private collection*)

These personnel are wearing the Australian Multicam Pattern (AMP), initially released in 2010 and worn in Afghanistan beginning in 2012, but only for a couple of years. One of the distinguishing features was a small AMF logo embedded into the design. (*Department of Defense*)

A RAAF officer wearing the General Purpose Uniform (GPU), adopted in 2014 and exclusive to Air Force personnel; the design is based on Multicam design but has a blue colorway. (*US Air Force*)

Adopted in 2014, the Australian Multicam Camouflage (AMC) pattern seen here, differs from the AMP in having a coloration more in line with traditional Australian DCP and is now the official pattern of Australian ground forces personnel. (*US Army*)

FIJI

The island nation of Fiji was a part of the British Empire until 1970, when it was granted independence. 1987 saw two military coups d'etat, the results of which were that the traditional Fijian monarchy and the Governor General were replaced and the country officially changing its name to the Republic of Fiji. The country was readmitted to the Commonwealth of Nations in 1997. The Fijian government was again toppled in 2000, followed by two

Although not universally issued, a copy of US M81 woodland camouflage has been worn by some Fijian Infantry Regiment personnel.

mutinies staged by members of the armed forces; a general election in 2001 restored order. Once again in 2006, the nation's top military commander, Frank Bainimarama, orchestrated another coup d'etat; three years later the country experienced a constitutional crisis that resulted in censorship, increased police powers, suspension of the constitution, and severance of diplomatic relations with Fiji by some nations.

Although relatively small by international standards, Fiji has a reasonably large armed force based on its population. The Republic of Fiji Military Forces (RFMF) consists of the Fiji Land Forces, the Fijian Navy and a small Air Wing that ceased to exist in 1997. In addition to its obligation as part of the Multinational Force and Observers (MFO) in the Sinai, Fijian military personnel have been actively engaged in a number of peacekeeping missions internationally, particularly in East Timor and the Middle East. The Fiji Police is responsible for law enforcement.

Fiji has never adopted a camouflage uniform as standard service wear for its military personnel. However, some Fijian personnel have worn camouflage for special duties.

NEW ZEALAND

In the post-war years, New Zealand recognized the importance of allying itself to neighbors and friendly allies in the region, first signing the ANZUS Treaty in 1951 (a collective security agreement between Australia, New Zealand the United States). The country later joined the South East Asia Treaty Organization (SEATO) in 1954. Military personnel were sent to Korea, and to Malaya in 1955 during the Malayan Emergency. Beginning in 1964, New Zealand was drawn into the Vietnam War via its ANZUS obligations, eventually sending combat units, support units, special forces, and military advisors in the form of the New Zealand Army Training Team Vietnam (NZATTV). The war was not popular at home, however, and by 1972 all troops had been withdrawn. Contributing to the Global War on Terrorism, New Zealand deployed members of its Special Air Service (NZ SAS), as well as a Provisional Reconstruction Team (NZPRT) to Afghanistan. The NZ presence lasted from 2001 to 2013.

The country has made significant military contributions to international peacekeeping efforts, serving in Kashmir, Lebanon, and Rhodesia as observers, and joining the Multinational Force and Observers (MFO) in the Sinai beginning in 1982. More recently NZ personnel have served in Somalia, with UNPROFOR in the former Yugoslavia, East Timor, the Solomon Islands, Iraq, and Tonga.

US issue ERDL or 'leaf' pattern camouflage uniforms were worn by New Zealand Special Air Service (NZSAS) personnel operating in Vietnam, and became an unofficial operational uniform for the unit from 1968 onwards (until replaced by DPM). (*Private collection*)

The New Zealand Defense Force consists of the NZ Army, Royal New Zealand Navy and the Royal New Zealand Air Force. The use of camouflage by NZ military personnel was limited to members of the NZ SAS, until the late 1970s when a shelter half printed in a 'brushstroke' camouflage design began to be issued. This was followed in 1980 by the first issue of British DPM camouflage, which would be the standard operational and working uniform pattern for NZ forces until the turn of the century.

Adopted in 1979–80 as a general issue poncho/shelter half or 'basha', this 'brushstroke' design was never implemented on combat clothing.

The first issue DPM camouflage pattern was obtained from the UK and the same as used on British 1968 pattern uniforms; this was issued between 1980 and 1983.

The second series of DPM was produced locally and featured a drastic change in dyes, using brighter colors; this version was issued between 1984 and 1986.

A third DPM series began production in 1986 and was the first truly tropical weight uniform issued to NZ forces. Production continued until 1990.

Universally disliked due to its poor quality and tendency to fade quickly, the fourth series of DPM was issued between 1994 and 1995, and nicknamed 'diesel' pattern.

This Kiwi trooper deployed to East Timor is wearing the last series of DPM, issued from 1996 onwards. (*Private collection*)

New Zealand soldier serving with ISAF in Afghanistan wearing the British-type desert DPM pattern adopted in 2003. (*Private collection*)

Multicam uniforms were worn by members of the NZ SAS while serving in Afghanistan.

New Zealand Army Artillery personnel wearing the Multi-Terrain Camouflage adopted in 2013 and designed by Hyperstealth Technologies® of Canada. (*US Marine Corps*)

PAPUA NEW GUINEA

This country was under Australian administration until 1975, when it became an independent Commonwealth realm and was also admitted to the United Nations. The island of Bougainville experienced a secessionist movement between 1975 and 1976, which resulted in the granting of province status to eighteen different districts. In December 1988, another Bougainville uprising brought this part of the country into full-scale civil war, pitting the armed forces against the Bougainville Revolutionary Army which supported the interim government of the district. Over the course of the war, more than 20,000 lives were lost, until a peace agreement was finally reached in 1998.

The Papua New Guinea Defense Forces was created 1973 and consists of Land, Air and Naval elements. It receives considerable training and military aid from neighboring Australia and New Zealand.

Several types of DPM pattern camouflage have been worn by this country since the 1970s, where it is known locally as Kumul. (*Private collection*)

A member of the Royal PNG Constabulary Special Services Division wears a DPM pattern variant. (*Private collection*)

TONGA

The Kingdom of Tonga was an independent British protected state until 1970, at which point it joined the Commonwealth of Nations. In 1999, the country was granted membership in the United Nations.

Originally called the Tonga Defense Service (TDS), His Majesty's Armed Forces consist of a Land Component, Maritime Component, Air Wing, Support Units and reserves. A Tongan military contingent was deployed to Bougainville for peacekeeping operations during the civil war there. Tongan personnel also joined the Multinational Force in Iraq from 2004 to 2008, which consisted primarily of Royal Tongan Marines. In 2011, Royal Tongan Marines were sent to Afghanistan, returning home in 2014. The Tonga Defense Service was officially renamed His Majesty's Armed Forces in September 2013.

Soldiers of the Tonga Armed Forces wearing the woodland variant pattern in use for several years. (*Private collection*)

Royal Tonga Marines in Iraq during a briefing by US Navy Admiral Timothy Keating in 2007 wear US tricolor desert camouflage uniforms. (*US Navy*)

Royal Tonga Marines in Afghanistan in 2014 clad in British MTP pattern camouflage, now in service with the entire Land Component. (*Private collection*)

Formerly known as the New Hebrides, when it was jointly managed by France and Great Britain, a movement towards independence began in the 1970s under the New Hebrides National Party. Although the two countries agreed to grant independence in 1980, the Nagriamel anti-independence movement on the island of Espiritu Santo spurred violence and full-scale rebellion, which ultimately descended into a two-month conflict known as the Coconut War. Troops from neighboring Solomon Islands and Papua New Guinea joined native forces in quelling the Nagriamel rebellion, and by September the war was over and a new country, the Republic of Vanuatu, had emerged. During the 1990s, an unsuccessful coup d'etat was attempted by the Vanuatu Mobile Force.

There is no standing military force in Vanuatu, law enforcement and national security both falling under the wing of the Ni-Vanuatu Police (Vanuatu Police Force) and its paramilitary branch, the Vanuatu Mobile Force (VMF).

An officer of the Vanuatu Police Mobile Force (VMF) wearing the brown-based woodland pattern historically worn by this unit. (*Private collection*)

These members of the VMF wear the currently-issued DPM pattern in 2017. (*Private collection*)